September 11, 2001
American Writers Respond

Edited by William Heyen

etruscan press

ETRUSCAN PRESS
P.O. Box 9685
Silver Springs, MD 20916-9685
telephone 301.946.6228
www.etruscanpress.org

*Views expressed by contributors to this anthology
are not necessarily those of the publisher or of the editor.*

1 2 3 4 5 6 7 8 9 0

Publisher's Cataloging-in-Publication
(Provided by Quality Books, Inc.)

September 11, 2001 : american writers respond / edited by
William Heyen. -- 1st ed.
    p. cm.
    ISBN 0-9718228-0-8 (paperback)
    ISBN 0-9718228-1-6 (hardcover)

    1. September 11 Terrorist Attacks, 2001.
    2. September 11 Terrorist Attacks, 2001--Literary
collections.   I. Heyen, William, 1940-

HV6432.S47 2002   973.931
                           QBI02-701381

CONTENTS

PREFACE

I live in a small village on the Erie Canal in western New York State. Behind my home, at the back of my one acre, I have an 8' x 12' cabin—Thoreau's was 10' x 15'—under ash and silver maple, surrounded by wild rose, honeysuckle, and red osier bushes. I retired from teaching a year ago, and now get back to this hideout most mornings, usually write something in my journal, then read for a while or draft a new poem or prose piece, or work on revision in almost the same state of intense reverie. As if by themselves, books gradually form, but I have no sense of program and little of direction. I believe that most of the writers in this anthology would say the same. In the main, we are not journalists, scholars, political scientists. We're often not sure how our writing gets written, or if we'll be able to do again what we've just done. We compose by way of what Emerson called "the flower of the mind," and can only hope that our text, in the end, by way of its interfused music-image-story-thought, knows more than we do and will continue to be evocative and meaningful.

Just before noon this past September 11th I left the cabin and came inside. I turned on the television. My mind still elsewhere, I saw a plane flying into a skyscraper. As did countless others, I thought I was watching a clip from a new disaster movie, then wondered if this could be a hoax updated from Orson Welles. But I recognized the anchor's voice, and began to absorb the events of that morning.

At 8:45 a hijacked passenger jet out of Boston had crashed into the north tower of the 110-story World Trade Center in New York City; at 9:03, another hijacked liner crashed into the WTC's south tower;

at 9:43, a third hijacked plane hit the Pentagon in Washington; and between the total collapse of the south tower at 9:50 and the north tower at 10:29, a fourth hijacked plane crashed in Somerset County, southeast of Pittsburgh. The scenes of death and devastation—thousands dead, including hundreds of firefighters and police, sixteen vertical acres of people and buildings in smoking ruin, a section of our military headquarters burning for days—were overwhelming as we tried to comprehend what had happened.

Thoreau once said that the news is always the same—a fire somewhere, a sultan's wedding somewhere, a war somewhere—and this was all the more reason for us to mind our own business, even to hide out. But he and the other American transcendentalists, if they were listening, if in their afterlives they were sensing the violent upheavals of this material world, must have lost their immortal breath that morning. Their faith was, as Emerson said, "that within the form of every creature is a force impelling it to ascend into a higher form." And even cataclysm could translate, eventually, given time, given sufficient perspective, to beauty, to soul. But it seemed to me that the trauma of this day would abide, soul-deep in our village and across the country.

A few days later, I was asking unfashionable questions in my journal about what our creative literature, given the magnitude of these iniquitous events, must and surely would now become if in the future it could hope to be of any practical use or relevance or moral value. I cautioned myself against optimistic over-reaction, reminded myself of America's accelerating amnesia when one headline event takes the place of another (as now these attacks would at last displace months of gossipy reports about a U.S. congressman's relationship with a missing intern), but I continued to feel that the events of September 11th had awakened us and shaken our senses of identity and security. I proposed this book to Etruscan Press. A day later, I withdrew my proposal, afraid that such a project was untenable for creative writers who, as William Butler Yeats says in "On Being Asked for a War Poem," cannot set a statesman right and who are only meddling when they try to do more than please "A young girl in the indolence of her youth, / Or an old man upon a winter's night." I guessed that others might be feeling the same contraries, the same paralyzing complexities that I felt as the desire for art disintegrated with the prodigious symmetries of the Twin Towers.

But I changed my mind again, and soon wrote to a wide-range of potential contributors. (Later, too, by the e-grapevine, word would spread and I'd receive hundreds of submissions, including some of the strongest in this book.) My letter of invitation read, in part:

> It goes without saying that we now feel ourselves living in a charged and fast-changing America. September 11, 2001, will be a fulcrum date for us as few others have been. It may be that our lives as writers and as citizens, our assumptions, our theories of beauty and necessity, our senses of audience cannot now be what they have been. This anthology will be a forum by as many as a hundred poets, fiction writers, and creative essayists who will cut to the quick of their thinking on the origins and implications of the grief and anger and dread now engulfing us.

> I'm asking for intensive contributions of no longer than 4-5 pages. I'd prefer in this case that most responses be direct, in essay form, but would welcome a breakthrough poem, or a flash fiction that strikes through to psychic ground zero, or a *sui generis* piece that seems to catch and hold our quaking reality as does no other traditional mode of discourse.

Poet Philip Brady wrote me and put into words what was my hope for the eventual anthology, that as a whole it be instrumental in "focusing the diffuse but immense powers we bring to our separate works every day."

But who has any right at such a time to say anything at all? What person who was not there or did not lose a family member or friend has a right to talk personally? I doubt that there will be a contributor to this book who has not asked himself or herself this question. Writing anything at all can seem like an obscene indulgence to us, and we remember Theodor Adorno's famous declaration that *"Nach Auschwitz, ein Gedicht zu schreiben ist barbarisch"* (to write a poem after Auschwitz is barbaric). His is the ultimate argument for silence, and much of my divided self nods assent to his injunction. But—and this anthology will exist by way of this *but*, this *conjunction*—as Czeslaw Milosz says in *The Witness of Poetry*, "Whoever invokes genocide, starvation, or the physical suffering of our fellow men in order to attack poems or paintings practices demagoguery."

I write this preface, as I must, before seeing what the writers will send me. Where are we? What is the state of our union, or disunion?

William Stafford, a conscientious objector during a vastly-different WWII, reminded us that "justice will take us millions of intricate moves." And as millions of new flags appear along our streets, on our baby-strollers and bikes and gasoline-powered vehicles, in our advertisements, and on our bodies as tattoos, these symbols themselves must remind us that the result of blind patriotism is always, in Robinson Jeffers' words, a blood-lake: "and we always fall in."

But, too, as our writers try to have their say (I'm thinking of Walt Whitman musing in his old age that he was content because he'd had his say), whatever their say and however they say it—in the end, of course, the way something is said *is* what is said (this being the secret heart of all creative writing)—we must understand that the September 11th hijackers were filled with such hate for American aspirations and were of such fanatical (from the Latin *fanaticus*, of a temple, inspired by a god, mad) fervor that they would with a sense of great fulfillment have killed all 280,000,000 of us, every man, woman, and child, if they'd been able. Theirs was not the flower, but the hellfire of the human mind. Such mania evokes new dimensions of fear and realization and commitment in us, disrupts and challenges the romantic American imagination as perhaps never before, and demands from us a different retaliation, an intricate move toward world justice for each star or stripe on every Old Glory now or to come.

William Heyen
Brockport, New York
September–October 2001

As the book you are holding in your hands was coming together, I dreamt I was driving a bus along the edge of a cliff. At the bottom of the abyss was chaos, madness, trauma, death. But the bus was filled with all the writers here, and all together they leaned the opposite way, toward that other life we all hope for, and kept us from plunging into the void. How could I, how could any of us ever thank them enough?

September 11, 2001

American Writers Respond

W. S. MERWIN

To the Words
(9/17/01)

When it happens you are not there

oh you beyond numbers
beyond recollection
passed on from breath to breath
given again
from day to day from age
to age
charged with knowledge
knowing nothing

indifferent elders
indispensable and sleepless

keepers of our names
before ever we came
to be called by them

you that were
formed to begin with
you that were cried out
you that were spoken
to begin with
to say what could not be said

ancient precious
and helpless ones

say it

TAMMAM ADI

Anthem September 11, 2001

Salaam, shalom and peace to you, thousands of martyrs
Of the towers, the planes and the Pentagon.
Your killers want America to make the bloodiest war.
Now watch how America will make the fairest peace.

I am an American Muslim.
I believe in God, Allah is God.
The God of peace and justice.
I believe in Moses, Jesus, Muhammad and all the prophets.
I believe in the Torah, the Gospel, the Quran and all the scriptures.
Thomas Jefferson believed in God.
But he knew that despots always used the clergy.
I believe "there is no god but God."
It means "be free and help others be free."
It means "no clergy in government."
It means "get rid of monopoly and oppression."
I am a Muslim from the Thomas Jefferson Mosque.

The Quran told Muslims "fight to protect churches and synagogues."
The Founding Fathers said the same.
I'll fight for Jerry Falwell's right to speak against Islam.
I'll fight for the Zionists' right to speak against Islam.
But let's sit down and talk it over
To protect our homes and temples.

It's all right to review America's foreign policy.
America has wronged the Iraqis.
America has wronged the Palestinians.

But nothing America did justifies September 11.
Clinton defended Muslims in Kosovo and Bosnia
And taught America "Islam is not the enemy."
And President Bush is protecting Muslim America
And reaching out to Muslims everywhere.

It's wrong to say "Muslim fundamentalists did it."
Did we call Timothy McVeigh "a Christian fundamentalist?"
Did we call Baruch Goldstein "a Jewish fundamentalist?"
Why don't we just say "criminals did it."

Hitler's song was "Jewish terrorism." It created the Holocaust.
The media keeps singing "Islamic terrorism."
"Terrorism experts" keep singing "Islamic fundamentalism."
Do they want a holocaust against Muslims?
Hey journalists, you know better.
Hey Fox, ABC, CBS, NBC, CNN, you know better.
Hey talkshow hosts, you know better.

The terrorists are not "them, the Muslims."
They are not "them, the Arabs."
Muslims do not know who the terrorists are.
If history is a teacher,
The terror masterminds are colonels in some states
Who brainwash kids to blow up things.
So find the states and find the colonels.
Do not prosecute all Muslims.

I am a Muslim from the Thomas Jefferson Mosque.
I pray in the corners of the White House.
I pray in the hallways of the Congress and the Pentagon.
I am a liberal, I am a conservative.
I am a democrat, I am a republican.
I am a pacifist, I am a soldier.
I am a feminist, I am a masculinist.
I love responsible corporations. I hate tyrannical corporations.
I am on the left, I am on the right.
I am in the middle.
Come together, right now, over me.
Drop the labels, talk about it,
Find a common ground.

I am a Muslim from the Thomas Jefferson Mosque.
I love Christians, Jews, Buddhists, Hindus and atheists.

I love Arabs, Europeans, Africans, Hispanics and Asians.
I love the East, I love the West.
But I love America best,
The America that will free the world from hate and injustice.

I am a Muslim from the George Washington Mosque.
Although I love peace, I will fight for freedom.

I am a Muslim from the Abraham Lincoln Mosque.
I will fight against my brothers
To free my brothers from slavery.

I love the star-spangled banner.
A star for Texas, a star for Iowa, a star for New York,
A star for Iraq, a star for Iran, a star for Afghanistan,
A star for Palestine, a star for Israel,
A star for Russia, a star for China.

A star for Jesus, a star for David, a star for Muhammad,
A star for Buddha, a star for Krishna, a star for the Great Spirit.

A star for Abraham Lincoln, a star for Mahatma Ghandi,
A star for John F. Kennedy, a star for Robert Kennedy,
A star for Martin Luther King, a star for Malcolm X,
A star for Yitzhak Rabin, a star for Anwar Sadat,
A star for John Lennon.

A star for 9/11.
A star for you and me.

We need a bigger flag.
We'll make a bigger flag.
Come together, right now, over you.
We'll all shine on. Like the moon and the stars and the sun.
On and on and on.

A I

Fairy Tale

The first time I heard the story
of Red Riding Hood,
I was so afraid of the wolf
I dreamed he ate me for dinner.
The next morning,
mother found bite marks on my arms.
Even though I swore they weren't my teeth,
she punished me for lying
by tying me to a chair,
facing the object of my dread—
a woodcut of the wolf in grandma's bed,
but I knew it wouldn't make a difference
because the wolf had chosen me.
At twelve, I turned to model airplanes
and my dreams became a means of escape.
High above my body, looking down,
I'd find the wolf in my bed,
as if he too had been released
from some nightmare
and finally could sleep.
Eventually, I dreamed of girls,
but even so, my nocturnal emissions
often ended in visions of the wolf
dressed in women's clothes
whispering my name seductively.
I came to him every time he came to me
just like the kamikaze did in nineteen forty-three,
when the United States was at war with Japan

and I was a pilot.
For some reason, neither of us fired at first.
We just flew side by side,
staring at each other
across the great military divide.
He wasn't wearing goggles
and I swear I could see his eyes
gleaming like black opals
and the expression on his face
was the one the wolf wore
the first time he tasted me.
I think we Catholics call that look transfiguration.
I don't remember how long our strange communion lasted
before I fired on the bastard.
I flew through the smoke and flames
of his disintegration sure that his death
had left me changed and whole,
but today, when borders and oceans
can be crossed as easily as tossing a coin,
as I am on my way to San Xavier Mission,
suddenly, I hear an explosion,
while all around me, the desert steams
under an empty turquoise sky
and once again, I feel as if I am a fragment of myself.
The highway stretches forward and back without traffic.
I am alone, yet I know the wolf's returned to haunt me
as I stop the car by the side of the road.
When I close my eyes,
I remember watching with horror and relief
as the kamikaze's burning body
shot from the wreckage of the plane
and dropped into the ocean below.
I made it home in one piece,
at least on the outside.
Now I'm retired, in good health,
relocated to Tucson, Arizona from Baltimore
and I've returned to the Church
after forty years of drifting between the New Age
and whatever "this" is.
I breathe deeply, open my eyes and start the car.
I drive the few miles to the Mission,
where I learn of a terrorist attack on New York City.
I ask Father Anthony if what I experienced earlier
was a premonition,

but he says, "my son, I don't know."
"A miracle then," I ask.
"Only if you pass certain tests.
You didn't save anyone, did you?
But if you saw the Virgin, or a saint..."
"Only a wolf," I answer, "and a dead man."
"Was the dead man a good man?"
"Maybe once upon a time." "So was Adam before the Fall," he says.
"Perhaps it was Satan you saw, for this is his work."
"Yes, Father," I say, "but I don't believe that either.
The kamikaze was only a man
and the wolf, I must admit at last, is me."
"You aren't the wolf," he says mysteriously.
"I'm not?"
"Don't you remember I absolved you of all that?"
"No, I'm getting old," I answer.
"So are we all, but some of us moreso.
You know the wolf is not necessarily evil.
To some Indian people it is a protector spirit."
"But what could the wolf protect me from?"
"Yourself?"
"I'm not convinced of that," I say.
"Then come have coffee," he says.
"We can chat about this latest manmade disaster
and wait for the Second Coming with bated breath."
"You are so eloquent, Father,
but I'm not in the mood for conversation.
I'll just pray, until I run out of words,
then I'll howl."
"Have you noticed the absence of bird song?
It's as if they know of the tragedy."
"All right, all right I'll go."
"You know the way," he adds,
laying a hairy hand on mine
and I glimpse behind his benign gaze
the face I know so well.
The reports say people jumped to certain death
when the jets rammed into the Twin Towers.
Rather than let death come to them,
they went to him,
their clothes billowing in the wind,
making them look like the kamikaze
in a fiery tailspin.
I kneel, staring at the altar,

trying to connect the dots of my life
and not getting anywhere,
as mother looks at me with a wolfish grin
and pinches my cheek,
encouraging me to repeat with her,
"the end."

JOHN ALLMAN /
DAVID ZANE MAIROWITZ

Letters

(Excerpts from a spontaneous exchange of letters)

22 September 2001

Dear David,

I'm somewhat over my wrathful state, and I'm trying to fend off a
deep depression—which pretty much describes everyone in the NY
area. We may seem to be getting back to ordinary life, but there's a
heavy grief overlaying everything we do. The other day I was wondering why there were so few people in the supermarket, until I realized
that there are thousands of us missing from our communities,
incinerated or entombed in the rubble of the World Trade Center.
Thousands more injured. And now, many thousands out of jobs. We
are dealing with a terrible evil, not to be explained in the usual
geopolitical terms. I am already disgusted with the "Give Peace a
Chance" movements—people whining (and I mean just that, making
high-pitched sounds through their noses) about the deaths we might
cause in a war, while they do not even stop to mourn the thousands of
us already killed here. It's not simply an issue of limiting war. It's a
matter of recognizing WHAT REALLY HAS HAPPENED. Of course,
once we do that, we're afraid to travel. Afraid of going to public
events. But gradually, the sports world is getting back to normal,
attracting crowds into stadiums. There are planes in the air again.
And though we know there are other terrorist targets such as our
water supply, our power plants, we seem to be shrugging that off. No
one quite contemplates biological attacks—yet.

We are already getting bogged down in endless talk. Endless analysis. Infinite second-guessing about what we should have done back
when. What we have to do is use a real and credible threat of major

force to affect international cooperation in tracking down terrorist networks. It's not a new problem. But the scope of it is new, and now we know that our will to pursue these crazy bastards must be as intense and as long-lasting as their hatred of us. It's fine and clever to generate metaphors as a German intelligence official did, referring to terrorists as cockroaches. You fumigate one apartment or building, they just move to another. The terrorists count on us throwing up our hands and saying it's too much, we'll never find them all. We have to challenge that in our thinking. We have to be patient and long in our memories. We have to be Simon Wiesenthal.

Ruth Ann Lief, who has not been able to speak for over three years, unfortunately heard about the attacks from a WQXR news broadcast. She has a headset plugged into a radio that is permanently turned to WQXR, which she listens to for classical music, one of the few enjoyments left to her as a former cellist. When she heard the shocking news, she cried out loud. But not being capable of normal vocalizations, her cry was a long, dry moan, a keening sound that chilled me to the marrow. We are not telling her that her daughter-in-law's brother and the brother's partner and their adopted child were on the hijacked flight out of Boston that was destined for San Francisco. Can you believe that Jerry Falwell and Pat Robertson, on TV, said the attack was a punishment for homosexuality, abortion, feminism, sexual promiscuity? We have our own Taliban.

Rockland County, where I worked for 26 years, is the home of many NYC firemen and policemen, as well as many office workers in the World Trade Center. On almost every street, there is someone lost.

So my mood is grim.

*

The casualties have been and are deeply felt, and I doubt there's much sympathy for the wounding of "civil rights," though that in time will surface. It already is, as Senator Patrick Leahy is developing his own bill to counter the Administration bill that would shrink constitutional protection. It's something we have to be careful about, to preserve the best of what we are. No fucking jihad should be causing us to eviscerate our own institutions. Our own struggle for tolerance. And—let's say it—freedom. There's nothing wrong with love of country. I feel it strongly. I want to kill my enemies. But first, I want to find them. Bombing the dust bowls and pulverizing the naked crags of Afghanistan, thrusting thousands out of their homes as they rush to the borders of Iran or Pakistan, will not turn up a single terrorist. We have to look under the rocks elsewhere. We have to find their moneys. We need the help of every country in the world, but we won't get it unless we seem very serious about making war. On a massive scale, it's like playing chicken, two cars speeding towards each other head-on. Either we're going to kill a lot of people, or nations will say, okay, let's find these guys where they are in our own countries. If it all turns out to be a global jihad, after all, which is what bin Laden and his ilk desire, then at last we'll know the face of World War III. I don't want the word "God" mentioned in my presence.

.... It's a perilous time.

Love to you and Avril and Liesl,

Jack

30 September 2001

Dear Jack,

Of course, I'm sitting in the south of France while you're on the spot. It's natural that our reactions are divergent. My first thought was for my brother, who sells spare elevator parts often in the WTC. But I got a call from him a few hours later, so I could relax on that score. You know, it may sound horrible to you, but one of the thoughts that passed through my mind when I saw the towers go down—apart from sheer horror—was: thank goodness at least it's not the Chrysler Building or the Empire State Building. All I mean to say by that—and certainly nothing more or macabre—is that the WTC was built after my departure from New York and I have no direct emotional attachment to those buildings as I do to the art-deco skyscrapers. This is only a question of geography, to position myself in the debate.

I agree with what you say about getting bogged down in endless analysis. But at the same time, as anyone can see, people need to talk. I was appalled that on Sept. 12, Avril had three hours of philosophy class, where the theme was "conscience" and the teacher didn't utter a syllable about the events. On the French radio there were a lot of good discussions, and don't forget that France has not only a tradition of Arab involvement, it is a day-to-day fact of life for us here. The Moroccan and Algerian ghettoes here are fertile terrain for the fundamentalists to recruit. Just yesterday a French court acquitted a cop who had shot an Algerian boy in cold blood. My first thought on hearing his raging brother scream revenge on the radio was: we've just created another terrorist.

Naturally, there is an overflow of oversimplification. Nobody has a ready answer to this. Comparisons with Pearl Harbor I find ridiculous. This was not a military attack on a military installation by an identifiable power. To me the central problem is religion. I have always said that, it's not new for me. When I hear Bush telling Americans to pray, so that good will triumph over evil, I see a group of Muslims on their prayer mats facing Mecca and praying to Allah, so they can triumph over the "Great Satan USA." Religion is power, a means of robbing the human race of choice. Islam, of course, does not sanction suicide, as many people believe. So, where do these fanatics get the will to commit such actions? From the Imams with a political agenda. Killing is absolutely unfathomable amongst Jews and yet those Brooklyn fanatics who murder Arabs in Israel are encouraged by rabbis with a political agenda. Northern Ireland might have found itself a solution years ago were it not for men like the "Reverend" Ian Paisely and Catholic priests who listen to IRA killers in the confessional. And the fascist American Taliban—Robertson and Falwell— also have a political agenda when they link the attacks to homosexuality and abortion. The current Pope—whom everyone takes for a great liberal— has also caused untold harm in the modern world with his medieval notions concerning abortion and the role of women. Don't think it was an accident that a Pole was chosen for this job in the middle of the Cold War.

*

The Cold War was also a time in which the term "Evil Empire" was used. Once again, this was a holy war. And, such notions (in my opinion) have guided American Foreign Policy ("policy" is, of course, a misnomer) for the last seventy years. Lately, it has been pointed out that the CIA helped create the Taliban and bin Laden as well, in order to fight the Russians in Afghanistan. But, in fact, this kind of thing happened throughout the Cold War. Endless fascist dictatorships supported in Latin America and in Asia. There is a direct relationship between the American support for the Shah and his torture chambers and the coming to power of Islam in Iran (with a knowledgeable hatred of the US). And Henry Kissinger (yet anoth-

er mass murderer with a Nobel Prize) backing Pol Pot! because he was at war with Vietnamese. The list is endless and goes on right up to today.

*

Does the new fight against terrorism (and countries that harbor terrorists) also mean that the US government will stop turning a blind eye (as it has for the last quarter century) to internal collections of money to buy arms for the IRA, at the risk of offending the Irish-American lobby? Does it mean that England will have to re-think its position as the heart of European Islamic fundamentalism and openly terrorist cells, despite the enormous tax revenues it collects from the oil sheiks who drive their lim-ousines around Regents Park?

Let me make it clear where I stand on the current situation, so there is no misunderstanding. I'm for rooting out "terrorists" and dealing with them in any way necessary. Freezing their assets, for whatever it's worth (not much, I expect) is a good thing, but why wasn't it done before? Who is hiding what? I'm also against appeasing the Taliban in any way. These guys are crypto-fascists and the women of Afghanistan will breathe more easily (literally) if they are driven out of power. I am against indis-criminate bombing of the civilian population. I also think the US has to force the Israeli government to give up its colonial territories in Palestine and make peace with the Arabs. All of this goes hand in hand.

Lots of love, and to Eileen (I'm back on Oct. 21)

How about the Yanks? How about Barry B?

David

MELISSA ALTENDERFER

Pittsburgh, 9/10/01, 7:30 P.M.

From the wide and generous porch
of my house, notable to strangers
only for its age and sick-colored
peeling paint, I watch the sun weld
its way into the sky between the houses
across South Winebiddle Street.
My front yard sneaks like a grin

through matching pines planted
by some Industrial-Age daughter
who loved growing things. The older,
sad oaks give up their curry-yellow
leaves early, which scatter across the street
like the crumbs left by an eraser on a clean

sheet of paper. Brownish children
perform wheelies for each other's cheers.
Everything else here is still green—
kelly, forest, the dusty olive

shade of the pine whose branches threaten
my driveway with their weight
and wear black lightning marks less
like scars and more like tattoos.

My dog's yellow stains have ruined
the strip of grass along the fence.
The tight-faced girl from next

door sidles up to me, wanting to talk,
as we often do, about Narnia and Oz,
and to show me her new kitten.
She tugs on her left braid and apologizes

when her father yells—is it in Hindi?—
for her to come inside. Front door
lights around us begin to blink on
and fall to the ground like the last
of the summer's fireflies.

This poem began as a simple documentary of life in my little corner
of Pittsburgh—a neighborhood called, without irony, "Friendship."
Rents here are relatively inexpensive, and Friendship is a blend
of artists, young families, blacks, students, whites, recent immigrants, retirees, and young single professionals. I grew up in a
bland, homogeneous suburb, and I wanted to communicate some of
the wonder I still feel at the diversity I've found in Pittsburgh.
Before September 11, all these people living so easily together
seemed like a small miracle.

After September 11, I reworked the poem to stress the underpin-
nings of dread and vague threat I hadn't noticed in the earlier
drafts. I still think living here is a miracle, though I no longer think
it a small one. The Pittsburgh I tried to show in this poem seems,
now, as fantastical as any world dreamed up by L. Frank Baum or
C. S. Lewis.

ANTLER

Two months before the terrorist attack
a 16-year-old walked into a hospital
in New York City
handed the receptionist a note—
"Please donate my organs in case of death"
then blew his brains out in front of her.
Six hours later his removed eyes
were transplanted into empty eye-sockets
of a 60-year-old woman
blind since birth
who two months later
turns on morning TV to see
skyscraper apocalypse.

A week before the terrorist attack
a woman stopped her car
on a bridge in Seattle
during morning rush hour traffic,
got out, climbed over the railing,
stood on the ledge looking down.
Commuters caught in the traffic jam
fearing they'd be late for work
started yelling "Jump! Jump!"
even started making a banner
encouraging her to jump
till she finally did.

The terrorist at the controls
and his fellow terrorists
in the cockpit
had big grins as the jet
slammed
into the skyscraper
believing they were instantly transported
to an endless orgasm
in a paradise of beautiful girls
because their suicide terrorism
was a heroic martyrdom
that made God happy.

No one ever saw two
of the tallest buildings
on Planet Earth
burn and collapse
in less time than it took
the Titanic to sink.
Till now.

Play the film of the Towers
being struck, burning, imploding
in slow-motion over and over.
Freeze-frame close-up of lovers
holding hands the moment they jumped.

Flashback to Walt Whitman 150 years ago
standing where the World Trade Center Towers
would stand
looking up at circling seagulls
looking down at him
little knowing
skyscrapers so high
would be built
or jet planes exist
hijacked
by deranged fanatics
deliberately crashing
into those skyscrapers
murdering thousands
because they think
God wants them to....

How the jet appeared to be
swallowed by the Tower
entering it like a hangar
and a split second existed
before
the explosion—
just enough time
for office-workers sipping coffee
reading their newspapers
to drop through the demolished floor
and through the torn-off roof of the jet
to suddenly be side-by-side
with airplane passengers
gaping each other in horror
as the fireball engulfed them....

Flashback to victory parade
in downtown Manhattan
after Persian Gulf War—
snowstorms of confetti
wafting down on drunk celebrators
from triumphant skyscrapers above,
from soaring and mighty skyscrapers above.

How does it feel to be exploded into human flesh confetti?
How does it feel to be crushed, squashed,
decapitated, dismembered, disemboweled,
tongues torn out, lungs torn out, livers torn out,
hearts torn out, stomachs torn out, bladders and kidneys torn out,
skeletons torn out, how many breasts how many buttocks
how many genitals how many jaws how many noses torn off?...

One American said
he wouldn't be satisfied
till he saw children in Afghanistan
running down the street on fire screaming.

Another said he wouldn't feel right
till he could be in Afghanistan
and throw a grenade
into a schoolbus full of children....

If only the terrorists had been more into
tightrope-walking between the Towers

to the delight of cheering onlookers
to draw media attention to their cause
and debate it in pastoral settings
with fountains and jugs of wine.
If only the terrorists had been into crashing
model airplanes into model skyscrapers
instead of real planes into real skyscrapers.
If only the terrorists had gone to costume parties
dressed up as their favorite skyscrapers,
got drunk, lit each other's skyscraper on fire
and laughing jumped in the swimming pool.
If only the terrorists had believed
cutting snowflake designs from folded paper during a blizzard
and unfolding them in front of each other
pleases God more than explosions of body parts.
If only the terrorists had been more into
watching butterflies emerge from their chrysalises
or dragonflies emerge from their nymphs.
If only the terrorists had been more into pterodactyls,
believing the more life-size models of pterodactyls
the more we are in awe of Allah's handiwork.
If only the terrorists had spent their lives trying to prove
the world annihilates itself and reappears just as it was
a million times a second.
If only the terrorists had embraced as their mission
to evangelize to every nation and religion
there are enough advanced civilizations in the Universe
for a trillion different utopias
from a trillion different planets
from a trillion different galaxies
to pay Earth a visit every nanosecond.
If only the terrorists had been more into wandering
snowy midnight winter neighborhoods
looking for snow angels children made
to lie down in them and ask their blessing.
If only the terrorists had been more into deer
eating from their outheld hands.

Have the winds blown enough
that by now all of us have breathed
particles of the burned-up corpses?
Sooner or later all of us will inhale
invisible remains of the incinerated victims,
their atoms and molecules spinning in space

transported by breezes little-by-little
dispersing outward spreading outward
till all of us have inside us through breathing
the vanished corpses that will never be found
but that found us and became
buried within us....

Meanwhile four miles from ground zero
in the Frick Gallery near Central Park
in a room next to the marble courtyard
with its pillar'd colonnade and arching skylight
with its fountain pool with two gold frogs at either end
spurting continuous long arcs of water—
St. Francis in Ecstasy by Giovanni Bellini,
painted the same year Columbus set sail
in search of a New World,
still shows St. Francis barefoot in his monk's robe
emerging from his hermit cave
leaving behind his desk with closed Bible and human skull
looking up with arms outstretched in awe
to fields and woods and mountains
as the sunrise engulfs the world
in the light of another day.

PHILIP APPLEMAN

What We Have Lost, What We Must Save
NYC, 11-15-01

After the violence of September 11, 2001: first, a succession of
emotional blows—shock/horror/pity/sorrow/rage—then a firm
determination to punish those responsible—and, upon sober
reflection, the earnest wish to remain a decent people in a civilized
nation. But at this painful moment in history, both the attackers'
jubilation and the victims' vengefulness make it difficult to talk
about decency or civilization.

Consider the Al Qaeda/Taliban's hypothetical strategy:

A) America must be destroyed, but the Taliban alone cannot
accomplish that, so Muslims everywhere have to be united in wrath;
this can be achieved by viciously attacking America, whereupon

B) the Americans, meeting violence with violence, will strike back
with their powerful but often inaccurate bombs, inevitably killing
thousands of innocent Muslims; and then

C) the blood of the Muslim dead will unite in hatred a billion
Muslims across two-thirds of the world, all dedicated to the honor,
the glory, and the visceral satisfaction of killing Americans. (In a
related scenario, Pakistan becomes a Muslim theocracy with a
nuclear arsenal, directed by the simmering moral imperatives
of Muslims everywhere.)

In other words, this struggle is not about who wins or loses the military conflict in Afghanistan; it is a long-term plan to rally the devout
against an infidel American hegemony.

The Taliban strategy having already been alarmingly successful, we
can glimpse a hazy image of the grim future. Now think about the

past—from the bloody Christian crusades to the Western colonial dismemberment of the Islamic world—and consider also this stream of personal memories.

·Fifty years ago, in the Algerian Sahara—still occupied by France—Noubli Laroussi, a young Arab with whom my wife and I had shared a long and dusty desert trip, invited us into his oasis home, gave us dates and cool water, and presented his wife, without her veil.

·Forty years ago, in one of the miserable Palestinian refugee camps in Jordan, an old Arab told me, "It took us centuries to drive you out before, and no matter how long it takes, we'll drive you out again—an Arab always gets revenge."

·Twelve years after the British withdrew from India and Pakistan, we were walking the streets of a squalid village, with a local journalist—the ugly smells of poverty about us, black flies swarming, pitiful grimy children running in the streets, the newsman's face a mixture of humiliation and hostility as he bitterly commented: "This is what the British left us."

·Generosity/vengefulness/pride/resentment: the contradictory and combustible feelings of the powerless.

We Americans have been pleased to think of ourselves as the most envied nation in the world. People tend to like being envied, but often forget that envy can breed hostility—and, if coupled with the perception of economic exploitation (as "our" prosperity feeds on "their" poverty) can also beget a persistent hatred; and if that in turn is coupled with ancient religious antagonisms and intense religious fervor, it can produce a fanatical malice both homicidal and suicidal. This is nothing new in history; but in times of local-ized peace and prosperity, the fortunate ones tend to put it out of their minds, and then react with innocent surprise when confronted with the virulence of their previously faceless enemies. But hatred and its offspring terror are not spontaneous—they are spawned and nourished by a profound sense of grievance; and until the grievance is recognized and effectively addressed, the hatred and terror will always be with us.

The many causes of Arab/Muslim hatred of America are no secret; we have known them for decades. By far the most potent is the Israeli-Palestinian war—a war now half a century old, with no sign of an end, a war that daily produces more and more bitterness and intransi-gence, as more and more people are killed by it. The Muslim nations see the U.S. as the perpetrator and protector of their enemy, and until a lasting peace is accomplished in the Middle East, the Muslims will always view Israel and America together as legitimate enemy targets. Beyond that primary cause, our continued bombing of Iraq, the starvation of thousands of Iraqi children by our economic sanctions, and our support of repressive Saudi and Egyptian regimes (and assorted other military dictatorships) are all among the causes of Muslim anti-Americanism, and justifications for "holy" war.

But the present struggle is not so much a "war" as it is a blood feud, a feud with an ancient pedigree, Hatfields-and-McCoys on an international scale. Wars can be fought and won (or lost), and relegated to history. Blood feuds go on and on, fueled by their own internal fires, generation after generation after generation, as each side tries to "get even"; the lust for revenge is a hungrier beast than the mere desire for battlefield victory. So we must face the fact that "terror"— the weapon of the weak against the strong— is here to stay.

Making matters far worse is the fact that this conflict is fundamentally about religion—that beneath the surface of today's glaring atrocities lies the long, dark history of religious slaughter. We read with appropriate revulsion about the murderous Christian Crusades and Muslim Jihads, and the genocidal Protestant/Catholic carnage of the Thirty Years War. Those righteous passions have gone underground from time to time, but they resurface endlessly. So we now live in a world where Catholics are killing Protestants (and vice versa) in Ireland, where Muslims are killing Hindus (and vice versa) in India, where Hindus are killing Buddhists (and vice versa) in Sri Lanka, where Muslims are killing Christians (and vice versa) in Egypt and Algeria and Azerbaijan and Nigeria, where Roman Catholics are killing Orthodox Christians (and vice versa) in the former Yugoslavia, where Sunni Muslims are killing Shiites in Iraq, and Shiites are killing Baha'is in Iran—to name only a few examples of contemporary religious bloodshed. And now, of course, the lethal faith-based initiative of September 11, and our retaliatory bombing, with its increasing numbers of the inevitable innocent victims.

Our own country was lucky to have founders who remembered and understood the tragedy of religious warfare; and one of the invaluable provisions of our Constitution is religious freedom, based upon and guaranteed by the strict separation of the power of the church from the power of the state. Thanks to that benevolent restriction, we are now a nation of diverse religions—as well as secular free thought—all existing side by side, with the toleration that makes civilized life possible. Unfortunately, members of all three branches of our federal government are now actively conspiring to tear down Jefferson's "wall of separation" between church and state, so that the ability to live in our unprecedented condition of diversity-with-peace is now threatened as never before.

So, in the wake of September 11, 2001, beyond our immediate emotional distress, three kinds of problems have become obvious and pressing.

1) American military tactics in Afghanistan have accomplished the second stage of the Taliban Strategy, with all of the fully anticipated "collateral damage." (The thousands of dead in the World Trade Center were also "collateral damage;" is anyone in this country consoled by that euphemism?) The Afghan people, victims of many years of vicious tribal warfare and foreign invasion, are among the world's most pitiable: war-ravaged, homeless, and faced with famine. To add to their misery carelessly or needlessly—or to bomb them back into the internecine chaos of the pre-Taliban years, leaving them with no viable central government—would be as shameful as our carpet-bombing of neutral Cambodia a generation ago. Of course, it is manifestly difficult to locate and "surgically" destroy a network of elusive terrorists, who can hide in the caves and mountains of Afghanistan, but to take wholesale revenge, in our frustration, by punishing the innocent for the crimes of the guilty is not only cowardly; it is simply not a solution to anything, and will only serve to galvanize our enemies and rally their sympathizers (the Third Stage of the Taliban Strategy). Just as "the blood of the martyrs was the seed of the church," the blood of each Muslim will generate hatred and vengefulness. A billion Muslims are witness to our actions: either a billion people willing to live with us in peace, or a billion potentially implacable enemies, who will remain our enemies long after the fighting stops in Afghanistan.

(Noubli Laroussi, who welcomed us into his desert home so long ago—would he welcome us today?)

2) While our attention is focused on military, diplomatic, and economic sanctions abroad, we must not let our attention be diverted from matters that momentarily seem less urgent but are of immeasurable long-term importance.

A) Domestic social programs, including education, scientific and medical research, environmental protection, social security, health care etc., must not be hijacked by political opportunists during the excitement of martial enthusiasms. And we must protest against the swarm of profiteers who want to drill for oil in wildlife refuges, exploit the resources of our public lands, contrive massive tax giveaways to the wealthy, promote ruinous "missile defense" boondoggles, and a host of other domestic frauds.

B) We need to be on heightened alert not only against foreign threats but also against the home-grown terrorists who, maddened by anti-government hate groups, bombed Oklahoma City, and maddened by Christian fundamentalists (the American Taliban), continue to bomb clinics, murder doctors, and mail anthrax threats to planned parenthood workers with the message, "We are going to kill you all. –Army of God"

c) International problems, notably overpopulation, will continue to imperil the entire human race, and should be addressed vigorously. If the world population continues to outstrip food, water, and fuel supplies, thus causing poverty, relentless hunger, and environmental devastation worldwide, then political unrest and widespread warfare will surely be inevitable.

3) Our personal freedoms must not be compromised in the name of "National security." Personal Freedom, the Democratic Process, Civil Liberties, if our nation stands for something special and valuable, those are the key words. To ensure these liberties, our vaunted "free press" should begin doing its proper job again, fully informing Americans about the facts of the real world, not self-censoring harsh truths or performing like puppets for the political and military establishments, in the name of "patriotism."

Which brings me to another, still older memory: sixty years ago, on October 3, 1941, the commander of the American Legion post in Indianapolis declared: "Traitors have got to be stopped—the time for freedom of speech has passed." That was two months before World War II started. I was reminded of those words by the current White House press secretary's recent threat to us all—"Watch what you say, watch what you do"—the language of Stalinism, not the language of America. As we fight the terrorists, we must not begin to resemble them.

At the end of his powerful novel *The Plague* (in which plague symbolizes despotism), Camus brooded about "what had had to be done, and what assuredly would have to be done again in the never ending fight against terror," by thoughtful people who know "that the plague bacillus never dies or disappears for good; that it can lie dormant for years and years" and then "rouse up its rats again and send them forth to die in a happy city."

Here in our own once-happy city, the rats have done their work. Now we remember the dead and mourn with their survivors. With pain and difficulty, we pluck up our courage and energy, and dedicate ourselves to rebuilding, to binding up wounds, and to punishing the guilty. Meanwhile, we must keep in mind the crucial difference between justice and vengeance, and we must cherish and protect our traditional civic virtues, stated so clearly in our Constitution, our Bill of Rights.

MICHAEL ATKINSON

The Accountant's Exodus

The bridges stood, pulling and pushing upon nothing at all.

One day this September my friend Ed
walked across the Manhattan Bridge.
In his blue suit, a silk tie, leather shoes.
A policeman in a stairwell said, Get out.

On the street, towers falling, Ed turned and walked east.

He carried nothing as he crossed the river
except car keys, and the morning
blazed like a fourth-generation rose
fulminating a newly-deepened, unknown gold.

He left the island behind him, and the bridge
filled with his countrymen, migrating
in the direction of the Old World.
Ed, quiet and balding, has three children,

and that brilliant morning he walked across
the river and the dead cities and
the deserts of Brooklyn and the thresholds of Jericho to reach them,

them and his wife who smokes too much
and treasures the cartoon-Calvin tattoo on her ass,

all of them and the promised land they've staked their lives on,
its shaped shrubs, its plastic yard castles,

its exhausted, late-night love made
as the children snooze down the carpeted hall,

the dark, silent ceiling
patiently waiting for witnesses.

September 28, 2001

How do I put this:
the huge acorns rain down upon our roof at night
like God's stones pelting the Egyptians,
and yet in our house, in our bed,
we are blessed from calamity;
the maple leaves this fall may fall
in a storm of bloody handprints,
but, for the life of me,
I cannot imagine the groundwater turning,
the hyacinth bulbs sickening as they wait,
the ant factories panicked by plague.
The grackles search the grass I haven't mown
for whatever grackles lack,
their prisming indigo plumages
struggling toward a crow's black,
wanting to be that black and devil-may-care.
How do I put this:
flowers we forgot we'd planted
show up without applause,
and though I'd sunk only violet impatiens this summer,
the wound-red blooms of 1999
appear like ghosts, flowers
that don't know they are not alive.
For what it's worth, the raspberries
have been reluctant, or perhaps
preemptively filched by squirrels.
Thus is the apocalypse of the dooryard,
while the sky has been pullulating with havoc.
For the life of me, I cannot figure
why it is I have been so fucking lucky.

Missing

O children of the demiurge,
spindly twistings of tissue in the flame,
are you my city ghosts,
too sweet to slam the midnight doors?
Are you the ripped corn of our autumn?

Even red leaves can be found, if not
by their trees: you evaporate
into mucous, misted over the river
that's purled unhindered for five thousand years.

Bedevilment, the stricken zodiac of you.
The shrine posters: streetcorners and station walls
overrun with statistics-this tall,
this heavy, this young, this flush with family.
This Rocco, this Ruth, these Franks.

So many photographs of barbecues.
By just such love shall we know you?
Will the wanderers make it
to 49th Street, stumbling
from the mouth of what's so much of this world?
Will you know your way home,
or have you forgotten all but the sirens' roar?

But, of course, we know where you are,
buried, treasure buried
in the underworld beneath a new mountain,
thrumming secretly with fortune and portent

in the city's cellars like fossils that could,
undug and reconstructed, reveal
the bones of this mysterious creature
so lately extinct but already as distant
as a mammoth carcass
in the Icelandic ice.
Who remembers this beautiful being?

If we recover them and clean them
carefully with sable-hair brushes,
softly blowing our breath across their cheeks,

MICHAEL ATKINSON
THE ACCOUNTANT'S EXODUS / SEPTEMBER 28, 2001 / MISSING

they'll tell us more
than our quaint skulls can imagine
about that day and age.

DAVID BAKER

Late Blooming Roses
(September 18, 2001)

The sun cracks through
   the bracken sky—
      week of

black clouds, rain, spit-
   mist of fog,
      the streets

gripped with terror,
   and mud against
      the curbs.

Now the dog down
   the street's racked with
      barking,

and the red flag
   waves on my e-
      mail screen.

I want the petals
   bright, the whole
      nine yards:

so when the hel-
   icopter thumps
      over

from somewhere to
   somewhere, I
      feel once

again the heart-
   rattle, that old
      great fear,

—that thrum—as in
   a movie of
      the war

that everybody
   watched, though no
      one won.

On Tuesday, September 18th, I received a phone call from the *Chicago Tribune*, inviting me to write a poem for their Sunday Arts and Entertainment section. This poem, my caller stipulated, should respond to the terrorist attacks of September 11th on the World Trade Center. My first and immediate response was to say no—that since the attacks I could hardly speak, let alone write a good poem. It takes weeks, months, longer, I explained, for me to write and release a poem; and further, hardly ever have I been able to write a poem on command with an assigned subject.

Four days later I emailed "Late-Blooming Roses" to the paper. Alas, I was too late for their deadline. The poem is not a specific description of the attacks, but rather it wants to describe an eternal irony: that beauty, unbidden, persists and blooms in the same world where terror and agony reside. This is not news. And yet, of course, every day it is newly true.

Poems may console. They may accuse. They may memorialize. They may rouse, enflame, woo, and bemuse. I am amazed, but finally not surprised, that so many people have turned again to poems, to the rigorous consolations of the art, during the weeks since the first attacks. Poems, as William Carlos Williams reminds us, shape our passions and connect our imaginations and our sympathies in ways that may yet keep us from killing each other. That's where my faith remains.

ALIKI BARNSTONE

Making Love After September 11, 2001

The ghosts of the people killed crowded into our room,
each one a rainbow where skin would be,
and some slid along us, the women and the men,
sharing in our bodily bliss, passionate with us,
as if they lived. Some swam in the air
between the bed and the walls, and between
our breaths I could hear their longing.
The children hovered in the corners silently
and saw what they would never know,
their little mouths only glimmers
moving without words now,
their lips a dark without a kiss.
The dead crowded in our room, like light twisting
on the surface of night waters, they made love
with us, they wanted us and to be an us, wanted
to be flesh against warm flesh, wanted to hold
the beloved and pleasured body close again.

For me, consciousness itself changed on September 11. In the past I
was loath to describe the autobiographical sources of my poems
because I wanted readers to focus on my poetry as the imaginative
transformation of experience, and not as a therapeutic record of my
personal life. But after the catastrophe, I think this reserve is a silly
theoretical conceit that might even have the dangerous effect of
divorcing art from the real and from its power to witness.

The simple story of "Making Love After September 11, 2001" is there in the poem. When my husband, Joseph Clark, and I made love after the catastrophe, I saw and felt in the room the ghosts of the people killed, "sharing in our bodily bliss," actually making love with us, as in a Dionysian orgy. It wasn't horrifying at all. It was as if the dead were reveling in our bodies, taking joy with us. But it was profoundly sad because I felt how much they longed to have bodies again.

Afterward, I forgot about these ghosts until Joseph reminded me. Then all came back. He said I was distracted by the others in the room and not wholly there with him. I think it is paradoxical—I was and was not connected to him. I was with him in the sense that I felt so lucky to be alive, to be in my body with the love of my life whose body I have loved and pleasured and desired, always thrilled by him, as if our love were new. Yet our ecstatic newness is coupled with the familiar—we also love in the way that people who are long married do—we know each other, know how to make the other happy, and that intimate knowledge gained over time is sexy. I feel giddy watching him walk into the room or make a cup of coffee. I've learned how his body moves. How extraordinary his body is as he performs mundane tasks! I praise Joseph now not to show that our love is unique, but to show that intimacy feels extraordinary yet is common. Each person who died or who lost a lover lost "being flesh against warm flesh." When I sensed the ghosts in the room, I felt the sorrow of the survivors. The poem is informed by their feelings and my own, but I didn't include much of the perspective of the living because the poem wants to be inside the consciousness of those who were killed. The poem comes out of my (involuntary) empathic union with the dead, who were robbed of the pleasures of their own bodies and their loved ones' bodies.

Another part of the poem deals with children. We have a beautiful four-and-a-half year old daughter, Zoë. Zoë, whose name means life in Greek, has been fully conscious of the tragedy. She has been trying to work out the difference between dying and killing and she says: "When you die, it's something your body does, but killing is something someone does on purpose." And, "Why do our bodies do that? Why do we die?" And, "I don't want to die." She focuses heartbreakingly on the body, on her body. We love our children's bodies more than our own, more than our lover's. Would I be a mother if I didn't love to touch my daughter's luminous skin? If I didn't love to see her skip ahead of me? Or dance on her long legs? I think people also tend to be uncomfortable when they think of their children growing up and having sex. But it is intolerable—isn't it?—to imagine your child never growing up and never making love. Because Zoë is always close to me, I also saw the dear lost children in the room. I saw them "see what they would never know," the joy of their adult selves making love. And I saw, too, they would never speak again, for there can be no words without flesh, lips, tongue, throat, lungs. Nor would the children kiss or be kissed. No mothers or fathers would marvel at that most ordinary thing—as Joseph and I do daily—to see how tall their children had grown. The children's "little mouths [were] only glimmers / moving without words now" because they told me what they had no voice to say—it is unbearable to be kidnapped by killers, ripped away from one's lovely body and the arms of parents and the future.

I hope the poem succeeds in making the term "making love" larger than "having sex"—and I hope that it is the children who make the term more inclusive—or perhaps familial is a better word. For me, making love at its best is like making poetry at its best: both are ecstatic, spiritual unions, both are utterly empathic with the other, the lover, the subject, the reader. If my poem works, then my readers will be, as I was, inside the souls who yearn to have bodies, for bodies allow us "to be an us." The god I believe in is inside each of us and in the space between us. I hope Emerson is right when he says, "Grief too will make us idealists," which is why the title of the poem is "Making Love After September 11, 2001." I hope we can hope. I hope after our tragedy we can make love for everyone, that we can all make love in the space between us, which must mean holding others close, body and soul.

WILLIS BARNSTONE

Our New York Rooms in the 1930s
Remembered in September 2001

We faced the park and sometimes a big swan
over Manhattan rose from the small lake
where I went with my Dad to row and scan
the New York skyline. Each year Mom took
a glass with wax in it, and lit the wick,
her hands hovering over it like a well
she fell into. She wasn't nuts or sick
but I didn't get it and broke her spell
with blabber. Whispering for her dead, a Jew
on a few days, she never could parade
her feelings. This evening I stood out on
the street for Mom and her high skyline that
had no Twin Towers then, nor now. Some prayed
(a lily tolls a day and night comes through).
My candle lingered for the thousands gone,
the child in the swan, burning where she sat.

I happened in my vagabond travels into many war sectors—in Greece
in 1949 at the end of the civil war, in Spain in 1951–52 during the
armed years of Franco, in China in 1972 during the Great Proletarian
Cultural Revolution, in Argentina in 1975–76 during the "Dirty War"
and its disappeared, in Guatemala during the long genocide, and
even in Chiapas on January 1, 1994, the morning of the Zapatista
rebellion. There is one commonality to all slaughter, which resem-
bles the present horror: the face of the victim. From the corpses of
fugitive Andalusian republicans caught in the Sierra Nevada mountains, sprawled across donkeys as they were paraded through the
main square on their way up to "the pit of the poor," *la fosa de los*

pobres, on the cave hill overlooking our village, to the bodies I could see on any morning in Hong Kong, almost clogging the Pearl River, as they floated down from Cultural Revolution China in the north, all these victims looked less glamorous than their adventurous killers. All war is execution. All executions, from electric chairs to the killing fields of Cambodia, the gas chambers, and the Twin Towers in New York, hide behind a proclaimed virtue of justice. My Quaker education sees no execution as ever permissible, in "good countries" and "bad ones." And the New York and Washington plane bombs were executions. Like the Holocaust which used crude science to augment the numbers of the executed, so too the people whose faith was hatred and death invented a new weapon of mass extinction, the passenger-filled plane as bomb.

The night before the catastrophe, I was thinking of my parents, who died young, and of death the equalizer in nature, always ready to seize our breath and time. I saw my mother with her candle glass (which I also saw a few days later in Oakland when I was in the street with a candle). A Yiddish proverb says you never bury your parents. So I have not mine. Nor did they, nor will the new bereaving survivors. The night before the catastrophe, I was back in our apartment overlooking Central Park and its swans of innocence flying over Manhattan from the rowboat pond, and the next day the swans were the plane bombs executing the poor. I say poor, because anyone whose life is absurdly shortened is poor as are the loved ones who grieve. The lines I refer to in Matthew 6:26–30 speak of "the lilies in the field," who, in a forecast of oven and fire, are all victims: "even Solomon in all his splendor / was not clothed like one of these lilies / yet the grass of the field today / is tomorrow thrown into the oven." In the last line the child was sitting in the swan—one of so many children burning—strapped to her seat.

"He must be thirsty," someone in the crowd
is saying. "You think even he's not scared?"
another says. He whispers from his cloud
of agony, "I'm fading!" He too cares
to live. Who doesn't? The trapped jumpers soar,
some holding hands. For love? Or terror? They
can't last in the building a second more
of smoke and flaming clothes. Hung from spikes he
too wants more breath like every visitor
to earth. The sheep are leaping out of hell,
hurling from windows, floating down the sky
to nothing they can see. Last breath of air.
They pole cheap wine to his lips. He cries, "Why
have you left me?" And sags while jumpers fall.

One might ask, how can a secular Jew find in the execution of Jesus
(rabbi Jeshua ben Josef) a parallel to those who leapt into the sky
from the Tower windows. The name of Jesus has been raised to
occasion the countless murders of other Jews, but Yeshua the man
was a victim of dumb political hatred as were millions through the
millennia, including the victims in the Tower buildings. The one
historical fact in Jesus's life that scholars do not quibble about is
that a man named Yeshua ben Yosef was crucified by the Romans.
And if the mocking placard THE KING OF THE JEWS (Jn 19:19) is
true, then he was crucified among the thousands of crucified Jews as
a seditionist for opposing Roman rule. So witnessed is a victim on a
cross or in a tower. All killings—and worst of all the killings for a
label—are as stupid as kicking the wind.

One long Sunday morning in 1975 in Buenos Aires, I was walking
with Jorge Luis Borges through the streets. This was the grim Dirty
War period. We went from one book store to another. Then we sat
down in the Saint James Café and he said from nowhere, "You know
the two greatest deaths in history were of Socrates and Jesus." And he
compared the nature of each one. One of the last poems that blind
Borges wrote is "Christ on the cross" in which it is man who feels the
fire of the nails: "Christ on the cross. His feet touch the earth. / The
three beams are of the same height. / Christ is not in the middle.
He's the third. / His black beard hangs over his chest. His face is not
the face of the engravings. It is severe and Jewish." And then, "He

knows he is not a god and that he is a man / who dies with the day. It doesn't affect him. / What affects him is the hard iron of the spikes."

I have been haunted by another image since my youth, that of my father's suicide in 1946, when he climbed the tallest building in his city in Colorado and leapt into the May sun. Like those who flocked into the sky from the Tower windows, he was pursued by intolerable pain that caused him to jump into the release of blind air and oblivion. From my childhood on, surely coincidence, I was into the act of floating. During high school and college I was a team diver, every day testing gravity. When I was forty I parachuted. I also translated a book of poems of the sixteenth-century Spanish mystical poet Saint John of the Cross, who chose the rising and falling through space as a dominant metaphor of love, fusion, and "death in life." In "Full of hope I climbed the day," he wrote, "I had to fly so high, high / I floated unseen and became / lost in that dangerous day…. Dazzled and stunned by light / as I rose near the sun, my greatest conquest was won / in the very black of night…. The higher I began to soar / the lower I felt—more sore / and broken and depressed." I could not know what my father had experienced, but somehow I moved in his ways, toward his last instant of soaring and dropping. I can't express but feel why. Now we have the image and knowledge of a multitude driven to jump.

These examples of the man hanging from spikes and the people leaping from fire are continuations of the unnecessary horror that we humans do to others in our few days of life. And my father's leap to extinction is as close as I have come to knowledge of such death. It never leaves my mind. As for answers, solutions, consolations, they are mainly language, without much earthly truth. And for the killings, there are strategies but never a good in extinguishing the light of being, in a condemned human, inside a giant stone Buddha, or in a stone tower alive with people.

WENDELL BERRY

Thoughts in the Presence of Fear

I. The time will soon come when we will not be able to remember the horrors of September 11 without remembering also the unquestioning technological and economic optimism that ended on that day.

II. This optimism rested on the proposition that we were living in a "new world order" and a "new economy" that would "grow" on and on, bringing a prosperity of which every new increment would be "unprecedented."

III. The dominant politicians, corporate officers, and investors who believed this proposition did not acknowledge that the prosperity was limited to a tiny percentage of the world's people, and to an ever smaller number of people even in the United States; that it was founded upon the oppressive labor of poor people all over the world; and that its ecological costs increasingly threatened all life, including the lives of the supposedly prosperous.

IV. The "developed" nations had given to the "free market" the status of a god and were sacrificing to it their farmers, farmlands, and rural communities; their forests, wetlands, and prairies, their ecosystems and watersheds. They had accepted universal pollution and global warming as normal costs of doing business.

V.   There was, as a consequence, a growing worldwide effort on behalf of economic decentralization, economic justice, and ecological responsibility. We must recognize that the events of September 11 make this effort more necessary than ever. We citizens of the industrial countries must continue the labor of self-criticism and self-correction. We must recognize our mistakes.

VI.   The paramount doctrine of the economic and technological euphoria of recent decades has been that everything depends on innovation. It was understood as desirable, and even as necessary, that we should go on and on from one technological innovation to the next, which would cause the economy to "grow" and make everything better and better. This of course implied at every point a hatred of the past, of all things inherited and free. All things superceded in our progress of innovations, whatever their value might have been, were discounted as of no value at all.

VII. We did not anticipate anything like what has now happened. We did not foresee that all our sequence of innovations might be at once overridden by a greater one: the invention of a new kind of war that would turn our previous innovations against us, discovering and exploiting the debits and the dangers that we had ignored. We never considered the possibility that we might be trapped in the webwork of communication and transport that was supposed to make us free.

VIII. Nor did we foresee that the weaponry and the war science that we marketed and taught to the world would become available, not just to recognized national governments which possess so uncannily the power to legitimate large-scale violence, but also to "rogue nations," dissident or fanatical groups, and individuals—whose violence, though never worse than that of nations, is judged by the nations to be illegitimate.

IX. We had accepted uncritically the belief that technology is only good; that it cannot serve evil as well as good; that it cannot serve our enemies as well as ourselves; that it cannot be used to destroy what is good, including our homelands and our lives.

X.   We had accepted too the corollary belief that an economy (either as a money economy or as a life-support system) that is global in extent, technologically complex, and centralized is invulnerable to terrorism, sabotage, or war, and that it is protectable by "national defense."

XI. We now have a clear, inescapable choice that we must make. We can continue to promote a global economic system of unlimited "free trade" among corporations, held together by long and highly vulnerable lines of communication and supply, but now recognizing that such a system will have to be protected by a hugely expensive police force that will be worldwide, whether maintained by one nation or several or all, and that such a police force will be effective precisely to the extent that it oversways the freedom and privacy of the citizens of every nation.

XII.   Or we can promote a decentralized world economy which would have the aim of assuring to every nation and region a local self-sufficiency in life-supporting goods. This would not eliminate international trade, but it would tend toward a trade in surpluses after local needs had been met.

XIII.   One of the gravest dangers to us now, second only to further terrorist attacks against our people, is that we will attempt to go on as before with the corporate program of global "free trade," whatever the cost in freedom and civil rights, without self-questioning or self-criticism or public debate.

XIV.   This is why the substitution of rhetoric for thought, always a temptation in a national crisis, must be resisted by officials and citizens alike. It is hard for ordinary citizens to know what is actually happening in Washington in a time of such great trouble; for all we know, serious and difficult thought may be taking place there. But the talk that we are hearing from politicians, bureaucrats, and commentators has so far tended to reduce the complex problems now facing us to issues of unity, security, normality, and retaliation.

XV.   National self-righteousness, like personal self-righteousness, is a mistake. It is misleading. It is a sign of weakness. Any war that we may make now against terrorism will come as a new installment in a history of war in which we have fully participated. We are not innocent of making war against civilian populations. The modern doctrine of such warfare was set forth and enacted by General William Tecumseh Sherman, who held that a civilian population could be declared guilty and rightly subjected to military punishment. We have never repudiated that doctrine.

XVI.   It is a mistake also—as events since September 11 have shown—to suppose that a government can promote and participate in a global economy and at the same time act exclusively in its own interest by abrogating its international treaties and standing aloof from international cooperation on moral issues.

XVII.   And surely, in our country, under our Constitution, it is a fundamental error to suppose that any crisis or emergency can justify any form of political oppression. Since September 11, far too many public voices have presumed to "speak for us" in saying that Americans will gladly accept a reduction of freedom in exchange for greater "security." Some would, maybe. But some others would accept a reduction in security (and in global trade) far more willingly than they would accept any abridgement of our Constitutional rights.

XVIII.   In such a time as this, when we have been seriously and most cruelly hurt by those who hate us, and when we must consider ourselves to be gravely threatened by those same people, it is hard to speak of the ways of peace and to remember that Christ enjoined us to love our enemies, but this is no less necessary for being difficult.

XIX.   Even now we dare not forget that since the attack on Pearl Harbor—to which the present attack has been often and not usefully compared—we humans have suffered an almost uninterrupted sequence of wars, none of which has brought peace or made us more peaceable.

XX.   The aim and result of war necessarily is not peace but victory, and any victory won by violence necessarily justifies the violence that won it and leads to further violence. If we are serious about innovation, must we not conclude that we need something new to replace our perpetual "war to end war"?

XXI.   What leads to peace is not violence but peaceableness, which is not passivity, but an alert, informed, practiced, and active state of being. We should recognize that while we have extravagantly subsidized the means of war, we have almost totally neglected the ways of peaceableness. We have, for example several national military academies, but not one peace academy. We have ignored the teachings and the examples of Christ, Gandhi, Martin Luther King, and other peaceable leaders. And here we have an inescapable duty to notice also that war is profitable, whereas the means of peaceableness, being cheap or free, make no money.

XXII.   The key to peaceableness is continuous practice. It is wrong to suppose that we can exploit and inpoverish the poorer countries, while arming them and instructing them in the newest means of war, and then reasonably expect them to be peaceable.

XXIII. We must not again allow public emotion or the public media to caricature our enemies. If our enemies are now to be some nations of Islam, then we should undertake to know these enemies. Our schools should begin to teach the histories, cultures, arts, and languages of the Islamic nations. And our leaders should have the humility and the wisdom to ask the reasons some of those people have for hating us.

XXIV. Starting with the economies of food and farming, we should promote at home and encourage abroad the ideal of local self-sufficiency. We should recognize that this is the surest, the safest, and the cheapest way for the world to live. We should not countenance the loss or destruction of any local capacity to produce necessary goods.

XXV. We should reconsider and renew and extend our efforts to protect the natural foundations of the human economy: soil, water, and air. We should protect every intact ecosystem and watershed that we have left, and begin restoration of those that have been damaged.

XXVI. The complexity of our current trouble suggests as never before that we need to change our present concept of education. Education is not properly an industry, and its proper use is not to serve industries, either by job-training or by industry-subsidized research. Its proper use is to enable citizens to live lives that are economically, politically, socially, and culturally responsible. This cannot be done by gathering or "accessing" what we now call "information"—which is to say facts without context and, therefore, without priority. A proper education enables young people to put their lives in order, which means knowing what things are more important than other things; it means putting first things first.

XXVII. The first thing we must begin to teach our children (and learn ourselves) is that we cannot spend and consume endlessly. We have got to learn to save and conserve. We do need a "new economy," but one that is founded on thrift and care, on saving and conserving, not on excess and waste. An economy based on waste is inherently and hopeless violent, and war is its inevitable by-product. We need a peaceable economy.

PATRICK BIZZARO

Houses of History Are Made of Words:
A Short Essay About Feeling and Language
(9/12/01 Greenville, NC)

I am writing here about a feeling—but more than that. A feeling, of course, but more importantly where that feeling originates. I want to write about the kind of feeling that makes you anxious about what happens to all those hundredths when you round numbers to their tenths, or where all that money goes when you round to the nearest dollar. My grades in algebra, my checkbook, my most basic instincts about mathematics, and the world make me doubt that it all eventually evens out. I have become royalty of the round off as a result. But life experience has made me think that rounding off causes problems: national debt, wars, perhaps even loss of love. At a minimum, the consequence of such approximations is the uncertainty, perhaps even dread, that many of us feel today, September 12, 2001, and may feel for some time into the future. So, then, let's not think about numbers. We're better off not thinking about them, Hemingway might say.

Let's think instead about language. Recently a well-respected poet sent a list of words to an editor for possible publication, permitting the editor the apparent honor of deciding upon the order of the words. A concession to our postmodern condition, I suppose. But there are other concessions, less conscious than letting someone else decide which word goes where. Let me give an example. If I say in a poem, as I do, with words in a specific order, "people good with money / are also good with time," saying so doesn't make it true anywhere but on the page. Language too suffers from approximation. We round off language to the point where it no longer matters to some people what order you put their words in. We round off language to the nearest truth, general though it may be: not all people who are good with money "are also good with time." But something happens when language enters the world we live in. In that world, approximations of truth leave us with the feeling of dread, the anxiety that arises when we feel we are drifting toward something we cannot define. As most of us have learned, defining it won't help anyway. I want to argue here that these approximations contribute to feelings we have but cannot name directly. Consider the world news (CNN, as a fine example) not as media event, but as language event: approximate and threateningly incomplete.

As a writer, I must confess complicity in making approximations that generate tentative understandings—since it is fragile language with which I have chosen to work. There is, in my mind, a consequence for inexactness and uncertainty, for using language that by its very nature prevents us from conveying exactly what we mean. What happens to our language, how it is used, tells us something about what has happened to our culture. George Orwell warned my father's generation: "...the decline of a language must ultimately have political and economic causes." This was written when we still believed in words, when we felt some certainty that they had some magical relationship to the objects they represented. But things get more confusing, if not worse. Let me add to Orwell's warning Ferdinand de Saussure's announcement, one that has left some members of my generation drawing and making music rather than writing: "The linguistic sign unites not a thing and a name, but a concept and a sound-image." For Saussure, theorizing about language in 1959, there is nothing in an object that, by its very nature, requires that it be called by a specific name. Rather, according to Saussure, "the linguistic sign is arbitrary."

Like numbers, then, all language is a rounding off, an approximation. People of my generation who have known about it (it wasn't intended to be a secret, you know!) have lived with this threat posed by our language as we have lived with the threat posed by nuclear weapons: going about our daily business as if everything's all right. And I'm feeling increasingly certain, writing here today, September 12, 2001, that things aren't all right. In final analysis, after all, bomb shelters will do no more to protect us from words than they will from nuclear bombs or chemical contagion. Clearly, we must accept this as one fact of our lives as we plan to continue living them: reading is misreading. Information, misinformation. And both contribute to the dread we all feel but cannot quite name.

We may, of course, insist upon our innocence in our uses of

language—you're not guilty and, naturally, neither am I. We didn't do anything intentionally; it's more like something was done to us or happened while we weren't paying attention. Maybe we were talking about nuclear weapons or bio-warfare or poetry. Whatever. While we weren't paying attention, language grew a life of its own and we simply cannot control it anymore. Today, considering the world's condition, I tend to agree with James Berlin, who insists that "language is never innocent." But I want to add that because we cannot trust in the innocence of language, we feel instead. But we do not know where our feelings come from or have an exact name for what has thus moved us.

Thinking recently about history—about how the Civil War is told in the north, where I was born, as compared to the way it is told in the south, where I have lived (as a damn Yankee) for the past twenty-five years—I wrote a poem I would like to end with, in the belief that history is the story of the teller who is also the victor. And, given the vulnerabilities of language, its ability to betray us as writers though we love it dearly and depend upon it for our very existence, we should remember that houses of history are, in fact, made of the very words that trick, befuddle, and eventually betray us.

HOUSES OF HISTORY

FOR JASON, MY SON

In the lot
across the street, four men enter
my vision, all doing almost
what I think they're doing,

all building a house together
cooperating with the movement of dirt
to a designated spot across the yard,
all building one house
from a single plan.

But as I watch, I see
ahead of their weary motions
the house of my understanding
and the house of theirs
though all the while
they ignore me

as if the structures we live by
differ at the brick foundation,
and the house this will become
is finished as they begin it,
stretched to its imaginary
posts, so people
we have never seen
can enter
and make it a house of their own.

KAREN BLOMAIN

Sisters

Sisters. In foggy semi-darkness of 6 a.m., feeling a little of the wine from last night's traditional sleepover behind the eyelids, we drove Bucks County lanes. Donna, who yipped from trees during the student rebellions of the 60's; who, disenchanted, hitchhiked cross country, followed the Marahaji to India and came home weighing 85 pounds; who grew her own food and lived beside a river in a house without electricity. We had gathered to celebrate Donna's cronedom and fiftieth birthday.

Tent-sheltered wares dimly visible in the gray morning, the hectic, the idle motion of a makeshift village—from a distance so like the CNN footage of Kandahar Bazaars we would soon get to know. Around us, the flash and chatter of many cultures invited us to consider the knock-off watch, the exact copy of the Kate Spade bag, the stack of CD's, three for ten dollars, the genuine earrings with imitation diamonds as big as the Ritz. We had come to worship at a particularly American altar, the quintessential melting pot: the flea market.

Sisters. Our best conversations take place when we're doing something else. Give me a stack of ironing and a telephone and I'm a philosopher. Set me near a sibling and a blueberry bush and the words fly as fast as my picking fingers. No one gets our jokes as quickly or appreciates our well-honed harrangues and paeans. We talked as we walked the rows of splendid stuff, intricate copies of middle-class dreams; we talked about our parents, dead now and, therefore, both more terrible and more interesting than they had been during their long, fretful, wonderful earthtime. "A regular League of Nations," Lucie smiled, imitating our father's dated comment and tone of voice. Childhood nights we snuggled back into the sofa under his sheltering arm and shivered at his stories of ships and cargo and ports, the swelter of humanity and tongues. A Merchant Marine during WWII, he had set his foot on every continent. Proud. "Tell us again about Africa." We begged stories of dark skin, exotic facial ornaments and lively cloth wraps instead of trousers. "You learn," said my father who had been raised in a Pennsylvania coal patch, "people are just people, no matter what they wear or how they talk."

Mother stood in the doorway, a forgotten cigarette between her fingers, its smoke tentacling toward us. Afternoons, called into the room in the basement where she had put cots and blankets, food and clean water, we worried our abandoned dolls and books, sunlight and birds, the games we had run from at the sound of her whistle.

By nine, slivers of sunlight had pierced the morning fog. Already laden with bundles, we began the second section of the market. "Ray Bans," Donna said, pointing to the stall where a large Jamaican man poked the earpieces of sunglasses onto a revolving case. I tried on a pair of sandals, held my foot out for sisterly inspection.

Nearby, a woman wailing. A sharp plume of sorrow jarring in the market's tranquil air, a cry like the soundtrack you imagine for those same refugee scenes. Staggering, the woman clutched the edge of table, her face distorted in stroke or ecstasy. A radio played softly in a van behind the shoe tent. Like the mother who hears her own child crying over the din of an entire nursery, she had picked out the words that meant terror. "Aiaee, aiaee," she shrieked: The primal intensity of her cry froze the people milling nearby. A man dropped the black boots he was examining and flew to her side. "My God, oh God. My daughter works there ..." the woman howled. His shoulder muffled the rest.

The man pointed skyward. "Aero planes," he said, "aero planes," forming the words carefully through a heavy Russian accent. Across the way in the clothing tent, the Korean family stopped unpacking boxes. The father retrieved a radio from their car and placed it on the front of the u-shaped table where it caught the sunlight. He adjusted the antenna as we waited. The Latino touting the sucking power of a vacuum killed the motor and joined us.

In the glitter of faux gems, the scent of spices and candles drifting from the Indian stall, we clustered together, jostling politely for a view of the radio. Someone handed the worried mother a cell phone. She punched the numbers. Breathless, we watched. She shook her head. New people came upon us and someone whispered them into our growing community of fear. "Twin towers," someone said. It became clear that both had been hit. The young daughter of the Korean family, her eyes table height, stared questioningly.

Word leapt like gossip across the acres of the market. More radios and a few tiny televisions were positioned for optimum viewing. We shaded our eyes against the glare for a glimpse of what had happened. On a nine-inch screen, the towers looked as insubstantial as a child's play set, the make-believe of cardboard box cities crumpling as the planes disappeared inside. Smoke, an imaginary dragon breath, billowed from the frangible columns. We searched the horizon for proof of what was happening fifty miles away.

Sisters. Speechless, we clung to each other for comfort as we had in childhood when the sounds of anger woke us in the night. I felt the breath of their grief on my cheeks. We were old suddenly, our own pasts tamed and receding like the images of our parents. My body felt weak and insubstantial, unequal to the task. How could we fix this thing? What lesson, what warning could we write or speak? I imagined my children, their place in the wheel of history, an end to the long illusion of peace, the face of the planets dreaming, fierce jewels still hidden in the morning sky.

BRUCE BOND

The Language of Disaster

We all know the image, if not the many images, the many angles. We see it still, the second plane's irrevocable penetration, its wounding spectacle going deep into the national psyche. Unreal perhaps, the sheer magnitude of tragedy and our ensuing sadness reminiscent of some Hollywood fiction. How fascinated we are by the dream of our collective demise, and yet this object of our disbelief derives its obsessive magnetism from its hyper-reality, the hard fact of enormous loss distilled into the primacy of the image. Confronted with the hyper-real, the imagination feels overwhelmed by what resists any adequate response, let alone the troubled pleasures of art. As much as the World Trade Center, the Pentagon, and the assault on each stand as emblematic, the interpretive mind is likewise humbled by what refuses to be reduced to symbol, what fails to be reinvented. In the freshness of our grief, we honor the dead with silence, their native tongue.

And yet the very language of such prayerful intimacy is the language of distance. A space in which the literal banishes our dreams is finally uninhabitable, unresponsive to the needs of the living. If all we have to offer in difficult times is our silence, however briefly honorific or healing, is there not in time something unsatisfying in its receptive passivity? "No art after Auschwitz," Adorno writes, summing up the crisis of the imagination hushed by images from death camps, so hard for any art to mitigate or stand beside. Given such difficulty, it's tempting to pick through the rubble with the most barren of poetics, as if to measure up to the literal power of the newsreel, or try, or perhaps to mirror fragments with fragments, chaos with chaos, distrusting speculation as foreign to emotional truth.

But it is precisely in such times, such crises of meaning, that we may crave the imagination's transfigurative potential to make new myths of the moment, new reasons to love the world. It is precisely in such times that the literalism of the newsreel, the poverty of the fragment, the radical irony of a poetics that believes in nothing may strike us as meager sustenance, insufficient in terms of commitment. Part of art's allure is likewise its threat, how it compromises our boundaries, investing the self. It is exactly when such boundaries have been violated by great disaster that we become most vulnerable to withdrawal and disenchantment. The challenge of all politically charged art is for the authority of the work to reside not merely in the given situation, charged as it is by ready-made pathos, but in the quality of spontaneous imaginative participation in that situation, what calls us to drag the newsreel to the recesses of the unconscious, to wed a passionate authenticity with expressive freedom.

With the rise of nationalism and all its implicit aggression, collective narcissism, and delirium of projection, it is especially important to keep vital those forms of consciousness which assert the reality and significance of the individual, which deepen and complicate our sense of our lives, our dependencies, our affections, and the shadows we cast. It is important to feel connected to the world without losing our mobility within it, not to mention our creative self-awareness, our capacity to surprise ourselves. As many a violent fundamentalist demonstrates, little is more dangerous than blind conviction intolerant of a plurality of voices, both within the self and among selves.

Recently I read the following new poem, "The Altars of September," to a group of students at USC and admitted some uneasiness I felt with the work or rather with the reading of it. "Is it because you don't have enough distance?" one student asked. "Yes, that's true," I said. "I don't." And yet it's also true that I have too much distance, that there are other voices that can speak with greater authority, and will. Still, it felt good to talk with the students that day, to begin one more conversation that, thanks to their insight and good nature, shed a little more light on our respective emotional difficulties, that worked in turn to animate the conversation within each mind, the silence of each room broken.

THE ALTARS OF SEPTEMBER

That night she closed her eyes and saw
the trapped birds of voices shatter
against the crumbling walls, like a scene

in a movie replaying the disaster,
lighting up the back of the brain.
With each collapse the glass rose up,
restored, bright with sky, the fist
of God a shadow-plane approaching.

And it felt so distant, the numb
comfort that would bear this image
into the first cold regions of sleep,
the blackboard of the body wet
and remless, as if those towers
fell still deeper through the floor
of the mind, gone the way of the pill
she took in faith, swallowing the world.

However many nights she clicked
her TV off, its spark of light
dwindling into the clear stone,
it would take time for any shape
slipping through her hands to lie
down in clay or paper, any lip
of paint to redden her brush.
White was its own confession.

She always imagined the distance
between a painting of a day
and the day behind it as a path
that carries us into our lives,
giving us more room, more reason
to move, luring us on and in
like sleep so deep in the body
all we see is of the body.

In time, looking out this way
through the window of her canvas,
every cloud dragging its anchor
becomes a burden of the flesh,
not hers alone, but the skin
of what no solitary gaze
can tear there from heaven's fire,
what no frame can ever shelter.

Just that morning before she heard

the news, she took the shore drive south,
set up her easel, all the while
an unaccountable strangeness
drawn down over the folding cliffs,
a stillness unlike any day,
the uneasy silence of the skies
that hour tender as an eye.

EMILY BORENSTEIN

from "Twelve Meditations"

4.
The Days of Awe
are upon us. Our feelings are carried,
bleeding and raw
on gurneys through the streets
of Manhattan.
The sun streams into windows
as though it were just
another day.

6.
The crater still hisses and spits
like a snake.
Fire erupts from the pit of the
snake's belly.
Above, engineers pilot cranes,
excavators, front-loaders,
and wrecking ball.
They crash, rip, tear, scoop.
Ironworkers and carpenters assist.
There are flashbacks.
A return to Viet Nam.
The stench of dead bodies.
Smell of festering wounds.
Anything that looks out of place
in a load is spread out
on the ground
as firefighters scour
for body parts.

8.

Numbers don't begin to tell
the story.
Numbers don't quantify hurt,
reveal the depth of grief,
the amount of sorrow.
Numbers don't say how
desperation grows.
Numbers don't show the pain of
putting dreams on dialysis,
then removing the needle
and letting dreams die.
Numbers don't add up human loss.
In the *Encyclopedia of the Unexplained*,
disbelief and denial give way
to pain and grief.
We suspend old assumptions.
Mourning continues.

9.

We move in solitude, bewildered
and confused.
Death might be acceptable
when we live to old age and die
peacefully, our lives fulfilled.
But not these deaths!
You who died in terrorist-flown
planes,
you, unable to escape the burning
towers,
you who jumped to your deaths
holding hands,
you, the firefighters who climbed
the endless stairs to rescue
men and women trapped on the higher
floors,
for you we recite the mourner's
kaddish:
yit-gadal v'yit-kadash
shmei raba ...
We remember you for a blessing.

On 11/29/01 the author wrote: "Dear Bill, late this afternoon I pho-
tocopied and sent you my new "Meditations" poem.... If I were to die

tomorrow, not that I plan to, I would be happy that I accomplished this final re-working of the original poem. You may not agree, but I feel this is one of my very best, possibly the best poem I've ever done. I've accomplished what I set out to do, but I can't even begin to tell you what it's cost me physically, emotionally and spiritually and how utterly drained I am. I am a very intense, passionate person and I've lived every thought and feeling in the poem just as I've lived the Sept. 11 disaster without let-up since that day."

JONAH BORNSTEIN

Blackout

Days later, in the safety of hills, lights go out
without a sputter, the speaker
crackles. Then silence. You imagine war.
And go to the window.

Four miles away the town is dark. You watch several cars
move down the highway, cautious
in blackout silence

as if something might descend on them. You understand
the scope of the sabotage, see power grids
blinking off across the country,

and you prepare for darkness lit by fire and candle.

You think this might be the beginning of something new,
fear grated through life; you will hang on
for a time as others must,
a world shadowy

and silent, no television, no music tugging an uncertain
pulse through wire, only the murmur
of lovemaking, the drone of a jet high overhead.

Then the lights come on, and you return to the present,
the ceramic cocoons of power plants
reappear on steelworks, the babble

of the radio smoothes into distinct voices and notes;

no longer do you trade glances over candle flames
when your son turns to the window
at the sound of rain; tomorrow you will

not forage for food or water or light, you will not form
alliances with neighbors, you will not
reconfigure yourselves in caves, in piles of leaves.

You bend to blow out the candles.

Return to the City, A Dream

Left outside the hotel, the man turned back to the street. Papers swirled in a gust of wind, then settled back into the ash. The quiet reminded him of a first snow on a dark morning. He had read about the new camaraderie in the city, the populace linked by tragedy and trauma. He looked up at the façade of the hotel to what he estimated to be the 37th floor, where his wife would spend the evening. He wanted to be alone with the city, to wander the streets he had owned when young. He wished a stranger would come for him, put an arm around his shoulders and walk him to a neighborhood bar, where the people gathered in the evening. He walked down Broadway and cut across Canal as far as he could. He looked south toward the site, the sky glowing from the rescue lights. The streets were almost empty. He wanted to return to his wife, put his head in her lap, and cry. He headed north, toward the Village. Without a word, she would understand and stroke his head and begin to sing. He was so lonely. But he knew she would only look down at him, say, "You don't need me, you want a mother." He would want to reply, *Yes, be my mother a little will you?* But her words would restrain him. He turned a corner. Up ahead, Sixth Avenue. He realized he was on Waverly Place. A movie at Waverly Theater sounded good.

In the first days after the attack, my instinct was to fly to New York, or drive across country, since the airports were closed. I wanted to help physically. My initial reactions to the bombings were common: wrenching tears of grief and anguish for ten days, a patriotism I had never before felt, desire for revenge, fear of a broader war and inno-cent lives lost. I can't pretend to comprehend the enormity of the tragedy, and I won't in writing. What I have done is approach it, as I do now with most of my poetry, through a personal experience that touches on the psychological effect of September 11. Thus my poem describes how the attack indelibly altered my reaction to a power blackout, a not uncommon event. In my dream piece, I seem to walk into great sorrow, but manage, at least for the length of a movie, to turn away from it.

DANIEL BOURNE

The First of October, We

Suddenly we can say last month,
that small flip of calendar between us,
September 11 now out of mind
at least in the way we might want it,
somewhere beyond, not quite reaching
here to the swamps and Amish of Ohio
the way Kafka's imperial messenger,
by the end of the story, never
quite arrives and we have to dream
the emperor's last words, first instructions
in this new world no one thought would happen.

The icon of the month: Dalmatian
to Schnauzer, alpine lake in Colorado
to an autumn hayfield in Vermont,
April's swimsuit model and the endangered
species for May. A bomb made
from a jetliner hits the World Trade Center
in New York City. A jetplane flings
a bomb on the Taliban in Kandahar. These
are the transformations of the world,
one thing leading to another, one God
picking up the phone and phoning
the second God, saying hey you
keep the racket down. Meanwhile,

we also want to put down distance,
get away from collapsing shard and myth.

We want to speak metaphorically
and not then have someone die. We want
the person next to us to be
our neighbor. We want to turn to him and say
remember. We want the version of the fable
where we have still survived.

October 1, I was sitting in my brown Plymouth Sundance in the middle of Wooster, Ohio, listening to the latest news on NPR when I first heard "last month" being employed to describe the time of the attack on the World Trade Center. Right then, I realized how much of an emotional buffer such seemingly mundane words as "last month" can be. As the attack recedes more and more into the past, we might end up feeling it less acutely. In the same way, here in the middle of the country, we could maybe, just maybe, keep up the facade of "it can't happen here." O the grace (and distortion) of distance, both temporal and geographic.

But such veneers of separation are so thin—as thin as glossy paper. Similarly, engrained in our culture is the visual ritual of flipping from one image to the next as we change months on the calendar. One month you have this, the next you have this other thing.

Usually, these changes are just superficial, image only a paltry transformation of world-view. Well-intentioned, but also frequently saturated with kitsch, such variations do involve a switch of adorable puppies, of tourist landscapes and "bathing beauties." Even well-meaning activities such as saving endangered species becomes trivialized by this "poster-child" mentality. One month it's pandas, the next it's Javanese tigers. Thus, to the skeptic in me, there's the fear that the shift of emblematic image from one attack (on the World Trade Center) to the next attack (on Afghanistan) is just one more swerve of our short media attention span, just the flavor of the month in terms of mass entertainment.

But as I worked to the end of my poem, as the poem appeared to me on the page, I decided that what has happened is not just a switch of image from one thing to another, from America being attacked to America attacking. In fact, the world has turned out not to be just an image on the screen, whether this world is New York City or Afghanistan, Amishland, Ohio or a dreamed empire in Kafka. It's as concrete as our neighbor, as concrete as our need to have our neighbor speak our same language, to remember the same history as we do—the same history in which miraculously we do come out (will we come out?) intact.

PHILIP BRADY

Letter to Bill Heyen

October 5, 2001

Dear Bill,

*I have held off writing anything (thanks for asking) though the conversa-
tions are incessant, obsessive, and I wake up every morning and click the
remote even now that they are down to interviewing compassionate
restaurateurs and families who donated their penny jugs. The reticence
comes from spending so long trying to be a poet—I think, "what would
Yeats say?" when the media have replayed over and over the scene now
marked on our collective psyche and even as I write "psyche" my ears pop.
Years I shied from writing directly about anywhere in poems: Africa,
Ireland, California. I layered every line to sift out the exotic. I didn't want
to be a tourist (I went to graduate school, took theory). But what's left? I'm
from Queens. Flushing. Fresh Meadows. St Kevin's parish, 111th precinct.
True, I lit out. I've been to Ujiji, where Livingston met Stanley, and to
Oisin's tomb in the Antrim hills, where John Hewitt's cairn reads, "My
Chosen Ground." I'm homesick for the world. I never go back to Queens,
except to fly. The neighborhood's all changed—my brother drove by the
ancestral row house and told me the Pucerellis were the last of the old
crowd. I still see Ronnie Pucerelli's windmilling fists. I remember when the
twin towers were built. They got placed on every tour I gave to friends
visiting New York, who thought I'd be a great guide. Sometimes my father,
a retired cop, went with us. But his New York was all rancor and nostalgia: Coney Island, the Botanical Gardens, the trattorrias where mafia
kingpins got hit. I did time in the Bronx. From Fordham, Manhattan
seemed exotic as Khartoum. If I'd stayed, I might have gotten there. Others
did. McGorry became a broker, why not me? Or a fireman, like Vinnie*

Halloran. He was my brother's pal, one of his Irish cronies—Duffy and Hogan and Halloran, firemen all. I haven't seen any of them since high school. I'm so sorry about Vinnie, and Marie, his widow, and the five kids. How can I say anything? The country is so vast grief must be conducted via satellite; our horror packaged and desiccated (there I go) by the screen or page; I recoil from theory (honest reticence is rooted deeper—my business is circumference, says Dickinson). It's horrible that we're stuck with who we are, that we can't ululate or tear out our hair, burn effigies or flay skin. I feel awful about leaving Queens, as if my failure to woo Mary Ellen O'Brien in eighth grade, therefore not dating and subsequently impregnating and marrying her and raising our family in a duplex in Astoria, was the pivotal moment in my life and that of my ghost family. Are words more real? Or the ground I've chosen? Can a poem live up to the dead? Bill, it was me who sent your dragonfly to that eejit who told us to shut the fuck up. Sorry. I needed all the words. I loved the e-mails from the Great Mother conference (bomb them with roses, send shamen). I've shut up for years, trying to be a poet. Yeats loomed, with all the ghosts "who converse bone to bone." I'm moving toward them now. I'm strapped in. Sometimes language just takes off and I get that knot in the pit of my stomach, thinking, we will never land alive.

Late Elegy
October 11, 2001

First, silence. The phone floats in your hand.
Then four quick syllables, obscene.

You breathe. You sip your coffee. You're alive.
You feel ashamed of being so far off.

TV, occasional sin, engulfs your days.
The towers collapse and rise again like toys.

There's Flushing, your old childhood friends.
Vinnie Halloran's gone. You try to imagine

A grown man, but all you picture
Is an eighth grader running toward a fire.

The million final thoughts—is there a trace
Of spectral consciousness in that absence

Above the smoking rubble? And the planes—
When did the people know they would not land?

At night, the old ghosts gather in the distance—
Whitman, Dante, Tu Fu, Yeats, and Horace—

They can't be coaxed with blood or psychobabble.
Their silence weighs you down. How they recoil

From every line you scribble until the bombs
(Though retribution's regular as iambs)

Drop. Now they've dispersed. You're on your own.
One foot lockstepped in language quickens

To rhyme. The other glides like vapor
Into the open structure of the future.

DAVID BUDBILL

Budbill and Parker Together Again

Poet David Budbill and world renowned bassist,
multi-instrumentalist and composer
William Parker will present a new work:

PHOENIX RISING;
Improvisation and Incantation for 911 and Beyond

*

FRIDAY, NOVEMBER 16:
at 7:00 p.m. at Studio Place Arts,
Main Street, Barre, free, pass the hat.
Contact: Eva Schectman, Studio Place Arts,
201 N. Main St., Barre, VT 05641, 802-479-7069
spa4arts@sover.net, www.studioplacearts.com.
SEATING IS LIMITED

SATURDAY, NOVEMBER 17:
at 6:30 p.m. at The Full Moon Café,
South Strafford, the performance and a supper of soup and
bread included in the $15.00 admission fee, BYOB.
Contact: Margo Baldwin
802-765-4869 or mbaldwin@sover.net

Sunday, November 18:
at 7:00 p.m. at The Unitarian Church,
Main Street, Montpelier, VT. $10.00.
For more information call The Onion River Arts Council at
(802) 229-9408 oremail: orac@together.net.
Tickets can be reserved in advance
with a credit card by calling or emailing
The Onion River Arts Council.

Well known for their collaborative performance and double CD, Zen
Mountains, Zen Streets, with which they toured Vermont in 1998,
David Budbill and William Parker are together again in Vermont, this
time to create and perform a new work called PHOENIX RISING;
Improvisation and Incantation for 9/11 and Beyond. Part poetry
reading, part jazz concert, part meditation on the events in our
lives since September 11th, PHOENIX RISING promises to be
improvisitory, incantatory, soul searching and passionate. This is
a performance piece for the spoken word, upright, acoustic bass,
pocket trumpet, Gralle (Barcelonan double reed), Shakuhachi
(vertical bamboo flute), and slit drum, various whistles, bells,
wood blocks, noise makers, pots, pans, gongs and ringing bowls.

for future bookings contact David Budbill at budbill@sover.net

What Issa Heard

Two hundred years ago Issa heard the morning birds
singing sutras to this suffering world.

I heard them too, this morning, which must mean

since we will always have a suffering world
we must also have a song

FRED CHAPPELL

The Attending

Let us, in this time of bitterest lament,
       Go awhile apart and meditate
       And reverently attend the ancestral choir
       Of prophets, sages, founders of the state,
Who lend us strength and solace when the world is rent
       And everywhere besieged with fire.

Let us linger, as we may, within the grove
       And hear those voices in the heat of day
       Speak like gentle winds stirring the silence
       Softly in their never-ceasing play
Of loving variations on the theme of love
       And weary descant against violence.

For we are nothing without the ones who came before,
       Those who with palette, loom, and graceful pen
       And sculpted stone, with treatise and debate
       Built up our world and built it up again
When it was brought to rubble by incendiary war
       And the towering, sword-blade flames of hate.

And let us join with them in spirit by going to
       Their words and deeds that make our history
       A matter of some pride, if we will know
       The best of it, forgoing vanity
And boast and doing calmly what we ought to do,
       As they did then, a world ago.

(Fred Chappell wrote to the editor: "I have not written about September 11 in a direct fashion. But I was asked by Governor Mike Easley to write a poem, as NC poet laureate, on the occasion of his proclaiming October 'Arts and Humanities Month.' As I worked on it, the horror came into it, quite without my planning it that way.")

KELLY CHERRY

A Writer's Pledge of Allegiance

I believe one must speak, and speak truly. I believe in the power of language to show, to move, to solve, to heal, to build. I believe nothing is beyond language—or, rather, that the Nothing that is beyond language is containable within art. I believe that that is what art is for: to contain the Nothing that is beyond language. What is unsaid can be said. What is said can be heard. What is heard can be sung. I believe that to be human is to sing. I believe there is nothing that cannot be sung. I believe that the music of humanity must and surely shall encompass everything, even the Nothing beyond, and that if we fail at first to recognize its strangeness as music, we will learn its dimensions and intricacies in time. For I believe nothing is beyond knowing. I believe nothing is beyond saying.

I believe this and am without words.

VINCE CLEMENTE

Footrace Along the Brooklyn Bridge

A native New Yorker and child of the Brooklyn streets, the vacant lots under the New Utrecht El—my first experience of the natural world—the lone sweetgum in our apartment house courtyard, I've enough poignant memories to go on writing well into my seventh decade. However, I've just three recollections, each salient and tarn-deep, of the Brooklyn Bridge: the initial two wedged in childhood and early manhood; the third, I fear, tied irrevocably to the World Trade Center, the day of September 11, 2001, and a young woman, my daughter, running for her life, across that bridge.

Let me begin, though, with a yellow coupe lumbering through five inches of freshly fallen snow, hardened to an oilslick sheen in the near-zero weather, along the bridge; a young man and his wife terrified as they pass abandoned autos, snowbanks, hayrick-high, the East River below, and a three year old, me, snug in a crawl space, a loft, really, under the coupe's rear window, just above a rickety rumble seat, enjoying the weekly jaunt to Little Italy, to Aunt Laura and Uncle Nick's walk-up flat on Mott Street, the tins of vanilla cake that await me. And suddenly catastrophe: something burning, acrid and foul.

"God, the radiator," was all my poor father could say; he had forgotten to check the anti-freeze, by now probably a curb-side puddle, somewhere in Bensonhurst, Brooklyn. In just seconds, dark, rank smoke billowed from the hood of the yellow coupe—then flames. In no time, it had become a conflagration. The diminutive two-seater aflame. We were above the East River, the moan of tugboats, like the call to morning prayer, trudging through ice and city flotsam.

As if following some hypnotic command, my mother lunged for me, grabbing the underlining of my winter coat. I came hurtling over the passenger seat into her arms. "I'm saving my baby!" she shouted to my father, still dazed, musing through the windshield, through the smoke and flames in stunned disbelief.

HENRY STREET EXIT 1 MILE, the sign read. How she got us there, that part of the story my mother forgets; but she sprinted all the way, dodging autos and snowmounds, petulant truck drivers, beckoning policemen, my melon-sized curly head, mortised in her small bosom. I felt her girl's heart beating wildly, heard her prayer to the God of her childhood, "Jesus, Mary, and Joseph, help us get to the other side. Please, please do." And we miraculously did, stopping off at the Terminal Luncheonette just under the bridge for hot chocolate, while I had the added treat of two Yankee Doodles. My mother could not stop trembling; it was more, though, than just the cold.

In no time, Uncle Nick came for us, drove us home to our Brooklyn apartment. Somehow, my weary father arrived just in time to go to work on Monday morning, matins-early, porting crates of mackerel, scallops from Montauk, lobsters just down from Maine, along the waterfront at Fulton Market. He never complained about losing a night's sleep; in fact, that Sunday was never talked about, became our own family secret.

For fifty-five years, my father Louie opened a padlock and raised the stall's corrugated metal door at four in the morning, too busy or tired—or both—to notice the sun come up along the East River, just above his stooping shoulder. All this, while the city slept. And like a metronome, he never missed a beat: food on the table, a roof over the family's head, all the bills paid. He staggered, a foot-soldier in the army of working stiffs. It was my good fortune, my initial two years at St. Francis College to make the journey with him every morning from our Bay Ridge flat, just above the Narrows, so close to the Verazzano Bridge, that on clear nights I could see the eyes of the toll attendants from the monk's cell of a bedroom I shared with a younger brother.

Up at 3:15 AM, we would drive along the Gowanus Expressway, awakened by the toxic, chemical fumes lacing the old canal, then through the Brooklyn Heights of Thomas Wolfe and Henry Miller to Brooklyn Bridge, and like Hart Crane I was reading at the time, under "the immaculate sigh of stars" and "above the sleepless river," that same bridge, where just fourteen years before, I was hurtled to safety in the arms of my mother. We said little, if anything at all, my father and I; but I had learned to understand his silences, his unspoken yearning for something better.

Borrowing money from an older brother, he had just opened his own place, one he called Gloucester Fish; and for two years, I did his work: porting crates to his stall from dockside; and like him, a packer's hook became a second hand, raised so high, those pre-dawn mornings, I swore I scraped the face of heaven. I recall in my sophomore year, being summoned from St. Francis College on Ryersan Street in Brooklyn Heights, not far from the site of Whitman's father's house, on Ryersan and Myrtle Avenue, where the poet completed the first edition of Leaves of Grass, to hurry on to the Fisherman's Bar on West Street, where my father had collapsed. He was at odds with my mother at the time and rudderless. And as I held him in my arms—he was a frail, slight man—and ran my hand along his face, he murmured, "I'm tired, Buddy, just tired." (I recall an early poem of mine about those pre-dawn drives to his Fulton Market stall, and how Brookyn Bridge loomed, "a cathedral I would never leave;" and, in a sense, I never have.)

"Dad, have you heard from Maryann? I can't locate her. Have you seen the Twin Towers attacked and crumble—God, I've never seen anything like it! Maryann's yet to arrive at work; I just phoned her office. I just don't know what to do—where to turn!"

It was our younger daughter, Gina, grief-stricken, helpless, calling from her flat along Central Park South. Like millions of Americans, she had seen the devastation on morning television. My wife Annie and I had not, but understood the panic in her voice. Maryann's law firm office on Maiden Lane was just blocks from the World Trade Center. Her morning subway commute from midtown passed under the Trade Center—and at about the time the hijacked passenger planes hit their target. We feared the worst, life's primal terror: losing a child.

We spent the entire morning, flitting between the ghostly replay of the Towers attack and phone calls: her law office and still nothing about her whereabouts; the Metro Transit System, with either a busy signal or a recorded message that "All city subway train service has been canceled;" and then the image of throngs of city dwellers, many the ages of our daughters, crowding the pedestrian span of Brooklyn Bridge, a frantic run to safety, from the Canal Street entrance to

Brooklyn Heights. And all day, phone calls to nowhere; the Towers dissolving, girder by girder, family member by family member; fleeing masses across the bridge. And for some reason, again and again, those lines in T. S. Eliot, out of Dante: "Unreal City ... / A crowd flowed over London Bridge, so many, / I had not thought death had undone so many, / Sighs, short and infrequent, were exhaled...." Always those lines.

And then, at about 3:30 PM, pointing to the TV screen, to the Brooklyn Bridge pedestrian walk, the victims so numerous by now that they had become an eerie blur, I shouted to Annie, "Why, that looked like Maryann, there, bottom of the screen. God, she's already gone! It was her, though, I swear it was!" I left Annie alone in the living room, monitoring the screen, waiting for a call—any call—as I collapsed in my study, prayed to the St. Francis of Assisi by Arezzo I have framed, and just to the right of my desk. And suddenly, and feeling like a pardoned sinner, I remembered Maryann at Bryn Mawr, our drives weekends from Long Island to the Pennsylvania campus to see her, and a poem I wrote for her many years ago, the concluding lines: "And you, my daughter, / rise from a clump of birch / in terracotta shoes, in a dress / of orange and red nasturtium. / You are a flowerbed!" And at that very moment, I called to Annie, certain as Grace is certain, "Our daughter's alive and well; we'll hear from her—and soon!"

And the call came, at about 5:35 PM, and from a flat on Montague Street in Brooklyn Heights. Yes, she was well; her train had been evacuated before it reached the WTC; and on pure instinct, she followed the fleeing throngs to Brooklyn Bridge, the pedestrian walk and the long, long journey to safety in Brooklyn Heights. Refuge was the Montague Street flat of a Bryn Mawr classmate, too ill that morning to report to work at her WTC office.

Next weekend, both our daughters were with us in our Sag Harbor home, still shaken, numb, speaking haltingly. Sitting alone with me in my study, and just under the di Arezzo St. Francis, Maryann paused, held my hand, and said, "Dad, do you know what kept me going, running to safety along the bridge? Now, I know you won't believe this, it was that older woman, small and delicate just like Grandma Rose, there ahead of me. I knew I had to follow her."

I could only smile and say, "I understand," recalling that Sunday morning, lives and years ago, and a wisp of a girl holding a child in her arms, running for her life, for the child's.

Numb myself, I still don't know what to believe, just how to sort out all that has happened. I've returned, though, to the evening prayers of my boyhood: the Sorrowful Mysteries; the Canticles to the Sun of St. Francis. I pray to my mother Rose, my father Louie; and finally to that span of cable wire, a nave, really, dallying high above a "sleepless river."

LUCILLE CLIFTON

9/11/01 – 9/17/01

TUESDAY 9/11/01

thunder and lightning and our world
is another place   no day
will ever be the same   no blood
untouched

they know this storm in otherwheres
israel   ireland   palestine
but God has blessed America
we sing

and God has blessed America
to learn that no one is exempt
the world is one   all fear
is one   all life   all death
all one

this is not the time
i think
to note the terrorist
inside
who threw the brick
into the mosque
this is not the time
to note
the ones who cursed
God's other name
the ones who threatened
they would fill the streets
with arab children's blood
and this is not the time
i think
to ask who is allowed to be
american   america
all of us gathered under one flag
praying together safely
under the single love
of the many tongued God

THURSDAY 9/13/01

the firemen

ascend
in a blaze of courage
rising
like jacob's ladder
into the mouth of
history
reaching through hell
in order to find
heaven
or whatever the river jordan
is called
in their heroic house

FRIDAY 9/14/01

some of us know
we have never felt safe

all of us   americans
weeping

as some of us have wept
before

is it treason to remember

what have we done
to deserve such villainy

nothing we reassure ourselves
nothing

SATURDAY 9/15/01

i know a man who perished for his faith.
others called him infidel, chased him down
and beat him like a dog. after he died
the world was filled with miracles.
people forgot he was a jew and loved him.
who can know what is intended?   who can understand
the gods?

SUNDAY MORNING 9/16/01

for bailey

the st. marys river flows
as if nothing has happened

i watch it with my coffee
afraid and sad as are we all

so many ones to hate and i
cursed with long memory

cursed with the desire to understand
have never been good at hating

now this new granddaughter
born into a violent world

as if nothing has happened

and i am consumed with love
for all of it

the everydayness of bravery
of hate of fear of tragedy

of death and birth and hope
true as this river

and especially with love
bailey fredrica clifton goin

for you

i bear witness   no thing
is more human than hate

i bear witness   no thing
is more human than love

apples and honey
apples and honey

what is not lost
is paradise

CHRISTOPHER CONLON

Safe House

What loads my hands down?
—Philip Larkin: "Going"

My wife and I just bought a house—a 1921 bungalow—in suburban Maryland. It's in what the realtor calls a safe neighborhood, which is especially important to us now with the arrival of our young foster daughter. But last night, September the tenth, a man was carjacked at gunpoint in his driveway not a block from here.

Admittedly the case has its comical aspects; the criminals were forced to ask the victim for the keys to his other car when they realized that their first choice had a manual transmission and neither of them knew how to drive it. It raises a laugh in me, if rather a shrill one. But the laughter cannot abate the heaviness I sense in myself this morning—an actual physical sensation, much like how it feels when I haven't exercised in a while. A kind of fatigue which begins in the brain but emanates down throughout my extremities like some kind of deadly radioactive fluid in my veins.

The nearness of chaos. Years ago, in another country, I was mugged: half-a-dozen South African youths surrounded me, pulled back my head, pressed a knife to my throat, and emptied my pockets. Yet I held on instinctively—stupidly—to a bag in my hands, a bag one of the young men tried to wrench from my fingers but which he had to abandon as the group fled. My prize, for which I had literally risked my life? Half a dozen paperback books.

Later, living in Washington DC, my apartment was robbed—cleaned out in a nearly surgical operation that even managed to include the food in my refrigerator and the soap in my shower. In a bizarre touch, however, my television, though it had been unplugged, was not taken. The police speculated that the thieves simply ran out of space in their van, truck, whatever they had.

With both incidents, the high, not-quite-hysterical laughter rises in me. But also the heaviness: the sense of walking on a planet with greater gravity than I'm built for.

I do not want to fear my new neighborhood. I do not want to fear for my wife's safety as she walks to the bus stop, or for our seven-year-old's as she heads off to school. (How much she has already endured, this child; how much my wife and I both want to shelter and shield her from everything; and yet already she is picked on by her classmates, chased by bigger boys, goaded into fights with girls.) The morning is filled with heavy shadows. I am skittish as I walk toward the school where I teach, past the sugar maples and dogwoods and black walnut trees that line our street. I watch others with nervous suspicion. I even wonder if the sky itself is darker than usual, convince myself that it is not my imagination, that autumn is drawing down, that as the earth moves farther from the sun the morning skies do indeed fade that much closer to black. Surely that's it.

Later—after the news, the endlessly repeated pictures and students weeping into their cell phones in the halls, after the school day disintegrates and everyone goes home—I walk along Georgia Avenue under a cloudless sky listening to the cars as they grind and gnash past me. Not a single stereo blares rap or rock from its loudspeakers; only the grim voices of newscasts. Indeed, it would be possible to follow the news just from these passing vehicles, like those of a certain generation remember being able to listen to Amos 'n' Andy while strolling through their neighborhoods at night because everybody—absolutely everybody—had the program coming from their porches and parlors. That, of course, was when people could stroll through their neighborhoods at night.

The public nostalgia for our lost innocence begins by dusk, but the country the TV talking heads speak of is not one in which I ever lived. No era is any more or less innocent than any other. It is merely different, and it is difference which scares us. Our daughter rebels against us every day, refusing to eat, refusing to wear the shoes my wife chooses for her, purposely breaking her glasses. She is afraid: afraid that we will abandon her, that one day it will suddenly, inexplicably be over, as for her it is always, sooner or later, over. She has lived in five homes already. And so she attempts to smash it all to bits right now: *I will reject you before you have a chance to reject me.* What scares her is difference, the possibility that this may be, could just be, the final stop—no more homes, no more lies. And if it is the final stop, what does that mean? How will she live? She was beaten by her mother, neglected by her. Yet she tells us how she misses her.

There is a phrase in Russell Banks's novel *Cloudsplitter* which captures it: "...I viewed my daily life with a nostalgia for a life that I had never led and never would lead." We miss what we no longer have, and it matters less what we had than the fact that we had it. But we must be careful not to believe that what we had was different from what it was. It was not innocence, unless ignorance can be viewed as a form of innocence. It was more like delusion—national delusion— and while it might abate temporarily, it will return. How many who forever swear off flying today will be careening down crowded freeways at eighty miles an hour tomorrow?

In the meantime night rises, and it is a brilliant, clear night, with fat cold stars doming our old house. Our daughter asks questions; we answer them hesitantly, glancingly, changing the subject as quickly as we can. It is not difficult. A girl called her a name today, a name she cannot say, and this is what matters, this is her world tonight. We have dinner, we put her to bed, we read her a story. Just before we switch off her light she asks, "Why do people do things like that?" and I am unsure whether she is referring to the day's events or the girl who called her a name. We say shh, go to sleep, goodnight. My wife and I sit up late looking out the window at the quiet street. I am thinking not of crashing airplanes or crumbling skyscrapers but of carjackers, of shadowy presences in the woods near our house, of men with guns and knives. Thieves. Murderers. The world, as before. But I feel that much heavier now, heavier even than this morning, lethargic, exhausted, a step or two closer to some kind of abyss.

We double-check the locks on the doors and windows. We go to bed, close our eyes. We wait.

LUCILLE LANG DAY

Strangers

I didn't know the man in black pants
who plunged headfirst
from the top of the north tower

or the young mother trapped
behind a locked door
on the eighty-seventh floor.

I never met the couple
crushed in their final embrace
and stuffed into one body bag,

or the fire chief quickly buried
under tons of concrete,
steel, glass, and ash.

Nor did I ever say hello
to the blond woman
who called her husband to ask

what she should tell the pilot
standing beside her
at the back of the plane.

I never shared coffee
with the six-foot-four executive
who said, "If we're going

to crash into something,
let's not let it happen.
Our best chance is to fight."

Yet I have felt sun on their skin
and tasted wine on their lips.
I have run using the long muscles

of their legs and felt air
rush into their lungs, their hearts
pumping in my chest,

and they have combed my hair
each morning, tasted
cereal from my bowl,

and held my children in their arms.
At night they have watched
stars shimmer through my eyes.

Now they have all returned
to earth and air, but I still feel them
stirring inside me, walking

the long corridors of my brain,
searching for something
irretrievable, precious, still there.

ALISON HAWTHORNE DEMING

Waking to the World's Pain

Two weeks have passed since I awoke to the words "explosion" and "Manhattan" on my alarm radio. It was a fall day in Tucson, the summer's heat beginning to subside so that the delicious sensation of coolness was new and palpable. I am accustomed to waking to the news, a sorrowful brew of tragedy and conflict, nearly always taking place somewhere else on the globe so that grief and fear have been remote. But with those words came the escalating series of images: smoke billowing from a skyscraper, a passenger jet aiming toward the tower's mate, bodies scrambling to the windows, men in suits falling like weighted rags having chosen a death gentler than the horror ignited within glass and steel walls, one building collapsing, and then the other, and then the human face of anguish, the human face of grief. Never have I seen so many men expressing their anguish in public—fireman, journalist, comedian, mayor, and cop— all wounded into expressing an anguish that cut to the soul. Grief and fear came home to everyone that morning. Everyone knew the hard truth: It could have been me. It could have been my lover. My daughter. My grandsons.

My own grief—a woman's grief, a poet's grief—is not an unfamiliar visitor to my life. The loss of a lover, the death of a parent, the impotence of being misrepresented or misunderstood can send me spinning under the breakers of that emotion. I don't welcome or invite such visits, but I appreciate their value as a measure of my love, whether it be for a person or for an ideal such as truth or justice. And so, like so many others I have embraced this collective grief, been addicted to the television images, to the stories that make real each singular tragedy, each expression of heroic resolve in meeting it. I have wanted its reality to penetrate my being so that I will never again toss off other people's misery as too remote to merit my compassion, sighing in relief that such things are dreadful, yes, but at least we are safe from them here.

I have wanted to understand the perpetrators, how the world looks from inside their passion—the arts of collaboration and sacrifice refined to gem-clear precision. For what would I compromise my belief that no one has the right to take the life of another? Put a weapon in my hand, put an adversary at the neck of my daughter, and I would kill with passionate conviction. When I tell my daughter this, she says, If someone attacked my boys, I'd kill them with my bare hands. Both of us finding it not inconsistent that we can be femi-nists, artists, pacifists, opponents of capital punishment, and fierce to protect what we love.

But those imagined maternal scenarios are not analogous to our situation after the brutal crimes inflicted on September 11, 2001. For one thing, the terrorists do believe they have the right, even the God-given duty, to kill those who hold beliefs that differ from theirs. For another thing, we don't face the crisis as enraged individuals, confronted with an obvious enemy. We are wounded and confused as a collective being. The enemy is here, there, everywhere, and nowhere. Somehow we must convince the ideologues of hatred that we are not a satanic people. And do not mistake that the nineteen men who gave their lives to inflict this wound hated every one of us— Catholic and atheist, girl scout and weapons dealer, movie mogul and janitor, CEO, and anti-globalization activist. It made no differ-ence to them which ones of us they killed. We have always been united in our freedom to disagree, though we have not always appreciated that freedom. Now we are united in grief and vulnera-bility. Not the least of our grief is the awareness that we have met an opponent against whom our prayers for peace will be only one of the weapons employed.

RICHARD DEMING

Ground/Zero/Ethics

Estragon: I can't go on like this.
Vladimir: That's what you think.
—WAITING FOR GODOT

Our present business in this, the aftermath of the terrorist attacks, is that of general woe. Tonight, a full two months since the attacks in New York and Washington, I was at a lecture. In the introduction there was again the suggestion that we, the United States, need to get back to "normalcy." For some time now, "normalcy" largely has meant, for so many of us, a blithe indifference to the daily imbalance of ethics in global politics. In the wake of what happened to the World Trade Center, a friend of mine from Sri Lanka calls and says, "I don't mean to be insensitive, but now you know how I've felt my whole life." What is "normal" to middle class America, is not normal for virtually any other nation. Nor is it in reality normal for here, or did we forget Oklahoma City so quickly? In any case this longing for "normalcy" is a kind of nostalgia for the near past, and nostalgia makes false Utopias out of memories. Hegel once described History as "the slaughter-bench at which the happiness of peoples, the wisdom of states, and the virtue of individuals have been sacrificed." That passage, at once disconsolate and inescapable, has haunted me since the morning of September 11th.

We are experiencing a crisis of representation. It's not lost on me that we've yet to come up with a catchy, albeit bleak, term for what happened: "The 11th", "the recent tragedy," "9-1-1," etc. We don't know what to say. Last week I talked with a woman who is a public relations professional who explained that her industry was hurting because clients didn't want to fly to meetings, and of course people in general weren't traveling anywhere. Since so many companies were directly affected by what happened, they would have to address it somehow in order to market products to assuage grief and to show they care. NBC has colored their omnipresent onscreen logo a glorious red, white, and blue. Give us this day our daily widget. During the middle of the day on the 11th, a mere three hours after a plane flew into the Pentagon, while my friend Roberto kept continual contact—he in Western New York and I in Western Massachusetts—his other line indicated he had a call. A moment later he clicked back to tell me that it had been a telemarketer. Normalcy is a great deadener.

I think I don't want us to return to "normalcy." If we've acquired any-thing from what's happened—which can only be weighed against that which we've lost, lives, yes, as well as civil liberties as the war machine heaves and sweats its way back to life—it's a similarity to countless nations around the globe where political violence is a daily issue. And frankly, far more people were slaughtered, people just as innocent and unsuspecting, in Rwanda only a few years ago. How many Iraqi children are dead because of U.S. sanctions that victimize the poor of that country? The rich Iraqi leaders can wait out these sanctions; those without wealth and power can't. I'm neither rationalizing nor forgiving the actions of the al Qaida, but at the same time it's clear that the U.S.'s ideological chickens have come home to roost.

On one hand, a condemnation of the U. S. might seem impertinent at this point. There are, one quickly points out (again), nearly 6,000 dead because of this terrorist action. No one will forget that. But a drive toward retribution, which is what the U. S. has embarked on, smacks too much of righteous fury for my tastes. We cannot, must not, do nothing but neither can we call this a battle of "Good versus Evil." How could we, when so much of what bin Laden is, what Afghanistan has become, arises out of the United States's exploita-tion of that area to our own ends? If our foreign policies, our insidious cultural imperialism, which subjugates people's culture as it simultaneously erases it, factors into what has happened, then how could anyone stand to see this as polarized metaphysics?

What is important is how we proceed: the manner, the tenor of our response must be rigorous, rational, and thoughtful. Again my criti-cisms will be seen by some as at least cynical and counterproductive, or at worst seditious. Already I've heard the joke, "What did the guy with five American flags say to the guy with four American flags? Go back to Afghanistan." Democracy should be, ideally, a forum for various and even competing discourses and positions, and yet these days rallies for peace which condemn the bombing, if they get any press at all, are treated as treasonous dissent. The news reports repeatedly tell us how Americans are bonding together, how there is a palpable sense of "brotherhood." Of course, the news plays down the countless death threats against Arab Americans, the beatings of Muslims in Chicago, Washington, and elsewhere.

One Sunday morning at the end of September, my wife and I were watching *The McLaughlin Group*. While a montage of scenes of violence against Arab Americans flickered horribly across the screen, the host's voice crescendoed as he described ghastly incidents, ones at least as "evil" and senseless as the initiating event in New York. Of course we assumed he was preparing to ask his panel of commentators how the nation might stem the tide of this growing, virulent racism. Instead he asked if Arab Americans were being sufficiently critical of the Muslim terrorists. I was shocked both at the question and at the fact that his esteemed guests all seemed to agree that, as they saw it, Arab Americans, many of whom are U. S. citizens by birth, in fact were not being critical enough. The violence depicted in the montage had thus seemingly been justified. If PBS, the network with a supposed liberal bias was spewing such jingoistic right- wing propaganda, what hope is there for anyone else? And there isn't. Bush calls the attack an act of war, thereby invoking the 5th article of the NATO treaty and our allies must be on board or else be in breach of that treaty. That breach would be a betrayal. The various national security changes are lumped together under the "Patriot Bill." The conservatives have packaged this well rhetorically: If anyone were to vote against the "Patriot Bill," they would have to be a traitor. "Normalcy" can only exist under operant conditions of binary opposition.

Every day I see the bumper stickers that read, "Don't Panic." Panicking isn't good for the economy. We need to "return to normalcy" to maintain productivity. When do we get to say that "normalcy" is a lie, an illusion that sacrifices countless people here and abroad to maintain that bourgeois, banal illusion? Perhaps I am cynical but part of that is because I see people making money from the grief, rage, and confusion that prevail in the wake of what's happened. The commercials appeared almost immediately, announcing how various corporations supported the Brooklyn Fire Department, and to show that support were having a huge sale. Down the street a salon's sign read, "God Bless America! Buy one tanning session, get one half-off!"

The terrorists weren't stupid. They attacked not just the tallest buildings in New York, they attacked an allegory. The WTC was the new Babel, a corporate Babel that wanted to make a single worldwide language of commerce. And again that tower fell. It didn't have to and of course the action was villainous. But it wasn't unmotivated, and in one day they pointed out the analogous connection between the U.S.'s military center and its financial center. They are, in the final analysis, the same target.

When I was six or seven, I had the poster for Dino De Laurentiis's 1976 version of *King Kong*. In the poster, Kong stands astride the World Trade Center, crushing, impossibly, a jet fighter in one hand. I remember looking at that poster again and again because although Kong had obviously been painted, I couldn't tell if the Towers themselves were real or painted also. No matter how closely I looked at it, I couldn't tell for sure. As I watched the news all day of September 11th and saw that airplane endlessly flying into the tower, I kept thinking of that poster, of not being sure of the reality of what I was looking at. In *Ways of Seeing*, the art critic John Berger tells us that, "We only look at what we see. To look is an act of choice." We cannot look away from the attacks on New York and Washington. These were acts "against democracy," perhaps, but against a democracy whose ethics needed to be looked at. As abominable and unconscionable as the attacks were, things are and have always been too complex for us to return to a somnambulistic normalcy.

If anything is changed now, it's the absolute necessity to look at what we ourselves are doing. "Ethics is born of natural suffering," the late French philosopher Jean-François Lyotard tells us, "the political is born from the supplement that history adds to this suffering." The suffering that has occurred, that still occurs, and that *will* occur is part of the violence of presence. If to *be* is to be amidst violence, it is an equation that we can neither accept or become inured to.

If I offer no consolation, others will. These are times that must be defined by a necessary complexity of thinking and feeling; such complexity must be kept possible in order to offer a multiplicity of approaches and responses. One can feel as I do: that I *am* an American, full of grief and anger, and that is not all nor is it enough. The personal act, the act of looking, is where ethics and politics come together. If this confluence is only academic, then the twisted steel girders and debris that bear mute testimony aren't the only wreckage that confronts us now.

ROSEMARIE DIMATTEO

Waiting Room

Lisa sits and waits for her therapist, Dr. Steve, who helps her deal with the emotional turmoil created by two years of chronic pain. She takes her various medications and sees him every Tuesday. He's her lifeline, her most important doctor. He keeps her from sinking.

"TV. We hear what they want us to hear," Lisa says.

"That's true," Lisa's mother says. "You think you're seeing everything, but ... And the generals ... they keep changing what they report, and they don't even think we notice."

"Yes. Exactly," Lisa says. And the president, too. It's like they're talking to sleepwalkers.... I can't watch this anymore. It gives me a headache. Anyway, I want to vacuum. It's gotten out of hand in here."

Lisa lives with her parents again. She's forty-nine. She has a son. Her parents have a nice house in the suburbs. They joined the great sixties exodus, taking their family out of the civil rights struggles, the threats of violence. That was over thirty years ago. For Lisa, several lifetimes ago. Her illness took her away from her third husband to search for medical answers. Maybe a cure. In his anger and grief, he divorced her. Now, when she's not in pain, Lisa cooks, cleans, and tries to give her parents their space. On TV, the world has changed forever. In her parents' home, life goes on and on. Coffee in the morning. Whatever for lunch. Maybe some thought to dinner. Roasted something with an appropriate starch and veggie. Lisa has grown tired of eating. And of TV.

"They're all nuts for God," she tells her dad. He lives for the news, but that life is one of consternation. "Osami ... what?" He's just getting used to the names. Where the nuts seem to congregate. Their cities. Their geography. "Osama bin Laden," she says." "Catching him won't solve this."

"No, it won't. They'll spend millions on his trial. Like that other one—Milo—son of a bitch. I say throw Old-sama in a pig sty. Let the pigs eat him. See if Allah still wants him as pig shit."

Lisa pictures pigs—huge, hungry pigs—feasting on the lanky body. The placid, beatific face. The flesh disappears. White bones poke up from mud.

CNN reports on the living room TV all day, now that the networks have resumed their normal programming of sound bites, vague political allusion, and ubiquitous commercials. Now and then, a new case of anthrax. A "case" is a person afflicted with the disease which came in a letter or puffed into the air at the post office in Trenton, New Jersey.

Lisa's mom calls to her, "A woman died. They don't know how she got it."

Lisa hauls out the vacuum. "Mom, do you mind?"

The vacuum's noisy hunger drowns out the audio. Serious mouths keep reporting and important sentences keep streaming across the bottom of the screen. Bits of dried bread and such rattle up into the suck and drone of the machine. It takes almost an entire day's strength to vacuum the downstairs. Lisa's been sick for too long. She's not exactly the strongest salmon in the river. During the back and forth motion, she looks over at the screen and sees it again: the steaming, smoking disaster; heaps of concrete, steel, and dust. Buildings that once met the hazy New York City sky. They appear now like ghosts in so many recent movies. At least she's alive, she tells herself.

"There's the Twin Towers," her son remarks, in case anybody in the living room, anybody in the country missed them.

"Chuck, do you mind?"

With "America Freaks Out," *The Daily Show* finds its way back to humor. For God's sake, even anchorman Dan Rather was crying on David Letterman. It couldn't go on. Things just had to lighten up. Eventually. Didn't they? Could they?

"How many al-Qaedans does it take to screw in a light bulb?" Chuck asks, leaning on the kitchen counter. Mouths open. Nothing comes out. "None," he shouts. "No light bulbs in caves." But Chuck's grandfather answers right back: "Yes there ARE lights in caves. They have EVERYTHING in there. Even the kitchen sink. And nukes. You can BET on it." Serious business, this war.

One morning, still September, the news carried images of people who had gathered somewhere near "ground zero" to hold pictures of loved ones for the cameras. For anybody who might have seen that face, the whole person, maybe alive, maybe lost and confused somewhere in the new New York. Lisa stood transfixed, staring at all those ordinary Americans holding pictures. Just like all those ordinary Palestinians, Pakistanis, Afghanis—all those who held up pictures for each other. For their countrymen and women. And for the assorted media over the years. Holding pictures of their beloved lost and dead.

At that moment, as though drawn into a vacuum, all the pictures of the world converged in Lisa's mind. All those "other" people in far-away places? They've felt all their lives like we do right now—for the first time. It felt to her like an epiphany, this convergence.

"The world has changed forever," says Lisa's mom. "I feel ... every-day I have this ... anxiety. I feel like this all the time. It's on the news. How we all feel afraid of what's next. And they tell us to be normal. So what's normal now?" Lisa's mom is talking loud. She's talking above the vacuum.

"You told me last week you loved music," says Dr. Steve. "Can you give yourself some time to listen? You could take a timeout and relax. Some time just for you." Lisa looks at Dr. Steve's face, but thinks of her mom. So dear to her. So kind and ageless. But confused, lately. And forgetful.

"Normal? Normal's a fantasy we can't afford anymore. But me? Well, I have my drugs." My doctors don't want me to feel too anxious these days, you know?" Her mom laughed.

***

So much of what's happened to us since September 11th comes back again and again to family. Countless families grieving. The family of humankind once again grieving its own potential to do unthinkable harm. Our grief takes countless forms of expression. Grief that must be expressed, or it will consume us.

I was born upstate in Rochester, New York, a small-change city, dwarfed by Manhattan. In fact, when living in the Midwest and asked "Where're you from?" I'd reply, "New York." The asker, instantly impressed, assumed I meant New York City. So I had to say, "Uh, no. Rochester."

My grandparents on both sides were Italian immigrants for whom becoming "an American" was both an honor and the realization of a dream. A decorated corporal in the seventy-seventh New York State Division, my grandfather, Manusueto DiMatteo, was one of the few who survived the Battle of the Meuse River-Argonne Forest during "the war to end all wars." I remember my grandpa saying, "United States of America: besta damn country on 'a the face of the Earth." My own love for this country began at his knee.

And I think of Walt Whitman: "O lands! O all so dear to me—what you are (whatever that is), I become part of that, whatever it is," in his *American Feuillage*.

A poet's prophetic admonition? How to respond when countless voices become cacophony unless we are brave enough to hear, even a few, one at a time.

We all do what we can to love America with open eyes and broken hearts. I keep writing, deeply grateful to be one voice here, among those in this volume of families.

ELIZABETH DODD

Zero at the Bone

For those who teach, students, and the predictable presence before us of their attention—their selves—remain a call to being. They are a responsibility, a summons to remain attendant and engaged with whatever texture of life unfolds all around. I was already in crisis when I heard Bob Edwards say, with some discomposure, that there were reports that a plane had hit the World Trade Center. Personal despair and loss had for months left me feeling pale and diminished, often just a personage whose feet, mechanical, went round.

There was nowhere I had to be on September 11. I planned to go for a jog, then spend the day grading student work, but those activities still lay ahead; I wasn't there, yet. With a dustmop, I was making circles across the hardwood floors of the house while the radio told the news. And then, like so many anyones elsewhere, I turned on the television.

Wednesday, three classes filled the morning. What to say? How to meet them? What, on earth, to do, there on the second floor of Eisenhower Hall, where the desks were squeaky and uncomfortable and the air often stale? It seemed impossible to discuss the assigned reading as if we'd all been going about our expected lives on Tuesday; it would be offensive, I thought, to expect the written work that was due.

Though it had been years—more than a decade—since I'd read him last, I turned to Rilke's *Duino Elegies* to read aloud. Not the whole book: that would be overwhelming, not only for my college freshmen, but for me. So I put together a medley, snippets from the first, the ninth, the tenth elegies. I read Yeats's "The Second Coming," too. What was I after? Comfort, surely, though these were not gentle poems. Company, too: to be in the presence of writers whose work spoke to extremity of feeling, psychic depth and despair, and yet offered the inherent hint of celebration that comes from making, poiesis. Some grave, serious response that transcended patriotism or religion, since those comforts would be offered in plenty, by others. And, finally, some voice beside my own in the classroom. *Someone to drive the car.*

In the days that followed, a great isolation and distance closed round the house, the streets, the sky just overhead. The silence came at night, after the television at last was off, when the phone didn't suggest the apparition of connection. But the isolation was always there. The personal is the political, the devil is in the details, and yet sometimes one feels in deadly close proximity with the impersonal presence—or absence—that is vastly larger than the self. Vastly. The body is no protection, then, nor are the body's consolations, vocabularies—pronouns. Even so, language seems, I think, to be the motion that's most nearly here.

Late Friday afternoon, a friend suggested we go out for a picnic dinner on the prairie, and when he came by the house, he bent to pick up the vulture feather I hadn't moved since it had first appeared, three days earlier, along the selvage of the lawn.

"That's unusual. You've got a turkey vulture feather," he said, and then he let it drop, and it spiraled back down from his open hand and we drove away, to sit under skies that were still, for a few hours, utterly empty of airplanes.

Zero

And if there were no one
whose hand you'd clasp, familiar
fingers in your
fingers touching the living
and intangible fond
creature, sweet belief—

If, in the leap
of static moment, panic—

If: the ever-
present branching, leafed

contingency, wind shifting,
blowing south— or
northward, changing
what we name as *course*.

Today rain courses
down the swale beside
the house, the somber-morninged
streets; it sheets the broken
surface of the driveway, banging
down each gutter's hollow
column. Beneath the
water's weight the goldenrod
leans horizontal, sodden tassels
inches from the grass.

How fast it happens.
Hearths, or paths, the images
of happiness the spirit
carried: dashed.

Wednesday I found a vulture's feather
on the lawn. Worn, tinged dimly
from a year of weather,
cast, most likely,
as the bird soared by or circled.

I didn't see the graceful helix
that it must have whorled past
the locust tree's brown
pods and husks from last
spring's honeyed blooms.

Downward to darkness on
extended
            things fall apart,
the center cannot
                        Hold this
plumage once connected

to the beating heart, the loveliness
you thought you'd found, bound now,
abruptly, to the shadowed,
sudden ground.

WAYNE DODD

The Third Tower

Hour after hour we watched them, day after day we watched them

Falling forward, falling over,
falling out of

as the heart stops.
Falling straight down

endlessly
in darkness

as well as light. Falling forever
out of the future.

Falling into memory,
into absence ...

Planes, people, towers—falling before our very eyes. On one bright
morning in September, familiar images of travel banked suddenly,
as through a heretofore unimagined opening, into another dimension as we watched. In a matter of minutes, soaring, once-symbolic
towers were revealed in all their despairing literalness. And soon,
around the wreckage of them, the walls of pathos, papered over with
thousands of intimate photographs, looking disturbingly like the
remains of a bedroom. And then there were the hijackers, always the
faces of the hijackers—wanted posters from a world beyond.
Appalled, held, we watched them.

The magnitude of these events was so great that we knew instinctively a fundamental change had occurred. Over and over we said it on
television, *Nothing will ever be the same again*, our new version of "all
bets are off." But what did such a declaration mean? That much of
what had been merely trashy and cheap in our culture would now be
recognized as such, and thus rejected? That we as a people would
become more serious now, reach for a deeper content in our lives?
That, as some commentators rashly declared, the horrors of these
events would mean the death of irony?

Or is it more likely that evidence of this alteration is to be discovered
at a subconscious level, at some primary locus of our humanity? And
if so, what images will be able to reveal to us here something of the
scope and the nature of that change, what inescapable recognitions?
These are, I believe, questions one should investigate in order to
"discover," in some fundamental way, what it feels like to be on the
present side of those altering events, here.

IN THE THIRD TOWER

And it came to pass that men could fly
they flew over mountains across oceans
through buildings nothing
we told ourselves
will ever be the same again
the grass the rocks the waters we sat beside
forever would be changed
the color trees become in September
would be changed
even the sounds children make
in their sleep would be changed but the faces
are the same
everywhere we look we cannot
not see them and they tell us
nothing will ever be the same
again yet men have flown
through buildings and we see them
eyes open eyes closed
they are always the same
faces they fly through buildings
with our soft bodies

SHARON DOUBIAGO

Jesus Was a Terrorist

FOR MY GRANDSON
WHOSE FATHER'S FAMILY HAS BEEN OF NAZARETH, PALESTINE FOR
2000 YEARS.

*"The most important deficiency in U.S. counterterrorism
policy has been the failure to address the root causes of terrorism."*
—PHILIP C. WILCOX, JR., FORMER US AMBASSADOR FOR COUNTERTERRORISM

1. *The week before September 11*

The novelist defined a terrorist
as one who has no heart, cares for nothing
but himself. Another character in her book
Mother Teresa
picks up a diseased beggar in the street
and carrying him in her arms sees Jesus.
The Jewish author gasped telling this.
I walked out gasping Jesus
would carry a terrorist in his arms
and see Himself.

I walked down to the pub. A terrorist,
the Christian on the stool beside me offered,
is one who has no heart, cares
for nothing but himself. He drank
to the oldest cliché, why can't
those people get along? They're
exactly the same people. I saw
the light then, televisions
the night before. I walked out
rather than be kicked out, walked
the foggy streets, hearing from somewhere Love
is all you need.

"We have the opportunity to forgive them."
—Doug Chateau

Jesus carries the terrorist in his arms and sees himself. An
Arab. An Israeli. A Middle Easterner. A
Jew from Nazareth. A Palestinian.
I am not being metaphorical. Exactly a terrorist
by definition of the State, the Western
occupying Army that executed him
for crimes against it.

A religious fanatic. A
suicide for his Cause. A martyr for us.
He gave his only body
that the prophecy be fulfilled. I'm not being
Christian, a Believer. Not
metaphorical. Why can't we get along? We're exactly
the same people.

Illegitimate from the start.
Conceived out of wedlock.
Born of a girl into poverty, born
homeless to a stepfather on the road in a
winter barn. Born wanted
dead or alive. The soldiers killed
all the baby boys in the land
in the search for him. His parents fled
across the border. Illegal

immigrants from the start. Terrorized
refugees at the exact heart
of our hate. When do we rise
above this oldest story?
Or is this the drama we're really nailed to
to live and relive until the Apocalypse?

At the exact root of Western Civilization, at the exact heart
of "the American Way of Life" hangs
a murdered Arab, an executed Middle Easterner,
an assassinated Palestinian
a crucified son given by his father
a son tortured by other sons, everyone of whom

denied his mother. A Jew
dead of Capital Punishment

who gave his life
in order that the old way—
"You have heard it said, an eye for an eye,
and a tooth for a tooth"—be overturned.
"But I say unto you resist not
evil: Whoever shall smite thee
on thy right cheek
turn to him the other also."

Who gave his life—without heart? for
nothing but himself?—in order
that the old way of revenge
be overturned.

"You have heard it said, thou shalt love thy neighbor, and hate their enemy.
But I say unto you: Love your enemies, bless them
that curse you, do good
to them that hate you, and pray
for them which despitefully use you and
persecute you."

He was not being metaphorical. He didn't mean
strike back. He didn't mean
bomb them. He said
forgive them.

He didn't mean God bless our money. He said
give to every man that asketh of thee. He said if any man
sue thee and take away thy coat, let him have
thy cloke also. Sedition and blasphemy! They crucified him

for overturning the tables of the money lenders. For teaching
carry not a purse, don't be afraid for your next meal, accept
the food of your hosts.

He wasn't a Christian. He didn't say
God Bless America. God bless our might.
He said blessed be the meek. He said
blessed be the merciful. He said
blessed be the peacemakers.

3. *October 7 Until the Apocalypse?*

We're bombing the Holy Land again. "Jerusalem
the mother of us all." We're bombing
the Tigris and Euphrates again, the cradle
of civilization. He said be like the creator
who made the sun rise over the evil the same as the good
and sendeth the rain to fall on the just
the same as the unjust. We're bombing
our only selves again, exactly
the Divine made flesh. We carry in our arms
exactly the terrorist who didn't kill anyone. Forgive us, we

don't know what we're doing. Face and body
of that dead son (not a father) our mirror, this Cross
roads of our insanity. Love
thy enemy means love thy enemy. Why

are we breaking the Cosmic Law? Why
are we committing suicide? When
do we turn the tables? I'm not being metaphorical. Why
are they nailing us up again? Who
are these soldiers? These old fathers
who call themselves Christian, Muslim, Hebrew?
Blasphemy and sedition! All the great religions
say the same four words. How

can they kill us? Why
will they make all the world
Golgotha? Love

is the easiest betrayal. Even so he said

be ye perfect.

I was born into Christianity. I studied it as I was warned, and as I exalted, for the salvation of my soul. The religious crisis of my early adulthood, the disillusionment, was painful.

The habit of prayer from childhood is so deeply engrained in me I have to continually renew my vow not to petition Jesus or anyone in Heaven. I write poems instead.

He said love your enemy. He said resist not evil. He said let them smite you. He said turn the other cheek. He said give to every man that asks of thee. During the three weeks after September 11, before we started bombing, I read the Sermon on the Mount for the first time since I memorized it as a girl. How profoundly, like from a trumpet, those words seem directed at our so-called Christian government preparing for "a long, difficult war." (But he said do not sound a trumpet before thee.) He was born, my mother always said, to change the world from the wrathful God of Jealousy and Revenge of the Old Testament to the God of Love of the New Testament. She was not being anti-Semitic; she always said Jesus was a Jew. (She always told of Sarah and Hagar and their sons Issac and Ishmael, how all three religions come from the same father.) The Old Testament says this is the only future. He will come. A major part of my adult crises was learning what Christian Germans did to Jews. A minor part was learning the most simple but shocking fact, that the Old Testament was Jewish and that the New Testament is not read by them. And that Catholics study only the New Testament. I was taught it is One Story. It is essential to know the whole story. It is one living book from beginning to end. The Holy Bible.

During those three weeks one of my most sophisticated (i.e. cynical) friends, whom I kept encountering in the Mendocino Bakery line for morning coffee, said, sincerely, "Look at it this way, Sharon, we have the opportunity to forgive them."

Then we started bombing.

Sign on the cash register at the Mendocino Corners of the Mouth Health Food Store: "If the 6000 deaths on September 11 have sparked a global war against terrorism, when are the 30,000 deaths of children under five every day going to spark a global war against child mortality?"

Death death death to your baby your grandpa your sister your mother your brother your lover your son your husband your father your neighbors your village your books your civilization your enemies in the name of Jesus Christ. It's a secondary issue to our evil deeds but how do we bear the insanity of our hypocrisy?

BART EDELMAN

Coat of Sorrow

It's early Tuesday morning. The radio is tuned to KFWB, a news station in Los Angeles. I'm awakened to a special bulletin I don't quite believe I'm hearing. There's been an explosion at the World Trade Center. I listen for more news, wondering if I'm drifting back to sleep too soon. A reporter in New York City believes an airplane may have flown into one of the two towers of the World Trade Center. I bolt up in bed. An airplane hitting the World Trade Center? Bad luck, indeed! I turn on the television, just in time to see another airplane rip into the second tower. We are now out of accidents, I remember thinking—dumbfounded.

Days, weeks, and months later it's been documented. News reports are broadcast around the clock. There are names and faces, shell-shocked survivors, smoke still rising from the devastating debris, bombs dropping night and day over Afghanistan, anthrax attacks and a host of other nightmares to jolt us into "the reality of the 21st century." Welcome aboard this new flight, planet earth. Strap yourselves in and say your prayers.

We're supposed to be digesting what's happened. We're supposed to be making sense of it all. We're supposed to explain this as best we can. We're supposed to know ourselves well enough to know what we know, even though we could swear we're out of things to know. And, yes, nothing seems to look the same, taste the same, feel the same, or fit the same since that September day. This malaise hovers above our heads and drapes us in clothing we now appear destined to wear.

And so it is that rage
Remains incomplete
In the beds where we sleep
Week after week, unable
To keep the pace
Of life steady, the dream
Alive and ready for what peril
Faces a nation in grief,
Impotent to speak its peace,
Except in whispered words
Which seek to explain how rubble
And twisted steel weaken
The faith we swore to follow.

We walk the crooked streets
In this arrhythmic city,
Watchful of a sky
Whose clouds billow and swell—
Ominous towers of smoke
Stacked high to blow us
From here to kingdom come
At a moment's notice,
Until we turn our backs
And beat a slow retreat home
To visit empty rooms
Where yesterday's clothes hung,
Long before they vanished
And left us wearing nothing
But a coat of sorrow.

KARL ELDER

The Silence

A wind will spread its windy grandeurs round
And knock like a rifle-butt against the door.
The wind will command them with invincible sound.
—Wallace Stevens, "The Auroras of Autumn"

I think for the first time in my life—no philosophizing here—looking out my third story office at treetops both green and gold, these could be the last words I write. My colleague Jeff has Packers tickets. He, two of our friends, and I will drive sixty miles north for Green Bay an hour from now. It's Monday night versus the Redskins, thirteen days after the attack. It's supposed to rain. We're leaving early from work. Word is that security will be tight—no coolers, no purses, no umbrellas. Barricades around the stadium. Aircraft prohibited from entering a no-fly zone six miles in diameter. I worry about my binoculars. Should I pull my poncho out of the zip-lock bag before we get in line? Assuming it's not raining while we're in line, I maybe shouldn't wear rain gear. People might think I've something hidden. After all, one of the four of us is Iranian turned U.S. citizen. Never mind that he's also a practicing Zoroastrian. What's a Zoroastrian to a cheezehead but another Arab? I cannot now know that my Zoroastrian friend will be confronted by a cop as he and I, separated from Jeff and Ron ahead of us, are squeezed through a bottleneck of fences toward the stadium:

Cop (to my friend, patting my friend's chest): *What have you got there?*
My friend: *My wallet.*
Cop: *Take it easy. Get it out slow.*

I don't catch my friend's response, and I'm packed-in so close behind I can't see him complying with the cop's order. I look over my friend's head. There's a kid facing us ten feet away, twenty-years-old, maybe, standing on scaffolding of some sort. He raises both hands to his face. A camera flash. I see the kid is certain to get my friend. Not for a second do I think he's shooting the crowd behind us, and by no means do I think he's shooting the cop or me. I unzip my case and tilt it for the cop to see the binoculars inside. He peeks in, but he doesn't look through the lenses. He's a nice enough guy. He smiles and motions for me to move on.

I wonder what we'll talk about on our way up to the game. Probably there will be jokes about how we're going to sneak someone named Mehreban Khodavandi in, a bag over his head, emergency plastic surgery, a nose reduction.... We'll talk about the traffic. We'll talk about the Pack. We'll talk about safety in numbers, that for three hours we will be merely four among fifty thousand sitting ducks. I might even tell of my dream last night in which Lambeau Field, aglow with electric light, floated beneath my blimp's-eye view, a cross between an ark and a cruise ship bearing the world's largest shuffle-board. I kept dreaming it was the wrong target because of the illusion it was moving. I couldn't bring myself to open the bomb-bay doors. Yesterday, Sunday, tuning into a couple of games on TV, I expected the next attack would be on a weekend, just to keep us thinking. But then they already have us thinking.

What I won't talk about is the silence. The silence is the subject of a poem I'd begun and abandoned called "Nine One One," which promised to be blank verse, of a kind—staccato at first. For days I counted syllables of numbers, and when, following some compul-sion to begin at the beginning, I'd come up short (*nine one one two zero zero one*, nine syllables instead of ten), I'd somehow forget how or what I'd counted (*nine one one two thousand and one*, for exam-ple), and I'd go back to *nine one one*. Just ... silence.

But it is a silence that swells, momentarily strangles imagination, and lets go like a blood pressure cuff, leaving thought flowing, throbbing. There is the silence after the initial impact, the silence between the assault and those of us in Wisconsin or even Tokyo who had not yet been told. (God bless the short-lived interval of our ignorance, silence soon to be broadcast over and over at the speed of light rather than sound.) Then there is the silence after the cries. There is the silence of the video cameras. The silence after the sec-ond crash, following the silence of the approaching plane. Even the bodies fall in silence.

It is the identical silence that feeds the clichés: *horrific, tragic, unfathomable, unimaginable*. Yet we go on, remembering afresh: the silence of the second collapse, that gray avalanche and cloud rolling through big city canyons like a slow belch from hell, the silence of the ash, of the smothered footsteps of survivors emerging from the ash, while elsewhere over D.C., over Pennsylvania—more silence, passengers' voices muted, cell phones gone dumb, silence on the one hand of coerced compliance and on the other hand defiance.

The tickets are good tickets—seats twenty rows up from a corner of the end zone. There's *Favre*—the first time I've seen him in the flesh. *Gilbert Brown*. The home team on our end, warm-ups. Moments pass, and Mehreban, my Zoroastrian friend, leans his right shoulder into me. *Take it easy*, he says. *Get it out slow*. There is this utterly strange mix of pain and giddiness in his voice as he draws out the syllables so that, by the close of the first quarter, he's repeated the cop's admonition a dozen times. Finally, Mehreban again leans into me, laughing, "I should have told him I can't get it out any other way."

Days pass, and I'm still thinking of the silence. I'm thinking of fifty thousand mouths chanting *U.S.A., U.S.A.*, both before and after an Air Force reservist, the staff of an American flag in his grasp, leads his fellow Packers' charge through the tunnel onto the field, just as I happen to spy to my left and slightly behind us a guy whose stern lips are sealed as he holds a cardboard placard high above his head that reads PEACE.

Yes. *Take it easy. Get it out slow.*

It's the Saturday following the game, five days since I received an invitation from Bill Heyen to contribute to this gathering and immediately sat at my keyboard and began to re-enter the rhythm of my life. Prose for a time, and then it's Saturday. I'm working in the yard, fall cleanup, thinking about the silence, which reminds me of a sequence of hard-won poems I've labored over for ten years—since before the Gulf War—called "Mead: 26 Abecedariums," for which I had not yet written a twenty-fourth. And while thinking of Mehreban and, yes, remembering the cop—that very moment the prose stopped and the poem began, that instant in my yard as I turned, quickened by a thing sensed, if not seen, if not heard, over a shoulder.

A transparent tarp you use to haul leaves
belies the eyes, inflates, rises, a great
cape slung by wind over its back, as if
donned by some invisible enemy,
entity without shape. For the form of
fear is never Bear, never Ghost, never
Ghoul. Neither is it evil or black of
hell. By flames or flashlight the mind still sees
inside the well, while fear's that ... that thing that
jostles, even should you dwell in certain
knowledge of its presence, your prescience
laughable to the mouth of the hand whose
magic's hardly the glove on your jacket
nor bite in your billfold—but a cold grip
on your heart. You awaken with a start:
Peace is apple pie without anthrax, the
quintessential mom's art, while you're outside
raking leaves and Dad's about to roll his
sleeves to adjust the carburetor and
timing. And while far more pastoral than
urban, Osama bin Laden's turban's
vacant the picture, which is not to say
war was then more pure, but that rather than
xanthic, leaves, when dervish-like they stood, spun,
yellow-red and blush-gold, in the face of
Zoids *you* stood, pretend sword in hand, deft, bold.

MARCIA FALK

Five Poems

AFTER ASTOUNDING EVIL,
THE PROMISE OF MORE TO COME

Sister Dolores says she believes that good will triumph.
I believe only in the necessities of evolution; hence
this may be the beginning of the end.

But why must it be so personal?
Could we not live coolly in an ice age
unaware that the glaciers will soon split
and part and heave us to the sea?
What about a meteor? Something sudden and huge
and instantly obliterating?
Not this unabating terror that we inhabit,
our jaws clenched, our necks twisted and stiff
from turning to see behind our backs, night and day.

Perhaps we will evolve, if there is time (which it seems there is not),
into a many-eyed, many-eared creature,
exquisitely sensed to danger, yet endowed with a great courage,
the kind we know now only through denial.

Or perhaps we will devolve, each of us, back to our infancies
when our imaginations were small, our fears simple and few:
Hunger. Cold. Wet.
That she will not be there when we need her.
Her largeness, that powerful presence
so able to leave at any moment,
our fingers so tiny, so weak, so completely unable to hold on.

The winter winds have started to blow in St. Joseph, Minnesota.
Outside the window, you watch the dance
of birds, grasses, trees,
while inside, confusion rises and falls without pattern.
The birds at the feeder pay you no mind.
They quarrel as usual over the opening to the feeder,
poking each other aside until one is forced to give way,
while the smaller ones wait their turns quietly or nervously.
The wind seems to make the birds move more quickly
from tree to bush and back to tree,
but this, you know, is the window's illusion.
Everything is moving too quickly this morning.

What must it be like there, on the world's other side,
where the skies fill with shapes that swoop and lower and rise,
some bearing food and medicine,
some whatever it takes to blow us to bits?
And some—merely mirages in the terrifying clouds.

Through the television window, a dance.
But when you walk away, a new thing rises in your throat,
thickening there,
this first Sunday of October, 2001.

APPRISED

Here you are again this morning, my birds,
awaiting me.
I used to read the paper to start the day,
but these days, I begin with you.

Last night, the nation was apprised of current dangers.
We were told there is a 100% chance
that something will happen.

What do I know now that I did not know before?
Was there a time when something terrible
was *not* about to happen
to someone, at some moment, somewhere?
It's just that now it could be me
or, worse—far worse—mine.
But even that is not new.

In the morning, I wake from my poisoned dreams
to my terrible thoughts,
yank up the shades and find you, my small friends,
still fighting among yourselves at the feeder, unreconciled,
still taking dips in the birdbath
even though they are predicting a freeze.
(What if the freeze came while your wings were wet?
Have you thought about that?)

Yes, I know—
you have your own plans.
They are there in the inner curve
of your strong, fast wings
and in your sharp, precise beaks
and in your tiny feet
which know so well to grasp and to hold on.

Yet all of you will die
and some of you will die soon
and for some it will be an awful, sudden thing
you could never have imagined—
a windshield slamming into your head,
a freshly washed, deceptively blank window
in a place you were sure you could freely fly.

For now, you are still eating, bathing, arguing,
oblivious to me and to all who wait on the other side.
While we take in facts and estimate our chances,
you are busy inaugurating the day.

VIGIL

Now *this* is weather!

Did I already say there's a dance outside the window?
Then how can I say it again and trust you will understand
I mean it differently?
How can I tell you that yesterday was nothing compared to this
and have you believe me?
Won't you say to yourself,
Yeah, sure. And tomorrow she will say today was nothing.
You will, and of course you will be right.
Where does it end? you will want to know.

Well, it doesn't.
Not with me, and not with you, either.
None of us can help it,
not one of us can still the constant motion
or cease our efforts to try and grab hold nevertheless.

Just look at the trees this morning,
struggling to hold on to their last leaves
while the wind keeps them working and vigilant.
Here, for example, is a moment's calm, and yet
you can feel the waiting in the tiny, almost inscrutable trembling
at the very tip of the thinnest branch
at the top of the tree.

And even after the last perfect flaming-orange leaf succumbs to its fall,
you will still feel the waiting—
if not here, then there,
if not there, then somewhere.

HAPPINESS

I was afraid.
I had been awake all night thinking about the warnings.
Thinking about being so far from my young son,
unable to get to him in time.

I went walking in the woods.
I walked and walked,
and the leaves were yellow and the leaves were red,
and I gathered some red and yellow ones and a few still green,
and talked aloud to myself, keeping myself company.
Under a huge maple tree, I stopped to sort them,
choosing them, one by one,
making a bundle to fill my arms.
Then holding them against my chest, I continued on.

I came upon another walker, the only other person I'd seen that day,
and she was weeping.
When she passed by me, she touched my arm,
riches on riches.

I was almost back at the field near the edge of the woods
when I stopped behind a big rock to pee,

leaving my armful of leaves at the side of the trail.
The rock was only a few meters away, but when I returned
I couldn't find the leaves.
I was distraught, and, even so, I reproached myself for caring,
blamed myself for trying to take so much with me
and for *still* wanting to, nevertheless.

And I remembered my son's face, perfect,
and the light wet touch on my arm.

RICHARD FOERSTER

Resolve

I'll put aside those images, the camcorded
streaks, for already I bear the raised, raw
welt, the thrust fiery brand of grief hard
upon the brain. I'll listen past the thunder
of gray blossoms bursting from the ground,
the snuffed cries deep within each petal's
heavy folds, for souls too fast are silent,
light as pollen in the air, and I
would hear them again, breathe them in again
though my lungs are full to aching. But how ignore
the Babel of opinion mounted stone by stone
that forever comes crashing into our lives
like vengeance? Better, I'll say, to think on where
that travel-weary Samaritan crouches
now, amid what rubble of the world,
faintly calling through the terror. The words
lodge like barbs on my tongue: *And who is my neighbor?*

Soon after September 11, the editor of *The York Independent*, one of
my town's newspapers, telephoned to ask me to write a poem "to
express the inexpressible" about what people were feeling in the
wake of the terrorist attacks. "Try somehow," he said, "to make sense
of the bewilderment, grief, and anger that we are all experiencing."
I had just recently returned home to Maine after nine months of
travel abroad—nineteen flights in all during a journey that took me
safely around the world. Before setting out on that trip, however, I'd
suffered the sudden loss of a loved one to cancer. Now back in my

familiar surroundings, I found myself still deeply mourning that death. And so the initial shock of watching those images of the jet-liners crashing into the World Trade Center towers, the realization that thousands of lives were being violently extinguished right there, live on TV, struck me to the core. Instantly, my own small grief seemed trivial within the broader perspective of the families, communities, governments, and nations that I knew would be forever altered by those brutal acts. Though I didn't feel up to the task, I told the newspaper's editor I would try to write something appropriate in time for his deadline.

Like most people during those confusing first days, I remained glued to my TV screen, insatiable for the latest breaking news that I hoped would begin to make sense of what had happened. But listening to the various official press briefings, I grew dismayed at the way the President and his advisers were casting the events in simple black and white: "America's new war" would be a "crusade" pitting the forces of Good (us) against the demonic powers of Evil (them). Dismay turned to disgust when I heard the small-minded, morally bankrupt pronouncements of Jerry Falwell, laying the blame for the attacks on the doorstep of homosexuals, pro-choice advocates, and other outcasts from his fundamentalist kingdom. First the Administration and now a supposed representative of God had spoken from on high.

Then, overnight, all those flags began snapping from car antennas—no doubt, soon to become wind-frayed tatters along the nation's highways. The display seemed to me a sadly inadequate means to express the resolve that we as Americans had to muster to face the uncertain times ahead. As the son of immigrants who left Germany at the rise of Nazism, I'd learned long ago to be suspicious of officially endorsed, homogenized sentiments of patriotism expressed on a mass scale. However well-intentioned, they invariably spring from a gut reaction, the herd instinct to find the easiest way through a crisis to some safer emotional ground.

And so, when I sat down to write my poem, I knew I had to try to "express the inexpressible" from an entirely personal point of view, with the goal that the "I" of the poet would be representative, the stand-in for a much larger group. I felt that any resolve to overcome adversity and grief must arise from within each of us as individuals before it can begin to operate socially within families, communities, nations, and the family of nations. As the poem took shape through several drafts, I realized there was a connection between the World

Trade Center towers and the biblical Tower of Babel: both aspiring to the heavens, both resulting in universal confusion. From there it was a short metaphoric leap in my mind to Luke's gospel and the parable of the "Good" Samaritan (the prejudice of the day being that Samaritans generally were a bad lot). Amid all the anguish and conflicting cries for justice and vengeance in the wake of September 11, the slippery lawyer's question that prompts the parable—" And who is my neighbor?"—is a painful one to contemplate. My poem doesn't pretend to offer a simple answer. Whether the travel-weary Samaritan in the poem is any well-meaning average Joe crouching among the rubble of a shattered life, or a heroic rescuer at Ground Zero in Manhattan, or someone on the minus side of the us-vs.-them equation (dare I suggest today's Taliban or tomorrow's Hezbollah), the events of September 11 have redefined the bound-aries of neighborhood on a global scale. Our resolve to set things right at home and in the world had better build on that realization.

NORA GALLAGHER

Lament for the World

Andrew has made you into grains of rice
all five thousand
and placed you in a basket as if to shield you from the flames

He asks at breakfast how something so large
as those towers
could stop existing, holding his coffee cup,

turning it around and around as if half expecting it
to implode in his palm

A dead fish rises from the lake this morning, gills spread,
white skin, it floats
in the dark water, the slow kill of acid rain

Everywhere we are ruined, our towers fall into
a dust of memos,
plaintive notes,
all life suspended, falling

How could something so intricate, so cleverly built,
so beloved as a body, as a fish,
cease to be

I wrote "Lament for the World" at the Blue Mountain Center in Adirondack State Park, a writers and artists colony on a small private lake. We had no television. The morning of September 11, someone called us, and then someone else turned on a radio in the main lodge kitchen. Andrew Ginzel, one of the artists, was not with us. He had returned to New York over the weekend to teach a class. His studio is on Bleecker Street. Andrew heard the first plane come over Manhattan as he was sipping tea at his desk. Then he heard the explosion. He got on his bike and rode down to Battery Park to find out what was going on. There he witnessed much more than anyone should ever have to see. He returned to us that night, late, driving out of Manhattan, watching the convoys of military vehicles, police, and ambulances driving in. In the morning, he told us his story. Having not seen any of the TV images, Andrew's account was the first I had heard in any detail. That was the first day I cried. Later, Andrew counted out five thousand grains of rice and placed them in a basket on our dining table. They stayed there for the rest of the session.

TESS GALLAGHER

I Have Never Wanted to March

or to wear an epaulet. Once I did
walk in a hometown parade to celebrate
a salmon derby. I was seven, my hair in
pigtails, and I wore a steel flasher strapped
diagonally across my chest like a bandolier
(which in Catalan would be *bandolera* from
bandoler meaning "bandit".) My black
bandit boots were rubber
because here on the flanks of the Olympics
it always rains on our parades.

I believe I pushed a doll buggy.
I believe all parades, especially military
parades could be improved if
the soldiers wore bandoliers made to attract
fish, and if each soldier pushed a doll buggy
inside which were real-seeming babies
with their all-seeing doll-eyes open
to reflect the flight of birds, of balloons
escaped from the hands of children to
hover over the town—higher than flags, higher
than minarets and steeples.

What soldier could forget about
collateral damage with those baby faces
locked to their chin straps? It is
conceivable that soldiers would resist
pushing doll buggies. Bending over

might spoil the rigidity of their marching.
What about a manual exhorting the patriotic
duty of pushing doll buggies? Treatises
on the symbolic meaning would need to be
written. Hollywood writers might be of use.
Poets and historians could collaborate,
reminding the marchers of chariots, of
Trojan horses, of rickshaws, of any wheeled
conveyance ever pulled or pushed or driven
in the service of human kind.

I would like, for instance, to appear
in the next parade as a Trojan horse. When
they open me I'll be seven years old.
There will be at least seven of me
inside me, for effect, and because it is
a mystical number. I won't understand
much about war, in any case—especially
its good reasons. I'll just want to be pushed
over some border into enemy territory, and
when no one's thinking anything except: what
a pretty horse! I'll throw open myself
like a flank and climb out, all
seven of me, like a many-legged spider
of myself. I'll speak only
in poetry, my second language, because it
is beautifully made for exploring the miraculous
ordinary event—in which an alchemy
of words agree to apprentice themselves to the possible
as it evades the impossible. Also poetry

doesn't pretend to know answers and speaks best
in questions, the way children do
who want to know everything, and don't believe
only what they're told. I'll be seven
unruly children when they open me up,
and I'll invite the children of the appointed enemy
to climb into my horse for a ride. We'll be secret
together, the way words are
the moment before they are spoken—
those Trojan horses of silence, looking for a border

to roll across like over-sized toys
manned by serious children—until one horse

has been pushed back and forth
with its contraband of mutually-pirated children
so many times that it is clear to any adult watching
this unseemly display, that enemy territory
is everywhere when anyone's child is at stake, when
the language of governments is reduced to ultimatums
and threats, when it wants to wear epaulets
and to march without
its doll buggy.

But maybe an edict or two could be made
by one child-ventriloquist through the mouth
of the horse, proposing that the advent of atrocities
be forestalled by much snorting, neighing, prancing and
tail swishing, by long, exhausted parades
of reciprocal child-hostages who may be
rescued only in the language of poetry
which insists on being lucid
and mysterious at once, like a child's hand
appearing from the peep-hole under the tail
of the horse, blindly waving to make sure that anyone
lined up along the street does not submit entirely
to the illusion of their absence, their
ever-squandered innocence, their hyper-responsive
minds in which a ladybug would actually fly away
with only its tiny flammable wings
to save its children from the burning house.

BRENDAN GALVIN

Fragments
(Against September 11, 2001)

1.

He breezed past me on a bike so thin
it looked bulletproof, another spandex
superhero, I thought, until he came back
slowly, sagging and loud, both hands
on the grips, talking to nobody
on this road given over to birdsong.
Both towers? He was almost screaming now.
Both? Another vacationer losing
his mind at his leisure, until I saw
the headphone clamped to his helmet.

2.

Way down the tideline where the dune
seemed to turn a corner, out of
mist and heat ripple, a single coast guardsman
comes walking the wet sandpack, Maguire's Beach,
1942: a sentry in black and white from squared
sailor hat to leggings, his police dog
leashed, rifle slung tight
to his shoulder.
             A boy, crewcut
and blond, between those women
and children around the driftwood fire
and the Atlantic bowling out of skies
up that shore. None has ever seen
a rifle. Their eyes unhooded,
lips without irony, those faces
will be open yet awhile.

3.

The smell of apples ambushes me
and it's Corn Hill Road again, September,
not the nowhere of my cluttered rage,
the jags of former things
jamming me up. Can a tree—
all pelvic scoops and spine—

                  sinking

among chokecherry and goldenrod
into the marsh's ferment, a leaf-out
flush with fruit, ever say again,
If you would compose obituaries, think on
the way my time keeps coming round?

Walking Corn Hill Road

Some of the walkers I encounter have cell phones in their pockets now, which go off with a fingernail-to-blackboard effect on the marsh's silence and birdsong, but that bicyclist wore the first microphone I'd seen on the road. It was so absurd in that context that I thought he was cracking up. When I got home, pictures of the airliners hitting the World Trade Center were on the tube: the tease for a new Bruce Willis movie, maybe. That lone coast guardsman with his dog and rifle, one of my earliest memories, began to stand for innocence in a much larger way, as have the unlined faces of people in photos from that period.

Days later, I walked Corn Hill Road in anger, locked into my head. Nobody appeared to recognize that dusted-off Vietnam War attitudes wouldn't work in this situation. Unable to distinguish between reason and wits gone astray, reporters and editors seemed willing to quote *anybody* with any opinion rather than suffer blank space and dead air. A retired "radical historian," a few days after the event, had told a local weekly that those people were expressing their "grievances" against us, and we should listen to them. If you read this man's footnoteless "history," which Oscar Handlin called a fairy tale, you would be forgiven for thinking that the day the Berlin Wall came down was the worst day of his life. Others said in various ways that the sneak-attack was our own fault. Why wasn't it obvious to Americans that we were up against an irrationality that couldn't be negotiated with? We should build them houses, people said.

The smell of apples on that old tree brought me back to where I was, on a Cape Cod road I've been jogging and walking for the last thirty-three years. The *New York Times* in its wisdom asked *critics* to comment on whether Art offered any solace for such events. Not artists, poets, composers, but *critics*! In the late '60s, during some of the worst hours of my young life, I had turned to *The Four Quartets* for sustenance. Recently my friend, the poet David Slavitt, had sent me a tape of Eliot's poem, read by Alec Guinness. I hadn't read it recently and was surprised at how much I remembered of it. Guinness presented it as wildly Romantic and lyrical, unlike Eliot's desiccated version, and I found as I read and listened that it moved me again in new ways. Maybe if I approached September 11 indirectly, circled around it. That old apple tree chimed for me with Thomas Hardy's "In Time of 'The Breaking of Nations'." I remembered a callow young poet in 1968 saying that anyone who wrote about a tree should be shot, that only poems against the war in Asia should be written.

DAN GIANCOLA

The Ruin

I'm screwed to my seat,
glued to the tube. Flight
175 repeatedly slams
its innocent freight
into Tower Two. The mum
of fire blooms. The twin
Niagaras shift atoms,
rumble and spill,
concrete and steel
cataracts pouring
through a mist of glass....

I imagine the hijackers gut-stuck,
pitched in a sty where swine
gobble their entrails....

At Ground Zero, open wound
serving as nation's tomb,
wind bullies and tatters
concrete genies
escaped from the shattered
tons of America's dream.
A Union Square candle sputters.
Lost faces on handbills scatter,
the sun bleaching their names.
Tomorrow is a ruin.
Tomorrow is fragile as flame.

The events of September 11th are scored on my retinae, thanks to the unconscionable acts of kamikaze terrorists and the media, which gratifies its existence by spooling the tapeloop of tragedy, the instant replay of death.

I watched all day, all night—my blood lust demanding satiation. As the middle stanza of "The Ruin" suggests, I was ready to advocate the most heinous response. A few days away from CNN, however, afford-ed me a new perspective: at whom would my righteous indignation and vengeance be directed? I began to worry about guarding against further acts of terrorism; after all, retaliation by the United States would certainly spur more terrorism, and my country was about to lock itself into the self-defeating cycle of exchanging violence for vio-lence. How could we "win" against a cowardly and resourceful enemy integrated like a dormant virus inside our citizenry?

Retribution fails to resurrect our dead. I have a 15-year-old daugh-ter and a 9-year-old son; I want more for them than a future charged with danger and fear, a future of ash. We must end our complacency and move, as a nation, from notions of simple Old Testament revenge to complex and far more courageous New Testament for-giveness. Our failure to do so further endangers the sanctity of human life and will make a ruin of all our fragile tomorrows.

DANIELA GIOSEFFI

Sept. 11th, Meagan's Birthday

I'd watched the rolling, billowing ball of fire thunder skyward, over and over again in my nightmares, heard the roaring blast as I stood stunned with the pain of lives being lost inside the huge towers. Some leapt to their deaths rather than be sizzled alive. An explosion that big, loud, and ugly had never been witnessed by any of us who stood on the roof deck that fateful morning breathing the blast of jet fuel fire and ash of workers' lives raining down on us. As the grey United Airlines jet deliberately crashed into the second tall tower on the horizon of the Manhattan skyline, I shouted, "Terrorist attack!" We ran from the roof as the fire thundered up, fearing for our lives. The superintendent of our tall building, just across from the Twin Towers, immediately ordered an evacuation. Minutes later, I stood at the edge of the Brooklyn Heights waterfront watching the World Trade Center collapse in clouds of grey smoke from the skyline just across the East River. As thousands died in one blasted instant, my daughter was in the hospital for an exploratory surgery, while my husband, ailing with a terminal illness was struggling for his life.

Three weeks later, on a bright autumn day out of a fairy tale, I'd seen my daughter through her surgery and she was okay. I'd dropped my ailing husband to visit with his grand-children—perhaps for one last time for all we knew—in Salem, Massachusetts. Shaken and distraught, I'd headed for a retreat in the Berkshires—my first time free from nursing my husband in two years. I'd visited the Nathaniel Hawthorne Wayside House in Concord—a home previously owned by Louisa May Alcott's father—a man of liberal, even progressive principles in his day—like Hawthorne an anti-Puritan, Alcott helped abolitionists run an underground railroad. He believed in open-minded education of the young, and decried fanatical ways of rearing children in strict Puritanical obedience. He wanted to allow them to question authority and communicate in a dialog of learning. For his views, he suffered a measure of poverty which his daughter, Louisa May, had to endure, as portrayed in her popular novel, *Little Women*.

Stunned with pity for the dying inside a burning Trade Center tower, I had watched from my roof as the second gray jet buzzed low over my head up the East River, turned suddenly at the Brooklyn Bridge, and smashed tons of exploding fuel into the second tall tower. I hadn't slept well since witnessing firsthand the "Attack on America" as CBS billed it. With Hollywood slick red, white and blue graphics and dramatic music, the networks showed that explosion over and over again like a special-effects movie, as America was numbed out of its mind with thirst for war. Young men with baseball caps atop their heads were shouting "Nuke 'em!" with Howard Stern in New York streets, while Muslim women and children hid in their homes afraid to go out and shop for food. Some of us marched in mournful peace demonstrations uniting our grief for the victims of the attack and our fear for the future in a hope for a rational reaction. Who did these baseball jocks think "'em" was? I knew "they" were only civilians like those dead in my city—except they were the poorest of earth's poor. They were orphans crippled by land mines, starving widows living amidst famine and drought in the rubble of Afghanistan laid waste by the US and USSR who had fought their Cold War—hot as Hell—there over the rich oil reserves of Caspian Sea area. The two warring superpowers had pulled out leaving land mines, starvation, and mass graves everywhere. "They" were the subjects of Taliban dictators which the U.S. military had supplied with weapons and CIA know-how. "You've already had your vengeance on the Afghan people." I wanted to tell the baseball caps, but it would have taken a small dissertation to explain their own country's foreign policy—a rare subject in a nation entertaining itself to death on sitcoms, sports, pornographic horror movies, Disneyland dreams, and opiates.

With the image of the exploding towers in my head, I lay awake nights listening to the jingoist slogans about liberty and freedom as thousands of American workers festered in lingering fires under tons of debris. My nightmares were full of their faces mixed with the cries of half-a-million Iraqi children starved as "collateral damage" by U.S. trade sanctions. I thought of how my country, "land of the free and home of the brave," had been kicked off of the Human Rights Council of the United Nations; how it had walked out of the World Conference on Racism; how it had voted "No" for reparations for the thousands of sexual slaves tortured by the Japanese military because of fear of having to compensate the heirs of African slaves brutalized here in the building of America. I thought of how the price of one nuclear bomber would build thousands of ghetto schools. I thought of how President George W. Bush had stepped out of the Kyoto Accord on Global Warming. I thought of how Henry Kissinger had been pursued in Paris to be tried at the Hague as a war criminal for his proven part in the assassination of Allende and sundry other war crimes which had caused the deaths of millions. This I'd read in a lengthy article in *Harpers*, weeks earlier, carefully documented with Kissinger's own papers, by Christopher Hitchens.

One night, I dreamed that Allende's ghost was weeping—and all the Chileans who were tortured or "disappeared" under the despot Pinochet, put in power by the CIA—were walking with me like shades amidst the moans of thousands of mothers, husbands, wives, and fathers lying under the rubble of the felled giant towers. These were working people from every walk of life and culture snatched from the moments of their lives. They expired calling on cell phones to speak of love. Allende took my hand and led me through the rubble. Then he sailed with me over the giant crater in the Pentagon and showed me a basement room in the CIA where Anthrax was being prepared by a psychotic, rightwing agent in an envelope destined for the office of the Democratic Majority Leader. The idea was to cause a renewed expansion of the CIA and embroil the legislature in another terrorist attack to make them vote right on a "Patriot's Bill" that eroded American freedoms—even as jingoists claimed we waged war for liberty. Allende's ghost accompanied me, like a guide from Dante's *Inferno*, to a Red Cross Hospital in Afghanistan where civilians lay under the rubble bleeding. "These Afghan dead are just like my Chilean dead and your American dead," he said, "all innocent and murdered by the same murderers." I woke with the taste of petroleum oil burning in my mouth, the smell of the jet oil fumes still permeating my bedroom in the city.

Was I awake and dreaming or asleep and living when I witnessed cheering hordes wave the bloodied red, white and blue over the collapsed hot steel of Rockefeller's big "edifice complex" as it melted and continued to crumble? The too tall death-traps designed to implode sprayed human entrails throughout their steel insides. Only the firemen and rescue workers trying to extract dismembered bodies seemed like heroes. I thought of how a huge arsenal of nuclear bombs can never protect an imperialist nation from the rage of box-cutters and plastic penknives. I thought of the targets of the terrorists, not the Statue of Liberty, symbol of freedom, but the Pentagon and the World Trade Center, symbols of military and industrial might. I thought of the huge demonstrations gathering strength among the workers of the world who opposed the famines wrought by The World Bank and the International Monetary Fund. Coincidentally, those mass demonstrations uniting workers and environmental activists from all over the world had been planned for the very month of September 2001. When the World Trade Center had been attacked, they were cancelled. I knew that bombs were not falling on Afghanistan to protect my freedom, because the bombings were only encouraging more Islamic fundamentalists to join the armies of the Taliban, destabilizing Pakistan, a shaky nuclear power. The sorrow in me grew large and would not let me sleep. Though I'd been an anti-nuclear activist for decades, this was a worry bigger than I could handle.

It was ordinary New Yorkers like me who died, as the sun swooned and the bright morning turned to a smoky nightmare and ash kept falling over me in the streets. For weeks, I choked on the ash of the budding hopes of these workers turned to dust which coated my face and clothes, and wormed in the wind up my nose. The burning smell was exactly, I imagined, like the dust of bombed and burning Palestinian and Israeli bodies; hot ashes blasted by Timothy McVeigh—blond blue-eyed American of the New Aryan Nation; fires of Hiroshima and Nagasaki, napalm of Vietnam, bombs blasting Cambodians; grenades of Granada and machine gun-smoke of East Timor. Was it also like the fierce fire-smell reported by astronauts— both Russian and American—of infinite outer-space in which we drift on our common earth bound by one bright thirsty sun, ruled by one magnetic moon, as we spin out and around caught in an eternally expanding blast of stars on our dying ecosystem composed of nearly all water? This was the beginning of the 21st century as the huge war industries of our outmoded nation states continued to kill and bomb each other's babies, mothers, fathers, sisters, brothers in unending bloodbath of misery. Earthlings murdering earthlings!

The twin terrorists, Bush and bin Laden, were blurring into one another in my mind. From my reading, I realized they were becoming interchangeable. Their guns, bombs, money, and drugs had been going around international loops for years together. The Stinger missiles that shot at U.S. helicopters were supplied by the CIA. The heroin used by America's drug addicts, traded for guns, comes from Afghanistan, and had been the fruits of a drug industry encouraged by the CIA. The Bush administration recently in Spring of 2001 gave the Taliban a 43 million dollar subsidy for a "war on drugs" which would buy more profits for guns for multi-national weapons dealers. I knew that my country was the biggest arms dealer in the world, and that Russia came in second on that score and was just as evil. The two Cold War Superpowers had amassed large arsenals of bio-terrorism, too. KGB agents and CIA agents had traded all sorts of spying back and forth until no one knew for sure who were the spies and who the counter-spies and that, no doubt, the same sort of intrigue had gone on in Central Asia during the Afghan wars which I was told by a Russian soldier who'd fought in them, were riddled with heroin addicted infantry.

Osama bin Laden, I learned, as I read unable to sleep, was an Afghan veteran who fought valiantly in the front lines against the Russians for the U.S. He spent his family fortune subsidizing the veterans of that war and their widows and orphans after America deserted them. He broke with the Saudi crown of his homeland in an argument over U.S. intrusion into Central Asia's Holy Lands. Osama—first trained as a business man who switched his studies to Islam—had been the only son of the big bin Laden clan to fight with the Taliban on the American side. He'd become legendary among The Taliban for his generous aid to the deserted veterans of the Afghan wars after the Americans pulled out, leaving the country in ruin—giving little to rebuild their promise of freedom from Communism. Osama was a six-foot-seven devout believer who walked like a king of mercy among the veterans' families of Afghanistan, dispensing alms from his family's fortunes. Many Islamic extremists thought of him as a Christ "turning over the tables of money changers" when he bombed the World Trade Center. He was the only rich son to have fought in the front lines among the starving soldiers. He was a fringe cult-figure of the despotic Taliban who controlled their countrymen and the Afghan women with murderous military powers bestowed upon them by the United States.

The cruelties toward women were unspeakably extreme on the part of the despotic Taliban. Thinking of Afghan widows buried alive in mass graves, and women stoned to death for not wearing their veils or for imagined or real sexual transgressions added screams to my nightmares. Osama was also the step-brother and son of Salem and Muhammad who once hobnobbed with the oil barons of Texas society before dying in unexplained airplane or helicopter crashes there at about the time of the Iran-Contragate scandals. I remembered, too, an article I'd read about Saddam Hussein seeing his father shot by Westerners before his own eyes when he was a boy of five. I wondered what psychological aberrations, what private vendettas, had helped to create these two fanatical Frankensteins: Saddam of Iraq and Osama, exile of Saudi Arabia.

I thought about George Bush, Jr., too. He seemed like a personable, not too bright guy, who loved baseball and really would rather not be president—if only being a baseball team manager would have satisfied Dad. He was a typical "frat boy" who had married a librarian. Laura Bush, I read in *Newsweek*, was a woman who had killed her classmate when she ran a stop sign, ramming his car with hers and breaking his neck. For this old crime or accident committed when she was seventeen, she'd never gone to prison, but served a little community service instead. Had she been a drinker like George W. had been? Had they helped each other to give up alcohol? I knew that he'd been chosen by his father, a former CIA director, and a wealthy political machine made of oil and pharmaceutical money, to steal the U.S. election in Texas. I thought about how except for some "hanging chads," Al Gore would be president. G.W. Bush came into office just in time to seal the about-to-be-made-public Reagan/Bush presidential papers with a presidential order claiming "national security reasons." G.W. Bush was an unschooled puppet who had never traveled abroad, who self-admittedly didn't like to read, who was funded by a powerful oil lobby more than any other president had been. The pharmaceutical giants were behind him, too. That I understood from John Loftus of the Holocaust Museum in Florida, a former U.S. Prosecuting Attorney for Nazi war criminals, who was quoted as saying: "The Bush family fortune comes from The Third Reich." I.G. Farben, big German financial corporation, had built the Bush and Rockefeller profits during World War II. According to *The Encyclopedia Britannica* I.G. Farben financed the building of forty death camps, including Auschwitz. I.G. Farben had morphed into investments in the big pharmaceutical corporations now invested in the genome project. Those same pharmaceutical giants were scalping our senior citizens for the drugs that kept them alive and killing AIDS victims with medication prices beyond their pocket books. Giant pharmaceutical firms were destined to profit, too, from the new bioterror threat sweeping my city and spreading throughout America. Bayer, maker of Cipro—the antidote to Anthrax—was part of the I.G. Farben group, too. Also, the I.G. Farben group of old had financed Joseph Mengele and his Nazi eugenics projects. It was the manufacturer and deliverer of Zyklon B to death camps. And, Bayer researcher, Professor Gerhard Domagk, conducted human experiments for the S.S. on Germ Warfare. My head spun with these newly learned facts.

Now the military industrial puppet of oil and nuclear barons, George W. Bush, and double-crossed Osama, Frankenstein of the CIA, were faced off in a tragic comedy of "blow-back." The people of my city were dead and my family threatened, as each borrowed the other's rhetoric. Each referred to the other as "the head of the snake." Both invoked God and used the loose currency of good and evil as their terms of reference. Both were engaged in unequivocal war crimes. Both were dangerously armed as they stalked my nightmares, one with the nuclear arsenal of the obscenely powerful, the other with the incandescent, self-destructive power of the utterly hopeless.

On September 29th, I sat alone over a bowl of New England clam chowder at a busy lunch counter in Concord Village—the seat of American transcendentalism. Even after enjoying my tour of the Hawthorne Wayside House, sorrow and disorientation still pummeled my spirit with a feeling I'd no right to be happy, to enjoy my soup or the sunshine. That sensation combined with a fear I'd never feel safe again in my city, living just five minutes across from Wall Street in Brooklyn as I had for thirty years. Worse, I'd never feel my daughter was safe working and commuting through the subways, tunnels, or over the bridges.

I looked at the map I'd placed on the counter next to my soup to check the route that would take me across the Berkshire mountains from Concord to Greenfield. It looked narrow and winding. I had only a couple of hours to get to my destination before dark. A young man and a blond child had just seated themselves to my right and ordered chowder. The young man looked alert and his young daughter with her long light-brown hair seemed well cared for. She smiled up at me. I smiled back.

"Excuse me, do you happen to know about this road across the mountains to Greenfield. Does it take very long to make it to Route 91?"

"About two hours or more. It's a beautiful road on an autumn day like this." He replied.

"So, it's a real highway? Easy driving. Not a lot of lights?"

"Two lanes, a few traffic lights, and you'll need sun glasses, because the sunset is coming right at you. There's no better view of the fall foliage right now though."

"Thanks, I appreciate your advice. I'm from New York City and don't know these parts well. I was just visiting Hawthorne's Wayside House."

"We were visiting Walden Pond," her father offered. "Nice and peaceful there."

"You're from New York City where the attacks happened? Gosh, did you see them?" His daughter's big blue eyes implored a thorough answer.

"Yes, I saw them from my rooftop close by. I live in the tallest building just across from lower Manhattan on the East River."

"Oh, it must have been terrible to see! Did anybody you know get hurt?" Her father wanted to be sensitive about the point.

"No, but my daughter was having surgery in the midst of the chaos. That was really the harrowing part for me, though she's okay now. I saw the second grey jet buzz in over my head up the East River, turn at The Bridge, and smash into the towers with a big explosion," I told him. "Debris and ashes rained down on me, but I'm okay." When I see his daughter looking at me in wonder, I hasten to add: "But most people in the world are good people. There are only a *few* very bad ones who do things like that. I'm sure you are safe up here in New England."

"I know everybody in our town. We all know each other and feel safe there and our teacher said that not all Muslims are bad people, only a few who call themselves Muslims, but are really just crazy criminals. There are lots of Muslims everywhere in the world, just like us," she offered with enthusiasm. "One of the kids on our school is Islamic and she seems just like us, too." Her good cheer was palpable and her vocabulary bright.

"Well, you sound like a very smart girl. How old are you, may I ask?"

"I'm nine. My name is Meagan and I come from Stowe, Vermont."

"I'm sixty. My name's Daniela, and I come from New York City. Pleased to meet you, Meagan! I was just enjoying seeing Nathaniel Hawthorne's house. He was a good man who opposed the fanatical ways of Puritans. It sounds like your teacher is giving you a good lesson against extreme ideas."

"I love my teacher. She's always telling us not to be prejudiced. This spring we studied the underground railroad for escaping slaves. We made believe we were running one in our class, and I played a slave. I got to feel how scary it is to hide and worry that you will be caught and put in chains and made to do all the hard, dirty work for other people who have good stuff to eat when you don't have anything to eat at all. The slave masters got to eat cookies during recess and the slaves had to hide in the cellar and got none. We traded places the next week. The masters had to play slaves and they got nothing. Only, Mrs. Stein says it was even much worse because they were actually beaten and starved and couldn't get to know their mothers or fathers. They couldn't even have a family name or go to school or anything. Mrs. Stein thinks African-American communities should have re-par-a-tions to build better libraries and schools." Meagan's earnest innocence touched me.

"I'm so glad you're learning all those things in school. I just learned about the underground railroad at Hawthorne's Wayside house which was run there by Louisa May Alcott's father. She wrote *Little Women*, about some smart American girls like you."

"Oh, I like that book. My Mom read it with me last summer. Dad, can we go see that house next time we come down here—please?"

"Sure." her father answered—used to pleasing her. "If you want to."

"Was it where she lived when she wrote that book?" Meagan asked me.

"Oh, yes, she wrote it right there at Wayside House when her father was having difficulty with money because people didn't agree with his ideas. He had ideas that children should have recess time and be allowed to ask questions when they learn. Some Puritanical extremists thought that was a terrible idea. You can see the staircase where Louisa played with her sisters. And the room she lived in, mentioned in the book. You can see the desk in the attic where Hawthorne wrote."

"We have recess everyday and our teacher is always asking us if we have any questions about stuff. We saw Walden Pond. Daddy says Thoreau was a nature writer. He lived there and swam there and planted a garden."

"Yes, he started the great national park movement with his essay on hiking through the wilderness. He was really good at appreciating nature, but not so good at knowing that women and girls can be just as smart as men and boys. He thought our brains were smaller, but you're living proof he was wrong." I smiled at her father and he nodded.

"Do you think Global Warming can be stopped? My Mom says there are lots of people working to stop it around the world. Dad says it won't come to Stowe, Vermont, to make floods so soon as it will to the coastlines."

"Yes, there are lots of people working to stop it, and you are safer in Stowe, but unfortunately the president we have now isn't very helpful about that."

"We have to get a better president who cares about children and their future on earth, Mom says." Meagan answered with characteristic earnestness.

"We need one who doesn't drop bombs on civilians, but really weeds out the terrorists with diplomacy and intelligence," I answered.

"Dad, what's diplomacy?" Meagan asked.

"A way for nations to talk things over instead of make war." Her father answered with a patience which I could tell was characteristic.

"That sounds better than war, for sure," she answered. "You know," she looked at me sadly, "September 11th was my birthday! Those attacks on America kinda spoiled my party."

"September 11th was your birthday?" My soup was finished and I had to be on the road.

"September 11th every year is my birthday!" She sighed with irony.

And, I don't know why my eyes welled up when I told her: "I'm so glad you told me that because every year when September 11th comes around, I'm going to remember that it's Meagan's birthday. That will make me happier every year."

"Thanks," she said, waving goodbye as I thanked her father again for his travel advice. "Remember your sunglasses!" Meagan called after me.

"I will and I'll never forget that September 11th is your birthday!

Never! Wherever you are, wherever I am I'll be wishing Meagan a happy birthday on September 11th every year for the rest of my life!"

"Thanks," she said, smiling her gorgeous all-American smile and giving a little wave goodbye.

I turned so she couldn't see the tears beginning to ooze from my tired eyes. I felt a lot better thinking of her as I drove over the Berkshires, wearing my sunglasses, viewing in awe the gorgeous foliage of those New England mountains glowing orange and red in the sunlight.

DIANE GLANCY

Lamentations

From above he sent fire into our bones.
—LAMENTATIONS 1:13

THE PROLOGUE

I have written about my mixed heritage, the fragmentation and era-sure, the conflict of American Indian and European descent, the brokenness I inherited. But I have not said much about my Christianity, which is itself broken into many denominations and interpretations. Because I want to be tolerant of other faiths, I do not speak my views on Christianity. They offend those who do not believe in Jesus Christ. And what I am talking about anyway is based on faith which has no actual substance.

The thought of a spirit war, of opposing forces of which we are not often aware, raging above us, is Biblical, though more of a possi-bility in Native American heritage than European. I approach the events of September 11, 2001, in acknowledgment of the visions of the Lakota holy man Black Elk in the late nineteenth century. I'm also reading billboards posted by Christianity along the road. Biblical surrealism and an Indian sense of the other world. Yes—that's it.

It seems more was planned than was carried off.
Did the spirits hold hands, bind their wrists together with rope, out-stretch their wings to deflect further planes from the air?

Why did it happen? There was a large banner in Islamabad, Pakistan: *Americans, think! why you are hated all over the world.* America is a part of the world community and is not always guiltless in its dealings and its history.

When the buildings fell, did the voices of those who died unjustly join the voices of all those whose lives have been taken? *How long, O Lord, do you not judge and avenge our blood on them that dwell on earth?* REVELATIONS 6:9

America has opened a conduit for attack by its misdeeds.

When the buildings fell, did the dead from Wounded Knee, and the buffalo, which were the Trade Center for the Plains Indian, look up? Is there a Native American left anywhere who did not say, now they know how it feels?

Her filthiness is in her skirts, therefore, she came down wonderfully. LAMENTATIONS 1:9
The pieces of metal sparked in the sun, the gray fingers of smoke reached down. Papers drifted over buildings and through the streets, blanketing St. Paul's cemetery in lower Manhattan with feathers blown off the spirits still in a holding pattern over our nation. The millions of slaughtered buffalo snorted and grunted. Their hooves were the dust clouds that rushed the streets.

And the people in Church. Is it Armageddon yet? Is this where the valleys run with blood?

The planes of the air flew into buildings, driving, as it were, the family van, with the family in it, into the family's own garage in a burst of flames.

America the target? *She that was great among nations, how is she become a tributary.* LAMENTATIONS 1:1
The terrorists attacked the seat of the military/government and finance. But the terrorists forgot the church. They forgot the people who think their prayers are weapons. They forgot the Christians who cry, *send us your spirits of the air.*

Christianity is entered with the confession of Christ as Savior. Once inside Christianity, it is a sacred lodge with teepee drawings on the wall. It is a large room with passages written all over the walls. Passages of startling thoughts you would never have on your own. EPHESIANS 6:1 *We wrestle not against flesh and blood, but against principalities, against powers, against the rulers of darkness of this world, against spiritual wickedness in high places.*

I PETER 5:7 *Be sober and vigilant, because your adversary, the devil, like a roaring lion walks about seeking whom he may devour.*

Osama bin Laden, the Muslim extremist, the terrorists, the Taliban housed in Afghanistan, the Iraqi, the Pakistani, all of them, masks for the powers of darkness that would take America in its teeth.

A new war is upon us. Global and de-territorialized. The enemy is faceless and placeless. Who should we attack? The air? They are the powers of darkness behind the powers on earth. They would love to get Israel most of all, the seat of God's government, though Israel does not recognize the Messiah.

The spirits of darkness hate Israel. They know Zion is God's holy mountain. It is what they want to destroy. The darkness has put hatred in the terrorists. They want Jerusalem. But who is standing in the way? Who is the ally of Israel? America. That's what has to be gotten out of the way.

Christians know the importance of Israel. God blesses those who bless Israel. In Numbers 25:1, Balaam saw that it pleased the Lord to bless Israel. *Blessed is he who blesses you, and cursed is he who curses you.* NUMBERS 24:9

We are attacked for our goodness also. We side with and protect Israel. *Get America and then you can get Israel.*

Who will go with us into the rural mountains of Afghanistan to find the Taliban? It is not a force we can appease. It is not a force we can conquer. We have gone too far. We have had our finger on the world. We have pushed hard.

In the quietness. In the still smoking rubble. In the dust and ash that covers the streets. We remember the attack on our nation, and the desire for justice. May the maker have mercy upon us, even the group that made its attack.

All our enemies have opened their mouths against us. They hiss, they say, We have swallowed her up; certainly this is the day we have looked for.
LAMENTATIONS 2:16

After the blizzard of ash and rubble, we are planes headed for the other side of the continent full of fuel.

It is a spirit war. Not sacred, but spirit.

The war talkers plan the machinery of war. You can hear their engines rev.
Revenging America which is what the dark powers want, so they can retaliate with nuclear war.
America does not know the checkered, shape-changing place into which it goes.

PATRICIA GOEDICKE

Crash

This motorcycle is no Ariel it's a banshee it's a flat shriek
and it's coming towards you and you're at the same time
riding on it speed lines streak out of you like stars and
stripes but this is no comic book rain on the windshield slices at you
on the sleek coast-to-coast highway knives slash at you

and the saddlebags that were once bulging are skinnier now
what you thought you had brought for us is seen to be nothing
to anyone the flap is a single sheet
of illegible leather the corrupt papers inside it are crumbling
like shredded wheat as you slide into the gas station on your face

and the motorcycle guns itself now the body you thought was yours
roars right over your shoulders and almost up to the carbon
dioxide layers barely visible through the rising fumes
the choking fog of the smokestacks and other exhaust pipes
of America I mean we're not just talking about industrial
fat cats here we're talking about other kinds of

flatulence as well bad conscience behind you and coming
after you on the road however you zoom away from it
what you had thought lost you do not care to remember
perfectly good or bad it can return
anytime from a complete standstill take off at 150
miles per hour with you struggling to see through the tears razoring
straight back from your eyes into your hair well why not

let all throttles out hate the world that hates you

you haven't a clue why because whatever you did
or didn't do of course you didn't mean it
personally one man (or woman) one motorcycle
in the long run makes no difference
at all no one can take care of everyone though your actions
and non-actions are not that bug-like still it's a tough
life isn't it you do what you have to even if it's yourself
you're screwing hate is such a fast trip even self induced

rage takes you right out of yourself tastes like high ozone doesn't it
fast action champagne spurts up and goes on and on
forever and the excuses for it are everywhere
and nowhere always there are these gigantic who could have
     expected it
Bangs suddenly two or three jet engines the unfolding
smoky petals the implacable descent

and the smothered sound of air hissing out of your mouth
thin spittle filled with pieces of white steel and paper
ash and high octane flames daggering up
over the skyline as you scrape up your smashed helmet
and bloody jeans from the pavement and slowly haul yourself back
for a pit stop to your own back yard in the country

as far from the action as possible you sit down with a beer
on the back steps at evening with your two house cats
rubbing themselves against you but then out on your brooding
late summer lawn where have they gone
with their small red mouths and their sharp claws you can't
quite make them out two tiny spurts of color
against the dim grass you can't tell where they're coming from
one gray one even darker shadow stealthily moving towards you

ABOUT "CRASH"

The date in my spiral notebook tells me I started writing "Crash"
(then called "Motorcycle") on August 8th, 2001, in response to a set
of rather drastic changes I'd recently experienced in my own life. I
left the first draft at home while I gave a reading at the Woodstock
Poetry Festival in New York, after which I flew on September 10 to
visit dear friends in Virginia. Next day we awoke to the sight of the
two topless towers of America's own Ilium disintegrating, over and

over, into Ground Zero. Added to the horror was the strangeness of the fact that we'd been in Dulles Airport just the day before, a few scant hours before the plane took off that demolished so much of the Pentagon.

·

When I got home to Missoula I was shocked to pick up "Crash" and discover how closely the headlong rush of the poem paralleled the rush of America towards a cataclysm I believe we in part brought on ourselves. The drive towards God-like power *and* self-immolation in the first line's reference to Sylvia Plath's "Ariel" was the beginning of many clear parallels, an eerie experience which—I'm still stunned by the sudden appearance of that banshee in the first draft of the poem—is the sort of thing that so strangely occasionally does happen. That first draft (about my personal crash), seemed to me to voice something central to the tragedy of September 11.

It's the kind of horror which begins as the poem begins; when, just as one's beginning to really feel the power one's lusted for (over motorcycle or world, no matter), suddenly one loses the fine edge of control. In the hurtling rush that follows, the vehicle swerves recklessly, turning its presumed driver into victim as it takes over utterly, runs rampant over one's whole body. Thus separated from the vehicle, the tool of one's own rampant desires, the driver feels innocent of any crime but knows otherwise. It is a suicidal inevitability which seems to me to attach itself not only to the attackers of September 11 but to the power of the United States of America, their intended victim.

That our comfortable ignorance of poverty may have assisted in the crash and our consequent loss of safety and security is hard to bear. Out of negligence, the rider and the gas-sucking motorcycle are accountable for their own downfall. But for the self to survive intact, such knowledge must turn elsewhere, must search angrily, a heat-seeking missile burning to find an evil other to blame. This anger intoxicates, overrides self-confrontation, until personal crash merges with the crash of the Twin Towers, the Stock Market, and the death, not only of thousands of innocent victims, but also of America's belief in itself as all good and powerful, secure from all danger.

There are surely other things going on in this poem, things that I'm not aware of any more than I was aware, when I first saw that *New Yorker* cover as all black, that next time I looked I'd suddenly see those ghostly two oblongs looming up at me just underneath it. The whole terrible event is a tragedy from which, just as millions of us did after September 11, the subject of the poem retreats into the sub-urban world of house cats and evening lawns—only to discover that a bad conscience will not be placated. For even though everyone is innocent and no one is guilty, at the same time everyone is guilty and no one is innocent.

LAURENCE GOLDSTEIN

Thinking About the Unthinkable, Again

Twenty-five years ago I published a scholarly book titled *Ruins and Empire: The Evolution of a Theme in Augustan and Romantic Literature*, whose purpose was to trace an obsessive anxiety of British writers about the seeming decline and likely extinction of the glorious civilization, down to the most humble rural habitat, that had nourished their sense of well-being and their pride of nationality. These writers had drunk deep of history and taken from their reading the single lesson that all great empires follow the Roman model: a period of flourishing growth and splendid achievement followed by a gradual sinking into exhaustion and, finally, conquest by barbarian tribes of a hardier stock and greater zealotry. In almost every case, from Spenser to Wordsworth, the message of such gloomy writings was cautionary, a plea to their countrymen not to allow the abnormal political crises of the day—the Spanish Armada, the Puritan rebellion, the American Revolution, the French Revolution and the ensuing Napoleonic wars—to shock them into the kind of fractious despair that invites enemies to contemplate invasion and subjugation.

Those writings were also directed at posterity, at us, and they have been much my mind in the aftermath of September 11. For all its bad dreams, England never had to undergo massacres on its own native ground, not until the aerial blitzes of the twentieth century. During the age of empire, England exported violence to other countries, and part of the anxiety of authors I studied derived from their fears of retribution for imperial aggression, as in William Blake's prophetic poem *America* in which the plagues that George III sends abroad rebound upon his own head and those of his hapless citizens. One reading of the deadly attacks on the World Trade Center and the

Pentagon is that this is the dynamic at work in our time: having played the bully in the international arena, flaunting our power and privilege, we are now taking our lumps and will do so till the end of time because the grievances we have aroused are infinite and unforgivable. In this fatalistic reading of history, the former subalterns grow ever stronger as they batten on the blood of the former colonizers. Blake put such ideology into the mouths of diabolical characters who counsel despair to the divine figure Albion, the soul of his beloved country, who rises into renewed glory having shaken off his foolish king and unpatriotic ministers on the right and left.

Being a literary person, my thoughts about September 11 have been constantly informed by the wisdom of writers I have long admired, and even by the poems and essays of authors I have long disdained. There is nothing like a crisis of almost unimaginable, even apocalyptic proportions to drive one back to the bedrock texts of our tradition. I recognize that some of my retrospective thinking is defensive, escapist. The pain of gazing daily at the faces in the *New York Times* of all those extinguished lives is as harrowing for me as it was for my parents when they scanned the obituaries during World War II for the names of acquaintances. Yet I compel myself to read the daily mini-obituaries as a kind of spiritual exercise, and to remind myself that whatever political and cultural upheavals result in the near future, these lives, these deaths, are what our lives are now all about. Yeats had it exactly right when he fashioned his litany for the patriotic poem "Easter 1916":

I write it out in a verse—
MacDonagh and MacBride
And Connolly and Pearse
Now and in time to be,
Wherever green is worn,
Are changed, changed utterly:
A terrible beauty is born.

In our case too, the saving grace of all these fatalities must be the memory of their faces, their names, their truncated lives. We must resist the temptation to recreate their vanished existence in the persons of their killers, extending sympathy to those who are left standing, weapons in their hands, full of rote grievances. (Hitler could discourse for hours at a stretch about his nation's grievances, some of which were legitimate; but he had no right to start World War II by rolling into Poland, nor do terrorists and their apologists have the right to start World War III.) We should memorialize without idolatry: these are not martyrs in the sublime or sacred history of the Republic, but they may serve the social and cultural function of martyrs, if we can resist the temptation to turn them into mere statistics.

Why did these individuals have to die? Dolores M. Costa, who crocheted colorful afghans for her friends and fed finches, warblers, and sparrows in her backyard; Philip T. Hayes, a firefighter who rescued children from a day care center in the World Trade Center before losing his life when the towers fell; Michael Parkes, a scoutmaster intent on guiding young black men into top colleges and corporations "and teaching them true friendship." Literature helps me think about the motives of the killers, motives which may have something to do with Israeli settlements and American troops on Saudi soil, but also have deeper sources about which Milton and Coleridge and Szymborska and Heaney and Soyinka have more to tell us than the pundits on television. The poets tell us clearly enough that one of the most powerful emotions of human beings is the mordant envy stirred in us by the sight of people happier and more powerful than we are. The gut reaction of those reproached by the enriched life of fortunate Others is a destructive "spoiling of the object" (in Melanie Klein's phrase), a ruthless canceling out of the future well-being of those with advantages. Such are the dark impulses of Iago, Satan, the Ancient Mariner, or the mock-goddess Hatred in Szymborska's allegory:

She is always ready for new tasks.
If she has to wait, she waits.
They say hatred is blind. Blind?
With eyes sharp as a sniper's,
she looks bravely into the future
—she alone.

Rather than the normal push-pull of social and political contention, and the shared community of difference we call multiculturalism or globalism, such figures seek to annihilate what challenges them, till they stand alone, wrapped entirely in their irremediable grievances, emblems of triumphant ideological purity. What an archetypal figure is Osama bin Laden, in his underground caves, proclaiming that Muslims have a moral duty to kill American civilians!

Such figures, rightly or wrongly termed "fundamentalist" to mark their repudiation of whatever competes with the mindset they both projected upon and derived from their holy book, seek to fold everyone in their own dark cast of mind. If they cannot everlastingly punish others for being unlike themselves, they seek to become martyrs to inspire posterity to fulfill their dreams of violence. (Their stony-heartedness troubles the living stream, as Yeats recognized of the Dublin rebels, even as he praised them.) They hope to arouse anger by their obscene deeds, to provoke holy war. And so, even in my own anger, I step back from the apocalyptic. "Put off holiness and put on intellect," says Blake's figure for the human imagination, Los. I try to think my way through this crisis, which deepens and complicates itself each day as the dimensions of the terrorist networks and their conspiracies become clearer. I assume that my own country will commit some excessive and unpardonable acts of violence in the coming months and years, as it did during another just war, against the fascist powers in Germany, Italy, and Japan. I will continue to speak out against those actions as well, and for the individuals who perish in them. Nevertheless, I know that posterity will read our texts and acts with the cold eye we now fix on our predecessors, and find our self-pity and smoldering anger as disturbing as we find the preening melancholy of Edward Young in *Night Thoughts* or James Hervey in *Meditations Among the Tombs*.

Justice, with all its cold satisfactions, is the first order of the day, but only the first. I feel in myself, against my will, how the inexorable power of bad news—about the deaths in New York, Washington, and Pennsylvania, about anthrax attacks, about terrorist threats of the most extreme kind—distracts me from a lifelong commitment to rescuing the environment from its spoilers (who continue their pillaging under cover of the national crisis), and from all other humane affections. Even as I write this commentary, however, especially when writing it, I feel a compensatory zeal for the life-enhancing habits and values of my culture. I doubt that I will ever fully understand people who blow up monumental statues of Buddha, beat women in the street for letting a sliver of flesh show through their burqas, and stigmatize music and literature as unholy. Or fly airplanes into buildings. But I know that I am just as zealous in support of my beliefs and in support of the nation that protects them. If the writers I surveyed in *Ruins and Empire* could see England now, no longer the seat of empire but a thriving multicultural society, they would be relieved. Never have I wished so much for a crystal ball as this autumn of the year 2001, when history seems to be turning in the fearful gyre Yeats summoned in his visionary poem of the second coming. For many years to come, poems like his, not just about history but about love, art, nature, and the indomitable spirit of individuals, will have to do the work of prophecy, keeping our souls afloat as we ride out the storm.

RAY GONZALEZ

The Ladybugs

I walk into my university office the day after the World Trade Center and Pentagon attacks. Classes were cancelled the previous afternoon and I have not had a chance to talk to any of my students since the terror. I set my book bag down, turn to my desk, and notice a ladybug crawling up my shirt, its tiny red body moving over the buttons on my chest. My first impulse is to flick it off, but I like ladybugs and consider them signs of good luck. I gently place my fingertip in its path and the insect climbs aboard. I sit down and watch it move across my finger, then onto the desktop. Distracted by having to get ready for class, I flip through my lecture notes and check my email. When I turn back to the desk, the ladybug has disappeared. I search under papers and files, but it is gone. I don't want it harmed or find it crushed by a book, but where did it go?

I try to imagine how far I carried it on my clothes, when the exact moment of it landing on me took place. These thoughts in search of precise time come from the hours I spent in front of the television the previous day. After awhile, the unforgettable images of the collapsing towers melted into exact moments of horror, the news commentators repeating what happened at what moment and at what human cost. My ladybug has vanished, its invisible ride on me a microscopic act in a world where it seems like each tiny thing we do has now been amplified by fire and fear.

I bring up the subject of the terrorists' attacks in my undergraduate nature writing class, but no one wants to join in. I manage to connect the optimism nature writers present in their work with a sense of hope for the future, in light of the terrorism. I insist nature literature is the kind of writing we should read in a shocking time. Torn between discussing Henry Thoreau and talking about thousands of deaths, I look at the thirty students huddled in the small room. They stare at me in silence, events in the outer world pressing against the old, ugly walls of the building. Even the students who regularly contribute to discussions are quiet. As teachers, do we allow this sudden tragedy to come into our classes, or do we try and shut the door? It seems the attacks have entered during the first day of school after the tragedy, but we don't know how to proceed. How will a catastrophic event affect my lesson plans and the way young people, never having known an environment of war, respond to the assigned readings? It is too much to ponder as I stand in front of them and awkwardly get back to the sanctuary of Walden Pond.

Is the subject I'm teaching influencing their silence? Has Thoreau's pastoral idealism dictated a quiet atmosphere among these students? Perhaps history and political science classes are reacting in more vocal ways as I analyze Thoreau's reasons for wanting to touch a loon, even becoming the bird in one of the better-known chapters of *Walden*. Transcendentalism and Thoreau's warnings to his fellow New England citizens to not abandon an essential harmony with nature appeal to the students. We wind up having a lively discussion about the loon in the pond and why Thoreau insisted that hunting without a gun was one way to move beyond the boundaries of civilization—a belief that fell on deaf ears. There is enough time left in the period to discuss another famous passage in Walden—the battle between the red and black ants Thoreau gathered in a jar. I exhaust every metaphor about armies, good and evil, and human behavior in a time of war. The session ends as we isolate transcendence with the loon and nature's violent character as two key lessons for our time. The students pile out of the room and I feel a sense of triumph and relief. Several of them connected the previous day's events with the timeless lessons of environmental literature.

I stand alone in the empty classroom and can't forget the images on campus from the previous day. When classes were cancelled on the eleventh, and I walked across campus to my car, I saw dozens of students in tears. Many of them were huddled in small groups; cell phones in hand, a few hugging each other as they cried. The day after, I stroll the three blocks to my parking garage in silence, passing dozens of students and seeing that the fear and uncertainty is still on their faces. I reach my car on the fourth level of the massive garage after having momentarily forgotten where I parked that day. I unlock the door, throw my book bag on the seat, and climb in. As I reach for the magnetic card that will open the gate on the ground level, I spot a ladybug moving across my bag. Is it the same one that appeared in my office? My bag was on a chair near my office door and I never set it near the desk where the first ladybug appeared. Can this be a second ladybug and another sign of good luck? Why would I be getting these kinds of clues in the midst of a terrible and frightening time? Where are the ladybugs coming from, when I rarely see them at other times of the year? Instead of leaving the ladybug to disappear inside my car, I roll down the window, place my finger in the path of the insect on my bag, and it climbs on. I shake my finger outside and the ladybug flies away in a miniature dot of light.

I sit in my car for several minutes, not wanting to leave yet. The garage is located one block from the edge of campus, so the bustle and activity of thousands of students is muted. An eerie silence hangs among the rows of parked cars and concrete pillars. They remind me of the towers and how I had to finally turn off the television. The class discussion on Thoreau and his ideas on wilderness and the encroachment of civilization ring in my ears, yet they seem so far away. He was writing about America in the mid-nineteenth century and tried to encourage people to pause from their hard work on their farms and look around. The power of nature in its wild state on the continent had not been diminished by a great nation yet. One hundred and fifty years later, it seems the only wildness we know is one of crushed concrete, elusive enemies, and a state where the survival of our way of life has nothing to do with the natural power of the earth.

I pull out of the garage and turn onto the street leading to the freeway I take to get home. As I emerge from the shelter of the ramp, sunlight flashes across the windows and lights up the car. At that moment, I spot a ladybug clinging to the windshield on the outside directly at eye level. It stays on the glass as I turn into traffic. My impulse is to slow down, but I have increased my speed to keep up with the cars. As I switch lanes, the ladybug springs off the windshield, its flared wings the purest fire I have imagined that day.

GAIL GRIFFIN

How It Comes

1.

Moon like a milky fetus deep in Virgo. Changes spelled in shifting smoky winds, scraps of papery leaves, flights of outraged birds. Ending, beginning; snake swallowing its tail; New Year facing down the Day of Atonement.

From a bright sky, the growl of a plane.

2.

Does it come unannounced? Does it come tangled in crossed wires, mixed signals? What language does it speak? *What language do they speak there anyway?* Codes flashed across the night, prophecies written in lightning. *The local bureau chief speaks no Arabic.* Undistinguished briefcases slipping past the X-ray's eye. Hungers unassuaged, undignified, rumblings in the vast stomach of the world, angers pinned to a map. *Sorry no one in the office knows Farsi.* Messages from the long past catching up. And from the wards and black-windowed houses where women, once doctors, teachers, artists, rock themselves, moving their mouths— a roaring silence.

Deep in the desert, the Buddha's head bends as if to listen, breaks at the stem like a ponderous flower, and falls—falls the long meters to the hard ground, shatters, lies in pieces, here a benign closed eye, here a broken smile.

3.

They are promised heaven, of course. But they are also promised virgins. Virgins by the dozen. Even at Allah's gates we are handed out like door prizes. They with their enormous imaginings can not get past these simple bodies of ours.

When it comes, it comes loaded with promises.

4.

Or does it come out of the blue, an ordinary thing growing stranger as it comes closer, lit with obscure intention? We will see it and not see it, like the woman on the 102nd floor, opening her e-mail, glancing out and barely noticing a streak above the harbor, a silver glint in the morning's eye, moving east and then, as her eyes fall back to the screen, dropping a wing and banking left. And when we look up at last into the screaming face of it we will say

So this is how it comes

5.

He calls them *jumpers.*

I came out of the subway, he writes, *and saw body parts. On the sidewalk across the street there was a jumper.*

Like every kid I dreamed I could fly. One day I stood at the top of the stairs, the dream still so real I felt myself do it, leap out brightly, float down, drop like a leap onto the landing. My friend says the dream is memory driven out: after our parents turn out the light we fly around our rooms until one day we begin to forget. *Fallings from us, vanishings.*

Think of facing all that air, choosing to give yourself over, leaping out into the sky like Icarus. Imagine. Take your time. It will take time to see this, to believe in jumpers. But you know them now.

Fallings from us. Vanishings.

Already they're in your dreams.

6.

The legends scramble out like refugees. In one, a Juilliard student carries his violin downtown, places a chair in the smoking, rubbled street, and plays, solo, for hours. *Concerto for Strings and Chaos. Suite for Violin and Bass Continuo*—deep bass, the sound of a tremendous heartbeat, buried.

The day the stock market reopens, a trader takes his violin to work. He asks to play "Amazing Grace" before the starting bell. They confer, tell him thanks, but no. It would be, they say, too sad.

Time Magazine reports the following week that Einstein didn't like imagining the god of his universe as a kind of meta-engineer. What he would have loved was for god to be a violinist.

7.

When it comes, will time come scudding to a halt or yield an instant's grace to the greedy heart? One moment to reach for a man's fingers a thousand miles away, one breath to seek a sister's dark eyes? One beat for a line of Wordsworth, a scrap of Lennon-McCartney. A small space filled with lakewater lapping the shore, wind conspiring with the tops of pines, the deep night's breathing? A pause in which my lost brother turns to see me again?

8.

A gull crosses over the island. Below, the sinkhole of the West, smoking on into the days of November. Ashes, ashes, and silence. Such a silence fuming at the century's door. A silence five thousand voices deep. Five thousand bodies, unarticulated. It comes, in the end, so silently.

From here we walk with smoke in our throats. What story begins here?

What book follows Revelation?

9.

And this is how it comes:

In Kabul a woman begs in the street for something to take to her children in the abandoned building where they live. She tells the reporter *I hope the first American missile comes straight at me.*

10.

Out of the bright sky, a plane, too loud, too low over the chapel tower, a shadow along the grass, and on the sidewalk we stop, stop and stand. Sun pauses, wind dies. All of us together here, silent, looking up.

KIMIKO HAHN

Four Poems

IN THE ARMORY—

where we paid ten dollars
to view art from Asia
we could not afford to buy,
among the well-heeled who could—
are people with photographs
of mail clerks, research analysts,
waiters—
and I cannot imagine
trying to locate a beloved
with saliva from an old toothbrush,
zip-locked and tucked in a handbag
like a lover heading for a tryst.
It is too much.

AFTER SEEING OUR FIRST-GRADERS OFF

Carla and I would sometimes sip coffee
in the diner window seat
to watch the firefighters
lumber by in their large gear.
Not to flirt or fantasize really—
we were admiring them,
even as they shopped in a grocery

like so many fussy old ladies
organizing a Sunday social. And today,
I realize it was the excitement
of small girls seeing a rock star
or dapper uncle.
Wanting a kiss on the cheek. A wink.
Wishing to blush at a power
reserved for fathers. This
was my small association with
that neighborhood Engine Company
until yesterday when I heard from my neighbor,
also a firefighter, that you are all lost.
And I am full of such queasy emptiness
that all I can do is donate blood
and offer words of condolence,
such impossible rescue tools.
Such pitiful tools for thanks.

HER VERY EYES

A friend's sister, my daughter reports,
cannot close her eyes,
and I interrupt, it must be asbestos irritation—
until she adds,
she sees bodies falling from the sky,
she sees bodies breaking through the glass atrium
or smashing onto the pavement,
she sees one woman, her skirt billowing out like a manikin's,
and a suited man plunging headfirst.
And she hears them land in front of her
but cannot turn away when she closes her eyes.
And she doesn't know what to do.
This is what my daughter reports
upon coming home from school
last Tuesday.

the wife of a rescue worker
from that first maneuver
finds a son's transit pass, brushes
a daughter's hair, braids her hair,
slaps together a couple pb&j,
and believes her husband
lies under metal, concrete, glass, chairs, desks,
fax machines, souvenirs—
with a pulse. She waves
bye to their children,
late for school, and sits down
to collapse
for a second
then stand again
for the ordinary.

from Boerum Hill Tanka

Once an afternoon for groceries, it is still an afternoon for
groceries—and a fear once called the bridge, the subway, the rental
truck parked too long on the corner.

Day ten, after days of sun and two of rain, the soles of the rescue
worker's boots melt on the still feverish metal wreckage.

Taped to every lamppost on every corner are missing person
photos of the dead—6,965 to date. And after a thunder shower,
fresh fliers appear as if from nowhere.

After the two planes hit the World Trade Center towers, my older daughter and I jogged three blocks over to the harbor where we watched as smoke and flames billowed from holes several stories high. It was not real. I watched as if it were a spectacle and could not then know that people were jumping out of once-sealed windows. We looked on as the first tower collapsed on itself—then, amid thick smoke and debris, covered our faces and fled back to our tiny apartment. Not a day goes by without reminders: funeral services, altars, washing hands after opening mail, National Guard at toll gates. Not a day goes by without heavy doses of dread and denial.

Why do I stay? We have fought so hard to make a home in what really is the most amazing city in the world—and it is home—that it will take another crisis to force us into exile. And we have plans. And we have gas masks. So if we live through it, we will know what to do and where to go. But it is a choice I question every day. Meanwhile, I find myself at political odds with my colleagues at school: I am not a pacifist this time. Although my vision of democracy radically differs from the President's, I believe that what we do have is worth defending—and the defense is not against the poor or the "Third World," but against men who will not allow the most basic freedoms of expression: For a woman to show her face. For a child to fly a kite. For a girl to read words on a chalkboard.

JOY HARJO

When the World As We Knew It Ended—

We were dreaming on an occupied island at the farthest edge
of a trembling nation when it went down.

Two towers rose up from the east island of commerce and touched
the sky. Men walked on the moon. Oil was sucked dry
by two brothers. Then it went down. Swallowed
by a fire dragon, by oil and fear.
Eaten whole.

It was coming.

We had been watching since the eve of the missionaries in their
     long and
solemn clothes, to see what would happen.

We saw it
from the kitchen window over the sink
as we made coffee, cooked rice and
potatoes, enough for an army.

We saw it all, as we changed diapers and fed
the babies. We saw it,
through the branches
of the knowledgeable tree
through the snags of stars, through
the sun and storms from our knees
as we bathed and washed
the floors.

The conference of the birds warned us, as they flew over
destroyers in the harbor, parked there since the first takeover.
It was by their song and talk we knew when to rise
when to look out the window
to the commotion going on—
the magnetic field thrown off by grief.

We heard it.
The racket in every corner of the world. As
the hunger for war rose up in those who would steal to be president
to be king or emperor, to own the trees, stones, and everything
else that moved about the earth, inside the earth
and above it.

We knew it was coming, tasted the winds who gathered intelligence
from each leaf and flower, from every mountain, sea
and desert, from every prayer and song all over this tiny universe
floating in the skies of infinite
being.

And then it was over, this world we had grown to love
for its sweet grasses, for the many-colored horses
and fishes, for the shimmering possibilities
while dreaming.

But then there were the seeds to plant and the babies
who needed milk and comforting, and someone
picked up a guitar or ukelele from the rubble
and began to sing about the light flutter
the kick beneath the skin of the earth
we felt there, beneath us

a warm animal
a song being born between the legs of her,
a poem.

SAMUEL HAZO

September 11, 2001

The reaction of most people to the carefully planned and executed destruction of the World Trade Center and one section of the Pentagon—after the first shock had passed—was to call those they loved or to leave work and hurry to be with them. These, of course, are two of the most primordial instincts in human nature, and they have been expressed in literature since the age of Homer. What is the Odyssey, for example, but the saga of a man who yearns to be home with his family?

The consequences of September 11, 2001 have come to involve criminal investigations, war-plans, psychological insights, politics of all sorts, a renewed domestic interest in the possession of firearms, religious services and discussions, apocalyptic warnings, the public display of flags, and as many other variations as can be imagined. But the human reaction to the first shock of recognition transcends everything. It was at that instant that our souls were speared, and we lived thereafter with our wounds. It was not something that could be readily translated into prose or mere talk. The language of prose did not operate at such frequencies. The only language was poetry or silence.

SEPTEMBER 11, 2001

1.

The hawk seems almost napping
  in his glide.

            His arcs are perfect
  as geometry.

His eyes hunger
for something about to panic,
something small and unaware.
Higher by two thousand feet
an airbus vectors for its port,
its winglights aiming dead
ahead like eyesight.
                              The natural
and scheduled worlds keep happening
according to their rules.
                              "We interrupt
this program ..."
                              Inch by inch
the interruption overrules both worlds,
engulfing us like dustfall
from a building in collapse.
                              The day
turns dark as an eclipse.
                              We head
for home as if to be assured
that home is where we left it.

2.
Before both towers drowned
in their own dust, someone
downfloated from the hundredth floor.
Then there were others—plunging,
stepping off or diving in tandem,
hand in hand, as if the sea
or nets awaited them.
                              "My God,
people are jumping!"
                              Of all
the thousands there, we saw
those few, just those, freefalling
through the sky like flotsam from a blaze....
Nightmares of impact crushed us.
We slept like the doomed or drowned,
then woke to oratory, vigils,
valor, journalists declaring war
and, snapping from aerials or poles,
the furious clamor of flags.

MICHAEL HELLER

Mourning Field, Note Card

Slaughtered lamb broken in the shards and rocks.

Wasn't the cycle that the ant ate the carrion,
that the bear ate the ant, that the bush
surrendered the berry without sentience,
that the merry danced and lived,
that justice was that morning
only an afterthought because to have to think justice
in daylight, at all hours, signaled our defeat.

What broke the cycle? He who played
with the untimely and he who transgressed,
whose bloody mouth still hungers,
who is myriads of the unappeased.

And didn't we ring the cycle like a bell,
didn't we lull in the vibrato,
drowning the world,
oh lull, oh sleep oh stopped up ears
couldn't it be said that our singing
like the tenor's with the goblet,
cracked the bell.

And didn't the lamb lie broken
at the base of the towers,
staining the dream

and were we now to forego dreaming,

to feed the black crow of the real
our hearts and our children,
to offer carrion to the pigeon,
to let our fears blot the afterimage
of the city before the siege

to remember the ancient cycle littering
the walks with leaves, the blue cool
of the autumnal skies, to walk toward
the dull sound of the bell, to hear the tinnitus
of the imaginary ...

On the Mourning Field

The mourning field has no perimeter. The mourner on his path into
the depths of grief creates his own outer border, the starting block of
his own sorrow, possibly the remembered moment of first awareness, the picture on the television set. Sorrow has its own space-time
continuum, a yesterday or a last month when the heart was ready for
its heaviness. And because the mourner is both vulnerable and
political, he may cast aside the temporal frame altogether, may find
that his pain begins long before his own birth, blaming history and
its aftermath. For this reason, the outer perimeter of the mourning
field is not fixed. It can be moved at will. It can accommodate past,
present and future; it embraces anger and sadness. Since death confronts everything and confronts it uniquely in each of us, there is no
telling beforehand what we may need or where to begin. Adjusting
the fence lines of memory or imagination, back-shadowing our
pasts, these are the operations necessary to bring us to our grief. No
matter. Wherever he starts, he is creating a girding for his journey,
not so much to aid in mourning as to help in confronting the obsta-
cle that stands between himself and the ability to truly mourn. A
willingness to imagine death up close, to take it personally—only this
brings someone into true relation with mourning.

Freud in his essay on war and death writes that we often live
"psychologically beyond our means," that it would be "better to give
death the place in reality and in our thoughts which is its due." For
a moment, for an infinity of moments, the images we saw on
September 11th gave death its "due" with a vengeance, reconfiguring

death and dying in ways Americans had only seen in movies where reality and unreality swirled together in an intoxicating mixture of vicarious danger, a danger that did no more harm than to launch celebrities and box office hits. But now, after the events of September 11th, the images pouring out from the screen, ones to be filed alongside the others for the future, were "real" in a new way. No one could see these without being indelibly seared, whether one saw the buildings crumbling to the ground or the people jumping from the World Trade Center tower windows. There was even one of a couple who leapt hand in hand from a high floor, stepped together into the air above Manhattan as though going out on a date, an image deemed so awful for American television that it never aired again. Just hearing about it was enough. The television I watched showed a few such specks, distant and forlorn, minute against the grey-white vastness of the building. And the speck that I can't forget was tumbling in a cartwheel through space, head over heel on its way to the ground like a mad gymnast. What could it have been like for that person to contemplate the choice, to burn slowly to death or to end one's own life quickly, though how quickly would it be from such a height? Such images would tear at us forever.

On Saturday, September 15th, my wife and I took the M 15 bus down to South Ferry and walked to the northern tip of Battery Park. Smoke rose in billowing acrid clouds from the disaster site, burning the eyes and throat, and many people were wearing masks.

Slowly we made our way uptown, entering any street going west to see how close we could get to the disaster site itself. Up William Street, we peered along Fulton and Pine, gazing through the biting plumes of smoke and dust at the twisted bronze base of the north tower, the only recognizable reminder that a building had stood there. Its grid of window frames, rising to a height of five or six stories, was torqued out of shape, teased into a quarter spiral toward the sky as though by a fiery comb. Ash had collected everywhere, sitting on car roofs to the depths of three or four inches, powdering fire hydrants and shop windows and building ledges. Nothing but blacks and greys. In the disaster area, along with the lives and the buildings, light itself seems to have been reversed. Lower Manhattan was one grisly photo negative of itself.

As we walked along, I remembered that much of lower Manhattan, especially the eastern side of the peninsula projecting into New York harbor, consists of landfill, some of it comprised of rubble shipped from England after the German blitz had knocked down much of

London's East End. The rock and brick had been put on ships and dumped along the East River to make space for public housing and the seaport areas. Now it was likely that all of the southern end of the island was to wear a cap of ruins, including bits and pieces of human bodies that could not be found nor extracted from the rubble. Hardy's great World War I poem "Channel Firing," which imagines the conversations of the dead war victims, came into my head. I wondered if one of us would now overhear the dead of London and of New York speaking. Or probe even deeper into the spirit-life of the broken buildings to reveal how the stones of the two cities that now had in common the destruction wreaked upon them might be communing with each other across Wall Street and Broadway on over to the FDR Drive?

In Manhattan, grief's center was, for a few days, Union Square. On the 16th of September, I walked in the park past clusters of burning candles and incense, past long scrolls of paper containing messages and poems taped to the wrought iron railings that border the walkways. Many were illustrated with simple drawings of the twin towers engulfed in flames. Copies of slogans and statements plastered tree trunks and pedestals of statues. Some had an almost political cast: "a cry of grief is not a call for war" and most ubiquitous, "an eye for an eye only means blindness." Alongside the scrolls, the faces of lost ones gazed out of photos. Grim details surrounded these: the company worked for, a floor in one of the World Trade Center towers, and saddest of all, identifying body marks, scars, and moles. With words, the dead were being washed as in a funeral home, swathed in language, touched in secret places by words that only lovers or family members usually know. The disaster had traduced all intimacy. Similar photos and details papered the city. They covered phone booths and bus kiosks and were taped to the plate glass windows of storefronts and banks.

Like many faces on the notices, most of the those in the park were young. They stood and milled around as young people do. And they spoke, and their writings on the long rolls of paper spoke, with that intensity only the young seem able to summon at such times as these. A few guitars were being strummed, playing old folk plaints of solidarity, weariness, and misery. Overheard, the thick canopy of leaves, black against the night, absorbed these sounds, compounded and cupped them in the sickly-sweet smell of the incense and burning wax. The crowds had driven off the pigeons, but in Union Square, the notices of the dead flapping in the breeze formed a new immense flock of anguish and grief roosting together.

AL HELLUS

Maybe I'll Write a Poem About It Down the Road

When I looked down at my feet, I found that a very large pool of blood had formed under the left foot. I'd stubbed my little toe on the clothes hamper in the bathroom. At closer inspection, I saw that I'd torn the damn nail in half lengthwise. It didn't hurt until I noticed this. I wrapped the toe in toilet paper and had to change it several times before the bleeding slowed down. I'd just woke up. Was still in a bathrobe. I turned on the t.v. in time to see the second plane hit the second tower of the World Trade Center.

It was my birthday.

By nature, and everyone I know will roll their eyes and testify to this fact, I am one hell of a smart ass. This is so fundamentally a part of my Selfhood that it's imprinted in bold capital letters on my DNA. I can't even repeat here some of the smart-ass remarks I've written and uttered since all this happened. It's how I write, and, to a great extent, how I cope with a life which, after all, is no more or less difficult than the next guy's.

In these remarks, of course, I mean no disrespect to the people who died or the people who are still, even as I write this, cleaning up the debris and identifying corpses and body parts.

Nor do I mean in any way to make light of the horror perpetrated here by, no getting around it, no other words in my personal vocabulary for it, some goddamned crazyass genuinely twisted sons-of-bitches. I know, as a poet, I'm supposed to be more elegantly articulate than that, but sometimes there's nothing for it but the talk of the streets, the bars and alleyways. And there's poetry in that, too. And I find myself with nothing else quite as elegant and articulate to say than: Fuck Them. And I mean that from the bottom of my broken heart.

Everything changes. Everything stays the same. When I'm done writing this, sitting in a suburban garage in Saginaw, Michigan, on a beautiful autumn afternoon replete with laughing neighborhood kids, blue jays jawing in the back yard, and squirrels running across the front lawn, I'm heading over to a local grocery store for a bottle of cheap and potent red wine. I've got the radio tuned to NPR and they're talking about biochemical terrorism and how we ain't nearly prepared to deal with it. Yeah, you bet, I could use a big glass of wine.

So I'll say it again: Fuck Them.

And I'll tell you what: I'm damn well moving my birthday to an undisclosed location under an assumed name.

GEOF HEWITT

Harvest

Raccoons penetrated with such precision
Not a stalk still stood in the rubble,
Some corn crushed, some stripped or broken,
Just a bite or two gone from the tenderest ears.
I know it was raccoons because,
Coming home two nights earlier
From Sunday's annual, community corn roast
Where my contribution was the butter, I saw them
In their masks when I looped my car
To let the headlights illuminate the scene.
A whole damn family, the mother yawning at me
Like the yaw of a crane eager to pull apart
The piles of destruction she was still planning.
What to do? I chased them up the maple tree,
Laughed at the glowing sway of marbles,
Unblinking eyes reflecting my flashlight
From high branches, little pairs of stars
Floating like a butterfly, bobbing and weaving
Like Muhammad Ali, the little rope-a-dopes
On a limb who knew I had no gun and fucked
If I'd stay up all night anyway.
So I've taken my lumps when the coons have come,
Have planted late and hoped they'd discover
The neighbor's corn when it ripened mid-August,
I could wait for September, hoping they'd habituate
To gardens across the road. But see them
Or first damage, that's a sign
The corn is close to ripe and any night

They'll take the first good ear, then sample all the rest.
No fence that lets in sun will keep them out,
So of course I pick eleven ears, none really ready,
Which is how I manage to eat each one,
It's now or never, tonight could be the night.
And come deep morning, the meaninglessness of my work:
Plant a little extra for the wildlife? Give me a break!
I'm refusing to negotiate, they know no reason,
I think of all the lies I've heard about them.
They don't even wash their food before they eat.

Writing attempts to paste wings on chaos, then tries to teach it to fly. Even with the future of humanity in doubt, even with visions of all human expression, whether piles of rotting books, smashed computers, letters, checks, or pieces of crushed desks and telephones in the yaw of a crane, lifted from a pile of rotting trash and dropped into a bigger pile of rotting trash, there's a reason to keep writing; one writes to make sense of the insensible.

Yet how much shame in making art of others' pain? It seems an exploitation, so I'm uneasy about "Harvest," which reports an actual event in my Vermont garden sometime after dark, before dawn, September 11–September 12, 2001. Does the coincidence of my petty loss merit expression in a poem? Is it bad taste, belittling and perhaps malicious, to make public my attempt to comprehend the "Attack on America"?

Fascinated by the unfolding, 24/7, commercial-free, television coverage, I was nevertheless appalled by the banner, "Attack on America," soon displayed to herald CBS coverage. Given that the people who were killed and injured represented more than sixty nationalities, it was an Attack on Humanity; any title more specific was a sleazy inflammation of patriotic fervor.

I almost phoned George W. Bush to suggest that, instead of rallying the troops by calling for bin Laden "dead or alive," he privately accept that terrorism will not be eradicated as long as impoverished people can be lured by demonic humans who offer food, shelter, and lessons. I wanted to recommend that he quietly invite bin Laden to a day-long meeting, where the President would listen to the ways in which the U.S. might improve the world's situation. Perhaps they'd actually work out a deal where bin would call off his zealots in exchange for our President's promising, in partnership with allies, to eradicate global hunger, maybe with a five-year dead-line. Maybe Bush wouldn't have had to negotiate away U.S. support for Israel or make military changes or free a bunch of convicts. In any case, I was going to tell the President that it might be worth a try to ask, "Why?" And, "How can we work together to keep this from happening again?"

Of course I didn't phone the President, but I can't stop imagining other conversations he and I might have. I was again tempted to phone him last week, as I thought about the weaponry our ground troops will carry into battle. "Smoke them out of their caves" seems dangerous, sure to kill innocent civilians, and I was thinking of supersonic weaponry, helicopters blasting rays of sound as ground troops wearing hefty earplugs patrol with assault rifles lest any tar-geted individuals happen also to be wearing earplugs. Those sonic machines, developed for crowd control, can disturb and disorient (call it "D & D") without causing permanent injury. I'm told they affect the central nervous system so the targets immediately lose control of their bowels. Hence the disturbance and disorientation as everyone drops what they're doing to hunt for toilet paper and clean clothes. Our troops would simply handcuff the bad guys while send-ing the innocents home with a warm, damp towel and a bar of soap.

But then I realized that all those handcuffed terrorists, representing the end of the Taliban regime without the loss of a single life, will leave our government the disturbing problem of what to do with them! Prosecute each soldier individually? Free those who are found to have terrorist tendencies but committed no crime other than joining the Taliban army? How long will it take them to reassemble and resume their mission? Still, sonic weaponry may be useful, and I wonder whether our military strategists have considered it. They did say this would be a different kind of war, yet they're killing people indiscriminately, the business-as-usual bomb and strafe.

Throughout all this, my desire has been to make things better, to be helpful, if only to myself. Writing a poem that uses the event seems less an exploitation than an expurgation; the exploitation comes when one seeks to make it public. Yet what possible gain is there? Only, as always, the hope that some people will read all the way to the end and there recognize that, in this case, we have met the enemies and have no idea how to deal with them.

How can we make sense of the insensible before we perish, victims of our own frustration?

WILLIAM HEYEN

The Dragonfly

That evening, I wrote a prose piece, a parable of sorts. I knew it was-
n't much, but I e-mailed it to several friends. I've touched it up a little since. It's called "Elegy."

*There are windows above a workbench at the back of my garage, & a glass
door to the left of the workbench. A dragonfly was flying against this door.
In the light of this early evening, again & again it flew into the glass with
such force that I thought it might brain itself or break its wings. I didn't
want to get too close. I could see myself as enemy, looming gigantic in its
compound eyes.*

*Since my Long Island childhood, I've known these dragonflies. Their lar-
vae, if I've identified them correctly, are grotesque dead-brown skeletal
underwater walkers. Adults stay near water. This very dry Brockport summer, I'd seen one, maybe this one, by my birdbath—greenish thorax, bluish
abdomen. Among the orders of insects, these, Odonata—dragonflies &
damselflies—are classified as large, & this one was the largest I'd ever seen.
Ben Franklin wasn't musing on this one when he mused on ephemerae.*

*The earliest ancestors of my visitor go back to Pangaea, the continents as
one solid landmass. The fossil record reveals these largest flying insects of
all Time on earth to have had wingspreads of up to at least 29 inches.
Ten-foot lily pads supported them.*

*I held my left hand in front of my face & with my right hand reached for the
door handle. But before I could push the door open, the dragonfly brushed
past my eyes & flew to the windows above my workbench. It got between an
outer screen & inner storm-window, which was partly open. It got wedged*

in, its ovipositor at the tip of its abdomen bending to its head. Its wings were useless. I turned on the light above my workbench. Its fluorescence bleached this scene, & the trapped creature soon stopped moving altogether.

(September 11, 2001)

Some of my friends forwarded this piece to others. I received replies in various kind, many of us trying to compose ourselves and relieve our shock by writing something, anything. I sometimes felt comforted, part of a community. Then I received a message from someone I didn't know. He had "poet" as part of his e-mail address. He said that this was no time for talk, for self-aggrandizement, but for quiet resolve. His brief message ended, "Shut the fuck up."

I wrote back, too quickly, to tell him that on a day when our President had just asked us for unity, he should be ashamed of himself. Stung to the spine of me that feels guilty whenever I presume to understand or to say anything about others' suffering and death, I ended my message with three little words: "Eat dead dragonflies." So much for my own contribution to understanding and peace, to community.

I don't know what it was about my meager elegy that angered this "poet." In other writings over the years, I'd always associated dragonflies with poetry and the life-source itself. The one caught in my garage the evening before I first heard of the attacks had eventually managed, with my help, to get back outside. My prose piece, however, seems to kill it, and I thought I'd written as dark a meditation as was in me that day. Apparently my speaker—the self I was as I wrote it—does not want to think about what has happened/is happening outside his home, but has an experience that he somehow connects, at least emotionally, with those searing events. Within the matrix of his mind is the history of life on earth, which seems to culminate for him in his garage. In any case, was I told to shut up because I'd said anything at all while body counts were soaring, or because of a particular thing I'd said, or because of the personal/ egotistical and refractive way in which, this time, I'd try to say it? I was unable to unsend my e-mail. I became part of the problem.

There are romantic trappings in my piece, the colors, the awesome fact of giant Odonata, the ovipositor—tipped abdomen bending into ominous circle—these, while the corpse-filled & -suffused rubble was still smoking and would go on smoking for weeks, a month, months.... I think of my date in parentheses not only as referent but as epitaph: on this day since Pangaea, that dragonfly is dead.... But long may the one that escaped my garage live.

JOANNA HIGGINS

Kwi

It's September 24, 2001. Tonight I washed your hair, getting you ready for school tomorrow and your first-grade field trip to a cider mill. (Clean and silken dry, your hair looks like black lacquerware.) Then you got into bed, eager, as always, for the books we read you each evening. Prayers followed books, and brief statements of thanks for various aspects of the day followed prayers. Then kisses and I-love-you's and See-you-at-three-thirty, which is a joke because that's what we say to each other in the morning when you're heading off to school. Then all our rituals finished for the evening, you pulled the quilt in close and turned toward your pillows, and I drew up the yellow down comforter purchased three years ago, just before we traveled to China's Hunan Province to adopt you. At the bedroom door I paused, then returned to give you yet another kiss on your warm brow.

Tonight it's raining, the first heavy rain of the autumn season, tropical, with small-stream flooding predicted. But experienced from inside a house with a tight roof, a hillside house, that rain welcome, after our dry summer. And the pleasure heightened by having a child—you!—to tuck in on such a night.

But tonight it is a guilty pleasure as well as a blessed sanctuary, given what our country is now going through. A sanctuary battered by fear, though, for we are just thirteen days beyond September 11, 2001—not yet two weeks into our new and terrible world.

Tonight, in that drumming tropical rain, I left your bedroom and went down into my study to read about anthrax, for that is the latest fear, apparently warranted—that some of the terrorists have been learning crop-dusting techniques (in the United States) and will now try to dust U.S. soil, water, citizens, and animals with the deadly micro-organism *Bacillus anthracis*. Given the right conditions, this organism forms "highly resistant spores" that can live in the soil and in animal materials such as hides, fur, wool, and bristles for years. People who merely handle contaminated wool can become infected and swiftly die. The spleen enlarges. There is bloody diarrhea. Swellings, frothy discharges, chills, fever, abortion, cardiac distress, trembling, spasms, staggering, respiratory distress, suffocation possibly, and, in the acute forms of anthrax, certain death within hours or a few days.

Tonight my mind quavers before these appalling images: a dog, a dairy cow, a horse, a child staggering about, bleeding from every orifice. Since September 11, 2001, the inside of my head has become a gallery of—all adjectives fail here—end-time imagery. The United Airlines aircraft ramming into the north tower of the World Trade Center complex— The fiery growth suddenly erupting from the building's side, bulbous, red and black, raw, cancerous-looking— The geysers of smoke cascading from the other tower, struck minutes earlier by another hijacked airliner. The towers sliding down upon themselves under their mushrooming clouds— The skyscrapers of lower Manhattan rising from a lake of dust— The tiny figures jumping, holding hands— The photos of those missing— The Beckett landscape on Staten Island where workers in white protective suits and face masks lean over hoes and scrape at a field of mostly unrecognizable rubble and body parts—

All these images—and more—behind my eyelids tonight. And inside this body, a moil of emotion. Grief, sorrow, guilt, anger, hatred—yes, that's there, too, hatred and rage and fear—terror, actually, at what might happen to you, now. And fear of this rage, small yet, still relatively small, but monstrous and overwhelming—this I know—should something happen to you as a result of these terrorists. I can feel it coiling tonight.

I will become a sub-human. My Christian sensibility will suddenly rise off my skin like vapor. I will not be able to turn the other cheek. Nor will I be able to forgive those who trespass against us. It will be all raw rage, possibly helpless but rage all the same. There will be a terrible need to strike back. Strike at something, if only myself. There will be no transcendence. I will be in the emotional equivalent of *The Perfect Storm*.

Tonight I fear losing hold of the civilized world; or rather, its losing hold of me.

But tomorrow morning I will read you a Henry and Mudge book, while Papa makes us breakfast, and then you will dress in a warm outfit and visit the cider mill.

(sweet juices pressed from earth-things)

As I read over these words, we are into early November, and the war goes on in Afghanistan and here, on American soil, in its new form of bioterrorism. Anthrax spores have been contaminating government offices and U.S. postal centers. No crop dusters necessary after all; only a thirty-four cent stamp. Several have died of anthrax, and others are hospitalized. And the new threat is smallpox, and there is not enough vaccine, as of now, to go around. And the fatality rate for smallpox is one in three.

Each morning at school you say the Pledge of Allegiance to the Flag, then sing a patriotic song. The other day you asked if soldiers really killed people.

I had to say yes.

This you couldn't get over.

"Do they go to *jail* for it?"

"Ah no— Because— In war, it's all right to kill."

(I'm doing this badly, it occurs to me.)

"In war? What's war?"

"War is— War is when there's a big fight. Somebody does something bad and then there's a big fight."

"They *fight*?"

"Yes. They fight."

Your glance drifted away. Your eyes showed confusion. I'll have to try to do better later. Find some better words. I hadn't expected to have this conversation so soon. I thought we had time yet. And for this I am terribly sorry—and for the legacy of images that will one day be yours. And for your fears-to-come. (If we make it through all this.) You need so much more from us, so much better. You who are being taught at school to try at least two of Kelso the Frog's solutions for getting along with your classmates: Take turns and share ... Talk it out ... Ignore it ... Tell them to stop ... Apologize ... Make a deal ... Wait and cool off ... And if there is a big problem, tell an adult you trust.

Still, this scribbling helps. It's something, anyway. And a kind of prayer, maybe, this wringing out of consciousness words, after all.

(bitter juices pressed from earth-things)

Words, still

My job as a writer, I've always believed, is to write where the pressure is, the wound, the uncertainty; explore if not fully understand, portray if not resolve; walk out in the storm and find the words for it. Will this change now, in the aftermath of September 11, 2001?

No.

Will there be some greater sense of urgency?

Yes.

Living, now, with the previously unthinkable: bioterrorism—anthrax, smallpox, and who knows what other pathogens soon to appear as weaponry, I feel like one of those monks who nightly slept (sleep?) in their coffins. At times it seems almost foolish to sit fiddling with manuscript pages when one could be outside in the last remnants of this fall.

(the pun unintended)

Be with my husband, our child, the three cats who nap undisturbed. Or simply look out the windows at the variety and color of clouds.

I'm closer, now, to knowing how it must feel for a dying person to leave a tip under a saucer in a restaurant, thinking, Well, that's that. The last time.

The blessed ordinary exerting its pull within the extraordinary. And it's good to pay attention. To look, as if for the last time.

But not at our child in this way. That's a stab to the quick.

I'm afraid of what will happen if something happens to her as a result of all this. I will lose it and lose it in some grand way. This, for me, is the terror. The thing eating away inside and no antibiotics for it.

But getting back... A sense of urgency, yes, to do the work underway, at hand. To keep faith, as a writer, by writing. Escape into focus and moments of clarity of a different kind. The kind from Before. Visit there, anyway, and rest a while. Then emerge into this strange now and face our child's stunning innocence, her utter vulnerability, her magnificent small joys.

September 11 has catapulted me into some hyper-sensitivity. I suppose it's a form of grief. The ordinary world can be piercingly beautiful at moments, sharp as those box-cutters the terrorists used. Or it can be dull and far away when Thought takes hold.

But it's no longer "the ordinary world"; it's the extraordinary: a brown leaf, the amber eye of a cat, the purple fingernail of my child painted with a washable marker—

Who can get it all down now and get it right? The world is too much with us these days, and it hurts.

And who will read our words when and if they emerge whole again and not broken stutterings struggling toward some sense?
Does it matter?

No. Not any more. At least not for now.

There is a largeness now, and we are too small within it.

The thing is, now, to be and to love—where we can. And to do what we can. With our hands. Our words.

Such as they are.

Before is over. Now is now. And here we are. And it's not such a terrible thing, really, just terribly different. And hard. Harder, maybe, than wherever we've been Before.

Well, hard can be good, too. Think of rocks flecked with bits of metallic glitter in the sun. Think of rocks smooth as satin under a sliding waterfall. Think of rocks in a sandstorm.

Just there.

And I'm thinking, too, of Flannery O'Connor's story "A Good Man is Hard to Find." At the end, when the Misfit says, "She would of been a good woman, if it had been somebody there to shoot her every minute of her life."

Do theories of beauty matter? Now?

Theories?

Don't make me laugh.

Or wait. Yes. A rare pleasure.

What is beautiful right now is the sound of a Vornado heater warming this room. And the sound of natural gas whooshing into flame somewhere in the mystery of the boiler in the furnace room down the hall. Then off again.

In lovely regularity.

And the sound of one of the cats wheezing a little in sleep.

And the sound of this clickety-click on the keyboard.

And the white of these walls. And the thready striations of the lampshade pouring soft light over writer-debris.

And it's good. All of it.

LAURA HINTON

The Hole I Cannot See:
Smoke and Fragments in New York City

You saw nothing in Hiroshima.
(Screenplay for *Hiroshima Mon Amour*)
—MARGUERITE DURAS

Like the majority of New Yorkers on the morning of
September 11, what I saw, or did not see, was what I viewed on my
TV screen. Many report that seeing those commercial jetliners
crash into the World Trade Center towers, then watching them
fall like paper fans, created an odd sense of *déjà vu*, of having seen
that movie before.

It was not like a movie to me.

I saw nothing.

I rehearse again and again what I saw or did not see September 11. I
make words serve as placeholders for the hole in what I perceived.
I must have fed my crying cats that morning of the 11th. I must have
tried to feed myself, determined to go about some physical order of
the day. I decided I should eat breakfast. Blueberries in cereal would
be nice. I ventured down my walk-up apartment building to cross
Third Avenue for the Korean deli. Hit by a sudden wave of light, I was
hit by another wave, that of people marching up the street. People in
suits with haircuts, women in high heels toting briefcases. People
who did not belong to my no-name Manhattan neighborhood. Buy
berries, I told myself, trying not to stare. Lingering in the light, I
became one with the strangers streaming up the avenue, flowing like
a river running backwards, like salmon swimming upstream.

They were the downtown survivors. Polished, dressed, they brought with them the ashen black smoke that filled the widening sky of lower Manhattan and the hole I could not see. They came out of the belly of the smoke, automaton-like, mobilized in their unified stride. Silent, grim, they contrasted against the backdrop of my neighborhood denizens, who perched on corners and stoops, unshaven men, old women with bags, Indian restaurant owners wet from having cleaned their sidewalks.

I entered the deli. It was bustling with business. Employees struggled to fill orders for take-out sandwiches—although it was not lunchtime—and coffee. But a heavy silence penetrated the air. People waited in lines all too patiently for New Yorkers. A woman broke the silence, saying to no one in particular, "My mother, I called my mother." She was walking to her mother's house on 98th Street. She was wearing high heels.

"Where are you walking from?" I asked. Stupid question. I must have been thinking about blueberries. "I work at the World Trade Center," she said. I glanced at her elegant, pinched pumps and I wished I could have given her my tattered loafers. But I said nothing. It was my first venture into the hole, the place where I couldn't speak. And I no longer could see her anyway, because my eyes had this watery glaze coating them, smearing my glasses.

Blinded, gagged, I felt useless to help anyone at all. Uselessness would define the rim of my hole, which now was a vortex. In the hole was a powerful dark channel that had swallowed up my power to activate, to create, to escape.

My will had been metaphorically fragmented into smoke.

The next 24 hours I spent more or less alone. Classes at my university were cancelled. The bridges and tunnels into Manhattan were closed. My son was stuck in Brooklyn, my husband stranded in Westchester.

I did receive an afternoon visit, however, from a long-lost friend. She called from Penn Station. She had chosen this day to come in to Manhattan from New Jersey to buy her young daughter a snowsuit. The World Trade Center collapsed and she went to Macy's to buy the snowsuit. She didn't know what else to do.

Grateful to be helpful to someone, I said to come on over. A few minutes later, sitting on my sofa, she said, "What does one do on doomsday?" Indeed, what does one do?

We went to lunch.

So while the World Trade Center blazed, we sat in a local restaurant and had a sandwich. Its bar was filled with the strangers in suits, their briefcases strewn haphazardly around tables. People were drinking. Television screens blared everywhere. Every two minutes the World Trade Center towers collapsed and incinerated over and over. Television reporters tried to say something new every time. They repeated themselves, just like the image. Their voices would be over-ridden by the buzz of helicopters circling the air. The strangers sat in small groups drinking and smoking. It was hard to get a sandwich. None of the restaurant's workers from Queens and Brooklyn could come in to work, so the restaurant owner and a couple of friends were trying to manage everything. They were doing a lousy job. They were quickly running out of food. They charged my credit card someone else's amount. The sandwich tasted like salt and sand. I couldn't eat. Every few minutes I hopped from my table and saw some piece of the World Trade Center burn again and turn to dust. I saw the reruns. But I couldn't stand still long enough to really see.

Alone again in the early evening, I wandered the streets toward lower Manhattan. I went as far as police barricades would permit, to 14th Street, where the cops stood like tin soldiers all on alert. A few people were escorted in and out of the metal barricades, wearing face masks. Others there at the barricades were snapping photographs. I couldn't see what they were trying to see through their camera lenses. There was no marked gape in the skyline, for everything was darkness, everything covered in a huge black pall. Then I thought I saw the outline of the World Trade Center towers hovering in the air. It quickly vanished, a mirage of smoke. Of course, I saw nothing.

I worked my way back through Madison Park, where the street people were rolled up in their tattered blankets. There were other people, as well, a crying woman here and there, sitting alone in the descending dark on a park bench, wearing tennis shoes and nylon hose, perhaps a leather bag propped against her. These were the new "homeless." Perhaps they couldn't get over the bridge to husbands in New Jersey, perhaps they had lost someone downtown and were searching for him, for her. Really, who were they? Their heads in their hands, they looked unattached to the landscape. Women in nylon hose don't sit in parks alone, at night, in New York City.

I turned again to see what I wanted to see—the outline of the World Trade Center. The black pall now blended without distinction into the black of the night sky.

I wandered from Madison Park to Gramercy Park, through one of its wrought-iron gates usually closed to outsiders. Tonight, exclusive, lush Gramercy was an open oasis. Inside, students were holding a candlelight vigil. They were singing "Amazing Grace." I joined them on a chorus of what I would later e-mail my friends was "Amazing Grave." I had absorbed Mayor Guiliani's unintended pun from morning television news broadcasts, describing unknown but "grave" casualties.

I had seen the smoke. I knew those people had vaporized.

In the days that would pass, I did not watch TV. I could not watch the towering crematoriums burn and smoke, spin and turn to ash. But I did read the newspapers in search of information. I wanted questions articulated for which politicians had already made easy answers. Experts on Islam came out the backalleys of university corridors and wrote eloquent columns on the page. Yet I was combing for another sort of information. I was looking for mention of exactly who those people were at the World Trade Center on September 11. I was looking for some understanding of how to interpret so sudden an arrested fate.

I reconstructed stories and put them into my hole. This act was futile. The hole had swept through them. It was growing wider. Stories require a beginning, a middle, and an end. We had the beginnings, we had portions of middles. But we had no ends. No closure. Many have no identities. Those engulfed by the World Trade Center are still called the "Missing." As of now, most have not been legally declared dead. Relatives wait, hoping for better news. There are shadows but few bodies. No closure is in sight.

Without bodies, we cling to fragments. I cling to the fragments of stories I read, for example, in the *New York Times*. There, a daily page, euphemistically entitled "Portraits of Grief," provides short eulogies about the World Trade Center's "Missing." This page might better be called, "Fragments about the Dead." It is part of a new *Times* section published for the occasion of terrorism and war, which, too, bears a euphemism: "A Nation Challenged." This title might also be more aptly rephrased. I would call it, "A Nation Filled with Anguish and Horror," or, "The Nation of Paranoia" section.

I open up today's *Times*. One "portrait" is about a young Yugoslavian immigrant who had fallen in love with New York City. He recently had matriculated at Baruch College, one of the colleges constituting the City University of New York. I teach at another CUNY campus. This young Yugoslavian could have been one of my students. He could have been my neighbor. I teach uptown, but I live near Baruch. I could have seen him at the Xerox store on Third Avenue, where the students duplicate textbooks at registration. I could have bumped into him at the checkout stand at Duane Reade Drugstore. I could have passed him enroute to the subway as he kissed his girlfriend on the corner of Lexington and 26th. According to the girlfriend, "He loved everything" about New York. Apparently, he loved her, too. She is inconsolable.

Then there is the junior-high-school sweetheart who did not propose to his wife until they both had turned 26. When they finally married, the formerly wild party-boy and drifter settled down to a nice steady life as a bonds trader, at Cantor Fitzgerald, in the World Trade Center.

There is the young father that my stepson knew, another Cantor Fitzgerald employee. He would show photos around of his baby girl when coming in on his New Jersey train. His wife was quoted as saying, "He was enamored of fatherhood." He wanted nothing more than to be at home with his new daughter.

There was the fireman who also loved to paint. There was the police officer who spoke four languages and worked part-time as a translator. There was a butcher, a baker, a candlestick maker. There was a security guard who would feed the homeless every week at his Seventh Day Adventist Church.

These are the Missing, whose lives we try to narrate, as we excavate them, piecemeal, from newspaper accounts. We see their smiling faces everywhere on posters around town. These paper fliers, announcing they are "Missing," are tacked to walls, to store fronts, to light posts, to telephone booths—the sexy glances of the "Missing" catch my eye as I pass the New York Armory at Lexington. The

Armory was made an official "Crisis Center" in the first days after September 11. Two blocks from my apartment, it was the place to which family members were asked to bring toothbrushes and hairbrushes, along with descriptions of their "Missing." Innovative family members brought fliers, too, then vied for the media cameras and sensational spotlights that flooded street corners around Lexington for days. They thrust their "Missing's" smiling photograph into the media's face. They did not smile themselves.

Along the brick wall of the Armory, the fliers begin to shred and peel. The family members and the media are long gone. But the "Missing" fliers remain, a shrill call for help. "Anyone know Diane?" Or, "Call if you have information about William." "Diane," we learn, was born in upstate New York in 1964. She would have been 38 years old when she joined the "Missing". A handsome man of 28, William, we learn, is a father of two, who worked as an accountant on the north tower's 92nd floor. Call his wife if you have any information, his flier pleads. Information? I have none. Increasingly whipped by fall winds, some of the letters in "Missing" disintegrate, losing an "h" or an "n." The faces of the "Missing," however, steadfastly smile on.

The hole where the World Trade Center stood is hallowed ground. They are talking about making what was once the World Trade Center a memorial site. But, of course, they also want to rebuild Manhattan's prime office space; they want to rekindle the economic energy of a dying downtown. Politicians speak out of two sides of their mouth, as the fragments of the World Trade Center are moved in truck loads to a Staten Island city dump site. There, on Staten Island, they sift for pieces of identifiable objects. Retired police detectives and other volunteers pass gloved hands tenderly through rubble moving along a conveyor belt. They feel for fragments of a leather shoe or golden ring. On a good day, they find a warped police badge or a credit card whose numbers are intact.

This is the Amazing Grave of Staten Island, where they also find pieces of bone welded to fragments of fabric and steel.

Coda

It is the evening of October 11, 2001.

Tonight, for the first time, I went down to the World Trade Center. To where the World Trade Center once stood.

I went not as a tourist, and not to gawk.

I went to honor the dead who were my neighbors.

I went to Fulton Street and Broadway, where, over the grid-like barriers, the still-standing high rises are masked with huge protective canvas nets like veils of mourning, and where "rescue workers," who are really rubble diggers, make their way further into a hole I cannot glimpse from Fulton and Broadway, whose cavernous place I can only imagine.

I see the blown-out bits of what must have been World Trade Center 7. Beyond, I see a hulk of steel that I recognize from newspaper photographs, the remnants of one of the towers. It does not look like a tower at all. It looks like giant shark teeth propped against a faded sun.

The light becomes, for an instant, falsely luminous, and the twisted gauntlet of steel turns purple, then is shot by rays of pink. Red lights flow on the surface of the Hudson, which one now sees from Fulton and Broadway. Then, red flecks reach the shark's teeth, more surreal than real.

More nightmarish than dreamlike.

To face the vanishing lights, the traces, of the World Trade Center, I confront the hole I cannot see. The sun dips its belly into the fullness of the new horizon. There are dark eddies and swells and pools. Then the Hudson deepens and becomes part of the sea.

H. EDGAR HIX

October 11, 2001

I was so disappointed when the world celebrated the new millennium a year early. Since childhood I had looked forward to living in the 21st Century. Since grade school I had counted the years to see how old I would be in 2001. (Ancient ... ancient....)

Then, two days before my 48th birthday, they blew up the world. Even my father forgot my day. As was appropriate. It was bitter. It was draining. It was necessary. A man and a woman held hands as they jumped to their deaths, choosing air over fire. How would my birthday dare compete with that?

Today, missiles and bombs are falling on Afghanistan (I had to use my spell checker to spell the nation correctly). Osama bin Laden (I had to look in the news to see how to spell his name) is calling for more violence. Some of the cheaper flags that people hurriedly bought are beginning to fade slightly. The post office is planning to offer a "United We Stand" stamp in mid-November. There's Christmas stuff up with the Halloween stuff at Wal-Mart and Walgreens. (Who in Hell remembers Thanksgiving?) In Minnesota, we're talking about an early snow, possibly even this Sunday. The President spoke to the nation but I was busy with a computer game and besides, I didn't want to hear. My horror is now puddles left over from the thunderstorm. My fear is still nightmares, but further apart. My rage is indignation tempered by carefully thought out logic and equally carefully squelched emotions that ate my mind like dog food a month ago.

There's an e-mail rumor making the rounds that there will be an attack on a Midwestern mall on Halloween. I live a few miles from the Mall of America. A very few miles. It's right by the airport. I enjoy going and looking at the sharks, buying videos, eating oriental, and doing a little girl watching. I can get the postage stamps I may have missed at the Post Office Store. There's a good bargain bookstore there, too. Who believes e-mail rumors? Of course, who wants to go shopping on Halloween? It's just inviting pranks while you're out.

Jesus has come and gone and will come again. In the meantime, I will go to class and walk my dog nights. Tonight we could see Orion very clearly, just above the roofs and trees. Night had hidden all the autumnal glory of those trees. They'll be black and bare soon enough. I'll continue to go to class and walk my dog at night. Some nights I'll pray to Jesus. Some nights I'll see Orion. Some nights I'll remember September 11th. Some nights I'll remember other days when the world blew up, like April 19th (I'm from Oklahoma). Some nights I'll just let the dog pee. I promise myself I will.

H. L. HIX

Where We Were, Where We Are

I was in the basement on my exercise bike. My fingernails were dirty from digging up Dutch Iris bulbs at dawn, and a bead of sweat had dripped from my forehead onto the left lens of my glasses, leaving a salty streak. I will always remember the expression on my wife's face when she came downstairs to tell me.

Certain unforgettable events become "where were you when" events because they locate us, alerting us to or reminding us of who we are. Every life bears their scars. *I was washing dishes when I heard Pearl Harbor had been bombed*, or *I was driving to Chicago when it came on the radio about JFK*. We remember where we were physically when these events occurred, because they tell us where we are spiritually.

A few days later I received a short e-mail from a poet whose work I love and admire. "Nothing the same. Ever again." In five words, she arrived at the heart of the matter. We predicate our confidence in the future on its continuity with the past, which the events of September 11 severed. But the discontinuity, the fact that nothing will be the same, is not a statement about the world, which has not changed and does not change. September 11 was always there, about to happen. It is we who have been wounded, changed forever. Nothing the same for us, in us, ever again.

"Where were you when" events. Martin Luther King. Kent State. John Lennon. The Challenger. Oklahoma City. Now the World Trade Center. Days that mark the loss of innocence, that strip us of our consoling beliefs. We who thought we were just discovered we were not. Or we who thought our government existed for us learned it does not. Now we who thought ourselves safe learn we were not and never can be.

Such events, always unprecedented, disorient us. In the wake of September 11, the ambition for a subtle and complex understanding seems presumptuous, even absurd. Left only with fragmentary and enjambed thought, pursuing simplicities instead, anything I can grasp to steady my thoughts for a moment, I have sought refuge in a quincunx of plain ideas and level voices with this at its center:

We maintain some element of control over how we will respond to attack and to tragedy, and we can respond in better or worse ways. Unintimidated honesty supports a better response, self-deception a worse; goodwill a better response, ill-will a worse. "It is difficult to suffer well, without resentment, false consolation, untruthful flight," Iris Murdoch tells us, followed by the central fact: "*How* we see our situation is itself, already, a moral activity."

Around that center, four corners:

We *do* have enemies, as the murder of thousands of civilians clearly proves, but we ought not be indiscriminate in identifying them. That, after all, would replicate one of the moral flaws in the practice of terrorism: it is indiscriminate, it attacks a *substitute* for its enemy. Terrorism and terrorists are our enemies. Islam is not our enemy, either within U.S. borders or in other parts of the world. Individual Muslims are not our enemies, here or abroad. Fringe groups and fanatics and violent fundamentalists infect every religion. We should be wary of hasty generalizations and stereotypes, attending in this matter to the words of Islam's sacred book, the Koran: "I worship not that which you worship; nor do you worship that which I worship. And I shall not worship that which you worship, nor will you worship that which I worship. Unto you your religion, and unto me my religion."

One way of being indiscriminate in identifying the enemy is using the suffering and death of others as a platform for aspersions against the objects of one's prejudices. Jerry Falwell managed soon after the events to assert that abortionists, feminists, gays and lesbians, and members of the ACLU all "helped this happen." Such scattershot vituperation has more in common with terrorism than with goodwill. Mr. Falwell would do well to read Camus' *The Plague*, to be reminded by one of its characters that "there can be no true goodness nor true love without the utmost clear-sightedness."

Even when events are beyond our control, when we can exert little influence on their outcome, we have a stake in them. Even toward such events we can be responsible or irresponsible, a circumstance Elias Canetti formulates in this way: "Whether one has lived in vain depends on what happens to the world. If it devours itself, one is devoured along with it. If it saves itself, one has contributed something to this salvation."

Finally, the hope that remains after tragedy may not be *our* hope, not hope *for us*, but hope *does* remain, and Václav Havel's assurance of that fact makes a fitting conclusion. "Life may be subjected to a prolonged and thorough process of violation, enfeeblement, and anesthesia. Yet, in the end, it cannot be permanently halted.... [H]owever violently ravished, [life] always survives, in the end, the power which ravished it."

CYNTHIA HOGUE

In a Battle of Wills There Are No Winners

*Victory with vengeance is ultimate defeat in
the modern world. We can have peace or we can have
revenge, but we cannot have both.*

—QUAKER CALENDAR, MAY 1956

It is four weeks since the terrorist attacks on September 11, 2001. Like most of us since these attacks, I have been more aware of being alive as a gift. I have reached out to loved ones to tell them I love them. And like most of us, I am scared and wish I didn't feel so helpless. As I write, the U.S. has started bombing Afghanistan. The bombing does not make me feel safe. It makes me feel unsafe.

One of the radio commentators remarked on the day the bombing started, apropos of the origins of war, that the Vikings didn't have a word for the meaningless escalation of violence that comprises the plot of the greatest Icelandic saga, *Brennu Njals Saga*. *Njal's Saga* is the story of a wise man with an unwise family. What starts out as a small retaliatory exchange between two households escalates, despite Njal's best peacekeeping efforts, until two whole clans are involved in the rivalry. At last Njal and all his household are burned alive by their enemies. When the plot is reduced to its broad out-lines, the horror of the violence of killing so many people is writ large (one of the themes of this saga). When we reduce the September 11th attacks to the "plot"—nineteen young Muslim fun-damentalists (the sect is so sexist we need not denote their sex) hijacked four passenger airline jets and killed over 6000 people in one hour—these terrorist acts seem to us clearly mad. Crazy mad. The actions of lunatics. From our perspective.

Angry mad, from their perspective. Why do they hate us? Americans asked after the attack. "How do people reach this level of anger, hatred and frustration?" asks Professor of Conflict Studies John Paul Lederach. To call them lunatics misses a crucial point:

> By my experience explanations that they are brainwashed by a perverted leader who holds some kind of magical power over them is an escapist simplification and will inevitably lead us to very wrong-headed responses. Anger of this sort, what we could call generational, identity-based anger, is constructed over time through a combination of historical events, a deep sense of threat to identity, and direct experience of sustained exclusion.

From the terrorists' perspective, they are a David heroically fighting the bully-giant Goliath, who is spreading Western imperialism. If we do as they expect, which is use our power against a weak people or nation, we can expect without a doubt that they will engage in the future in ever-escalating cycles of revenge and violence.

The Vikings in fact did have a word for the senseless feuding that drives the plot of *Njal's Saga*, which is the word used to rationalize the violence by the characters. It is the same word as motivated the terrorists on September 11th, the same word as is motivating U.S. and British retaliation. It is a word for an heroic concept, a warrior's code. That word is *honor*, along with the component parts of the ancient heroic code: pride and shame, loyalty and betrayal. One of the men interviewed on the radio the day we started the bombing was a veteran of the Gulf War. When asked if he'd go back to war if drafted, he said, "Of course. It's the warrior's code, *to rip the living heart out of the enemy's chest.* I'm a warrior" (emphasis added). Honor requires us to retaliate, or the enemy will think he can get away with murder.

But honor, too, will require the other side to avenge such retaliation because we "deserved" the punishing "justice" they dealt us. At the dawning of the twenty-first century, we discover that we understand the saga's world of the blood feud and violent retaliation because, to our shock and horror, we are suddenly living it. However much we refuse to hear them, from the Muslim extremist perspective, the U.S. has been made "to pay" for past grievances to the Muslim world, for which we had never shown remorse. Now, we are making Afghanistan "pay" for harboring terrorists. But Afghanistan did not attack the U.S. So, the U.S. will eventually be made to "pay" for its harming Afghanistan. How far and how long will this exchange of violence go?

We desperately need another model for what is deemed an honorable response. That model also lies in *Njal's Saga*, in Njal himself. The saga was written after Iceland had converted in 1000 A.D. to Christianity. Thus, although its action takes place before the conversion, its theme is influenced by gentler Christian tenets. Njal is a pagan precursor of what I will call "radical Christianity" (to distinguish it from the bigotry of most versions of fundamentalist Christianity, much like the terrorists' Islamic fundamentalism must be distinguished from the gentler Muslim faith). Njal counsels tolerance and negotiates nonviolent alternative responses to violence. He wheels and deals for peace. He advises his friend, the Viking Gunnar, as well as his own truculent sons, "Never break the agreements which good men make between you and others." Although broken agreements and the violence of his pagan family eventually take him down with them, he represents an alternative that redefines the heroic code of honor. We need to do that now. What are the possibilities?

For a start, we could redefine "honor" as being able to hear both sides, both perspectives, not just our own. We could view violence itself as dishonorable, and every "holy war" (both sides have bandied this phrase about) as sacrilege. Certainly when we are the target, we call violence "barbaric" and "heinous." Why is it justified when we perpetrate it ourselves? We could consider our own possible responses in terms other than violence. And to those who say we will look weak to the world if we negotiate, we could answer: We need another definition of strength. Strength is the courage to wait and to make a considered response. Strength is *not* throwing our military weight around. Strength is seeking insistently—and, why not? aggressively-negotiated, diplomatic solutions.

We need to honor the memories of our own victims by listening to their families. Many of the families of the September 11th dead are not calling for retaliation, but for peacemaking. Touched so deeply and irrevocably by this tragedy, these families understood more immediately than any of us that no violence will return their loved ones to life, no retaliatory strike could suffice to comfort them in their grief. They say again and again that their dead would not wish other innocent people to die for their deaths. In escalating the violence, we risk making the deaths of over 6000 civilians truly meaningless, for we will have failed to understand the lesson in their deaths: that how we feel now is how civilians in Baghdad felt when we bombed them, how civilians in Serbia felt, how civilians in Japan felt. Is it not dishonorable that we were indifferent to the pain we caused? We need to redefine honor as caring about the consequences of our actions in the world, and as not hypocritically mouthing the rhetoric of democracy when we take geopolitical action. Now, we not only should care, because we can identify with grief felt around the world. Now, we must care—not as a rule of law, but as Barbara Kingsolver puts it, as one of "a hundred ways to be a good citizen,... to look finally at the things we don't want to see."

On September 11th our world changed. We Americans learned that we weren't safe in our own country—whether we are warriors or peacemakers, whites or people of color, men or women, gays or straights, legal or illegal residents. All of us will suffer for the policies of the few in power. But it doesn't have to be that way. This tragedy has produced a huge awakening. We as a people have the opportunity now to change as well. Instead of confirming the terrorists' portrait of the U.S. as a bullying superpower, as we have unfortunately done, we might still yet react unexpectedly, for example by beginning to address real grievances in the region.

We might yet throw ourselves into supporting sustainable peace between Israel and Palestine, and *stop now the bombing of Afghanistan*, thereby being as good as our word and proving to the Afghan people in our actions that we are not making war against them. In this way, we might begin to defuse the reason that young Arab men give their own lives to kill American civilians. Lederach writes, "I believe that monumental times like these create conditions for monumental change.... Let us choose democracy and reconciliation over revenge and destruction." If we have not ruined already this monumental chance for change by meeting violence with violence, that old model of honorable blood vengeance, the terrible deaths we have suffered will not have been in vain.

As Ghandi said, "We must *be* the change we wish to see in the world." Mary Oliver's question in her poem "The Summer Day" never seemed so urgently timely, "Tell me, what do you plan to do / with your one wild and precious life?"

TOM HOLMES

Letter

[11/12/01 4:35:11 AM Eastern Standard Time]
Bill,

So, I live in the can, where the most disadvantaged community in the state of Washington resides. I'm trying to help write a grant so the Women's & Children's Free Restaurant (WCFR) can get two new freezers so they can feed more women and children. (The WCFR does not allow men. This way women who have left horrible situations have a place to feel safe.) This grant writing class is teaching me so much. There is a very active world/community in Spokane that seeks to fund those organizations that aim to help others. It's so wonderful, esp/ w/ Spokane being so poor, which includes me.

Now I forgot the point of this letter. It's such a different world where the grant writers live. It's as if they see more. And those who direct programs see more and work together.

But where was I headed. And is it relevant anymore? Ah, yes. Art. Write grants for the arts, and there should be no more suffering. If the arts were popular and listened to, then wouldn't problems disappear? Don't the arts get to the root before things root?

So, I was at work today. I wash dishes now. Part time. It makes me feel like shit. But, tonight I was thinking. And I never think like this. I was grateful I have Michelle loving me. I was grateful I have books, and I can write. I was grateful that I get to proofread your anthology. It keeps me going. It sustains me. It gives me purpose in this desperate little can of a town. My book, when I have the time for it, accomplishes near the same.

But what I was thinking. This anthology could be huge. It could be the first seminal, giant, hugely important piece of literature of the millennium. I keep thinking like Al Poulin thought about *The Waste Land*. Everything last century goes back to it. And I think everything for a long while will go back to 9/11 and your anthology, or at least some pieces in it. Something in the anthology or the anthology itself will create, re-create humanity. It may make poets and writers become giants once again. It may revive art once again. It may be huge. I think everyone will eventually read it. I think it will cause people to think and discuss. I think it will be smarter than you could have imagined, even you with your imagination. And hopefully, it will travel the world.

It will be news that stays news.

Make it sing. Make it sing. I have freezers to bring.

Peace, Flowers, and Art.

Tom

JOHN HOPPENTHALER

Crash

Frantic icons leapt from a failing desktop
deep into the cyber abyss, & I knew
it was trouble—virus warnings that were

routinely ignored soon flashed
red through my brain. The screen: blank, useless
as keys I kept punching, trying to lock in

& energize like wily Scotty on Star Trek.
But whir, zap, dispersed & gone to who knows where—
detritus & satellites slapped into

darker regions of the mysterious
universe. Backed up on disks, poetry survives,
though not innocence, risky downloads,

the suspicious, sexy allure of **click here**
lost in space. *Danger, danger.*
And even as earthly debris of towers still

smolders, is picked over for clues & miracles,
I'm through being stunned, grateful today
for anger. It will take time till technicians

get the machine on line, offer reasons
beyond a simple grasp. With icons restored,
we'll build again toward heaven, hover as we

can between galaxies absurdly distant,
or so close we tend to forget they're here.
Fingers tap buttons, funeral pipers

summon the missing. Tether their smoke now
to lovers born in September. Recover them
like confessions tangled in uncertain histories.

MARK IRWIN

Elegy for the Victims and Survivors, World Trade Towers, N.Y., 2001

Stadium of sorrow where archeologists of terror
dig for a jet's
brief fossil.

Stadium of sorrow beneath the trampled clouds,
who now will police
the stars?

Stadium of sorrow, what child
could piece together
these mangled
towers'

puzzle? And why? And will
they, each one together
I mean, Stadium of sorrow where people queue

around the smoke with candles
lighting their way into the other unseeable
way we are

Stadium of sorrow,
the spectators, living, who are lost
and found over and over
by looking.

Notes after observing the floodlit arena of
disaster through the distance of media,
night after night

210

Stadium, a bit of immovable Latin fixed like a huge stone within our
more tensile English language; stadium, from the Greek *stadion*,
fixed measure of length, altered from *stadios*, standing. Stadium, a
track (for footraces or events) surrounded by tiers of seats for
spectators. Stadia, the plural and also a method of surveying in which
distances and elevations are obtained through the use of graduated
stadia rods.

Stadium, an incantatory word, especially when repeated, due to the
fixed hum in the third syllable, akin to that of the Sanskrit *om*,
intoned as part of a mantra, or as a mystical utterance of assent during meditation.

Stadium, a place where people or distances are united or lost.

Stadium of sorrow: How dark into the far do the dead sail?

MARK JARMAN

9/11/01: A Journal Entry

Amy and the girls and I went to breakfast together at Waffle House near our home. We had never eaten breakfast there, but we wanted to go some place together before Zoë went off for her freshman year at Northwestern. When we arrived at the restaurant and ordered, we found out they didn't take plastic and we had brought no cash. They did take checks. But instead of going home for the check book, I ventured into the sluggish rushhour Nashville traffic to find the nearest ATM and realized I wouldn't get back until breakfast was over.

While I sat in the jam, I switched on NPR. There was Bob Edwards narrating the events. A plane had hit the World Trade Center. What? Some private-prop plane? How stupid and sad. As he spoke he said another plane—a passenger liner—had hit the other tower of the Trade Center.

Meanwhile I raged at the frustrating traffic, thought of the missed breakfast with my family, finally got to an ATM. Bush had been in Florida and condemned this apparent terrorist attack. The Trade Center's upper floors were burning. Bob Edwards was giving the news.

Back at the Waffle House, Zoë had discovered that we were seated across from the country singing stars Faith Hill and Tim McGraw, and their little girl. When I returned, beginning to feel the combination of adrenalin and nausea that stayed with me all day, the Pentagon had been attacked, crashed into by an airliner. Amy had eaten only a quarter of her waffle, but the girls had finished their breakfasts, and mine was being kept warm. I couldn't eat. I told them what was going on. What I didn't know was that they were excited about Faith and Tim, who had already left. I had seen an attractive woman with a little girl by a black Mercedes in the parking lot, talking to a man in a business suit. I had thought about rich, well-kept women, the kind of women rich men chose, the understanding that they would remain shapely, well kept, etc. Senseless, sensual nonsense.

When we switched on the car radio, Bob Edwards described the collapse of one of the Trade Towers. He was clearly losing it. All U.S. flights had been grounded. There was news of another plane down. He was choking, his throat and mouth audibly dry. At one point he spoke to a New York City reporter and asked her if chaos was upon us. She assured him that it was not and that to think so was to give in to the terrorists. It was not Bob Edwards' finest hour.

At home we turned on the TV to a calm but concerned Peter Jennings. It was just in time for us to watch the other tower—actually the first to be hit—buckle and collapse. In both cases the gray billowing smoke and debris was reminiscent of the explosion of Mt. St. Helens over twenty years ago.

A free-lance photographer, working in Trinity Episcopal Church nearby, caught the second plane on video. The jet enters the tower sideways and as its nose emerges from the other side, it explodes. Channel 2 showed this several times, at different speeds.

People aboard the hijacked planes were calling 911 on their cell phones. The hijackers apparently had knives. They stabbed flight attendants and took over cockpits. They knew how to fly. At least those that hit the Trade Center and the Pentagon knew how. Some speculate that the jet that went down in Pennsylvania was heading for Camp David.

Was September 11 the date of the Camp David Accords?

Everything points to Osama bin Laden, but how do you make war on such a person? Some insist that we should hit the countries that sponsor terrorism against us. But how can you be sure which these are?

If groups are willing to commit suicide in this way, it is very hard to monitor them. But America will have to. We're all going to be part of a clampdown.

Meanwhile the entire World Trade Center, almost, has been destroyed. The effect on the nation's economy has to be bad.

Members of Congress gathered on the steps of the Capitol to sing "God Bless America."

Amy and the girls and I went to the Temple tonight for a service. Nashville's mayor was there. All the Jewish congregations, except the orthodox, were represented. A family with three little boys sat in front of us. One of the boys was badly behaved throughout the service, even making a paper plane from the program and threatening to fly it. His mother was no better, chatting with a friend during the prayers. Yet the father wore a yarmulke and asked one of the boys, the oldest, to take his brother out of the sanctuary. I thought of "Musée des Beaux Arts" about the children, as the old waited for the promised birth, who didn't specially want it to happen.

Home again, the news went on. The FBI was checking houses in Florida. People were saying America would come together. But who are we looking for? Against whom are we coming together?

And all those people who were in the midst of their lives, innocent of the charge leveled against them by their killers, people in those buildings who might have been lovers, people on the airplanes who thought the future looked bright, everyone thoroughly absorbed by their lives, having them taken from them by religious fanatics. In the name of a god. And as usual God watches—both gods—theirs (the murderers')—and ours—(the murdered's)—both gods watch. They merely watch.

One tries to imagine the terror on those airplanes as they traveled toward their destinations. One tries to imagine all that was on the minds of the people in the offices before the horrible collision that changed those minds forever.

I keep thinking of a chef in the restaurant at the top of the World Trade Center, accepting a delivery of milk and peeling a Yukon gold potato. Maybe not peeling. Just washing it. Slicing it. Getting things ready. Food that had ascended, by elevator, over 100 floors.

A vast expensive structure, important to the lives of tens of thousands—more. I didn't like the building. It was ugly. It was like a double phallic boast to the world. And now it's rubble and burning debris. And now, like everyone else, I mourn its loss.

I keep thinking of people in stairwells, and the firemen telling them to keep moving, as they ascend, when the whole thing comes down.

America doesn't feel the same anymore. Its fortress walls have been breached, through the wicked little wicket gate.

DENIS JOHNSON

Several times during the nineteen-nineties I did some reporting from what we generally call trouble spots, and witnessing the almost total devastation of some of these places (Somalia, Afghanistan, the southern Philippines, Liberia) had me wondering if I would ever see such trouble in my own country: if I would ever feel it necessary to stay close to the radio or television; if I would sleep with the window wide open in order to hear the approach of the engines of war or to smell the smoke of approaching fires or to stay aware of the movements of emergency teams coping with the latest enormity; if I would one day see American ground heaped with the ruins of war; if I would ever hear Americans saying, "They're attacking the Capitol! The Pentagon! The White House!"; if I would stand in the midst of an American crowd witnessing the kind of destruction that can be born of the wickedness of the human imagination, or turn to examine American faces a few seconds after their eyes had taken it in; if I would one day see American streets choked with people who don't know exactly where they're going but don't feel safe where they are; and if I would someday feel uncontrollably grateful to be able to get my laundry done and to find simple commerce persisting in spite of madness. I wondered if the wars I'd gone looking for would someday come looking for us.

Travelling in the Third World, I've found that to be an American sometimes means to be wondrously celebrated, to excite a deep, instantaneous loyalty in complete strangers. In the southern Philippines, a small delegation headed by a village captain once asked that I take steps to have their clan and their collection of two dozen huts placed under the protection of the United States. Later, in the same region, a teen-age Islamic separatist guerilla among a group I'd been staying with begged me to adopt him and take him to America. In Afghanistan, I encountered men who, within minutes of meeting me, offered to leave their own worried families and stay by my side as long as I required it, men who found medicine somewhere in the ruins of Kabul for me when I needed it, and who never asked for anything back—all simply because I was American.

On the other hand, I think we sense—but don't care always to appre-hend—the reality that some people hate America. To many suffering souls, we must seem incomprehensibly aloof and self-centered, or worse. For nearly a century, war has rolled lopsidedly over the world, crushing the innocent in their homes. For half that century, the United States has been seen, by some people, as keeping the destruction rolling without getting too much in the way of it—has been seen, by some people, to lurk behind it. And those people hate us. The acts of terror against this country—the hijackings, the kidnappings, the bombings of our airplanes and barracks and embassies overseas, and now these mass atrocities on our own soil— tell us how much they hate us. They hate us as people hate a bad God, and they'll kill themselves to hurt us.

On Thursday, as I write in New York City, which I happen to be visit-ing at the time of the attack, the wind has shifted, and a sour electri-cal smoke travels up the canyons between the tall buildings. I have now seen two days of war in the biggest city in America. But imagine a succession of such days stretching into years—years in which explosions bring down all the great buildings, until the last one goes, or until bothering to bring the last one down is just a waste of ammunition. Imagine the people who have already seen years like these turn into decades—imagine their brief lifetimes made up only of days like these we've just seen in New York.

ERICA JONG

New York at War

Some September days in New York the sky is blue as Alice in Wonderland's Victorian pinafore. Last Tuesday was a day like that. New Yorkers awoke with all their usual love worries, money worries, real-estate worries—and then in a roiling flash of orange flame—we were reminded of what really matters.

A little before nine and a little after nine on a workday morning, two hijacked planes blasted into the double phallic symbol of the World Trade Center, raped our innocence and let us know how vulnerable we really are. Now all of surviving New York is subdued, dazed, eerily quiet. From my 27th story window on East 69th Street, I can still see the billowing yellow smoke where the World Trade Center once was. Another building collapsed at 7 World Trade Center several hours after the initial disaster and more collapses may be imminent in lower Manhattan. On the uptown and midtown streets, New Yorkers are silent, polite, helpful. No horns honk. No one screams profanities. There are few cabs, few private cars. Many schools and businesses are closed and the weather remains glorious—so Central Park is full of people and dogs, little kids and parents. But the quiet is eerie. Banned from lower Manhattan, Ground Zero of the disaster, we watch the unfolding news on tele-vision. For most of the day of the impact, telephone lines in Manhattan were iffy. Cell phones didn't work at all, and even landlines often didn't provide dial tones. We stayed indoors, glued to television sets mostly, and then we got itchy and found a reason to go out. Between the eerie uptown streets and the blazing television sets replaying and replaying the moment of impact, there was a profound disconnect. The first day, everyone knew someone who almost died. In my case, it was a young friend who walked down fifty-one floors to safety from her office in the northern tower. When I talked to her she was still nonchalant about the events. It still hadn't struck her that had she dithered for five minutes she'd be dead. It was her decisiveness that saved her. She didn't wait to be evacuated. She left. Too bad more people were less decisive. Or were trapped on higher floors. Or, in some horrifying cases, told to return to their offices. Each tower became a chute in which the stories fell on each other, flattening whomever and whatever was underneath. Rescue workers have been amazed to find so few survivors, but a plan of the buildings made it obvious why. The skin of the buildings supported them. Once that was punctured, the floors cascaded down. By the second day, most New Yorkers knew someone who never came home. Within a week, we'll all know somebody who died. By day #2, the TV news was full of stories of relatives wandering the city from one hospital to the next, looking for relatives. Those of us who were, for the moment, spared a direct hit on our lives also wandered around vaguely, looking to make ourselves useful— queuing in endless lines to give blood, volunteering if we had medical skills, or just wandering to pass the time.

The number of stunned New Yorkers still wandering the city on day #3 is amazing. Each of us has a kind of waxworks expression. The real shock is that war has come to our shores. We can't believe it. It's as if God promised us immunity. All those towers pointing to the sky— would we have built them so tall if we believed we were vulnerable? New Yorkers believe themselves entitled to celestial views—if they can afford them. Celestial views don't credit the possibility of terrorism. Last spring there was an earthquake under the East River that shook the apartment tower in which I live. Looking back, it now seems like an omen.

There's an insouciance about New Yorkers that measured Europeans adore. It comes from living in a country that has never been ravaged by war and doesn't believe war can cross the Atlantic. On September 11th, we lost this insouciance. We will never be the same. We have joined the vulnerable human race.

The change started to sink in as the haze of yellow smoke started to sink into our bones. We could smell the city smoldering. By Wednesday evening eyes were stinging all over Manhattan. The yellow smoke drifted northward, reminding Upper East Side residents that the war had come home. Tanks and military trucks rattled up Fifth Avenue. The skies were eerily silent except for fighter jets circling overhead when they could no longer do much good. The mayor ordered eleven thousand body bags from the federal government even though he knew that the bodies to fill them might never be found. Anyone who has traveled around America by plane cannot be surprised that four commercial jets were hijacked simultaneously. Our airline security is a joke. The lowest paid workers, often with no language skills and minimal training, ask a few questions, check your photo and speed you on your way. If El Al were allowed to supervise our airline security checks, there would be no more hijackings. We'd have trained security people interrogating passengers. We'd have reinforced doors between cockpits and passenger sections of planes, and pilots would be forbidden to open them under the direst circumstances. We would not leave the safety of the passengers to each other. There would be guards on the planes. All this would cost money—but more than that it would mean a change in attitude. I'm not sure Americans are capable of changing attitudes. Between our worship of the bottom line and our Frank Sinatra-esque I've-gotta-be-me religion of narcissism, we simply fail to understand how easily our security is breached. We expect to win because we've always won. We resist becoming paranoid. But paranoia may be necessary in a world of terrorism. As the crisis goes into its third, then its fourth day, the feeling one gets in New York is that American altruism and innocence have grown, not diminished. Coffee shops and delis are sending free food to blood banks to nourish both workers and donors. One shop selling sneakers handed out free shoes to women in fuck-me pumps hobbling home on foot. People are falling all over each other to volunteer as rescue workers. Nobody seems to be locking up their apartments and taking the family car to Canada. We react to emergencies by becoming more ourselves, not less. Perhaps that will be our downfall.

Meanwhile, we wait for word from our leader. George W. Bush with his simian smirk has clenched his jaw in the hopes it will make him look "presidential." As usual he stumbles over his words—except for the robotic "God Bless America." Our New York politicians are eloquent by comparison. Senator Hillary Clinton, Governor George Pataki, Mayor Rudolph Giuliani have all acquitted themselves movingly and well. But more than that, New Yorkers have been positively benevolent to each other. Our normal love-hate relationship to our city has become all love, all the time. The city is hugging itself to its own wounded bosom. We are licking each other's wounds rather than rubbing salt in as you'd expect New Yorkers to do. Here is the strangest thing about New York—New Yorkers really love their exuberantly disgusting city. We have taken this direct hit on our island as if it were a direct hit on our hearts. Even as lower Manhattan was cordoned off, forbidden, declared dangerous, many of us could not resist sneaking into the war zone to see the huge craters, the mountains of rubble with our own stinging eyes. It was as if we needed proof that this was not just another disaster movie. It was far worse than television had foretold. Dust still hung in the air and the smell of burning was infernal. The sky was dark. The rescue workers still looked ghostly behind their masks. Their hands and faces were powdered gray with gypsum and asbestos. They were breathing in the poison as they passed buckets of debris to each other—buckets containing pulverized building material, twisted metal, the odd high-heeled shoe.

I thought of those writhing figures trapped by molten lava in Pompeii. I thought of the firebombing of Dresden, of Hiroshima, and Nagasaki. Here too, people had been vaporized and would never be found. Their relatives would wander from hospital to hospital, from morgue to morgue and finally, go home not quite knowing how to grieve. The firefighters and police would stop searching for human remains only when exhaustion felled them. Suddenly it seemed obscene to be one of the lucky ones who was spared. I wanted to crawl into the rubble and start sifting through it myself to prove I was a real New Yorker. I wanted to travel into the rubble and find a survivor or disappear. I wanted to slip my feet into those odd, orphaned shoes. For years I have watched disasters on television without really understanding disaster. Now Vietnam, Rwanda, and Bosnia are under my skin. New York's terrible rubble is a part of me. This dust is mine. As it sifts through my fingers, I know I am going to die.

X. J. KENNEDY

September Twelfth, 2001

Two caught on film who hurtle
from the eighty-second floor,
choosing between a fireball
and to jump holding hands,

aren't us. I wake beside you,
stretch, scratch, taste the air,
the incredible joy of coffee
and the morning light.

Alive, we open eyelids
on our pitiful share of time,
we bubbles rising and bursting
in a boiling pot.

Television—which, like most Americans, my wife and I watched continuously through the day of devastation—kept limning the nightmare. Over and over again, we watched that tower collapse, domino fashion. (One newspaper reported that some child, watching it, cried "How pretty!"—unaware that a terrible beauty had been born). The next day I woke with a selfish thankfulness.

I couldn't help feeling grateful that Dorothy and I had been spared—not that we were anywhere near the scene, but we do fly out of Boston's Logan Airport from time to time, sometimes cross-country. I didn't deserve to be one of the fortunate majority, tasting with fresh appreciation the little joys of ordinary days. And it struck me that the nature of the life is to hand us more than we deserve. But only some of us.

MAXINE HONG KINGSTON

Memorial Service*
University of California at Berkeley
September 18, 2001

I'd like to teach you a breathing meditation which I learned from
Alice Walker, who learned it from a Tibetan nun.

At the sound of the Bell of Mindfulness, breathe in and breathe out.
Breathing in, breathe in sorrow, suffering, anger, fear.

Breathing out, breathe out healing, relief, joy, love. Let's breathe
together for three silent minutes.

BELL
Breathing in, I breathe in the world's pain....
Breathing out, I send it healing love....

[3 minutes breathing]

May all beings be happy. May all beings be peaceful.
May all beings be kind. May all beings be free.

[Repeat 3x]

11 BELLS

"May all beings be happy" is metta, the oldest prayer on Earth.
I learned it from a Vietnam veteran.

I hope that as you breathed with the Cal community around you,
you felt our connection one to another. And the wider connection
to the people in the rest of the country, and the rest of the world.

That feeling of connection with all of humankind is an intimation
of the collective consciousness, the universal soul.

We have just sustained an attack on America,
and also on the collective consciousness. America is badly wounded.
The collective consciousness is badly wounded.

America is a historically special country.
We are a nation made up of people from every nation on earth.
Americans are people from every continent and island.
People from all nations become one people—Americans.

In war, we suffer a special American pain. Whomever we shoot,
whomever we bomb, we are shooting and bombing relatives,
brothers, sisters, cousins. All our wars are civil wars.
We go through, again, the horrors of our own War Between the States,
when blood relatives fought blood relatives.
The consequences of that war continue to affect us to this day.

It is possible to heal the wounds.
We heal our wounds with every act of compassion,
with every loving, kind action.
It is a law of human nature,
as sure as a law of physics or a law of chemistry.
Compassion, love, kindness, end suffering.
For the sake of those we mourn today, for our own sakes,
for the sake of the children,
the generations that come after us, be compassionate.
Be loving. Be kind.

*Maxine Hong Kingston wrote to the editor, "While I just cannot
write a new response, I can offer notes for the memorial service I
helped give at U.C. Berkeley. I think they would be appropriate for
your book. 12,000 of the Cal community were there—at the windows,
on the balconies, on the green-grass knolls."

STEVE KOWIT

The Equation

10/19/01

Heard you were doing an anthology. Realize you must be getting dizzy with the thousands of poems being submitted. Well, here's one more. With friendship,

STEVE KOWIT

THE EQUATION

Horrific towers of smoke, & those belching flames—
like nothing so much as Hanoi in that first
haze of rubble. That rain of corpses
not unlike the storm of unending death
we vomited up over Quang Ngai; or Pyongyang,
after Walker's 8th Army got through with the place.
Or Beirut, after Haig gave the nod to Sharon
and the Christian Phalange was let loose
on the refugee camps. Or the tortured corpses
America's client army planted all over Managua,
or the ones that we engineered for Pinochet's Chile,
though fewer by far than the slaughter
that Kissinger's White House unleashed on East Timor.

And always the same bloody equation: *Our lives
count; theirs are of no consequence whatsoever.*

Now the Trade Center's gone.

Who'd have believed it? The air thick
with some sort of festering stench
as the innocent dead are stuffed into bags,
and old Glory unfurls in the breeze.

Good Lord, what a fog
of feculent speeches! What a ghoulish intoxication!
When the eagle, that bird of prey, sharpens her claws
everyone knows what it means:
a lust to spill somebody's blood.
Whose, at this point, doesn't much matter.
No doubt the Iraqis will pay; the Afghans are toast.
Collateral damage, indeed: they're gonna be blown
away by the tens of thousands. Guilty or not,
it's gonna be open season.
The Ozymandian people are already waving their flags.
Nationwide polls have shown
that it holds, no less today
than a thousand years in the past—
the ancient tribal equation:

the massacre of a few hundred thousand
innocent souls will not cause more
than the shrug of an indifferent shoulder,
a rhetorical sigh or two of regret—
just so long, of course,
as the mangled dead aren't our own.

10/20/01

Steve,

*I've been given as much space by the publisher as the book takes, and the
more contributors the merrier. I'd like you to be part of the book, but, as it
stands, to me, "The Equation" is sort of a messy poem (and never mind
that affective fallacy stuff about its being about a messy situation, so has
to be disjointed itself—not that you've laid this on me). Look, I retired from
teaching a year ago, have no academic axes to sharpen (I guess, though,
what is engrained in us now comes to be engrained in us over the years),
and don't want to pontificate, but I think your poem could be strong and
good for the anthology if it got harder, surer, in places less obvious. Man,
I'd like to use it just for that brilliant "The Ozymandian people are already
waving their flags."... The first line is all cliché. Something simpler would
be better: "The burning towers—nothing so much as like Hanoi / in that*

first haze of rubble. That rain of corpses," etc.... Anyway, if you can get
some shape, some sound's shape into your poem, I'd like to read it again.
The ending is too obvious. I want the poem to convince me of its truths,
whatever the Truth is, as poems must. I don't argue with your arguments,
but things said are things as said, and this is what I'm looking for. Some
call it individual voice. This voice makes meanings beyond itself. Control
the passion here into a kickass poem. You don't make me believe that the
massacre of a few hundred thousand innocent souls will not cause more
than the shrug of an indifferent shoulder. The fact is, isn't it, that we are
trying NOT to kill hundreds of thousands? But, in any case, the poem, in
its bald declarations here and there, does not convince. Sing it with fire.
And remember, as Pound said of the poetry of the new century he looked
forward to, he wanted it free from emotional slither—harder, clearer,
nearer to the bone. Forgive my opinions, or don't. Pressure the poem some.
Come back at me, if you like. Oh, and I'd be glad to see some prose, even a
paragraph or three, accompany any poem....
Bill

10/20/01

Bill,

Thanks for the comments. I'm not enamored of my poem & don't
have any interest in defending its aesthetic worth. But the equation
is accurate, though everyone needs to deny it. There was no hyperbole. Today, as we speak, tens of thousands of innocent poor people
have already fled their homes, there will be hundreds of thousands if
not millions more, in Afghanistan, and those who survive are going
to be living in tents thru the winter (if Pakistan lets them into their
country). Many will not survive the winter. & the American people
will find the fact of minimal interest & will quickly find bin Laden or
someone else to blame. That we will try to rush food to them as they
die in those tents is nauseating hypocrisy. That night & day bombing
raids will terrorize the population should be evident to a nation that
has just been utterly traumatized into war-hysteria by a single
bombing attack over New York. But people don't make connections.
What poor powers of empathy our species has! Hundreds of civilians
have been killed in our attacks (Rumsfeld's flaccid denials notwithstanding) which are only in their second week, & probably many
more thousands of Afghanistan soldiers are dead. These too are
innocent people. I repeat this fact because we tend to divide the
Other into innocent civilians (about whom we care very little) &
soldiers (who are utterly expendable). Many are conscripts but even
those who are there of their own will (often to feed themselves &
their family) had nothing whatsoever to do with the NY bombing.

These are innocent victims of America's war of vengeance against the people of Afghanistan. Is there much of an outcry? Is there any public outcry? No. We get denials from Rumsfeld et al. in Washington & stone indifference from the compassionate American public. The relief agencies say hundreds of thousands, if not millions, are likely to starve directly because of the American terrorist war. Is the American public the least bit upset? No, they are delighted that tiny amounts of food are being dropped by our heroic air force, much of it food that is inedible by Muslims. Proof of our big hearts. That is public relations, obscene public relations, & the American public loves it. We killed upwards of one million civilians in our Korean debacle, much of it with napalm, & there has never been an outcry. In fact, barely any Americans know to this day why the war was fought. We still have troops there to make sure the vicious North Korean devils don't attack the south. It is a central reason why we don't sign the land mine treaty—America the compassionate indeed! The outcry over Vietnam was precipitated by the fact that we were losing the war & after years had no sense it was winnable. The vast numbers murdered (again something approximating a million civilians) was never of much concern to the general public—except when it was their sons! Which is precisely the equation. That sort of thing—the murder of a few million "enemy"—is always justified with a shrug of the shoulder. That is how human tribes function. The Other really doesn't count, his life really isn't of the slightest importance, several hundred thousand innocent civilians exterminated by Indonesia in East Timor after getting the green light from Kissinger on December 7, 1975—almost the whole Chinese population because they supported the popular FRETILIN government—went all but unnoticed by the American press. & I suspect 98% of the American public still has no idea that Indonesia invaded, & encouraged by Kissinger & Ford (who had flown out of Indonesia the previous day after meeting with the Indonesian junta) slaughtered hundreds of thousands of civilians. Yes, the equation is absolutely true, a rather obvious perception if one has one's eyes open. The Other simply doesn't really exist. Did you know that on September 11, 1973 a US engineered coup (directed by Nixon's White House) toppled the Allende democracy & installed the brutal pro-US Pinochet dictatorship? September 11. Day of American terrorist infamy against the Chilean people. It hardly needs saying that we have no interest in extirpating terrorism when it's our own terrorism against unfriendly democracies, whether Allende or Moosadegh in Iran. Surely neither Sharon nor our boys in the White House would avoid the hangman if terrorism were tried by an international war crimes court (the kind the US is desperate to insure we never have.) And our slaughter of the Afghanistan people today, as I write, is proof, if any was needed, that the equation holds. The overwhelming majority of Americans "support the war" as they always will & always have—just as the Good Germans supported the Third Reich. The death of the Other doesn't count! The equation holds. The day after the September 11 attack, Democratic Senator Zell Miller of Georgia declared, "I say, bomb the hell out of them. If there's collateral damage, so be it." Most Americans still believe that Bush's father tried to avoid collateral damage in Iraq. In fact, we wiped out the entire domestic infra-structure of the nation—utterly unnecessary—power plants, sewer treatment facilities—& purposely & purposefully terrorized the civilian population to destabilize the regime. Then we continued bombing for eleven years—to the present day—while keeping sanc-tions in place that UNICEF estimates have killed over a million peo-ple, half of them children under five. (When Clinton lobbed in Cruise missiles in 1992, several hit a residential area as is, of course, inevitable, Rumsfeld & the other pinheads notwithstanding, & Leila al-Attar, one of Iraq's greatest living artists, was killed!) Have you heard much outrage from the compassionate American public about the vast slaughter in Iraq caused directly by our inane sanctions? No. The rationalization is that evil Saddam is responsible for the deaths, not compassionate America. Those sanctions against Iraq, which the rest of the world wants to see ended, include, needless to say, mostly medical supplies. No less to the point—since it's the central reason for the hatred of the U.S. in the Middle East—the Palestinian people do not really exist for the American consciousness, & are not quite human enough to care about. That 100% of their land was stolen by the beloved Israelis still matters not a bit to the American public, which has been taught that the word Palestinian goes with the word terrorist. Not that their homeland was stolen—purposefully—by a nation that has always (from the earliest Zionist days of Chaim Weitzmann & David Ben Gurion) been trying to engineer the trans-fer of the Arab population. (All this, by the way, is easy to document. I am not speaking theory or speculation but hard fact.) The expulsion of 700,000 Palestinians from their homes & farms in 1948 so that Israel could steal their land is still a traumatic wound (al-Nakbar, the Disaster), but the American people know nothing of it ... anymore than they care to know what Israel has done to the Palestinian people since. For the Palestinians are the Other; the Israeli Jews are our own! Ah, but in America this is a taboo subject! It is tantamount to anti-Semitism to tell these truths.... (The truly heroic Israeli peace movement, Gush Shalom & Bat Shalom, among others, has been saying these things for years & are public enemies in Israel & are

never spoken of in the U.S. press.) No, the equation holds. It was not an exaggeration. It was not hyperbole. It's the way tribes behave and think. The Other is outside the circle of compassion.... A little tsk tsking to salve one's conscience (& that, perhaps, only necessary among the intelligentsia) is all that's needed. We are in the process of slaughtering hundreds of thousands of innocent Afghan people. Very few Americans care. A shrug of the shoulder is all the slaughter of hundreds of thousands will get unless they're our own. The equation holds.................. None of this has anything to do with the poem, which I suspect, is not yet terribly well made. I will take your comments seriously since criticism usually helps get a poem better. Many thanks for taking the time. Good luck with the anthology.....
Steve

10/20/01

Steve,

Your letter knocked me over. I propose this, and hope it will be okay with you: I'd like to publish your poem exactly as it is, then my letter to you (which deals with aesthetics, mainly, though I do fly the idea that we are not trying, purposely and purposefully, as you testify, to kill hundreds of thousands) and then publish your passionate almost raving letter. Because of your refrain—"the equation holds"—and other elements of power, it's what I want for the book. You sent a poem. I replied. You typed a letter back to me by way of brain and heart fused in rhythms. I admire the sheer power of voice that carries your letter along, unstudied, cataclysmic in its passion, convincing, worth our reading several times and then finding things out from there. If you're willing, I'll type the whole exchange up and send it to you for your okay. Steve, this is the honest wildness that the book will need. I hope you'll agree....
Bill

10/20/01

Bill,

Yes, of course. I'll be delighted. Please correct any spelling or egregious punctuation errors in my letter. It was done quickly & not carefully proofread. My address is Steve Kowit, PO Box 184, Potrero, CA. 91963.... I'd love to see your book about the Gulf War.... From what I've read, Saddam sent the U.S. three inquiries about his plans to invade, to all three of which the U.S. responded that we would remain neutral. So one thought I've seen expressed is that he was purposely set up. With friendship,
Steve

Bill,

I still never see or hear any estimates of the Afghanistan dead in the media. It's a non-fact & therefore a non-issue. No one asks, no one seems to give a damn. Nor is it often (if ever) pointed out that the tens or hundreds of thousands killed are entirely innocent of the Trade Tower bombing: that to avenge the death of 3500 innocent people in New York & DC we have slaughtered tens of thousands if not hundreds of thousands of innocent people.... But of course they are hardly real humans; their agony is rarely shown on CNN, and then only with disclaimers & in a context that assures the peace-loving American that we had no options, it's the fault of bin Laden, it's all accidental, we don't want to hurt a soul. Rather, what's shown are the jubilant celebrants at their liberation (into the hands of the hated & feared Northern Alliance ... out of the frying pan...). Yesterday, Congress voted down America's participation in the new International War Crimes Tribunal. Not surprisingly, we want nothing to do with such a body unless U.S. troops & politicians get immunity.... America should be thankful that God is not just. Trust this finds you well,

Steve

NORBERT KRAPF

Three Paumanok Pieces

I (OPEN LETTER)

When I sent a message to anxious family and friends here and
abroad, after the terrorist attack of September 11, 2001, I told them
that my family and I were OK. After giving some frightening details
of what the day had been like here on Long Island, some twenty-five
miles from the scene of unbelievable devastation, I was moved to
conclude, in all candor, that "one of the most unforgettable images
was of Palestinians dancing and singing in the streets of their West
Bank settlements." An English writer and a German professor of
American literature, friends from years of living abroad with my
family, both lectured me on this remark. While they were grateful
that we were not harmed, they implied that I did not understand, do
not appreciate the history of those who sang and danced.

It must be made clear that I sympathize with the Palestinian people
for losing their homeland and being discriminated against in
various ways, some by my government; but for any human being, no
matter what his or her history of oppression, to dance and celebrate
when the lives of innocent human beings are cruelly taken reduces
the humanity of the dancer, at the moment of the dance, to zero. Who
can indeed separate the dancer from the dance? as a great Irish poet
once asked. Who walks a furlong without sympathy walks to his
funeral dressed in a shroud, says America's greatest poet. But
Whitman was not talking about sympathizing with those who gloat
over mass murder.

My European friends were reacting with their heads. Their words expressed sympathy for the victims, but their hearts did not fully participate in that expression. Head without enough heart can make a language sound unfulfilled; the ultimate fulfillment for a language is to be driven by head and heart in balance. My friends may have wondered why I did not respond. I had neither the psychic resources nor the desire to enter into a dialogue with them once they revealed that they stood several removes from the tragedy and were not my brothers in grief. Their language of the intellect was not connected to heart, blood, breath, except in an abstract way.

The first weekend after the attack the English writer, now traveling in another country, sent a sarcastic message about the President's "Dead or Alive" remark and wanted to know who his speech writer is. That Wild-West poster proclamation is not the kind of language I would have used, and I hope to the God in whom I believe that I would not be so insensitive and inflammatory as to call for another "crusade." I would like my language to be more temperate, even though my heart may at times strain in the opposite direction. As a great English poet observed, heart (gale) needs head (map) to balance the ship and enable it to sail forward.

"I don't know anything about speechwriters," I replied to my English friend's query, "but right now I am beyond such trivialities. We have just returned from the funeral of the son of a friend. Peter was to be married in a few weeks. Instead of his wedding, we attended his funeral." In the hour of such profound grief, when the obligation to express one's sympathy to parents was impossible to fulfill without deepening their pain, the appearance of the term "speechwriter" on my monitor left a foul taste in my mouth and a cramp in my stomach. Who would provide a speechwriter to speak to the families of the forty lost in Manhasset, where my wife teaches, or the hundred in Garden City, ten minutes to the south?

Less than forty-eight hours before the funeral, my wife and I walked down the street, candles in hand, to the local firehouse for a service in honor of the Langone brothers of Roslyn Heights, Long Island. One was a fireman, one was a policeman. One was finishing the night shift, the other beginning the day shift. Tell me how the intellect justifies their meeting in death, their anonymous execution! Tell me, my European friends, how to make whole the heart of their mother? Who will help her find the balance to walk forward? Who will deliver to her the lecture or sermon about the need to forget—to not remember—the sight of people dancing and singing in the streets over the hard fact that her boys will not come home again?

Some of the most vociferous singers of glee in that rocky street were mothers. Perhaps we should indeed turn our eyes from the sight of their dance, and force ourselves to concentrate on whatever oppression and loss may have generated such a passionate response. Would my European friends like to explain this to Mrs. Langone? Perhaps the brothers were helping the wrong people at the wrong place at the wrong time at the wrong end of a long history?

I heard a priest of my religion deliver a sermon to the mother and father, whose son, and the sister, whose brother, was to have married in a few weeks. The priest's rhetoric and rising voice, the logic of his argument, and the energy of his gestures were unable to assuage the rippling grief of those who sat listening. We were respectful and polite, but not won over. The tearful but spirited reminiscences of the lost son's sister and best friend spoke to us more whole-heartedly, convincingly, eloquently.

The only song now is lamentation. The only dance is done on the torn flesh and shattered bone of the innocent dead whose spirit shall live, rise above the lingering smoke, and help us heal.

II (ELEGY)

for Connie & Peter Frank
(22 September 2001)

To hug a mother
who has lost a son
just when he was to marry

is to feel salty grief
well up warm & trembling
from the depths
of an underground source
& break against you
in waves that repeat

is to hear a sob
that comes from beyond
where you stand in the sun
outside the church
in which a priest

searched for the language
equal to the depths
of a mother's loss

but could not connect
the volume of his words
with the power of her pain

is to wonder how & why
you could find yourself
in bright sunlight under
blue sky huddling with
friends & family in the dark.

To hug a mother
who has lost a son
just when she expected
to gain another daughter

is to feel how lucky
we are that our sons
& daughters by some
act of fate we do not
comprehend continue
to draw breath

is to make us hold
our breath for her
whose grief moves
us to find the voice
to say our sorrow

is to feel her summon
the strength to invite us
to sit around the table
with her & the father

to exchange the words
& share the bread
that help us rise
together to our feet
& put down one   ·
foot after another.

Come back, Walt Whitman, we need you now in the hour of our
    grief.
Come back, Camerado, wind your way back to Ground Zero where
    you belong.
Wrap your arm around the shoulder of a fireman who lost his best
    friend,
tell the policemen how brave were their fellows at the moment of
    collapse,
rub your fingers between the ears of the dog that has sniffed hour
    after hour
for the smell of human flesh,
stand at attention when workers find in the rubble the body of a
    brother,
amble over to the Armory and say a word to long lines of those with
pictures of loved ones pinned to their chests,
tell the husband how beautiful and good his missing wife is,
tell the wife how courageous her husband was to help his col-
    leagues,
promise the sister you will hunt with her for her lost brother just as
    you hunted
for your own brother George at Fredericksburg,
hold steady the mother and father who lost their son weeks before
    he was to marry,
hug the student from Queens who, after her class in the suburbs,
    rode your word-ferry across time and space, sobbed to her
    teacher how they had found the body of her firefighter,
comfort the family of the Brooklyn student who came to this coun-
    try from Syria for asylum and will now return home only in
    spirit,
guide to sanctuary the refugees who, clothed in ash and ghostly
    powder, hobbled across Brooklyn Bridge toward your old
    haunts,
you who know so well the underbelly of this city and the pulse of her
    people.

Come back to smoking Manahatta, Father Walt, where you walked
    the streets
with immigrants from many lands and rode the omnibus and lis-
    tened to Italian opera
and American folk songs and applauded the singer and ferried back
    to Brooklyn,
convince us the lilac will blossom again and release its fragrance
    into the air,

help us believe the mockingbird will trill and caper and the hermit
    thrush sing
and children will smile, shout and play in these streets and parks
    again.

Come back, implore the wounded moon to pour her mysterious
    ministrations on us,
petition the splendid silent sun to come out and shine long while
    wounds heal,
teach us a language that rises into prayer as we lift one another,
help us not to fear our grief as we remember the thousands lost,
look over us as we read the poem-prayers that inform our resolve
to become larger than before, open-hearted, strong, wise, patient,
keep waiting for us in the grass that grows beneath our boot-soles.

NANCY KUHL

Some Thoughts on the Unthinkable

> *One of the extraordinary things about human events*
> *is that the unthinkable becomes thinkable.*
> — SALMAN RUSHDIE

1.

It is November, but it's seventy two degrees outside and I am wearing short sleeves. I have been sitting in the grass among fallen
leaves, because though it has, for weeks, been warm as spring, it is
autumn. There is an Air Force base to the south of the town where I
live and periodically, for some time now, what look like military supply planes pass over my house. They are huge grumbling machines,
slow moving, big bellied. Less than two months ago the World Trade
Center was demolished by terrorist attacks. I am 29, about to turn
30. I was born the year after the World Trade Center was completed.

2.

According to the *Encyclopedia Britannica*, the construction of the
twin towers was completed in 1970. PBS's *Wonders of the World* data-
bank says that construction on Tower One was completed in 1972 and
on Tower Two in 1973. I prefer *Britannica's* story. Yamasaki Minoru,
the architect who designed the towers, also designed the Torre
Picasso, the tallest building in Madrid. The towers were about three
times taller than the Torre Picasso's height of 515 feet. I grew up in a
part of New Jersey where the New York City skyline is visible from
certain hilltops.

3.

One friend who worked in the north tower of the World Trade Center was a few minutes late to work on September 11th, and he was walking up to the building when it was struck by a passenger jet. Another friend was at her desk on the twenty-fifth floor of a building three blocks away from the towers when she noticed that the air outside her window was filled with paper—white office paper, memos, carbon paper forms, sheets from yellow legal pads, and unspooled rolls from adding machines—all of it caught spinning in an updraft. She walked home to Brooklyn, stopping along the way, with others who were displaced by the attacks, to crowd around the open doors of parked cars and listen to the news reports sounding from their radios.

4.

The first hijacked airplane was American Airlines Flight 11, Boston to L.A. There were 92 people on board. I don't know if this number includes the hijackers. We assume those aboard who were alive when the crash occurred were killed upon impact. True or not. Many in the north tower must have also been killed immediately. We assume that some of the dead did not suffer.

5.

"How are you?" a friend asks. I say, "I am at loose ends" by which I mean: I am uncertain, uncomfortable, disoriented, afraid; I am nauseated, anxious; I am bereft, filled with grief; I am sleepless; I am confused, paralyzed, utterly bewildered. The word *bewilder* is from a root meaning to *lead one astray* as though I was following mistaken directions in this small town—take South Pleasant to Maple Street—and found myself lost.

6.

Some numbers are fixed, some are in flux: 343 firefighters, 23 police officers, 37 Port Authority officers; 21,800 windows in each tower; at the Pentagon, 125 workers and service members; from the towers, as many as 4,979 as few as 2,573; 44 aboard Flight 93, 64 aboard Flight 77, and on Flight 175, 2 pilots, 7 flight attendants and 56 passengers; the towers' completion date—70 or 72 or 73. Some numbers are a kind of unfinished business, marks of progress or withdrawal: in the first week, about 2000 trades people including ironworkers, teamsters, and laborers worked 12 hour shifts at the site of the towers; union scale is between $20 to $40 an hour; an estimated 1.2 tons of debris must be moved from the site; the first U.S. military action, on October 7, was the launching of about 50 cruise missiles from ships and submarines; some 43,600 U.S. military reservists have been called to duty; well more than one million Afghans have been displaced since September, becoming refugees; during carpet bombing missions, planes might drop as many as 20 bombs at a time; the Afghanistan/Tajikistan border is guarded by about 10,000 Russian troops who are there to prevent Afghan refugees, more than 10,000 of whom are camped along the border, from entering; the BLU-82 is a 15,000 pound bomb.

7.
A man who worked in New York, but nowhere near the World Trade Center, vanished on the day of the terrorist attacks. His wife doesn't know if he was there for some reason he didn't mention to her or his co-workers, or if his disappearance is unrelated to the attacks. She will likely never know. You've heard this one, too? It is, perhaps, a new urban legend. There will be other stories like this; there will always be stories like this.

8.
Passenger elevators didn't come into wide use until the middle of the nineteenth century when Elisha Graves Otis invented a device that prevented elevator cars from falling, even when their main hoist rope failed. To demonstrate his device at the Crystal Palace Exposition in New York, Otis, himself, rode his elevator high into the air above what must have been unbelieving crowds and ordered the hoist rope cut. Not long after, the first ever passenger elevator was installed in a New York City department store. It traveled five stories in less than a minute. It was 1857. And the sky was opened. Skyscrapers went up and up and up, floor by floor and story by story.

There were 104 elevators in each of the World Trade Center towers. Traveling 110 stories to reach each building's top, we'd become dizzy and lightheaded.

9.
We climb into blue-white air until we are breathless and undone.

KELLY LEVAN

Dragons and Sharks

I live about fifty American yards from Logan airport. From my four-by-six foot deck on top of the back porch of the apartment below mine, I can watch the hotel buses, rental cars, and taxis rounding the corner toward the terminals. I can make out the control tower with its shrunken head and five erect air vents, gleaming like nickels over the harbor. I can see airplanes coming and going, flying toward and away from the city in rows; on a clear day, I can see seven easy, before the point where my eyes give up.

When the planes are close, they are loud as dragons breathing. Whenever I am awake and home, I hear them above the pounding of the construction crew on the corner and the piercing tirade of the mother next door. I hear the dragons flapping their taut wings and arching their tails, spreading their great nostrils wide as city blocks. Blinking against the Atlantic wind and the cold, high sun.

After the September 11th attacks, Logan, like other airports across the U.S., closed; snorting and sparking, thrashing against the ropes, the dragons were reined in. I heard about this on TV before I noticed. I watched the towers fall again and again and my living room roared with the numbers: how many missing, how many running, how many flying in the dust. And I, too, was grounded under this huge sky, looking up without my dragons, without my myths.

September 12th, I started early, took Zooker, my dog;

The First Day Without Airplanes

In front of me, my dog's wet nose
planted in weeds and cans,
his black tail swinging
to the beat of his hips.

Beneath four floors of families
rising behind bare open windows,
a skunk, belly to gummy ground,
bouncing slightly on marble feet.

And through the fence, beyond
honest warnings of tire damage,
the airport, its rapid men and tow trucks
new under pindrop blue.

Absolute silence, no—a fighter jet would orbit by my porch every so
often, both a reassurance and a reminder that Boston has lots of tall
buildings.

***

My best friend lives in New York City. I have bobbed along the
mounds of crowds with her, obeying the mark of manic heels. I
have been to MOMA and the Matisses, Warhols, *Les Demoiselles
d'Avignon*, a giant floppy floor fan constructed of vinyl couch. I must
have glanced at the World Trade Center. I don't remember. I've
spent one weekend in Manhattan, mostly eating and running
between restaurants.

The Requiem Sharks

Oh Wally the last time
(written in brick letters,
scattered with gum and tourists)
your giraffe brown eyes
opened,
city in their pupils,
city in the whites,
I stuck my spoon

in your shoulder
and you stuck your butter knife
in my clavicle
and we both cried
under the smooth hound's-tooth
streetwear we were
accustomed to,
and nobody could see us,
even as the street filled with water and dogfish
and old worn-out memories of better food.

Next time I visit, the waitress might stand over six feet tall, barefoot. Maybe she will forget to check my license when I order the *vino veritas*. Maybe she'll want to see my national ID card, or scan my retina with something that only looks like a pen. I doubt it. I hope not. I hope everything is exactly the same: "Wally" and I will drink some $14 bottle while the waitress leans on the bar, talking with her friends, waiting for us to leave her tip on the sunlit table. I want the NY I'm accustomed to, and I fear that if anything is different, if the wine tastes funny, I might blame the sharks.

But I can't let my friend drink bad wine alone; I will go back. And besides, I have an idea in the works:

To the Towers

If I knew
how to
hold each
pebble

put them
one per pocket
'till I filled
my own

and yours,
there would be
just as many
rocks

as pockets
and we
would feel
sure

passing
on the streets
that we could
see Your

Heart.

I would like to see the towers in pockets of people riding the subways and standing by bus stops. We carry them right now, every day, but I can't see the edges, poking out at acute angles. If we each kept a piece, we could reconstruct the buildings, spreading them out from shirt to shirt along the city, along the country. Nobody could break our mortar.

In Samuel Beckett's *Molloy*, the narrator carries several like-shaped pebbles in his clothes. He spends a few pages rotating the rocks from pocket to pocket, trying, I think, to create a sort of chain: a pebble from his shirt pocket goes to his left pants pocket, a pebble from the left pants moves on to the right pants, etc. He has his system down perfect—then he realizes he may just be sending the same one pebble around and around while the others lie dormant and still. It tortures him. I don't understand why Molloy needs to revolve his pebbles this way, but I wonder if we could do it, we Americans. I could take my piece of the towers and give it to you. You could hand your piece to Wally. Wally shares her piece with our waitress, who hands off to a dogfish, who gives a pilot at Logan Airport his pebble, who carefully gives one to a dragon. Dragons have pockets. Of course they do. And this way, instead of a piece, we carry the towers, both of them, all of us. Shifting, all the time.

CLAUDE LIMAN

A View from Canada

I was out on a morning run on September 11 to train for the upcom-
ing cross-country ski season when a winter friend pulled up in his
car to tease me about how slow I was going. Suddenly he frowned at
his radio and said that a plane had just hit the World Trade Center in
New York.

I looked east and south from this hill-top in Thunder Bay, Ontario,
200 miles north of Duluth, to the homeland I'd left thirty years ago.
I'd grown up outside New York City in Westchester County, had
worked in mid-town Manhattan, lived in Greenwich Village. Over
the past three decades I'd often reached my old landscape by imagi-
natively stowing myself aboard grain ships leaving Thunder Bay,
crossing Lake Superior in slow-motion nostalgia and traveling the
whole St. Lawrence Seaway. Now, with the new urgency of worry, I
diagonally vaulted the industrial sprawl below me, leaped the
Nor'wester Mountains on the valley rim and crossed 1500 intervening miles of Minnesota, Wisconsin, Michigan, Ohio, and New York.
Somehow, I expected to see smoke billowing up from the distant
disaster.

I ran home, turned on my t.v. and saw the second plane hit.

September 11 was the anniversary of my first marriage. I had recently left wife number two and was feeling sort of shaky even before the
crash. Maybe we process these big, national catastrophes by means
of smaller, personal parallels?

I'd come to Canada in 1973 to teach American Literature and

Creative Writing. I had not fled north to avoid the Vietnam draft, though many people on both sides of the border read political motives into my career move. I was a Landed Immigrant in Canada, a complex patriot with an oblique view of my old homeland.

In my boyhood I'd rooted for the Yankees and attended many games in the Bronx with my father. It seemed entirely right that these Yankees of the 1949–56 era always won, for they were the best team (Dimaggio, Mantle, Berra), and they were also MY team. How could anyone be a Dodger fan or hate heroes in pin-stripes?

Now I, too, hate the Steinbrenner Yankees and wonder how I ever liked these arrogant, smug, self-assured bullies. Over the years the Seinfeld version of the Yankee boss has come to seem more like truth than satire to me. I brought my underdog Toronto Blue Jays home to two successive World Series wins in 1992 and 93.

My first reaction to September 11 was guilt: I should have been there. In 1970 I stayed in Colorado when my father almost died in Manhattan on the brain surgeon's table, but now I know that one heads home in family crises. But where *was* home, who *was* family?

Later that day, hiking on the Sibley Peninsula, 50 miles by car around the bay from my city but only 9 miles across by water, I felt guilty for being out of danger. Thunder Bay is such a backwater, definitely not the Big Apple. Climbing to the chest of the Sleeping Giant, a rock formation about the same distance above Lake Superior as the World Trade Center used to rise over the Hudson, I imagined planes banking from their approach to our city's airport and droning right for me. Unimaginable!

High on my glacier-scraped ledge of pre-cambrian granite, pawing at a few late-season flies, I suddenly thought of King Kong in the 1933 black and white version. He carefully puts Fay Wray down on the spire of the Empire State Building so that he can do battle with the airplanes, little buzzing toys, mosquitoes, that eventually sting him fatally. When he falls over the edge, he hits ledge after ledge all the way down.

In the September 11, 2001, scenario, the graceful Empire State Building becomes the monolithic Twin Towers, while single-engine planes mutate into jumbo 767s. Kong himself no longer appears on screen. No doubt the 18 Muslim fundamentalists at the controls of the four suicide-mission planes cast themselves as Kong: the healthy, uncorrupted spirit of mankind engaged in necessary battle with the cruel forces of the modern industrial state.

I am not a traitor: I do not believe that bin Laden and the Muslim world are innocent or right. Their attack on the World Trade Center was cowardly. However, the west has always been guilty of trespassing beyond the log palisades of various native cultures to capture valuable commodities for exportation home. We should at least understand why some of these ravaged cultures do not cheer for self-serving heroes in pin-stripes.

I cannot imagine how Americans feel now that the enemy has reached them in such a stronghold as Manhattan and threatens them everywhere else. I lack the imagination to feel what this new vulnerability is like because, here in Canada, I still feel personally safe, even if frequently bored.

I envy the stimulation Americans have received from this trauma. The U.S. is a better, less arrogant, more united country now that people are talking, sharing; now that the eagle flies during the national anthem and opera stars belt out "God Bless America" at the seventh-inning stretch. The Yankees will probably win this current World Series for their city and country. As I write this, they've come from behind the last two games to take a 3–2 lead over Arizona. Even Dodger fans may be pulling for them.

ANN LOLORDO

View Interrupted

from the land

there is light, more of it
though gray and ashen, plumes
filling the cathedral of the air
now a canyon, negative exposure,
twin shadows replaced by light
no fixed address, this way and that
easy to lose your bearings, at canal
and sixth, a view clear south to the river

from the sea

boarding the ferry, Wall Street
bound, suits at the rail, gulls circling
in the haze, their cries overtake
the roar of engines, a droning engine;
on approach not a word, to a man
not a word, uninterrupted view
interrupted, in the glare
of the sun, the Empire State
Building is what you see

from the air

a smoldering heap, the color
or ash, timbers of steel, debris
piled high, remains of the day
everlasting, the eye catches on a crane
draped in red, a tall building red
roofed, to the east green leafy tree tops
at the edge, a marble blue river
and the long, white wake of a ferry

JAMES LONGENBACH

A Reason for Keeping Silent?

On September 17, 2001 the German composer Karlheinz Stockhausen called the attack on the World Trade Center "the greatest work of art imaginable for the whole cosmos."

Jump back eighty-seven years. Britain declared war on Germany on August 4, 1914. The first war-poem appeared in the *London Times* the following morning—long before a shot was fired.

> Hast thou counted up the cost,
> > what to foeman, what to friend?
> Glory sought is Honour lost,
> > How should this be knighthood's end?
> Know'st thou what is Hatred's meed?
> What the surest gain of Greed?

The compulsion to speak. The recognition of impending horror mixed inevitably with the satisfaction of having something to say. Henry Newbolt's poem was the first of many, and within a few months Edith Wharton began organizing the publication of *The Book of the Homeless*, an anthology of responses to what quickly became known as the Great War. On February 6, 1915 William Butler Yeats wrote "A Reason for Keeping Silent," the six-line poem that would be his contribution:

> I think it better that at times like these
> We poets keep our mouths shut, for in truth
> We have no gift to set a statesman right.

The impulse to stand back. The recognition that anything said in the face of catastrophe can too easily seem pointless or, worse, like preening. Of course Yeats was no stranger to catastrophe, and neither was he unwilling to speak out. Recent poems such as "September 1913" had already recorded strong feelings about the fate of Irish nationalism. And after the quickly aborted Easter Rebellion of 1916 Yeats would no longer be recommending silence: "You say that we should still the land / Till Germany's overcome; / But who is there to argue that / Now Pearse is deaf and dumb?"

I have read these poems for years, taught them, admired them, argued with them. After September 11, 2001, much of what I'd thought about these poems seemed to me inadequately felt. The reasons for not wanting to be Henry Newbolt—the mediocre poet who is confident he has something to say—had always seemed clear to me. The reasons for keeping one's mouth shut—for emulating the caution of a poet who was in other circumstances often noted for his recklessness—seemed equally compelling. What I had never felt before was the collapse of all distance between personal sentiment and public grief. I had not felt sympathy for Henry Newbolt. Surely Yeats would not have written "A Reason for Keeping Silent" if a great many Newbolts had not been willing to speak out; the *Times* received as many as a hundred poems a day throughout the month of August 1914. And while many of those now forgotten war-poems were hard to swallow, it's only in their context that Yeats's little poem feels risky.

Art traffics in risk. We need to feel a poet courting the edge, and if we do not feel the pressure of what is at stake in keeping silent, then silence may seem glib. Karlheinz Stockhausen, born in 1928, has been making notoriously risky music for decades. I remember watching the pianist Maurizio Pollini return to the stage of Carnegie Hall, having shed his tuxedo coat in order to play the forearm tone-clusters of *Klavierstück IX*; no recording does justice to the variety of sonorities this work of breathtaking seriousness provokes from a piano. But lately, if we hear anything about Stockhausen, we hear that he appeared along with W. C. Fields and Bob Dylan on the cover of *Sgt. Pepper's Lonely Heart's Club Band*; we hear that his *Helikopter-Streichquartett* is scored for four instrumentalists playing in four helicopters, their presence transmitted to the auditorium via loud-speakers and screens.

On September 17, 2001, while this quixotic, ambitious composer was talking about the presence of angelic and satanic energies in art, the radio interviewer shifted the conversation to the World Trade Center bombing. Stockhausen has subsequently maintained (and transcripts of the interview confirm) that by referring to the bombing as "the greatest work of art imaginable for the whole cosmos" he was speaking of the darkest side of human creativity, not necessarily about art as such.

The sleeplessness of regret. The knowledge that what's been said can never be taken back, never be explained to anyone's complete satisfaction.

> All that I have said and done,
> Now that I am old and ill,
> Turns into a question till
> I lie awake night after night
> And never get the answers right.

Stockhausen's comment has been universally condemned; performances of his work have been cancelled around the globe. "Not for one moment have I thought or felt the way my words are now being interpreted in the press," Stockhausen has said, but his reputation may never be freed from this notoriety—no matter how clearly his words are contextualized, no matter how often he might explain that aesthetic ambition has always seemed at least potentially sinister. Yeats came to a similar conclusion in "Easter 1916" when he spoke out about the Irish revolutionaries who blew up the Dublin post office and declared a republic: "A terrible beauty is born."

In retrospect, it seems fair to say that Stockhausen's remarks were not just open to misunderstanding but (under the circumstances) showily provocative. Should he have kept his mouth shut? Other remarks have been made, and the desire to erase them, strike them from the record, has been equally intense. On September 26, 2001, speaking in response to comments offered by the host of the late-night talk show *Politically Incorrect*, the White House press secretary said ominously that in times like these "people have to watch what they say and what they do." Later, when the White House released the official transcript of this briefing, the remark was missing. A "transcription error" is what an assistant to the press secretary called this lapse, this wish to have kept silent.

ADRIAN C. LOUIS

Liberty Street
Marshall, MN (9-30-01)

She wore strange
spiked hair, but
her intent was clear.
She was walking it.
She was out walking
her pussy like some
strange dog on a leash.
It was pushed out
and leading her
down the sidewalk.
It was a big one.
Her tight, white slacks
held the beast in bay.
Flags were shuddering
on every street corner.

When she caught me
gawking, she halted,
put her hands on hips
and stared me down.
I turned my eyes from
her scornful frown,
pushed the sour fear
back down my throat
and drove deeper
into our shivering
heartland. That night
I bought a flag and
blended in with
the other sheep.

PAUL MARIANI

The Face of Terror

Eleven weeks since the attacks and still trying to make sense of what happened that day. A Tuesday, my wife Eileen's sixtieth birthday. We'd just returned from the Big Apple the day before. We'd been to see *Proof* on Broadway, visited the new Hayden Planetarium, where in a darkened room we'd listened to Tom Hanks' voice explaining the mysteries of the universe, and afterward walked most of the way down to the Village, with the towers in the distance like twin pillars at the entrance to New York's harbors. Now, on the morning of the 11th, I was preparing for the ninety-mile drive to Boston College where I would teach a writing class and then another on Hopkins' 1877 sonnets of praise. I was just packing up my books when Eileen, who was working out on the treadmill downstairs, called up to me. There was something in her voice which said I should come. At once.

And there it was on TV, the upper portion of the south tower hidden in a plume of dense black smoke. It must have been 9:10 or so, and the TV commentators seemed to be at as much of a loss as we were. A buzz of words, but very little yet in the way of clarity. Then, unbelievably, we saw a plane smash into the other tower.

All of this was unfolding at a great distance, as if we were standing on Mount Olympus, watching some catastrophe unfold. Figures began falling or jumping from the burning buildings, but mercifully—after a few close-ups—the cameras kept their long-range distance. Then images of the Pentagon on fire, followed by news that a fourth plane had crashed somewhere south of Pittsburgh. Then, as if that were not enough, we saw the first tower actually disintegrate, sending up a dust storm as it did so. Then—a short time later—the second tower fell away in a plume of smoke. No matter that from the time I was ten, twenty years before the towers were even built, I had had nightmares of part of New York someday going up in a nuclear conflagration. Here was the thing itself: more concentrated, yes, but no less devastating for all that. An incarnation of the Kantian Sublime: terror and awe before something so overwhelming it threatens to annihilate the observer. Except that instead of some natural disaster like a tsunami or an avalanche of snow hurling itself at you, an avalanche of twisted metal and concrete dust and human bodies.

I remember once watching some young well-fed, stocky bum working the stalled traffic down around First Avenue and Tenth, I think it was. I was down there searching out the places the poet Robert Lowell had lived in back in the late forties. But already I was thinking of Hart Crane, who had lived around here as well in the 1920s. Somehow the guy working the car windows with a dirty rag reminded me of Crane, which is why I kept staring at him from the supposed anonymity of the corner. Most of the unlucky drivers kept staring straight ahead, while I watched him work the cars just thirty feet away, for what must have been three or four minutes. Then suddenly he caught me staring at him, and what up to this point had been observation suddenly involved me. His face turned menacing, and then he was reaching into his pocket for something. "Get the hell out of here," he began shouting, just as the indifferent traffic began moving again.

I had a moment to consider my options. Hold my ground as he came toward me, or walk away. The inglorious truth is that I was totally unprepared for this in-your-face onslaught. I might have called a cop, or even scuffled with him, but for what? So I could sport razor slashes down my cheeks forever after...or worse? And so I walked on. But the sudden transformation of that face came to inform my understanding of how Hart Crane, drunk and on the prowl, managed to survive on his worse nights down around the Brooklyn Navy Yard or over in the Village. Call it the stuff of experience alchemized by time and the imagination.

Analogously, that's what September 11th seems to have done to me, on a much vaster scale. For a month after the attacks, as the nation sorted through its angers and griefs, I found myself paralyzed, unable to do anything more creative than read galleys and teach my classes. I went through the motions. I worked around the house, slept (fitfully), became a CNN and NPR and *New York Times* junkie.

Each night in the pre-dawn hours I found myself bolting upright in bed, counting off my loved ones: my wife, my sons, my brothers and sisters, my father, my in-laws, my friends. Most of them were safe, though my niece, who happened to be walking out of the subway at Ground Zero just after the first plane smashed into tower one, managed to find temporary refuge in a building before walking as fast as she could, with several co-workers, uptown, away from the crumbling buildings. Somehow she kept her head that morning, but later—as the reality of what had happened burrowed into her consciousness—the nightmares began. But it was American Airlines Flight 587 with 262 people aboard, all bound for Santo Domingo, dropping out of the skies over Belle Harbor three minutes after takeoff from nearby JFK International on the morning of November 12th, and smashing into five houses, less than a mile away from her apartment, that really did it for her, so that she will need months to get back to some semblance of normalcy.

Nearly four thousand—it turns out—died in the September 11th attacks, terrorizing and yet galvanizing a nation into action. I took to flying my flag from the front porch of my Victorian home here in the Connecticut Valley. And even as I write these words, American B-52s and 15,000-pound Daisy Cutters have had their effect on the Taliban. Defectors in Kunduz were being welcomed by Northern Alliance troops with kisses, and today several hundred of them died in an aborted prison revolt. In the city itself, the hardcore foreign troops fighting with al Qaeda—knowing it will not go well with them if they should surrender—are preparing to make a final stand. There have been reports of Pakistani military jets—with whom we have an alliance—evacuating their own Taliban troops from the airport at Kunduz by night, a report stoutly denied by our military authorities. In fighting among the Pashtuns and Uzbeks and others (of whom I knew nothing just two months ago and really little more today) will make an Afghan interim central government a wonder to behold. American Special Forces have been spotted riding horseback with local tribesmen. These tribesmen, by the way, have reportedly made direct asaults on Russian tanks, taking direct hits, while the rest scramble up onto the tank turrets and drop grenades down the hatches. Neither side often takes prisoners, as they rarely took Russian prisoners fifteen years ago.

The whole scenario has the irreality of Lewis Carroll's hunting of the Snark (and indeed Carroll's countrymen were twice repulsed in Afghanistan in the Nineteenth Century). Meanwhile Osama bin Laden—like Iago—remains at large, though several of his top lieutenants have already been killed in our bombing raids. We live a schizophrenic existence, told by our government to remain on high alert and report any suspicious activities as Anthrax makes the rounds, and yet to get out there and shop. In the weeks following the attacks, eight hundred foreigners were rounded up by FBI agents and these people have been kept pretty much incommunicado—without being formally charged—until such time as all this can be straightened out. Attorney General Ashcroft has asked for—and in part received—sweeping powers to investigate suspected terrorists.

Meanwhile we watch nervously and guardedly, wondering if things will ever be the way they were before September 11th, and knowing of course that they can't. We have been forced—many of us—to enter the same world that the Europeans and Palestinians and Africans and Russians and Colombians and Brazilians and Chinese and Japanese have been living in. If that is the case, and if we learn from September 11th that the face of terror is not something that happens only to other people but is something that lies closer to us even than our television sets and is—like that bum in New York that suddenly turned on me—something far more personal, we may have learned a necessary lesson. But at what cost?

DAVID MASON

A Survivor

A man sits down because his world has burst
and stares into the desert of his hands.
Though powder chokes him, he does not feel thirst.

His mind descends a million flights of stairs.
When suffocation thundered up the street
he couldn't remember any of his prayers.

A stranger touches him. He tries to stand,
but something's missing in his knees. He can't
turn at his waist to take the stranger's hand.

He hears fresh voices rushing under the din
just as he did before the ceiling fell—
the voices of more firemen going in—

and blinks back chalk to read the sweated lines
auguring in palms that he has years to live.
If only he believed these simple signs.

Where did the sparrows and the heroes go
when heaven dropped and rubble went on burning?
He asks ten fingers. None of them seems to know.

What were their names? How did he get away?
Mute fingers gather to a temple door.
Tomorrow he'll remember how to pray.

I wrote this poem in honor of New York Fire Captain Patrick Brown, who was killed in the collapse of the north World Trade Center tower, along with 11 other members of Ladder Company 3. They were attempting to rescue more than 30 severely burned people on the 40th floor of the building. Mr. Brown, one of the most decorated firemen in the city, was legendary for his courage. At his funeral on November 9th, he was eulogized by Mayor Giuliani, as well as by former Governor Hugh Carey and columnist Michael Daly, among others. A Vietnam veteran (winner of a Silver Star for valor) and yoga student, Brown was known as a quiet and much-loved man who had led an immensely colorful life.

DAN MASTERSON

The First Day of Infamy

That Sunday morning, I was on my hands and knees in a vacant lot a few blocks from my house, playing with matches. Mild weather had left only a dusting of snow on Buffalo, and the gnarled growth of weeds I knelt in was brittle and dry, the color of bamboo. I struck one match and the whole packet went up. I dropped it and took off down the street, smoke and flames billowing behind me. I slowed down as I passed the police station, but sped up at St. Paul's Church, flipped over Mr. Bannigan's rickety picket fence and landed in our back yard. When I reached the side door, the sirens were blaring. My mother was crying at the kitchen table and my father was comforting her. I wondered how they'd found out so soon. I was relieved to hear it was only some war on the radio.

The next day, after school, my buddies and I began lugging home cardboard boxes from behind Kay's Drugstore. We roped ten or twelve of them together in a long row and cut circles out from front to back so we could crawl through our B-25 bomber. Four flattened toilet-paper boxes, spread out on each side, became wings we smeared with silver paint from the cellar. Wooden guns that shot thick rubber bands cut from old inner tubes made shadows and trees fair game.

For years, my parents pulled black shades tight against our windows when the air-raid drills began, sending my father off to the street with his warden's hard-hat to watch for planes. Lots of little flags with gold stars in the middle hung in the windows around the neighborhood, and Mrs. McCormack put one in her sunporch window next to the sign that told the man, who drove the horse-wagon, that she needed more ice for the icebox. That's how we learned that her son wasn't coming back. And way down at the end of the street, a lady my mother knew chopped down a Japanese maple in her front yard with her son's boy scout hatchet the day she got a telegram from the War Department.

This morning, sixty years later, I stand at the curb, waiting for the mailman, wondering if I should have bought a gas mask and some rubber gloves.

JACK MATTHEWS

Reaching for the Other Hand

Many years ago I read an essay by Gilbert Highet on the classical age of Greece, in which he pointed out that the seeds of the extraordinary genius of that period could be found in two short words in the Greek language *men* and *de*, signifying "on the one hand" and "on the other hand." It is not fanciful to contemplate how these two words contain, within their five letters, the promise of dialectic, democracy, rational jurisprudence, and, by extension, the most cherished ideals of western civilization. Its reflection can be glimpsed in all sorts of contexts, including Heraclitus's reference to war as the "father of all things"—and, more complicatedly, in Epictetus's homespun saying that everything has two handles: the one by which it may be borne and the other by which it cannot. I even fancy I can hear its faint echo in the Irish saying that "one dog can't fight."

On the one hand this, and on the other hand that. And when we are faced with disaster, we instinctively grope for *that*, the other hand, the other handle, convinced that no matter how great the horrors that loom over us might seem, they will not prove unbearable if we are blessed with sufficient character, courage, and imagination. We take comfort from old wisdom and try to understand how interestingly complex disasters are. Like satisfactions, they are never undiluted, for behind the simplicity of their labels, they are cauldrons of complexity and contradiction, cunning admixtures of this and that. On the one hand they are nothing but what they at first seem; on the other hand, there is something else to be found if we know where to look, and how.

Good and bad. The older I get, however, the more difficult I find it to clearly distinguish between the two in their advent. What announces itself as one can turn out to be defiantly the other; furthermore, the one and the other are so often inextricably mixed that I fancy I can hear a snicker behind either mask that's put on them. Brooding upon such uncertainties makes one wary: if an event comes radiating joy, have the courage to savor it, but also step back for a good look. If, on the other hand, something falls upon you with the weight of a leaden doom, search in it for what might prove good or useful, then dig it out and make it serve. Whatever happens, insist upon being nourished by it.

This may all sound like wise counsel, but what nourishment can be found in that great infamy of darkness that fell out of the sky on September 11th? As a people, we now find that we are being tested as never before; our lives having suddenly, radically, interestingly changed. Can we prove worthy of the challenge? Do we have the character and courage and imagination to endure and remain recognizable to ourselves? The answer is yes. And yet, as with everything, we will have to pay a price. In our foreseeable tomorrows, there will likely be less adolescent fun in our lives and less frivolity. In compensation for such losses, however, there is the great and inspiring possibility that we will eventually be blessed with a prouder and deeper happiness. With thoughtfulness, determination, and luck, we might reverse time and become more like the early Romans, leaving behind the decadence, vulgarity, and moral entropy of their final centuries as they rotted into fecklessness and desuetude.

The vulgarity and decadence of our popular culture up to this awful and decisive shift in our history were, indeed, appalling—as extravagant as any depravity the Rome of Nero and Caligula could provide. From most of the media testimony, Americans were soft, lazy, shallow, and self-indulgent—obsessed with being rich, chronically titillated by the latest toys, dazzlingly attractive to the opposite gender (or, with compounded decadence, to their own) and maintaining an active sex life into their dotage. Whatever ideals one might find reflected in these epidemic obsessions, they are, at best, the ideals of an ignorant teenager and unworthy of a thoughtful and morally responsible adult.

Does this mean that somehow we *deserved* to have religious fanatics try to destroy the World Trade Center and the Pentagon—those proud symbols of civilization and authority? Of course not. The twin towers did not really constitute some Tower of Babel in America's Babylon;

even if they could be considered a monument to *hubris*, they did not deserve so infatuated and brutish a vengeance. The cunning fanatics behind those assaults are as benightedly evil and as viciously demonic as it is conceivable for humans to be, and their assumption of divine sanction for their slaughter is nothing less than obscene. "The God they believe in," a German proverb states, "he is my Devil"; and so it is with them and us.

Furthermore, the images of western vulgarity and decadence that obsess the terrorists have never adequately represented our totality, our country; they simply represent the cheapest, most vulgar, most publicized, and most puerile fantasies feeding upon and insidiously perpetuating the self-centered adolescent who to some extent persists in everyone. In contrast, however, there is, and has always been, a wholesome maturity and a stubborn decency of the sort that can grow only in a democracy. This happy strain might justly be called "a silent majority," if that term had not been pre-empted for largely discredited political partisanship some years ago. Nevertheless, we now discover that those homely virtues they were meant to celebrate are finally, and inevitably, alive and worth fighting for.

But how can one live with the horror and uncertainty of being engaged in a war without clearly identifiable battle lines? Switching off the TV set has been suggested; and that is not entirely bad advice, so far as it goes. But there are other considerations: there is, for example, the seemingly odd comfort of viewing things in terms of statistical probability, which we do all the time anyway, instinctively and without deliberation. We constantly, and in thousands of ways, play the odds simply to maneuver our way through the tortuous complexities of modern life, and now is a good time to pause and contemplate doing so with calculation, cherishing the perspective that knowing the odds can provide—while being aware that we do not live in the abstractions such perspectives afford but always in the particular confusions and agonies of the moment. On the one hand and on the other.

Since comfort like this is grounded in reason, we use and cherish it, contemplating the odds as we try to live calmly and rationally in the shadow of terrorism. After all, how traumatic is it really to face the possibility that our average lifespan might conceivably be short-ened by three or four years, knowing that even with that modest subtraction, our longevity will still remain greater than the dreams of history?

Furthermore, it is probable that even the most horrible scenarios of disaster will fall short of what humans have had to face in the past. Consider the great plagues of Europe in the 14th and 15th centuries. And yet, even then, with a death rate that was horrendously brief by modern standards, there were humans who were capable of joy and sweet reason, as testified in many and subtle ways: think of Chaucer, one of the wisest and happiest of testators to the richness of human life.

The contemplation of statistical probability can help us tolerate the more dangerous world we now live in, but it does not hold the promise of chronic bliss—but what does, other than the infatuations of television commercials? This is the lesson we have to understand and learn better than before, and what it adds up to is simply the challenge to be realistic, knowing that our weaknesses are commensurate with our strengths; for the larger and more complex a society is, the more vulnerable it is to malicious and obsessive cunning. We have been so lavishly endowed with instruments of luxury and comfort—far beyond the wildest dreams of past generations—that a challenge to live a more sober existence may prove hard to accept. Even so, we know that the rewards will be worth it, just as any alternative is unthinkable.

It requires that we understand and accept the fact that the danger and confusion introduced into our population may be very great, for one Mullah, as the saying goes, can cause more trouble than a hundred hooligans. So we wonder what defense there is against such a benighted hatred, and the answer would seem to be that there is no defense, although there are defenses. And in employing them, we will survive, and our lives will become more dangerous and more interesting. Will some of our freedoms be sacrificed? Of course, but that will be all right, if we're not too infatuated with the word "freedom" and think of it as an absolute possession that you either have or haven't, with no gradations in between. Absolute freedom is anarchy, and who needs that?

Finally, there is the Socratic conviction that life isn't in itself worth living, it is only the good life. And what is that? However it might be defined, we know that it must consist of some combination of courage, benevolence, civility, and a defiantly good cheer; we know that it will not be vulgar and decadent, nor will it be characterized by the cosmic stupidity of believing it is a sacred duty to massacre those who do not share our vision of the world.

JEROME MAZZARO

Notes During the Aftermath

Two weeks after the assaults on the World Trade Center, normal life is beginning to return to my Manhattan neighborhood. Police cars and fire engines scream down the street on their ways to local emergencies. The traffic on Columbus Avenue has resumed its constant hum, and occasionally, there is the pulsing whine of a car alarm. Everywhere on buildings, cars, t-shirts, windows, and headgear American flags are flying, and from my balcony, I see airplanes again silently sliding by, taking off from and landing at Newark and La Guardia airports. In the corner supermarket, after days of silent exchanges, the voices of cashiers and customers are once more chatting in Spanish of family, events, and neighborhood characters. No mention in their talk of the pennant race, politics, or the assaults, as if by not speaking of them, they might go away, and, indeed, although the neighborhood is little affected physically from the fire, smoke, ash, stench, and pollution that filled Lower Manhattan, it has been affected emotionally. One sees aspects of the damage on tv, along with Mayor Rudy Giuliani's periodic litany of the numbers of dead, missing, and identified—brave firemen and policemen and emergency medical people who had rushed into the buildings in an effort to save lives and, instead, lost their own—and workers in the towers who had gone to their jobs that morning not knowing they would never return to their homes and families. One also grows to admire the workers who, tirelessly through heat and rain searched the rubble first for survivors and then for remains, and hears of economic damage to city in lost jobs and empty theaters, restaurants, and airplanes.

Days after the assaults there had been an almost Sunday morning quiet. Streets were empty, and people were in shock and disbelief, trying to make sense of what had occurred, concerned that what had happened was not over, another "shoe" might drop. They were glum, self-absorbed, entrenched, and hardly speaking to one another. Only months before, I had risen from the subway stop beneath the twin towers to a charming and busy square crowded with people and asked directions to a lawyer's office where I would complete the purchase of my condo. Emerging from the depths, I was exhilarated by a sense of strength and realized human ambition that was conveyed in the buildings' mass and height, familiar to me from postcards, movies, and previous trips to the city. I expected to share the feeling with friends and family who would be visiting, much as one shares the discovery of a good book or restaurant or meeting-place. Now, I cannot, and I feel the loss made even greater by the massive loss of life that the buildings' destruction accomplished and must learn to live with that loss. Having in my adult life experienced and mourned the deaths of parents, my sisters, a sister-in-law and dear friends, I know that eventually the emptiness that death leaves grows less, however much our lives fill afterward with other kin and friends. In this knowledge and tv talk of a memorial, I am heartened, mindful of the grace of Bill Heyen's *Erika* and Irving Feldman's wonderful use of George Segal's white plaster figures to commemorate the Jews lost in the Holocaust and the use of names etched on Maya Lin's powerful Vietnam Memorial to evoke the lost of that war.

When the attacks occurred, I was transferring to my computer an essay on Robert Lowell's poetry that had been published in 1970. I was taking a coffee break and turned on the radio and heard of a plane crashing into the Pentagon. I went to the tv to view news of the crash and saw pictures of the second airplane crashing into the south tower of the World Trade Center. I immediately shut off the tv and went back to the Lowell essay, not wanting to believe what had occurred, only to be interrupted by a phonecall from my brother and sister-in-law. They had been planning to visit the next week and phoned to find out how I was and to cancel their trip. After their call, I returned to the tv and spent most of the day watching it, forcing myself to accept its images as real. Later that afternoon when I checked my e-mail, I found that other family members and friends had tried to reach me and, failing, sent me e-mails of their concern. The next day, I was again at work on the Lowell essay, thinking that, by concentrating on work, I might remain strong. On Thursday, the next phone call arrived from my niece's husband who wanted to know how I was. He had been trying to reach me all day Wednesday. Rather than consoling, I found the calls and messages were making me feel more vulnerable and fragile. I also found that I was now unable to get access to my e-mail and had to change my access numbers. Perhaps prompted by references to Pearl Harbor and World War II or by the incessant playing of Kate Smith's rendition of "God Bless America," I was also being taken back mentally to my boyhood and rationing and young men being drafted and letters from the War Department and was struck with a tremendous sadness for all the young who would be going through similar experiences.

I know that I am lucky. I had no relatives or friends that perished in the assaults; nevertheless, the attack left me angry and feeling sensitive to the pain that it caused. The mild state of shock, keeping me from work requiring concentration, has since dissipated. So, too, has the restlessness that, for days after, kept me from viewing anything on tv but news. I keep hearing that, because so few bodies of the nearly 6000 people killed were recovered, the full impact of the horror has yet to register and that the impression gained at ground zero is much more horrific and moving than what can be viewed on tv. Nor am I fully aware of the work that workers sifting through the debris at the Fresh Kills Landfill have accomplished; although, on a lighter note, I have heard that the vulnerability and need for comfort that the assaults generated will result in a spike in new births nine months from now. All the same, I know I must join others in contemplating how to respond to the attack's evil and to the terrorism that continues to escalate about us. Attorney General John Ashcroft has asked for new, more restrictive laws, affecting our freedoms, and I am hesitant. The government has yet to give a credible accounting of its use of current laws or explain how they failed and how the new powers will remedy that failure. Having gone through the "red scare" and McCarthyism of the 50's and seen how they affected the publication of ideas, I do not want a return to witch-hunts and loyalty oaths in the name of super-patriotism. Still, although I did not vote for him, I do agree with the direction that President George W. Bush has so far outlined. Evil exists and must be excised if healthy organisms are to live. One would like the excision to be quick and painless, but this will not be the case. Perhaps by the end of the operation, the distancing needed to understand the full impact of the assaults and the changes needed to prevent their recurrence will have occurred.

JAY MEEK

Imagination As a Democratic Principle

In "The Convergence of the Twain," the occasional poem Thomas Hardy wrote after the *Titanic* went down, we hear the elements of what might seem an elegy to those who died when hijackers turned airliners into navigable bombs that struck the Pentagon and brought down the World Trade Center. However appropriate some readers have found Yeats's "The Second Coming," among poems for our time, I return to the question Hardy asks as the White Star liner lies at the bottom of the Atlantic, "What does this vaingloriousness down here?"

What did bring us down? We as a literate nation cannot seem to attend to our best and worst imaginings. Construction of the Empire State Building on the site of the Waldorf-Astoria, where Willa Cather's Paul had a glamorously indulgent spree, was begun on October 1, 1929, just four weeks before the stock market crashed. In 1933, *King Kong* gave us a dramatically new image of the ways a skyscraper can be topped off, until airplanes sent him toppling to the street below. In 1945, a photograph shows the B-25 that crashed into the Empire State's 78th floor, killing as many as fourteen. The *Towering Inferno*, from 1974, will be remembered in ways Leonard Maltin didn't imagine in his gloss of the film as "All-Star idiocy about a burning skyscraper. Purports to pay tribute to firemen but spends most of its time devising grisly ways for people to die." By now, we know just how grisly. By now, in popular imagination, our corporate towers not only graph the Dow-Jones stocks, but stand as emblems of our national hubris: the pitiful vulnerability that underlies an equally pitiful bravado.

George W. Bush has become a master of the simple sentence. As a reader, he's learned to pace complex sentences by abrupt pauses, although his presentations often sound flat, as if the words did not live in him, as if he hadn't a clue that words carry moral, intellectual, and emotional meanings. One hears him after the attack, calling the terrorists "evil" and "cowardly," in that stock and unconvincing vocabulary politicians use when they want to swear in public. I deeply believe it is wrong to kill, on any account, but I also believe that however regardless of life the leaders of the attacks were, however hateful, they acted with a terrible purpose and passion, and their acts were not cowardly.

Looking at the Bush White House, we see him turn from the United Nations, the World Court, the Oslo Accords. We see him adopt an imperialist stance among world powers, separate and adamant, and we hear him stump for the dubious virtues of "globalization." We see his "economic stimulus" bill grant tax rebates of $25 billion to major corporations. We see him waging a propaganda war at home, asking for our vigilance and support, while he and members of his cabinet endanger individual rights guaranteed by the Constitution. Who has seen him read?

We elect the politicians we deserve. But it's tragic we seem to deserve so little, when we must do much to sustain democratic practice and principle, among which I number imagination high. It is dispiriting to think that the off-handed disregard Bush holds for foreign affairs might have helped bring on the terrorist strikes, which in turn could well have saved his stagnant presidency. Still, he is spiffied up now, his touchiness and contempt more covert, glazed over. It's doubtful we'll again catch him mocking in public a woman like the person he executed while governor, one of more than a hundred to die during his stewardship.

Poet Ted Kooser once remarked how much it would mean if a president, pausing on the platform before boarding Air Force One, simply carried a book in hand. Maybe George W. Bush could pack his Hardy and read lines that seem much a part of our time, recognizing that the hijacked liners and the towers would become "twin halves of one august event" when "the Spinner of the Years / said 'Now!' And each one hears, / And consummation comes, and jars two hemispheres."

BRUCE MILLS

Infinite Horizon

I.   THE VOCABULARY OF SPACE

Infinite Horizon: the phrase, sometimes used by pilots or air traffic controllers, to describe a sky that affords unlimited visibility.

Intuitive Space: the illusion of space that the artist creates through the use of converging lines, multiple vanishing points, and shifting perspectives.

II.   THE EARTH AT OUR BACKS

In northwest Iowa on winter nights when there is no moon, when the cold clears the air of humidity, the sky stuns the eye. Nothing stops the gaze. The flat fields stretch black just below the line of the horizon; small clusters of shadow from distant groves blot out a few low-hanging stars. But, above the dark silhouette of firm ground, there is no impediment to vision but the narrow window of the eyes and the limit of the imagination.

Three winters ago, I pulled my daughter from her sleep, wrapped her in a blanket, and carried her out into this dark. From across the quarter section, we picked out the few sounds interrupting the silence: the clank of metal lids dropping under the rooting noses of livestock, a muted barking, the lowing of cattle, the cadence of a single car on a county road.

When my daughter got too heavy, I lay down with her on my father-in-law's gravel lane. With the earth at our backs, we no longer had to fight the weight of gravity. She said, "Let's look for falling stars." Between us, we were able to cover the horizon. She, the left; I, the right. I said, "Isn't it amazing how the sky is endless?" And it was infinite, this night sky. And I told her again how she was born under a full moon. And I thought how the Milky Way looked like the stretching skin of a pregnant woman and how the chest fills when love deepens like the space between stars and how hard it is to breathe under the infinite horizon and how no one person can encompass the stretch of this night sky but two is a start.

III. VANISHING POINTS

To the left of Lower Manhattan, far West from the sun-drenched clarity of the World Trade Towers at commuting time, lies the first vanishing point. It is where I am on the morning of September 11. To the right, at a point infinitely distant, lies the second. I accept it on faith. It is a point of impending contact. Between these distant places converge invisible lines, widening slightly to give shape to the angles of buildings below the wash of blue.

On the morning of this infinite horizon, a child lucky enough to have gotten a window seat on a cross country flight from Boston or Washington or New York must have been reassured by the solid convergence of city skylines, by the beautiful glint of ocean beneath the wings of the plane leaning inland, by the various textures of urban sprawl, the veins of rivers, the peaks of the Appalachia.

When I learned of the terrorist attacks and listened to the reports of other planes still unaccounted for, I called my daughter's school and arranged to pick her up. I wanted the memory of this changing horizon to include someone who lived within the intimate space of her world. We needed the ritual of this meeting, the holding together of these images, the simultaneous burden of love and grief.

When my daughter and I got home, we watched together as the second tower collapsed in upon itself. Behind the broken angles of this falling—above the street level rush of billowing dust and ash and then the distant view of smoke trailing along the horizon—the blue sky began to seem surreal, a brilliant brushstroke behind the nightmare of a Dali landscape.

I felt my chest begin to give, the sinking in before weeping, and, for a moment, I did not know whether to turn away or let it go. When I lifted my head, I saw my daughter looking into my eyes.

IV.   HORIZON LINE

I am searching for that other vanishing point, the one on the distant horizon to my right. I type the phrase "Afghanistan images" near the search prompt and let my computer begin to pull in the websites of photographers and journalists. I click link after link: Kabul street scene, the Blue Mosque, Taliban troops, farmers in the field. And then I find this image: Afghan Children, on the Frontline.

Though it remains indistinct, the image begins to fill in. Along the top edge, behind the white touch of snow and mountain peaks, flows the familiar and uninterrupted stretch of blue sky. On the dirt and rocks in the desolate foreground sit two girls, wrapped in blankets. The girl to the right looks out at me, and then I notice a small mound of brown then green just left of her head. Centered on the horizon line, a tank directs its barrel toward the camera lens. It is a new perspective, this vision that the girl invites through her gaze. How has she lived with these simultaneous horizons: the divine stretch of sky and stars, the clump of tanks like chunks of concrete from a fallen building? Horizon line. Frontline.

What must the imagination be to hold together the breaking imagery of this infinite horizon? Can the eye hold it all—the memory of cold air in the lungs and backs against a gravel road, the endless video of descending steel, the ghost of city skylines, tangled bodies in the rubble, the huddling of two young girls?

We create the world through the intimate spaces of our imagination. In this space, the lines are fluid, and grief is as malleable as love.

JUDITH MINTY

Loving This Earth
Lake Michigan: 9/12/01

—and we, here in the middle of this country, unable to watch any
          more
as the plane stabs the tower, as the TV film
reverses, the plane withdraws, no scar, then thrusts again and again
flames burst, smoke rises, the tower falling into itself, over and
          over; unable to listen any more to the stories of orderly
          evacuation, those stairs
that took more than 30 minutes to descend, people
lifting and leading each other, arms around shoulders, heads
          bowed, firemen
passing them on the way up; we, unable to imagine again what they
          have done to us:
the awful stench of jet fuel and electric fire, the bodies
falling from windows, cries from the rubble; unable to take in
any more stories of the electrician, the law clerk, the stockbroker,
the kids who looked all day for their father, the woman who at this
          moment is going
from hospital to hospital in search of her fiancé, the story of the
          shoe store that
gave sneakers to women who had to walk 100 blocks in high heels,
          the deli
that passed out free sandwiches to those trying to get home, to
          those
trying to find friends, lovers; we, in our own searching, in our own
          gloom and dread
and helplessness, quit the house and run down the stairs to the
          beach.

Here, a slight breeze plays dune grasses that twist and dip, their
        blades
drawing artful circles in the sand; here, waves roll frothy tongues
        toward land.
The tourists have gone—yesterday's rain washed their footprints away—
now sun glitters the sand. Miles from here, across the water in
        Wisconsin,
and beyond in the western half of this country, the sun
will set in beauty after it leaves Manhattan and sinks below this
        Michigan horizon.
We begin to walk the shoreline south, and everything speaks:
pieces of driftwood scattered like bones, deer tracks leading to
        water,
gull feathers along the shore, a dead carp the gulls are scavenging,
birthday balloon still tied with red and blue ribbons, a man's rub-
        ber sandal,
more gull feathers, another balloon—how old was that child?—
empty wine bottle with no message inside, a broken sand pail, crow
        feather,
zebra mussels stowed away in ballasts of foreign ships now
clustered in a sharp-edged fist, plastic glass from Red Lobster,
beer can from Milwaukee, lady bugs imported from Asia,
a tampax roll, a tennis shoe, more gull feathers, a baby bottle.
On our way back, we pass the carp. He is half-eaten now.
We begin to gather scattered feathers, wanting to put together what
        has been
lost and broken, those thousands of white papers fluttering down
        from the towers.

On September 11th, 2001

Most of us have never contemplated our deaths. Here in these
United States we've been too absorbed in the immediacy of living.
We're so wrapped in schedules and their daily constrictions—getting
the kids to the bus stop, the appointment at the dentist, the sale at
the department store, our next vacation—that we barely save an hour
to sit down at the dinner table in the evening. Though we've been
vaguely aware that accidents happen, that, indeed, we might be
prematurely extinguished, we mostly take for granted that we'll
live out our lives in a sort of orderly fashion, and that there'll be
time enough, somewhere in our middling-to-old age, to plan for

death with wills made and papers put in order. We've never thought of terrorism. We expect we'll die slowly, but not too slowly, in our sickbeds, surrounded by family and a few close friends who have gathered to send us on our final journey.

*

The events of September 11th were an attack on the American psyche and they changed many of our preconceived notions. What happened in Lower Manhattan, in Washington, D.C., and in Pennsylvania reverberated across this land. In some way, television networks and other news media bonded this country together when they transmitted the horrifying images of disaster into each of our homes, land, cars, and workplaces. Together, at first, we sought to express our anguish, but what came out was more like the howl of a wounded creature.

*

I live in Michigan, in the center of these United States, not in a city but in a rural area near Lake Michigan. These Great Lakes—Huron, Ontario, Michigan, Erie, and Superior—which Melville described as "our grand fresh-water seas," are known by those of us who live here as the "Third Coast." In times of sorrow or confusion, I have always received solace from this natural world. Mostly, I am reassured by the cycle of living things: the daily ebb and flow of waves, of sunrise and moonset, of seasons—the April trillium in my woods, the maple tree that is always last to give up its leaves, that first thaw followed by another snowfall, deer yarding up in the winter meadow, the return of rosy-breasted grosbeaks, the goldfinch's changing color, the colony of blue herons nesting again in their rookery, sandhill cranes riding the currents south each fall. Every lesson I have learned from woods and river and shoreline has been lasting and meaningful, and I attend them regularly, those places which continue to be my church. It was not unusual then for me, on September 12th, to turn to Lake Michigan for answers in my grief, to walk for miles along its beach trying to make sense of what has happened to us.

ROBERT MOONEY

That morning ...

That morning I was completing a revision of a novel that centers on an act of terrorism, a hostage situation set in 1982 perpetrated by a World War II veteran demanding the return of his son, a soldier missing in action in Vietnam for twelve years. My intent, my hope, the operative writer's fantasy for this one was to compose a work that could be described as something like *Dog Day Afternoon* as conceived by Dostoevski and edited by Virginia Woolf—tense action rendering a kind of psychological realism that would examine something essential, or at least interesting, regarding the character of our culture and our time. There is no violence in the novel, only its promise, or proximate intent. But I was steeped in the idea of the imposition of one's will through brute force in the name of a "just cause," the terror of victims, the pontificating conjectures of news hounds, the scrambling of authorities, the excuses of government officials, all of it homespun—that is, distinctly, if not exclusively, American—sprouting through the cracks in our history, spreading over the ground of our shared and eternal present.

Then my wife Maureen, a nurse at the local elementary school, called and told me that the World Trade Center had been struck by a 767 airliner. We assumed it was a terrible accident, but moments after I turned on the television the second tower was hit. Then we learned of the bombing of the Pentagon, object of my own protagonist's wrath, only 65 miles southwest of where I live on the Eastern Shore of Maryland, close enough for us to receive the Washington TV affiliates, so it was now local news, too. But seeing the disaster unravel on a 13-inch screen forced a psychological distance far greater than the geographic, like watching an event occur through the wrong end of a telescope. It all felt less real to me than the events in the novel I was revising—too much like tricks of the camera for our entertainment, like so many Hollywood clips. But not only was it real, it became personal when, much later, I learned that an old college friend, Billy Minardi, never made it out of Tower One. At the time, I couldn't get hold of friends, the lines were jammed in New York and Washington, who knew what else was going to happen and perhaps was already happening just then. The not-knowing shoved me into a kind of panic of the type I remembered feeling in the early hours of the "Great Blackout" of 1965 that plunged most of the Northeast into darkness, and the rumors, at least in my neighborhood, had us under attack from the Russians.

But as September 11th darkened under the horribly multiplying cumulonimbus of vaporized brick and steel and human bone, it quickly (too quickly, it seemed) became the consensus that "everything" had "changed forever." Indeed, in the succeeding days and weeks it did begin to seem that even if life did find its way back to being something like "the same," what we would once have called "normal," there would be a different feel to it, a shadowed and shadowy ambience, as though not all lights could be switched back on after the terrible darkening. For a culture that tends to deny death, we were all the more sobered by having to deal with it on such a monstrous scale right here at home. Because the mass-murders were perpetrated in careful orchestration by a people other than us and famously hostile to us and declaring their enmity to be representative of a substantial portion of the world population, these crimes not only have us thinking of ourselves as more of a collective self, as a united people, but also perhaps more curious as to the nature of the supra-American world we have tended to ignore. It is almost as if the force of history itself slammed into us that Tuesday, as though it had been happening without us "out there" somewhere, gathering momentum, powered—disproportionately, and ironically—by our own energy.

This is not to say we or any nation or principality or tribe deserve to be molested by such barbaric acts planned by sociopaths and carried out by indoctrinated minions; it has been difficult for many, though, to ignore the concomitant approbation, if muted—though in some cases outright jubilant—demonstrated in more than a few corners of the world in response to our suffering. Before the events of September 11, even many of our allies were murmuring against our apparent disregard for the concerns and fears and legitimate interests of other peoples in the world. Some of this ill-will, these accusations of arrogance, may simply be part of the burden of having assumed the role of "world leader," being the most powerful, the richest, the most fortuitously positioned, the most historically blessed, for the nonce. Even so, it may provide occasion for us to reconsider the playwright Eugene O'Neill's warning after the Second World War when we were debating whether we should return to a modified isolationism or assume the status of what would come to be called "superpower": "What will it profit us," he asked, paraphrasing Matthew's Gospel, "if we gain the world and lose our soul?" There is no possibility of isolationism in this incredibly shrinking world, and we have learned through this disaster that there are no suburbs in the global village. But if we do, as a people, possess something like a soul to nurture or to lose, we might begin in greater earnest to consider that if we are to lead the world of nations, we first ought to join them more fully. That means that "their" own wishes and desires, "their" sufferings, a comprehension of "their" anguishes, even an empathic (as opposed to simply strategic) understanding of their psychoses, if they be that, might be undertaken as well.

When Stephen Dedalus in James Joyce's *Portrait of the Artist* prepares to leave Ireland, he writes in his journal that he means to forge in the smithy of his own soul "the uncreated conscience of his race." Literature is the conscience of every race, every society, every people. Out of the common material of our language, our novelists and short story writers and poets challenge our certitudes, remind us of the richness of our humanity, speak to the innermost in us, enriching and revivifying our spirit, re-identifying and activating something like a soul. Partaking in the literary endeavor, as writer or as reader, is, if nothing else, an exercise in empathy. At its best, it places us, often uncomfortably, in the skin of other human beings and offers parallactic perspectives from which it is more difficult not to understand sensibilities foreign to our given experience. Hatred, Graham Greene reminded us, is a failure of the imagination, and our best literature deepens our humanity by cultivating and guiding intimate understanding of other lives. Mohamed Atta, the thirty-three year old man who commandeered American Airlines Flight 11 and piloted it into One World Trade Center, could not have had much of an imagination. He could not have nurtured any true sense of empathy, a feel for the lives of people beyond the ken of his daily experience, or his willful myopia regarding what he had experienced—though he had ample opportunity to cultivate if not a magnanimity at least a common decency. He did not know my college friend Billy Minardi; he could not possibly have envisioned fully enough Billy's gentle manner, his ready generosity, his capacity to love, and what that meant to so many friends, to his wife Stephanie, to his three children—William, Robert, and Cristine, ages 12, 9, and 5. How could he, and do what he did? And then multiply that cruelty, that egregious and deadly paucity of imagination, that appalling dearth of empathy, by nearly 4000, and then hundreds times that to take into account the aggrieved loved ones. Me? I want to detest Atta and his cohorts and comfort myself with the nobility and righteousness of that detestation. I want to see these men as not-human, barbaric, soul-less, and wish good riddance to the whole murderous lot of them. If Graham Greene is right, though, I have to consider that even the malfunction of the human heart that plans and executes mass murder and devastation can, somehow, be comprehended, must be understood, and so even as my anger rises against these simple men devoted to their desperate causes, my own heart, such as it is, must go ever further out to them, too, else I end up their comrade in all that we hate.

FRED MORAMARCO

Messages from the Sky: September 11, 2001

From the towers, from the planes,
Love, and again, love.
Stuart Meltzer from the 105th floor, to
his wife: "Honey, something terrible
is happening. I don't think I'm going
to make it. I love you. Take care of
the children." From the Towers, from
the planes, Love, and again, love.
Brian Sweeney from Flight 175 that
shattered the South Tower, turned
lives to gray ash: "Hey Jules, it's
Brian, I'm on a plane and it's
hijacked and it doesn't look good. I
just wanted you to know I love you
and I hope to see you again. If I
don't, please have fun in life and live
your life the best you can. Know that
I love you and no matter what, I'll
see you again." From the Towers,
from the planes, Love, and again,
love. Kenneth Van Auken from the
102nd floor: "I love you. I'm in the
World Trade Center. And the
building was hit by something. I don't
know if I'm going to get out. But I
love you very much. I hope I'll see
you later. Bye." From the Towers,
Love, from the planes, love.
Mark Bingham from Flight 93
before it crashed into a field near
Pittsburgh: "Hi Mom, this is Mark.
We've been taken over. There are
three men that say they have
a bomb. I love you, I love you,
I love you." From the Towers, from
the planes, Love, and again, love.
Moises Rivas, a chef at the Windows
on the World: "I'm O.K.—don't worry.
I love you no matter what. I love
you." Love from the Towers, love
from the planes. Jeremy Glick from
Flight 93 to his wife Lyzbeth: "I love
you, I love Emmy. Please take care
of her. Whatever decisions you
make in your life, I need you to be
happy and I will respect any
decisions you make." From Thomas
Burnett on Flight 93: "I know we're all
going to die; there's three of us who
are going to do something about it. I
love you honey." From Daphne
Bowers, somewhere in the Towers,
"Mommy, the building is on fire,
there's smoke coming through the
walls, I can't breathe. I love you
Mommy, goodbye." To mothers and
wives, to husbands and friends, to
fathers and lovers, to brothers and
sisters, to aunts and uncles, to the
inert tapes of answering machines:
Love from the towers, Love from the
planes, from the towers and the
planes, Love and again, love,
"I love you Mommy, goodbye."

Quotations from the *New York Times*
Sunday, Sept. 16, 2001

ANDY MOZINA

Missing in Action

He said we should have kept going right on to Baghdad. It was a civilian-type mistake. Civilians didn't understand the logic of power. Civilians didn't understand how to make the world right.

I said, what about the rule of law, what about sovereignty, what about the innocent Iraqis? I had such a huge need to be right, I couldn't explain my reasons.

Once, he admitted something about a training mission in Germany that hadn't gone well. A black night, hunkered under a truck in the rain, at the wrong coordinates, trying to read the goddamn map. He was the only captain for miles in every direction. Water ran down the cold barrels of the howitzers. No civilian really knows the burden of 150 heavily armed men.

When his tour was up, he resigned his commission and took an unsatisfying job as a systems integrator at General Electric.

I said, walking with him through an upscale mall in Williamsburg, VA, what is it you really want to do?

He said, I want to be a gigolo. He said, I want to write a novel. Instead, he got an MBA and said, I want the corner office.

Soon he was working at One Wall Street, for the Bank of New York.

I called him and said, I have some money, should I invest in your company? Because I thought he would respect the question.

He said, there are many ways to measure management's effectiveness. He said, examine the incremental relationship between revenue and accounts receivable. He said, take a look at the return on equity. Just look at the return on equity.

The next quarter's results were good and I sent him a congratulatory e-mail. But he'd changed his e-mail address, and the message came back.

He married a former Miss Hawaii, bought a house in suburban New Jersey, bought a Jaguar for cash with his annual bonus. He was a vice-president now, commanding hundreds again.

*

On September 11th, from his office window, he saw, heard, felt, and eventually smelled the second plane go in, while I watched it on TV.

When I saw the North Tower collapse, I didn't fear for his life. I called home, but I didn't worry for a second. He was all right. He was temporarily trapped in his building, a few blocks from what would be called Ground Zero, but he was all right.

I called him that night to see how he was. Just left a message. I said, "Maybe you feel too weird to talk about it, but I was just checking." What did I mean by "weird?" What did I mean by "just checking?"

I called him again a few days later, just to see how he was. And left a message.

I heard from our mother that he had decamped with a team of crack system specialists, with the CEO of the Bank of New York himself, a man with a personal net worth of hundreds of millions of dollars, the proximity to such wealth enough to make my self-respecting banker's own ten-dollar bill stand on end, decamped to White Plains with this highly trained team, where they were working around the clock to get the bank's transaction processing capabilities up and running for the re-opening of the markets on Monday. I learned from the internet that nearly one trillion dollars a day passed through his bank. I thought, how perfect for him, to be in a war, to be in charge of so much. (Maybe now a little less envy of his peers' service against Iraq.) Each enabled and recorded and stored transaction like a bullet in the heart of Osama bin Laden and his ilk.

All enemies concerned say they must destroy each other. It is a clash of belief systems. He has no illusions. Why shouldn't he himself be the target of an assassination? For what he stands for. For what he enables, records, stores. Who could be blamed for trying to kill him, if they think he is wrong, is enabling some harm? He doesn't quibble with the enemy's logic. He knows that none of this is incomprehensible, senseless, or inhuman. However the enemy confronts him, he will neutralize it. The superior system will win.

He still hasn't called me back, but I'm anxious to get through to him. I'd like to give him a certain type of encouragement, a certain type of gratitude. I'd like to try a joke on him. I don't think I could persuade him to accept anything else. In my weird, myopic way, I think of him as the United States, and I would like to tell him to take care.

HOWARD NELSON

Irrelevant Thoughts

I knew someone who died in the World Trade Center. She was a childhood friend, not close, but someone I knew growing up; her sister was my classmate, her parents friends of my parents. Though I had not seen her in years, it nonetheless added to the shock of that day to think of her among the dead. Word came through the network of family and old acquaintances. She had been at her job high up in the second tower hit. After the first plane struck, she had called home to tell her family that she was OK. Very soon after that, the second plane slammed into its tower.

Those two planes, and the collapsing towers, were explosions and collapses felt in the psyche of everyone in this country. The plane that hit the Pentagon was a further blow, like a kick to someone who already had the wind knocked out of him. The plane that crashed in Pennsylvania felt like a weird aftershock. In the talk about heroism that followed the disasters, I don't think that the passengers on that flight, Flight 93, have quite gotten their due, although Senator John McCain has proposed that they all receive the Congressional Gold Medal, Congress's highest civilian honor. Some acts of great courage, decisiveness, and self-sacrifice took place on that plane— acts that one would hope to be able to perform. The details of how their courage was enacted were lost in the crash that was no doubt intended to take place elsewhere—the Capitol? the White House? A black box may reveal more someday, though that doesn't matter so much. I'm grateful in many ways that those people were able to do what they did.

I am a Quaker—an uneasy Quaker. Not a birthright Quaker, but one by convincement, as the Quakers say, though I am not totally convinced, especially regarding pacifism. I've had many discussions of pacifism with my Quaker friends over the years. They cite Gandhi, and I cite George Orwell's essay on Gandhi, in which he says that there is something inhuman in saintly idealism, and that there is a difference between dealing with the British and dealing with Nazis. I've been especially interested to talk with older Friends who held to their pacifism during World War II. These are men whom I respect very much (more than I respect myself), and I believe any sincere person's refusal of military service is valid and should be honored. But I have never heard a convincing explanation of how pacifism could have been an adequate and effectual response to Hitler.

On the Sunday following September 11, the mood in our Quaker meeting was somber and troubled. A few people rose in the silence and spoke about the attacks. One person spoke about forgiveness, and about how this was the key element in the Christian message. My impulse (which I did not follow) during and after his comments was to get up and leave. Not out of an inflamed sense of patriotism, but from a feeling of how irrelevant his comments seemed. The passengers on Flight 93 were not in a mode of forgiveness when they realized what the hijackers were doing. They met force and malevolence with some kind of force. They could not have acted out of a sense of "that of God in all persons" in the hijackers. Would they have killed the hijackers if they could have? No doubt. Pacifism in those moments was irrelevant, and it seemed irrelevant, to me at least, whether my friend in meeting could find it in his heart to forgive the hijackers (now dead) or Osama bin Laden. I may be revealing my own low level of spiritual insight here, but his concern for forgiveness in these circumstances seemed a supreme irrelevance, almost a self-indulgence. What were we going to do to address these attacks, and those that their planners would no doubt be pleased to carry out to follow them?

The two weeks between the attacks and the start of our retaliation in Afghanistan now seem long ago, as I write, in early November. Like many others—the editorial pages were deluged—I felt I should say something. I wrote a letter to my local newspapers:

> I have been feeling thankful for this period of restraint in the U.S. response since the terrorist attacks. I do not know what lies ahead. But if the United States can continue to exercise such restraint, we may accomplish something rare.

Bombing is a blunt instrument that kills the innocent—and it would bring us closer to the level of the terrorists. At the moment, we seem to be recognizing that the suffering Afghan people are not our enemies. Governments and people around the world are sympathetic to our losses and united in opposition to terrorists—but this could quickly change if we begin throwing around the weight of our arms.

The terrorists must be pursued and stopped as criminals. It would be both moral and intelligent, and a relief to the world, for the United States not to use its enormous firepower.

One paper printed the letter on October 6. The next day the bombing began. The other paper printed it a few days later, omitting the first paragraph. Now my own opinion felt irrelevant. Was it a naïve hope, that this crisis could be dealt with by means other than bombing? Others—Molly Ivins, the local Green Party—proposed legal rather than military response, but they were short on details. What was I imagining? Send Columbo after them? These were not criminals skulking in apartments; these were criminals with military training bases, who had already declared war, holy war.

Holy war. There is much in these events about which I am unclear and conflicted, but one thing that I am clear about is that I don't want to hear anymore the phrases "Allah willing" or "Allah be praised" in connection with conflicts between peoples, nor do I want to hear the phrase "God Bless America."

Whether or not a different response would have been effective, it now seems a naïve and irrelevant thought to have hoped that the U.S., with its enormous arsenal, its overwhelming fleets of bombers and fighter jets, and its bellicose, self-righteous, and simplistic president, would not respond to the situation with bombing.

So now we are a month along in the bombardment of Afghanistan. There is a growing list of accidents and collateral damage—Red Cross warehouses, hospitals, mud-brick houses, pulverized by our bombs. The bombing grinds on, and it begins to feel like a continuation of our previous bombings, in other places, other wars. So much bombing, almost always by the U.S. The Northern Alliance, whose record is apparently not much better than the Taliban's, is poised to advance once their new allies, the U.S., have bombed sufficiently. The Islamic world watches, and much of it sees us as acting out the worst that has been said about us. I am struck by the huge contrast between the anti-terrorist actions of the passengers on Flight 93 and the explosions of our bombs on the ravaged cities and barren landscape of Afghanistan. The massive engines of war are in motion, and all other options seem irrelevant now. When we capture or kill Osama bin Laden, whose presence, lest we forget, was the justification for our bombing, will that bring an end to terror?

NAOMI SHIHAB NYE

To Any Would-Be Terrorists

I am sorry I have to call you that, but I don't know how else to get your attention. I hate that word. Do you know how hard some of us have worked to get rid of that word, to deny its instant connection to the Middle East? And now look. Look what extra work we have.

Not only did your colleagues kill thousands of innocent, international people in those buildings and scar their families forever; they wounded a huge community of people in the Middle East, in the United States and all over the world. If that's what they wanted to do, please know the mission was a terrible success, and you can stop now.

Because I feel a little closer to you than many Americans could possibly feel, or ever want to feel, I insist that you listen to me. Sit down and listen. I know what kinds of foods you like. I would feed them to you if you were right here, because it is very important that you listen.

I am humble in my country's pain and I am furious.

My Palestinian father became a refugee in 1948. He came to the United States as a college student. He is 74 years old now and still homesick. He has planted fig trees. He has invited all the Ethiopians in his neighborhood to fill their little paper sacks with his figs. He has written columns and stories saying the Arabs are not terrorists; he has worked all his life to defy that word. Arabs are businessmen and students and kind neighbors. There is no one like him and there are thousands like him—gentle Arab daddies who make everyone laugh around the dinner table, who have a hard time with headlines, who stand outside in the evenings with their hands in their pockets staring toward the far horizon.

I am sorry if you did not have a father like that.
I wish everyone could have a father like that.

My hard-working American mother has spent 50 years trying to convince her fellow teachers and choirmates not to believe stereotypes about the Middle East. She always told them, there is a much larger story. If you knew the story, you would not jump to conclusions from what you see in the news. But now look at the news. What a mess has been made.

Sometimes I wish everyone could have parents from different countries or ethnic groups so they would be forced to cross boundaries, to believe in mixtures, every day of their lives. Because this is what the world calls us to do. WAKE UP!

The Palestinian grocer in my Mexican-American neighborhood paints pictures of the Palestinian flag on his empty cartons. He paints trees and rivers. He gives his paintings away. He says, "Don't insult me" when I try to pay him for a lemonade. Arabs have always been famous for their generosity. Remember?

My half-Arab brother with an Arabic name looks more like an Arab than many full-blooded Arabs do and he has to fly every week.

My Palestinian cousins in Texas have beautiful brown little boys. Many of them haven't gone to school yet. And now they have this heavy word to carry in their backpacks along with the weight of their papers and books. I repeat, the mission was a terrible success. But it was also a complete, total tragedy, and I want you to think about a few things.

1.

Many people, thousands of people, perhaps even millions of people, in the United States are very aware of the long unfairness of our country's policies regarding Israel and Palestine. We talk about this all the time. It exhausts us and we keep talking. We write letters to newspapers, to politicians, to each other. We speak out in public even when it is uncomfortable to do so, because that is our responsibility. Many of these people aren't even Arabs. Many happen to be Jews who are equally troubled by the inequity. I promise you this is true. Because I am Arab-American, people always express these views to me, and I am amazed how many understand the intricate situation and have strong, caring feelings for Arabs and Palestinians even when they don't have to. Think of them, please: All those people who have been standing up for Arabs when they didn't have to.

But as ordinary citizens we don't run the government and don't get to make all our government's policies, which makes us sad sometimes. We believe in the power of the word and we keep using it, even when it seems no one large enough is listening. That is one of the best things about this country: the free power of free words. Maybe we take it for granted too much. Many of the people killed in the World Trade Center probably believed in a free Palestine and were probably talking about it all the time.

But this tragedy could never help the Palestinians. Somehow, miraculously, if other people won't help them more, they are going to have to help themselves. And it will be peace, not violence, that fixes things. You could ask any one of the kids in the Seeds of Peace organization and they would tell you that. Do you ever talk to kids? Please, please, talk to more kids.

2.

Have you noticed how many roads there are? Sure you have. You must check out maps and highways and small alternate routes just like anyone else. There is no way everyone on earth could travel on the same road, or believe in exactly the same religion. It would be too crowded; it would be dumb. I don't believe you want us all to be Muslims. My Palestinian grandmother lived to be 106 years old and did not read or write, but even she was much smarter than that. The only place she ever went beyond Palestine and Jordan was to Mecca, by bus, and she was very proud to be called a Hajji and to wear white clothes afterwards. She worked very hard to get stains out of everyone's dresses—scrubbing them with a stone. I think she would consider the recent tragedies a terrible stain on her religion and her whole part of the world. She would weep. She was scared of airplanes anyway. She wanted people to worship God in whatever ways they felt comfortable. Just worship. Just remember God in every single day and doing. It didn't matter what they called it. When people asked her how she felt about the peace talks that were happening right before she died, she puffed up like a proud little bird and said, in Arabic, "I never lost my peace inside." To her, Islam was a welcoming religion. After her home in Jerusalem was stolen from her, she lived in a small village that contained a Christian shrine. She felt very tender toward the people who would visit it. A Jewish professor tracked me down a few years ago in Jerusalem to tell me she changed his life after he went to her village to do an oral history project on Arabs. "Don't think she only mattered to you!" he said. "She gave me a whole different reality to imagine—yet it was amazing how close we became. Arabs could never be just a 'project' after that."

Did you have a grandmother? Mine never wanted people to be pushed around. What did yours want?

Reading about Islam since my grandmother died, I note the "tolerance" that was "typical of Islam" even in the old days. The Muslim leader Khalid ibn al-Walid signed a Jerusalem treaty which declared, "in the name of God ... you have complete security for your churches which shall not be occupied by the Muslims or destroyed.

It is the new millennium in which we should be even smarter than we used to be, right? But I think we have fallen behind.

3.

Many Americans do not want to kill any more innocent people anywhere in the world. We are extremely worried about military actions killing innocent people. We didn't like this in Iraq, we never liked it anywhere. We would like no more violence, from us as well as from you. We would like to stop the terrifying wheel of violence, just stop it, right on the road, and find something more creative to do to fix these huge problems we have. Violence is not creative, it is stupid and scary, and many of us hate all those terrible movies and TV shows made in our own country that try to pretend otherwise. Don't watch them. Everyone should stop watching them. An appetite for explosive sounds and toppling buildings is not a healthy thing for anyone in any country. The USA should apologize to the whole world for sending this trash out into the air and for paying people to make it.

But here's something good you may not know—one of the best-selling books of poetry in the United States in recent years is the Coleman Barks translation of Rumi, a mystical Sufi poet of the 13th century, and Sufism is Islam and doesn't that make you glad?

Everyone is talking about the suffering that ethnic Americans are going through. Many will no doubt go through more of it, but I would like to thank everyone who has sent me a condolence card. Americans are usually very kind people. Didn't your colleagues find that out during their time living here? It is hard to imagine they missed it. How could they do what they did, knowing that?

4.

We will all die soon enough. Why not take the short time we have on this delicate planet and figure out some really interesting things we might do together? I promise you, God would be happier. So many people are always trying to speak for God—I know it is a very danger-ous thing to do. I tried my whole life not to do it. But this one time is an exception. Because there are so many people crying and scarred and confused and complicated and exhausted right now—it is as if we have all had a giant simultaneous break-down.

I beg you, as your distant Arab cousin, as your American neighbor, listen to me.

Our hearts are broken: as yours may also feel broken in some ways, we can't understand, unless you tell us in words. Killing people won't tell us. We can't read that message.

Find another way to live. Don't expect others to be like you. Read Rumi. Read Arabic poetry. Poetry humanizes us in a way that news, or even religion, has a harder time doing. A great Arab scholar, Dr. Salma Jayyusi, said, "If we read one another, we won't kill one another." Read American poetry. Plant mint. Find a friend who is so different from you, you can't believe how much you have in common. Love them. Let them love you. Surprise people in gentle ways, as friends do. The rest of us will try harder too. Make our family proud.

HUGH OGDEN

Northwest Maine, September, 2001

It was a wide water day with the lake at peace
and the wind
revising September-end-of-summer shore waves
and it was
the silence of the wood stove percolating and
then it was
the wake-up call on the air waves, the break,
the interruption
of the Brahms symphony by a bulletin slipped in
after trumpets
and violins were suddenly silent and it was the
beginning
of what has always been the ending of quiet water:
a voice
saying a plane had crashed into the North World
Trade Tower
at the end of pure harmonies, flames replacing
music
until the radio was awash with fear and bafflement
and quickly
terror that thousands were dying, had died and then
a second bulletin
that Washington had been bombed, a second plane
had plunged
into the South Tower and I drove back down to southern
New England
past the Androscoggin, the unfolding untouched
forests,

the northern tip of the White Mountains, deep
with what
the newscasters had left me, thanked the still green
translucent
maples, the wide space of the timbered valleys,
the fact
that my car radio was broken, the speeding season
held
by road curves, river curves, in the drive down into
the hurt
of what would become the everywhere broadcast
of war.

ALICIA OSTRIKER

the window, at the moment of flame

the window, at the moment of flame

and all this while I have been playing with toys
a toy superhighway a toy automobile a house of blocks

and all this while far off in other lands
thousands and thousands, millions and millions—

you know—you see the pictures
women carrying their bony infants

men sobbing over graves
buildings sculpted by explosion—

earth wasted bare and rotten
and all this while I have been shopping, I have

been let us say free
and do they hate me for it

do they hate *me*

As to words about the poem—it was precipitated by exhaustion with the rhetoric of journalism and politics, debates over whether poets should or shouldn't, could or couldn't write about public as well as personal events, expressions of patriotism, anti-patriotism, flooding my e-mail. I felt very small, very helpless, very sad. I think we here in the USA, in our arrogant simplicity and our enviable and hated liberty, make a beautiful target.

ERIC PANKEY

Falling Towers
(Fragments September 11–October 1, 2001)

The metallic taste of anger on my tongue as I look for words not burdened with bigotry, self-righteousness, wrath, and retaliation. In my powerlessness, I want to kick someone's ass.

Or, at least, save someone's life.

*

Simone Weil: "If someone does me injury I must desire that this injury not degrade me. I must desire this out of love for him who inflicted it, in order that he may not really have done evil."

(Translated by Emma Craufurd)

*

These fragments I have shored against my ruins, T.S. Eliot writes in the final stanza of his poem "The Waste Land," a hetero-glossal, poly-vocalic, and wildly fragmented poem written in the wake of the first great war of the last century, a war precipitated, it could be argued, by a terrorist act against an empire. One wonders what lines will commemorate our contemporary loss, and one wonders if, as we read Eliot's wonder and dread at the devastation of great cities, of battered empires, we might not add under our breath the names of American cities: *Falling towers / Jerusalem, Athens, Alexandria / Vienna, London / Unreal*.

*

The pathos of those taken unaware, caught in the diurnal—waiting for an elevator or busy at their desks, leaving the restroom or filling a cup of coffee while talking to a friend—brings tears this morning, the pathos of our faith that the next moment, the next hour, the next day, the next season awaits us, as it did at Pompeii, the pathos of our faith that the future is foreseeable, that we have penciled it in our calendars and planners as if we would be there on that day.

*

A ruin is the aftermath of trauma, the aftermark of the ephemeral we believed to be beyond erasure, beyond effacement.

*

What the press has called "heroism" *is* a rare thing and deserves the attention it has received these days. But what does it say about us as a people that we are so surprised by the presence of goodness, compassion, and selflessness?

*

As troops are mobilized and the indeterminate enemy is characterized through hyperbole as *demon* and *animal*—devils we must exorcise, pests we must "ferret out" and exterminate—it is hard to remember that justice is patient. It is hard to imagine the scale on which we might weigh such justice and how the scales might be made to balance. It is hard to imagine a justice not corrupted with the blood of further innocents, stained with anger and vengeance, ruined by our own acts of injustice. I pray for patience, for peace.

Note on a visit to the Viet Nam War Memorial: There it is before our eyes, the tragic inventory of our error and our loss.

How rarely we are asked to imagine the loss of our adversary.

*

As I attempt to make sense of the motivation of the terrorist attacks and of the tensions as our nation prepares to respond, I am reminded of lines by Archilochus, ancient Greek mercenary and poet:

> In the hospitality of war
> We left them their dead
> As a gift to remember us by
> (TRANSLATED BY GUY DAVENPORT)

*

Poetry is a speculative mode. The tendency of poetry is wholeness—it dares to speak, it dares to give shape, to attempt wholeness within complexity, when other forces long for division and fragmentation. If politics is the enactment of power—force, violence, control—its language is the language of lies, deceptions, misinformation, rumor, and the withheld. Politics prefers innuendo. In politics, one admits only to the most recent revision and never the existence of the earlier drafts. Poetry is no match for the political, because the political has its mind made up.

*

A *crusade*—the President slips up again. *Infinite Justice*—the Defense Department offers as the apocalyptic code name of a forthcoming war. The members of Congress singing "God Bless America." Our secular government announcing, it seems and sadly so, a holy war of its own.

Bob Dylan, 1964: "For you don't count the dead / when God's on your side."

*

In *Art News* and *The New York Times Magazine* these past two weeks, I have seen sketches and proposals for memorials to the victims of the attacks. And certainly there must be a memorial to honor those lost. A memorial not only honors, though, it also reminds. In planning and building a memorial, we will admit to a future in which the unforgettable just might slip our minds, in which the unspeakable might be left unsaid.

*

Simone Weil: "The cause of wars: there is in every man and in every group of men a feeling that they have a just and legitimate claim to be masters of the universe—to possess it."

(Translated by Emma Craufurd)

BETTE PESETSKY

You were *where* when ...

People ask: where were you? Can you answer that you were here? Here, here, here. That's how you wrap your mind around September 11, 2001 as if where you were lent credence to the impossible. Oh yes, where you were. When planes bombed Pearl Harbor you were going to the movies with your sister. The theater was called the Tivoli. A generic theater name. You no longer live in that city so you don't know if the Tivoli still exists. You forgot the name of the movie. That's not like you. Maybe your sister picked it. She liked romances. You were a little kid and you didn't. Now your sister is dead twelve years. When President Kennedy was assassinated you waited for your car to be serviced. You sat in one of those rooms that dealers use for non-car buying customers. A row of chairs covered with nauga-hyde and the splits on the upholstery mended by strips of tape of a different color—green on brown. The tray that held free coffee had a scattering of freeze-dried granules and the cream was powder. Did you hear what happened? The volume on the television set bolted high on the wall was turned up. People appeared from the showroom to stare at the screen. Your child says that he doesn't want to be president any more.

Where you were and what you were doing—only events in ordinary life.

September can be a good month. Autumn in the big city. Everything the songs say it is. Where were you on that day? September 11, 2001. You were on your way to the cleaners. You went to pick up your go-to-meeting suit in a polyethylene wrapper. When you fly, mostly it's from LaGuardia. You know the World Trade Center. Know the towers best from up high. Quick glance and then back to a magazine. Some years you fly often. All those horizon bookmarks—buildings, bridges, ribbons of cars—meant you were close to home.

You're not flying on September 11th. When the first plane hit that World Trade Center tower you were still home having a last sip from your coffee cup. You said to your husband that it must be a commuter plane. Maybe the pilot had a heart attack? There would be a rescue from the roof. A dramatic rescue with helicopters. That could be what you said, and then you went to your car, because it was a day of appointments. You drive ten, fifteen minutes. And when you leave your car you click the automatic lock button. Always lock the car in the city. That's what you've been told.

The second plane already hit the other World Trade Center tower when you reached the cleaners. You stand with a group of strangers staring at a tiny television set the owner brought from the back of the store and placed on his counter. You had been to the restaurant—to Windows on the World. You were there for celebrations and to show off the view to others and to look at the lights.

You paid for your cleaning. No one in the store talked much. Their mouths though, fell open to form those anguished circles seen in pictures. Torment outlined in thick black lines.

You moved on with your day. You were with people you knew after the third plane hit the Pentagon. When were you last in Washington? Four, five years ago. You used to go to that city once a month wearing a go-to-meeting-suit.

Every day more things happen. Can you remember where you were all those times? Names of dead scrolling down a screen. People asked if you were acquainted with anyone on those lists. Any name? You shook your head.

Planes were locked to the ground in other cities. Do you know any-one in Denver? A friend of mine was stranded there. Know anyone she can have dinner with? You try to think. You've from the Midwest. Midwestern people scatter. There's you, for instance, in New York.

Facts about the unknown dead achieve a new importance. No pattern emerges. All the details become too much. Crying children. Desperate parents. They saw him just yesterday. He came to dinner with that girl. Where is she?

You forgot your cleaning. It languished in the trunk of your car. The meeting was cancelled. You find the now-wrinkled suit and hang it up in the closet. News sliced the days into segments. The screen with its racking coughs of grey dust. For days all you did was read the newspapers and watch the retelling of what happened on television.

The accounts of the lives of people who died grew more detailed, more complicated. People who vanished. A woman who didn't come home. Her home was in a high-rise apartment building. Her neighbors didn't know—not at first—that she was missing. She was nice. Wasn't she? A pleasant good morning in the elevator said with city wariness. Now her mail no longer fits in her box in the lobby of that building where she lived. The doorman says that her cleaning was delivered on September 11th. A garment in a polyethylene cover. It waits in the little room off to the side by the entrance door where packages accumulate.

You used to live in an apartment building where the doorman would hang the deliveries of dry cleaning on a rod in a similar little room. You know nothing about the real life of the woman—the woman with the unclaimed clothing. Her life belonged to her not to you. A city life. City lives can be solitary or people you work with can be your closest friends. Surely her relatives will come soon and enter the apartment that belonged to the woman and stare blindly at the appointment book on the desk open to that day, open to that week. Should someone be called? The names written are unfamiliar. After all it was her life and not theirs. The relatives weep over the coffee cup left in her sink that morning. Who knows when it is their last morning? And if you knew, what would you do? Wash the coffee cup. Straighten the cushions. Throw out yesterday's newspapers. No. You would do nothing, nothing, nothing. There would be nothing to do. The mail will come. The next day's newspaper will be delivered. The cleaning will arrive, and the doorman will accept it.

You cannot comprehend certain numbers.

You hear that they are removing the World Trade Center towers from scenes in movies. Blacked out in pictures. You think that it is wrong to obliterate history. The towers were there. They had a right to be there. They should be seen and noted.

The doorman won't remember to tell the woman's relatives about the cleaning delivered on September 11th. The doormen work in shifts.

The relatives came in the morning and now it was evening. The evening doorman didn't see them leave. His attention focused on residents returning and picking up what's theirs. Packages pile up in these little rooms. Other people's cleaning. Small deliveries. No one will remember to tell that woman's relatives that her cleaning waits. Later when they hear about it, those people have already returned to their own homes. And how can it matter? Give the cleaning away, they say. Throw it out. The representative from the building management shrugs. The woman's cleaning might stay forever and be pushed further and further back in that little room.

A go-to-meeting-suit. You decide that was what the cleaners delivered to that building for that woman who didn't come home. The suit under a paper-thin-plastic covering that ripples in the wind whenever the door is opened. A reluctant sail incapable of flying away weighted down as it is by the go-to-meeting-suit. To think that it might go up like a balloon is as unreal as removing the World Trade Center Towers from a picture. That doesn't mean that they weren't there. Doesn't mean that none of this happened?

ROBERT PINSKY

Enormity and the Human Voice

In the first days after the enormities of September 11, I received a lot of poetry by e-mail. Some were poems I already knew, some not. Some of the poems came from friends, some from strangers.

Part of this outpouring reduced the art of poetry: to the rhyme department of clinical psychology, or to a secular alternative to religious comfort. But some poems seemed simply and terribly appropriate, like Carlos Drummond de Andrade's "Souvenir of the Ancient World" with its concluding gasp of exclamation at a lost, suddenly remote reality. Here is the poem in Mark Strand's translation:

Clara strolled in the garden with the children.
The sky was green over the grass,
the water was golden under the bridges,
other elements were blue and rose and orange,
a policeman smiled, bicycles passed,
a girl stepped onto the lawn to catch a bird,
the whole world—Germany, China—
                    All was quiet around Clara.

The children looked at the sky: it was not forbidden.
Mouth, nose, eyes were open. There was no danger.
What Clara feared were the flu, the heat, the insects.
Clara feared missing the eleven o'clock trolley,
waiting for letters slow to arrive,
not always being able to wear a new dress. But
she strolled in the garden, in the morning!

            They had gardens, they had mornings in those days!

I knew this poem, sent to me by my poet friend Gail Mazur, who had read it to her classes at Emerson. But I had sort of forgotten it, had not realized its tremendous relevance to the transforming violence of September 11, until Gail pointed it out to me. The poem perhaps made me feel closer to my friends and to poetry itself.

There were also poems that seemed grossly inappropriate, as when someone on the Internet suggested Yeats's "Easter 1916," with its refrain line "A terrible beauty is born." No to that, and no to the comparison of the Easter Rising in Ireland. (Many civilians died then, too, but as the result of government action against the hapless, romantic rebels who had occupied the Central Post Office and other government buildings. That is the reverse of our September 11.)

I can't go along, either, with the people who have cited W.H. Auden's scornful, superior "September 1, 1939" as a suitable resource. He did write that poem on the brink of war, and it does mention towers, but I don't see the relevance of his tone: "Into this neutral air / Where blind skyscrapers use / Their full height to proclaim / The strength of Collective Man." This weary cynicism seems deeply wrong in relation to these particular lost towers. The capitalized "Collective Man," as in Auden's later lines "The windiest militant trash / Important Persons shout" fight a battle different from our current one: some windy militant trash is being shouted, but the phrase actually doesn't catch the tone of Colin Powell or of President Bush, who at the time of my writing this (still in the first weeks after the attacks) seems to be over his head but trying.

Everybody is different. I find more relevance in E.A. Robinson's "The House on the Hill," which Leslie Epstein e-mailed to me. I've known Leslie to claim that as a fiction writer he's no judge of poetry. But he chose well; Robinson's lines are adequate to total loss, total destruction:

They are all gone away,
  The house is shut and still,
There is nothing more to say.

Through broken walls and gray
  The winds blow bleak and shrill:
They are all gone away.

Marianne Moore's "What Are Years?" a poem I have read many times, and thought I knew well, came to me in a new light. In the context of a massive, successful stroke of terrorism, Moore's discourse about courage has a new quality for me—a kind of ringing understatement:

> What is our innocence,
> what is our guilt? All are
> naked, none is safe. And whence
> is courage: the unanswered question,
> the resolute doubt,—
> dumbly calling, deafly listening—that
> in misfortune, even death,
> encourages others
> and in its defeat, stirs
>
> the soul to be strong? He
> sees deep and is glad, who
> accedes to mortality
> and in his imprisonment rises
> upon himself as
> the sea in a chasm, struggling to be
> free and unable to be,
> in its surrendering
> finds its continuing.
>
> So he who strongly feels,
> behaves. The very bird,
> grown taller as he sings, steels
> his form straight up. Though he is captive,
> his mighty singing
> says, satisfaction is a lowly
> thing, how pure a thing is joy.
> This is mortality.
> This is eternity.

Even the verticality of the bird that "steels / his form straight up" reminds me of the image of the twin towers made of glass and steel. Maybe with poems, as with people, once you give your heart away you find great and good things in the recipient.

But the interesting question may not be which poem to read, or who chooses which one. Beyond those matters, why have so many readers turned toward poetry in response to this calamity?

My best answer has to do with scale. "Enormity," for those of us who fuss about words, is supposed to mean something like "outrageous evil" or "extreme indecency." In actual use, the word may be gradually sliding, incorrectly but logically, toward meaning, simply, "something enormous."

Both meanings apply to the visible and unseen horrors of September 11, especially in New York. One of the largest structures in the world, housing tremendous undertakings, with the dual buildings' very name signifying global scale—and sailing into it the massive, graceful airliners. The dimensions, the numbers, the awful scale of destruction, threaten to dwindle individual pain and loss.

Television, with its immediacy and ubiquity, made the enormous spectacle vivid to people all over the globe: our vast, helpless and inescapable eye. Poetry cannot accomplish any such spectacular immediacy, nor can it touch emotion as swiftly and surely as music. Poetry cannot provide comfort as reliably as religion, and it cannot dispense information like a newspaper.

What can it do? A poem can provide vocal intimacy: a human scale of emotion and understanding. A poem penetrates inside us—literally, into the chest and voicebox and ear, as well as into the brain. The medium for a poem is one person's voice-breath, and very likely the breath of the reader, not necessarily that of the poet or of an expert performer.

And vocality implies other people. Beside that inherent intimacy, poetry has a social, communal quality: it is made out of language, the words and sentences that people exchange all day like dollar bills and quarters.

The poems that readers are still sending one another and publishing formally or informally—great poems, feeble ones, everything in between—answer a need for something on the scale of individual normal life—while we are still sorting out how much of that life belongs, suddenly, to a lost, as if ancient, life together.

STANLEY PLUMLY

The Morning America Changed

That afternoon I'd finished up early, at about two-thirty, and decided, since it was a particularly pristine day, to make the descent into town. Maybe to get a coffee, shop, whatever. We were fifteen minutes getting ready and it would take at least fifteen minutes to reach the exit gate.

I should mention that we were in residence at the Villa Serbelloni, centerpiece of the Rockefellers' fifty-acre holdings spread out on the high hillside overlooking the village of Bellagio. The villa and its grounds and gardens are a sight to behold, located among some of the most beautiful mountain scenery in the world—the Pre-Alps, as they are called, which serve as green and granite precursors to the real Alps, great mountains whose ghostly and snowy forms loom visibly just behind. All of this height and majesty are grounded, so to speak, in water, in the famous Italian lakes out of which they rise. The lakes are vast, and the rich moraine shore that makes up the hemline around them is peopled with innumerable lovely towns, of which Bellagio is the "Pearl of the Lake," as Shelley once wrote. The lake he refers to is Lake Como, the largest and deepest.

Judith and I had been at the villa for close to a month and would be leaving mid-September. Trips down into town were always fun, though the climb back, especially on a warm day, could be exacting.

I cannot say enough about the beauty of Bellagio, its special lakeside, mountainside character (sans its chic boutiques) and its central place in the midst of what surrounds it, sitting as it does at the very tip of Punto Spartivento ("the point that divides the wind"). The boat and ferry traffic on the lake is not only necessary but, from a position of perspective, gorgeous to see, and the long drives around the lake are no less spectacular, if slow. Indeed, much of the charm of the whole area, with Bellagio at its heart, is its narrow-road and water-borne separation, even isolation, from the otherwise busy north of Italy. Isolated in time as well. For some, such insularity, after a week or so, might be a problem; for me, it was paradise.

This was a warm, sweet day. Big clear blue overhead, blue-green in the distant view of the water. *Veduta* means view in Italian, and from top to bottom, from the villa down to Bellagio itself, and from the tops of the cobblestone village streets down to the diamonds on the lake, the view is everywhere, at every level, from every moment. And walking the elegant stone switchback path into town it is all visible at once—sky, Lake Como, and the green and sheer mountains in between. You could lose your balance by stopping and looking too long.

We reached Via Garibaldi, the main one-way one-lane through-road, at around 3:00, which meant it was 9:00 in the morning on the East Coast. Judith went into the pasticceria for some biscotti and to chat with Maria, the owner. I sort of lingered on the street, people-watching and looking up at the open sky. Then I heard this tv loud American voice coming from the coffee bar close by. I hadn't heard an American voice amplified for quite awhile. It was strange. I'd had countless coffees at the place where the voice was calling from but never noticed a television.

And there it was, a great glass tower on fire, with an equally great smoke cloud billowing from a few floors from its top. On the screen, it all looked smaller than it should—I remember that—and I wasn't certain where it was happening—Boston, perhaps, the Hancock Building maybe; something about a plane. My first thought was—as it was for many people, I'm sure—how is this possible? Planes run into mountains, not high buildings. CNN was going back and forth between English and Italian, both of which constituencies were beginning to fill the bar. Then we saw what came to be known as the second plane swoop in and make its turn and crash into a now suddenly apparent second tower. This was live. Tourists from several countries had filled the little room, and many were in tears.

It was the World Trade Center, Manhattan, New York, the most powerful cultural, economic, and international city on earth, and we were here, on another kind of island, almost, it felt, on another planet. It tested one's sense of reality, especially since the messenger was television, the ultimate verisimilitude, the medium that needed to print *live* in a lower corner in order to distinguish the living from the taped. Had we or had we not landed on the moon or was it a staged video event? Mankind cannot bear too much reality, T.S. Eliot had said. Even in that moment I was sure there were people right there thinking to themselves that this was a movie, a bad tv movie at that.

I went outside to find Judith, who was just emerging from the pastry shop, and pulled her in among the rest of the witnesses. I didn't have to say anything, the scene here and there was immediately apprehensible. Long after, she would stay in front of the bar t.v., and for the remainder of the day into the night. The barman had switched it to English exclusively for her. But I couldn't watch anymore.

It was now 4:00 or so, Italian time, and all of the shops in Bellagio had reopened from lunch, and it was the 11th of September, the day on which John Keats had had to return, in 1819, to London from Winchester in order to try to raise money for his brother George in America, who had been swindled into bankruptcy by John James Audubon. Keats would fail, though a week later he would write his last and greatest lyric poem, "To Autumn." ("Where are the songs of Spring? Ay, where are they? / Think not of them, thou hast thy music too—"). I had been writing about this interlude in Keats's short life when we'd taken our break to walk the long walk down into town.

JEFF PONIEWAZ

from September 11, 2001

Pity the poor innocent people diving into the cool air
from the inferno forcing them out the windows.
Pity the poor innocent humans burned by a hell
created in the human brain. Pity the poor affluent
innocent humans burned alive and crushed like flies
between the layers of the arch-cathedral of Commerce.
Pity the poor innocent know-not-what-they-do people
caught in the inexorable Karma of the god of Gasoline
enshrined and worshipped in the Temple of wailing Wall Street.
Pity the poor innocent people trapped and doomed in the
larger-than-its-father progeny of the Imperialism State Building,
up which the natural world climbed with humanity in its fist
while U.S. Airforce planes tried to shoot it down
causing the natural world to plummet to the pavement
(the Gorilla species close to extinction a mere half century after the
RKO plane circled the planet before the opening credits of *King Kong*).
Pity the poor humans trapped and doomed inside the twin progeny
of the Empire State Building that soon overtower'd
the Chrysler Building that Lorca cried out from the peak of
decrying Rockefeller's poisoning of the Hudson River.
Pity the innocent bystander minions of Rockefeller
crashing an oil-laden *Exxon-Valdez* into the Bay of Cortes.
Pity the poor commuters sardined into the twin Molochs
that punctured a vast hole in the ozone layer, and crashed
a billion two-car garages through the Great Wall of China.
Pity those innocent accomplices aboard those skyscrapers
rammed into the sky sabotaging the atmosphere of the entire planet.
Pity the poor reality TV hostages cowering in front of their televisions,

their favorite commercial-riddled soap operas, sitcoms and
    gameshows
pre-empted by the bad news that not everyone buys Madison Avenue,
cowering in front of televisions where this terrorism gets reported
while the terrorism of a global economic Godzilla is not.
Pity the poor people who died for Rockefeller's sins.
Pity the poor people who died for Hitler's sins
that caused a Jewish state to be carved out of Palestine.
Pity the souls who were snuffed because Commerce rules
rather than an interfaith ecumenical spirituality to foster
compassionate harmony among all the peoples of the planet.
Pity the poor humans trapped and doomed inside the karmic
bull's-eye of the nature-blind cyclops on the U.S. Dollar.
Pity the poor ignorants who knew not what they do
and got a good paycheck accomplicing the eco-cide.
Pity the poor children seeing this on their TV screens
even more violently psychologically indelible than
the exploding Space Shuttle. This explosion hit HOME
more than all the explosions in movies—more than the White House
blown up in *Independence Day*....

People who live in glass skyscrapers
shouldn't hurl jetfuel fireballs into the sky—
even if the jetfuel is exploded gradually over the breadth
of the entire continent rather than in a splitsecond
into the face of the Temple of the god of Oil & Money.
How many fireballs dramatic as the inferno'd Trade Center
are exploded daily into the atmosphere to hasten
the Eco-Apocalypse that will ultimately generate more suicides
than jumped from those twin pinnacles of human hubris.
Icarus falling with wings of flame from the 110th story.
Lovers jump holding hands as mythic as Paolo
and Francesca da Rimini in Dante's *Inferno*.
There are a million stories in the Naked City—
5000 of them have just had a horrific ending.
People who live in flammable houses
shouldn't drive tankfulls of explosives
even if the infernal combustion is hidden under hoods
bearing art nouveau hood ornaments
in internal combustion engines and the pollution
is filtered through catalytic converters
and the roar muffled by Midas mufflers
(guns with silencers kill just as deadly
as the Bang-Bang-You're-Dead variety).

People who live in flammable houses
shouldn't drive tankfulls of explosives,
then complain if the price approaches
the price of milk they feed their children.
How dare the Powers That Be charge
as much to poison the lungs of our children
as we pay to put milk in their Sugar-Frosted Flakes
while Tony the Tiger is devoured alive
by the unrelenting overpopulation of Asia.
People who want peace shouldn't drill
oilwells in Holy Lands so the God of War
and the God of Religious Fanaticism can turn them
into cyclones of soot for the whole planet to breathe....

Whitman took his stand at the tips of peninsulas
     and on the peaks of high-embedded rocks
to cry "Salut au Monde!" 75 years before Lorca
took his stand at the top of the Chrysler Building
at the southern tip of the peninsula called Manhattan,
and shouted out danger, shouted out warning—
shouted a warning to Guernica and Warsaw:
        The Luftwaffe is coming!
        The Luftwaffe is coming!
and shouted out a warning to America and the world
about the Hudson River getting drunk on oil
40 years before a U.S. river caught fire,
and 58 years before a million gallons of diesel fuel
went down the Monongahela.

I take my stand on the tip of my tongue
and on the tip of my heightened brainlobes
to cry: Salut au World Peace! Salut au World Joy!
Salut au ever-expanding appreciation of this
beautiful precious endangered planet!
Salut au Peace in every language
that ever evolved in the human skull!
Shalom Salaam! Shalom Salaam!
Shalom Salaam! Shalom Salaam!

MAJ RAGAIN

Note to My Friend the Reverend Rufus Lusk

This morning, I read your sermon
delivered Sunday, September 16,
at the Prince of Peace Lutheran Church in Gaithersburg.
The waters do roar and foam,
the mountains tremble.
The peaceful life is a dream
from which we have awakened.
I think of you as the devout pilot,
your congregation the passengers in their pews.
Faith is the pole star.
The Prince marks the true north.
I am no pilot; neither am I winged.
I am earthbound with words.

All love is crazy in its presumption,
top to bottom, agape, caritas, eros,
that we must give ourselves
unto the keeping of the other.
There is no other way.
What is not love is fear.
Mercy and patience are the same face,
mercy looking outward, patience inward.

The rabbis, while believing He
is the judge of the universe,
delighted in calling him *Rachmana*—
the merciful—and taught
that the world is judged by grace.

The poet Hafiz: 'Even after all this time
the sun never says to the earth,
you owe me. Look what happens
with a love like that. It lights up
the whole sky.'

The judgment is to love, like that.

September 19, 2001

My poem continues a conversation with Reverend Lusk which began the summer of 2001 at the Fine Arts Work Center in Provincetown, sunny afternoons at a weathered picnic table, the cape a spit of sand held in immensity. My initial thought was to answer each of his weekly sermons, subject and spirit, with a poem, he and I diggers in the same sky. I got this far.

The poem is a linkage of gifts. The line "What is not love is fear" comes from my daughter Megan who wrote these words in the border of a photograph, the two of us. The notion of the two faces, mercy and patience, one looking outward, the other inward, is transcendental, connecting matter and spirit, based on rummaging in Emerson. Crazy love is a nut I cannot crack. It fits in no pocket I know of. The stanza yoking judgment and grace grows out of reading in the *Talmud*, a used copy through the mail. The lines from Hafiz were inscribed by another friend on the cover page of Jack Kerouac's *On the Road*.

After reading Reverend Lusk's reflections on the events of September 11, the webbing began. The passengers in the doomed planes were the parishioners in pews. Reverend Lusk is a devout pilot, a protector, navigating by the pole-star of his faith. I am grounded, without transport, rolling the big hickory nut of crazy love at the who-set-these pins, mercy, judgment, and grace. The judgment, that we must love as the sun fills the whole sky with light, is both merciful and severe.

DAVID RAY

Over There

Over There, Over There,
it was always Over There,
a tune we knew well
as the soldiers went marching,
traipsed up the gangplank—
off on a Liberty ship,
off to France, off to the Pacific,
off to Nam, off to Korea
(the one I'd have died in).
The hawkers told us
we had to have them—
wars unavoidable, wars
that were graded—Good,
Better, and Best. It took
a really good one
to convince the stubborn,
who desired their sons
to stay on the farm. Meanwhile
our cities grew upward,
piercing the clouds. Then
one day I woke to my wife
standing beside the bed,
teacup trembling in her hand.
"The Trade Towers," she said,
"the airplanes." It was now
                    Over Here.

The destruction of the World Trade Center was reality, metaphor, and metonymy for Apocalypse. Can we even rejoice that only a part of the city was destroyed, when the deed was such a clear preview of more to come unless we surpass the reasoning ability we have so far displayed? After September 11th, our president did not immediately unleash our military, and instead undertook diplomatic negotiations that were impressive, promising, and admirable. Weeks later he abandoned the ethical high ground and overnight turned our persecutors into apparent victims, alienated a large part of the world, and guaranteed terrorist martyrs and unimaginable acts of retaliation. We could say our civilization has regressed to the madness of the Crusades.

Can we take comfort that the worst has not yet been visited upon us, when the next time it may be? Pouring out grief in *Hippolytus*, Euripides spoke through Theseus:

O city, city! Bitterness of sorrow!
Extremest sorrow that a man can suffer!
Fate, you have ground me and my house to dust,
fate in the form of some ineffable
pollution, some grim spirit of revenge.
I am like a swimmer that falls into a great sea:
I cannot cross this towering wave I see before me.

(TRANS. DUDLEY FITTS)

And like the grieving families of those lost on September 11th, the chorus sings out its lamentations:

Woe for the house! Such storms of ill assail it.
My eyes are wells of tears and overrun,
and still I fear the evil that shall come.

A poet who wrote in India about the time of Christ reminds me of the spirit shown in the World Trade Tower ruins:

In the ruins of the village
they brought the scorched
clay cups to their lips.

These passages remind us that though the scale of technology may be different, the horrors ever expanded, humanity has been here before, and something deep within us recognizes another karmic encounter with disaster. We suffer the past anew.

The tragic hero is destroyed because he has made an error of judgment or has a deep flaw in his character—hubris. That is the error from which comes the horror. With our desire to control we bring down the fury of the gods. Have we done it again, the destruction of dozens of earlier civilizations mere practice?

For many poets, annihilation is as familiar as the asthmatic's wheezing, ever one breath away from death. In a poem called "Spies," about weapons encountered in a house in Hawaii sublet from airmen, I come across my lines as if they were written by a stranger:

> Christ, it is sickening,
> the world poised on the brink of disaster
> for years now, just waiting for the worst.
> Intolerable! And yet what can one do?
> We left Quaker pamphlets in the living room
> and tried not to think of fireballs and gas masks.
> You'd have to get drunk to bear it, not think
> of those who will die.

My visions have always been Apocalyptic, and my dreams, like those of war-lovers, may add their power to making the unthinkable happen, for I have not, as Quaker testimony recommends, banished the cause of all war within me.

During the Vietnam War I wrote, referring to a crashed nuclear bomber that scattered its radioactivity over the Spanish earth:

> These are the end-of-the-world days
> and that black kite or crow
> in a tree in Spain is no bird or iron-
> sculpture, but a dark sign of the end—
> the spilled radioactive junk, the unconcern.

As a child I was often terrified, for as an asthmatic I wheezed away, ever one breath away from death. Some of my poems are "dread satoris." Such *Angst* seems manifest in the poets and writers I admire—Sir Thomas Browne, John Donne, John Keats, Emily

Dickinson, T.S. Eliot, Stevie Smith, *et alia*. Randall Jarrell, in the five lines of "The Death of the Ball-Turret Gunner," expressed an anxiety far deeper than that of an airman risking his life for his country and losing it. His rage and helplessness—and his betrayal—were imposed by the State, the Behemoth that survives its errors and misjudgments while provoking and rationalizing war's horrors. The gunner is washed out of the ball turret like a child aborted from the womb of an unloving mother. Now even the survival of such unloving mothers is at risk as airliners are converted to bombs.

Carl Sagan worried about nuclear winter, a man-made extinction. In that event, the carbon of all we are and possess, our bodies and our cities, would enshroud the earth in an impenetrable dark cloud. And whose error would have triggered that horror, all too similar to St. John's vision in which "the third part of the sun was smitten, and the third part of the moon, and the third part of the stars; so as the third part of them was darkened, and the day shone not for a third part of it, and the night likewise." (Revelation: 8:12) Those black roiling clouds of nuclear winter would be composed of matter similar to what has been passed bucket by bucket, hand to hand, by rescuers sorting through the rubble of the World Trade Center.

We hope that Carl Sagan's concerns erred on the side of caution and the empowerment of prevention, but we have seen little humility or seriousness about arms control or nuclear proliferation since his Nuclear Winter Conference of 1984 at Bellagio, Italy. He worried about hubris, he told me, saying he feared far more the nuclear arrogance of America than that of any other nation.

Annihilation has always been the fear and concern of poets, though they have had little power as "unacknowledged legislators of the world" to prevent it. We can only hope that those who have shared with the world their dark visions were false prophets.

E.M. Forster's story "The Machine Stops" uncannily predicted a society in which individuals exchange information instantaneously with anyone in the world. They worship this machine, but have been diminished and threatened by their technology. "Man, the flower of all flesh, the noblest of all creatures visible, man who had once made god in his image, and had mirrored his strength on the constellations, beautiful naked man was dying, strangled in the garments he had woven. Century after century he had toiled, and here was his reward."

Carl Sandburg, confined to oblivion by the critics, had his moments of prescient wisdom, as in "At the Gates of Tombs":

Civilizations are set up and knocked down
the same as pins in a bowling alley.

Civilizations get into the garbage wagons
and are hauled away the same as potato
peelings or any pot scrapings.

Civilizations, all the work of the artists,
inventors, dreamers of work and genius,
go to the dumps one by one....

Such words resonate as one thinks of the debris of the Trade Towers being carted away. "A bar of steel—it is only / Smoke at the heart of it, smoke and the blood of a man. / A runner of fire ran in it, ran out, ran somewhere else, / And left smoke and the blood of a man." He didn't have in mind the melting of skyscraper steel, but the question he asked in "The People, Yes" seems relevant today:

The first world war came and its cost was laid on the people.
The second world war—the third—what will be the cost?
And will it repay the people for what they pay?

Where do we find hope and light to offset such darkness? How do we keep our errors from becoming horrors? In our obsessive focus on war, the most exotic of diversions, how can we reserve energy for problems that must be solved if mankind is to survive?

Other errors will become horrors unless we heed the warnings. Thomas Malthus, much scorned and derided, warned us in 1798 that earth would inherit disease, war, and pestilence if humanity does not choose to hold population down. Though history has proved him right, Malthus is not even considered a philosopher, but a quack, an oddball, an hysteric, as the world wallows in denial. Even bin Laden's fifty-one siblings suggest an overpopulated family of origin.

Darwin maintained that prey and predator are as one, engaged in vicious interplay of challenge and response. Challenge demands death or mutation to immunity or symbiotic tolerance. But how do we mutate enough to develop immunity to threats from all sides and from within, from an enemy skillful in using our own genius against us—cryptography, the chemistry we thought was for better living, jet planes, computers, nuclear weapons, and the leniency of our laws? Are all the impressive gains of success—as symbolized by the Trade Towers—to be brought down by rage and envy?

If we could, like fruit flies, go through the necessary generations needed for mutation we might emerge immune to radiation, anthrax, smallpox, and all the rest of the terrorist arsenal. We would grow body armor thick as an armadillo's. But we don't have that luxury. So the only solution is symbiosis. Auden put it in one line he later excised from his *oeuvre*: "We must love one another or die." Quakers suggest that even the use of the word strangers instead of enemies is a gesture toward that goal.

If we go on assuming we can afford the luxury of hate and from time to time settle things at the O.K. Corral, we must die as failures. None of our wars to end all wars banished the root of war within us. Our dreams of wiping out war, famine, and pestilence can turn to nightmares in which that dread triumvirate reigns.

The challenge demands no less than learning to live symbiotically with all nations, thus earning bragging rights for the first mutation in history to be willed by man within a single generation.

Preparing the Monument

They are hard at work on a monument
while the smoke is still rolling out of the pit,

raising the question of how much effort
it takes to pound the present into the past

and quickly convert a disaster still in progress
to the status of an ancient and archaic attraction.

They have chosen a fire truck mangled and twisted
to set on a plinth, along with a few smashed cars.

They are extracting relics not yet gone cold,
and unearthing what is already entombed.

Though the dust has not settled and the smoke
is still noxious in nostrils, they are braving

fouled air to assemble debris, and have discussed
the notion of choosing an unknown victim

to be interred in salvaged aluminum. For any
design calling for names stamped in bricks, tiles,

frieze or entablature they have been given a list.
Once their monument, centered on a smooth terrace

with a few tasteful trees, is in place they can gaze
upon this space called Ground Zero and not be blinded

or overcome by the stench, and when their work
is complete and every surface polished and gleaming

and ready for tourists, they themselves will be free
of fear, as if they are dealing only with the archaic—

dessicate, bloodless, and cold, with no smoke
in the air, and no catastrophe in progress. Once

I too sought out the archaic and found it on an island
in Greece, a fragment in marble that had once

been the foot of a lion, but he was already a thing
of the past and I did not have to chase him there.

As for the present, Buddha said it well—
everything is burning—everything—

and to enshrine the flames is hardly a task
for mere mortals.

ISHMAEL REED

America United

They are saying that we should join hands and show
solidarity with our new friends,
that we should burn candles and sing "God Bless
America" and "Amazing Grace" and stand tall
with Sir Rudolph Giuliani, the Mayor of New York,
The Joker among Racial Profilers, under whose
rule 35 thousand Hispanic and Black Men
were stopped and frisked
"No one group should be targeted
as a result of the WTC bombing," Sir Guliani said
They say that we should link arms with the
killers of Amadou Diallo, shot 44 times while
minding his own business
That we should march with
them to that gleaming City on the Hill, preceded
by the Albany jury that acquitted them, who
play Yankee Doodle Dandy on their piccolos,
fifes, and drums
They say that we should form a big strong line
with Sir Colin Powell who said that he's
against the bombing of civilians and buildings
"I'm against the bombing of civilians and buildings"
said Secretary of State Powell, MacWorld's Black Knight
They say that we should show our gratitude to the
woman whom President George Bush, Jr. calls Condi as in
"Get me Condi"
Ms. Condoleezza Rice, daughter of the
Hoover Institute and Chevron Oil,

murderer of the Nigerian Delta people
He calls upon her when he lacks the facts
which is often

Maybe we should send her a carton of
nail polish, hot combs, skin lighteners,
and pocket mirrors to show
our gratitude, our affection
She said that there was no reason for
the US to attend the Race conference in Durban
South Africa
She said that "We are a country that does not
judge people by their skin color or religious beliefs"
They say that we should bow our heads and pray along
with George Dumya Bush, who said that the
citizens of South Carolina should decide whether
the confederate flag should fly over the state capitol,
who said that every black man who was electrocuted
in Texas received a fair trial
He said that he wanted the "evil doers"
"Dead or Alive," smirking, eyes squinting

send them all to Boothill
which is how we do it in Texas
why shucks, we're going to smoke
them out of their holes because
they're the bad guys and we're
the good guys so
you're either with us or you're
with them
He said that he would bomb Afghanistan
as soon as Condi showed him where it was
on the map
Bombs upon which they write "Hi jack this, fag"
because they is the man
they is civilized
And they cluster bomb hundreds of men, women, and children
because they are with them
And they bomb the Red Cross because
they are with them
And they bomb hospitals and senior citizens' homes
because they are with them
And they bomb thousands of goats, sheep, pheasants,
donkeys and geese because they are with them
Osama bin Laden who, if he is a modern equipped

cave ogre, had his fangs, hooves, and horns supplied
by American taxpayers
If the Russians had built a bigger soccer
stadium we would have even more room
to punish women who read books and don't
cover their ankles!
Dumya Bush, bin Laden's comrade in oil, thinks
All I wanted to be was baseball commissioner
but hell being president is more of a blast than I thought.
Everytime I open my mouth, thousands flee their
homes and head for the borders. When I visited Italy
a few months ago, the police beat up demonstrators
while shouting Il Duce. Who is this Il Duce? Get me
Condi.
They say that we should place flags in our
windows and join Dumya in his
Crusade, I mean campaign
They say that we should bond with
the neoconfederates and All-American Union Busters
Trent Lott, John Ashcroft, Gale Norton and
maybe join them in burning a cross because
that's what brotherhood means, doesn't it
joining together
and standing around fires and stuff
Won't Generals Nathan B. Forrest, Robert E. Lee,
and Stonewall Jackson, American patriots all
be proud of us and
beam up to us from their permanent residence
as we stand shoulder to shoulder with Dixie

I got it. Maybe we would fly the Stars and Bars
along with the Stars and Stripes to
show that not only is one country united
but both countries, I mean shucks
two for one is a good deal ain't it
Ain't that what they say at Wal-Mart
They say that we should chant
USA! USA! with people
who shadow us down the aisles
of department stores, hassle us
for living while black
who voted for proposition 209, 187,
and 21, who try our children as adults
and place them in jail with predators

They say that we should chant *USA! USA!*
with people who say that it's the poor's
fault that they are poor

They say that we should chant *USA! USA!*
with people who drag us from behind pickup trucks
and beat us for taking a walk in Bensonhurst, New York
People who
send our kids to special education classes
who say racism doesn't exist
It's just us playing the race card
Why don't we sing "America, the Beautiful"
with those who red line
and gentrify us into oblivion
Why don't we join Gov. Gray "Lights Out" Davis
who reduced our community colleges' budget
by millions
and Jerry Brown, The Imperial Mayor of
Oakland in a recitation of
the Pledge of Allegiance
I mean, police brutality is the price you
have to pay to get people to shop at the
Gap
They say that we should stand with
Rev. Billy Graham
Pat Robertson and Jerry Falwell
Christian soldiers
who want to hammer the infidels
"Why those people over there are
Manicheans. They see the world in
black and white," said Stephen Cohen from the
Brookings Institute
They say that we should belt out a chorus of
Cumbaya with
Pfizer Pharmaceuticals, experimenters on
African children, applaud them
for donating to the recovery effort of those thousands
who perished at the WTC

sacrificed on the chainsaw of ignorance and
arrogance, the twin brothers of mayhem and death
They say that we should give a warm patriotic
embrace to those who say they're fighting for
freedom abroad but deny us freedom at home
they always say that

We're fighting for freedom
they said it during World War I, World War II
the Korean War, the Vietnam War and the Gulf War
They say now Mose and Mosetta and
Li'l Abner and Daisy Mae
Jose and Maria if you
die for us in the steaming stinking jungles
and in the mean Afghanistan winters
we'll maybe let you
have a grilled cheese sandwich at Denny's

They say that we should unite
that we should display the flag
wear red white and blue headrags
and help rebuild Wall Street
"More than two weeks after the
terrorist attacks, costume retailers
report that the good guys are out-
selling the bad. Grownups and kids
are bypassing black capes and picking
up patriotic gear such as Uncle Sam hats"
They say we should empty our pockets and max out
our credit cards on Christmas
to show our loyalty
"We must not put our buying
decisions on hold. Go out and
buy cars, and automobiles, and
electronics, and appliances" said
the economist.
"The market is a forward looking
beast. We must hunker down with
the Beast," she said
"Santa is going to look a lot
like Uncle Sam this year" predicted
Monk Rivers, a spokesman for the
Mill corporation, which operates 12
malls
We should show our determination
to vanquish our enemy
by emptying our wallets
We must hunker down with the beast
for this crusade, I mean campaign
Operation Noble Eagle I mean
Operation Infinite Justice
I mean Operation Enduring Freedom

I mean—
as soon as we can find out
who the enemy is
Their unpronounceable names
Their strange customs
Their scraggly beards
Their writing that looks like
wriggling worms
Their baggy pants
The diapers on their heads
By jiminy, I heard that these A-rabs
expect to be surrounded by
25 virgins when they blow
themselves to kingdom come
They hate modernity
They hate "The Pink Flamingo"
Britney Spears
theme parks, diet Coke, corn syrup sucrose
obesity and novels whose
length exceed 500 pages
Why can't they get with the program

WHY DO THEY HATE US
Major David Letterman asked General Dan Rather
THEY HATE US BECAUSE THEY'RE EVIL
THEY HATE US BECAUSE THEY'RE ENVIOUS
said General Dan Rather from his blow dried and
tanned silver foxhole at Black Rock
Let The President Tell Me Where To Go
and I'll show up, he said

"We should invade their countries
kill their leaders and convert
them to Christianity," said Admiral Ann Coulter
the Daily News's ersatz blonde
We should join Dumya in his crusade
I mean his campaign as soon as we can
locate the enemy. It keeps changing
like a chameleon, it seems to be always
one camp, or cave ahead of us
What did the woman on C-Span say
on Sept. 23, phoning in to Washington Journal
Where do I go to get the understanding of
what I need to understand
in order to understand the president

who wants to invade Afghanistan or is
it Pakistan
or is it Tajikistan or is it
Uzbekistan or is it
Turkmenistan

I can't stand all of these stands
Hey, don't we have someone who can speak Arabic
Hey! what happened to those shining
seas that were supposed to protect us
from all of this PC nonsense
All I wanted to be was baseball commissioner
Get me Condi!

F. D. REEVE

·

Sunset, New York Harbor

As the full moon rises, the national twilight
    floats down river. Old Glory sinks
behind the city's gold-skin towers.
    Remember how Sohrab died
        in the spider web of his father's blindness,
            man avenging man?

So kindred slaughter each other mindlessly;
    blood flows, belief leeches the house;
fire mutilates white and black high-mindedness;
    the green hills of Africa
        and the sweet salt sea of the southern ocean
            dry up like the moon.

From the far side of the harbor comes a native song
    bending the sky in a rainbow, breaking
the sullen stones, proving no man is wrong
    whose strawberry heart will mend
        and whose dulcet genius transforms
            a terrifying end.

A premonition of New York City's decline, or fear of some violent happening—perhaps the whole island sinking—began haunting me at summer's end. The fighting in Israel became hopeless; I thought of David and Goliath reversed. I felt our own country going down faster and faster, politically corrupt on a new scale since the Supreme Court's unconstitutional selection of a president and the reinstallation in public office of oligarchs familiar from a dozen years ago. The rich were getting more tax benefits while public faith in the political process spiraled downward. The monstrously evil, clever attacks of September 11th provoked a gross response, also devastating to innocent bystanders. Worst of all, war abroad quickly became an excuse for repression at home. Obsessed with fighting, the government came to resemble Rustum, who, in his frenzy, couldn't tolerate his own son's appeasement. And the popular media have offered no dissent.

If there were Manhattoes on the west side of the Hudson now looking back on the island their ancestors sold for $24, what would they think? What would they do to assuage present suffering and to let us off the hook?

HELEN MORRISSEY RIZZUTO

Letter

December 8, 2001

Dear Bill,

For the past few years, I've enjoyed receiving your newsy Christmas letter; even though I personally know no one mentioned, I always feel that everyone is an extension of my own family and friends. Well, last year, I was determined to write back to you before this Christmas—that conference out at Southampton where we met so long ago, seems now to have taken place in another lifetime—but yes, I was determined to write on a number of occasions: the morning I saw a red-winged blackbird down near the Point; the twilight I had driven back from my sister-in-law's, and as I crossed the Jones Beach Bridge, saw six (!!!) seals swimming in the inlet (this, after an entire season spent seal watching in Parking Lot something-or-other). But I never did write, and then my sabbatical year ended and I returned to teaching, and then September 11th came ... and has stayed, will probably, I realize now, always remain a boarder in my house.

I hope that you and those you love didn't lose anyone close. Like so many New Yorkers (I guess you can take the girl out of the city, but never the city out of the girl), I lost several dear ones "once removed": a friend's son; a friend's brother-in-law; a friend's cousin; my nephew's best friend on the force who became a firefighter and had just finished in the academy in April, and on and on. My neighbor across the street is the Battalion Chief who was buried under the rubble, but whom they were able to dig out, and then, a few weeks after the attack, I learned that one of my students perished there. I went down to the site shortly after, to just be with her, strange as that sounds, and there really aren't words for what I did and did not experience there. The ghosts that people talk about are certainly there, and a friend who got on the LIRR two weeks after the attack told me that she could feel all those who would never board that train again. Down at Ground Zero the day that I went to remember Jennifer, there was an air of respect, of quiet grieving, of disbelief.

Unfortunately, the "air" surrounding Ground Zero has changed, and I'm not speaking of the smell, unmistakable whether you were driving over a bridge or downtown closer to the site, that was there until just recently, when the weather turned cool. On weekends, I volunteer at a restaurant that feeds the wonderful rescue workers (firefighters, police, state troopers, construction workers, morgue employees, etc.), and the other day, when I went down to work, I noticed that at least where I was—on Canal Street—an almost carnival atmosphere had begun to assert itself. Camera stands had been set up, and suddenly everyone seemed to be "packing" a camera. One obviously L.I. mother and daughter were sporting such expensive equipment and making such a to-do of their picture taking that I suddenly thought of "Show and Tell." It's interesting that the young man from Stuyvesant H.S. who took the photographs for *The Spectator* that appeared in the *New York Times* suggested that we should go out in our neighborhoods and into the city and take pictures, because these are the only documents there will be. I did give that some thought at the time, but somehow, I think there is a sacredness to much of what I have seen, and such heartbreak … down in the West End, for instance, across the porch of one of those converted bungalows, a huge banner above a crucifix and an American flag reads "Long Beach, Thank You, for giving Michael *'The Best Summer of my life!'*" Michael was a young firefighter who had just moved here. When Captain Fuentes came home, there was a home-made red, white and blue sign on the garage, "WELCOME HOME, DAD," and then there are all the funerals, and all the memorial services that make me think of the plague; there is no escaping the hundreds of men and women in blue, the bagpipes, the "pictures." On September 11th, I watched the towers burning from our windows on campus—that picture is registered in my eyes and in my mind; I reassured my students whose parents worked down at the Trade Center, and my friend whose child is asthmatic and had to flee Stuyvesant, and I did what was expected of me, but I feared for my daughter's life (she's one of those people you see running across the bridge into Brooklyn); I worry about my son who would also have graduated from the Academy in April, and who now is on the list the Fire Department is calling from. When I stay up past midnight working on lessons or writing or studying Italian (September 11th has also given us the gift of appreciating the moment and making the very most of it), I hear the fighter jets start their nightly watch—you can always tell them from the commercial flights—the steady drone, the sound that never goes away, the plane that never lands—and I know my dreams will not be good ones. So, no, I think I'll let others take the pictures, let life go on. I have gathered together all of my students' journals, and I took notes when one of their dads who is a lieutenant in the FDNY came to speak to two of my classes; I have the very moving responses written to my students and to me by all the Emergency Service Unit Police and Rescue companies and individual firefighters; I have my poems that I continue to write and work on, and all of that will go into a box until I decide whether or not anything should be done with it. Right now, in between all the academic demands, my classes are putting together a number of "gifts" for firefighters and police—they baked cookies and cakes and went and visited with them on Thanksgiving, or they "adopted" someone—a sister who goes to Stuyvesant and is having a hard time, a friend who lost someone, little children in their Sunday schools— who need special caring. There are thousands and thousands of stories, Bill, and thousands of examples of such goodness in people that I never expected to see in my lifetime.

A few weeks ago, I decided to get my sister, brother and our childhood friends and all our spouses out to dinner, to celebrate life and friendship and the reassurance of places once cherished that still support us with their mere presence. We had all grown up together, in that small gem on Jamaica Bay, had played games of G-H-O-S-T, had fallen in love, had stopped our rowdy games of running bases and stickball and quieted down when taps would travel to us on the air from Fort Tilden. So, we went back to Belle Harbor to visit our friends who still live there; went back to the restaurant on Newport Avenue and 130th Street we had been taken to as children, the restaurant that now is owned by a retired NYC firefighter whose son died on 9/11. It was a wonderful, wonderful evening, and we decided to get together like that every few months. You know the rest of the story, or at least the parts of it that made the news. The following Monday morning, the plane bound for the Dominican Republic crashed right on that corner; again, I began the hours of trying to get through, wondering if our friends were alive or dead; again, we were spared. When I went down to the Point for tea the other morning on my way to work, I picked up *The Herald* because on the lower half of the page was a pretty face I knew from around the neighborhood down there. The "face" belonged to the flight attendant on that plane. That's the way we live now, with the constant, constant reminders to embrace life, knowing inside ourselves what we always knew intellectually, that everything is gift or lesson or both, and that time doesn't come with the option of holding onto it.

This is a sad time, Bill, sometimes—often—achingly so, but it's also a beautiful time in which the kindness of people is sometimes astounding, a time in which so many things are truly possible. When I drove down the street the other evening all the lights were strung across the trees and shrubs outside our neighbor, the Battalion Chief's home. I think if I were to take a picture, that would be the one I would take and share with everyone. I hope that you and everyone you hug close, Bill, and all the world, will find peace, will *make* peace the gift we give one another now as 2001 comes to a close, and forever.

My love to all,
Helen

MARY ELSIE ROBERTSON

Birchbark

On the afternoon of September 11, driving from Asheville, North Carolina to the Hambidge Center, an artists' colony in the northern Georgia mountains, I was haunted by the images I'd spent the morning watching on television—black smoke pouring from the Twin Towers, both horrifyingly collapsing into rubble. I was at the mercy of my imagination which forced me over and over into one of the doomed planes watching the Tower loom like a mountain and listening to the cries of people moments from death.

So it was with great relief I climbed out of my car at the Hambidge Center where the late afternoon light lay golden over fields of wild asters, and butterflies flitted from one cluster of buddleia blossom to another, stepping into a peace that was worlds away from news of horror. It seemed the familiar peace I've always felt when I've driven into the grounds of an artists' colony, entering a space like that of Zen meditation where the hubbub of ordinary life stills to make room for the life of the spirit.

But my joyful relief in arriving at Hambridge on September 11 was quickly tempered by an uneasy feeling it took me a while to recognize as guilt. On other visits to artists' colonies, I'd been happy to let the life I'd left behind float away from my attention for a few weeks while I gave my energies to writing. On that particular evening, however, I could not so lightly turn my attention from what was taking place in the life I'd left behind where, I knew, families and friends were huddled together watching the unfolding of events, forming a common community of suffering that I felt removed from. The pleasure I'd felt in arriving at Hambidge suddenly smacked unpleasantly of escapism.

In the days to come, the other artists—three visual artists, a composer, another writer—and I talked about this dilemma during conversations at dinner. We couldn't deny that we were relieved to be in our Shangri La in the mountains where there was no television, radio reception was erratic, and even newspapers were four miles away. Few people in the country could have been as cut off from the news as we were. But the flip side of this isolation was that we were also cut off from common American experience during a time of grief and anguish. After September 11, the work we'd come to Hambidge to do seemed pointless, maybe even frivolous. In our isolated studios, where our only companions were pileated woodpeckers and hooded warblers, we feared we were merely doing the equivalent of fiddling while Rome burned.

Still, even if what we did in our studios might be pointless, we continued painting, writing, composing. And it gradually became clear that although our little group of artists was cut off from the wider world, we were nevertheles obsessed by what had taken place there.

After I'd been at Hambidge a couple of weeks, a visual artist asked us at dinner to write on pieces of birchbark our thoughts about September 11 and our hopes for peace. Later that evening we placed our bark vessels in the creek running through the property, sending them downstream in a ritual we thought of as a kind of prayer.

Another of the visual artists gave an open house at her studio, showing the rest of us, with some trepidation, abstract paintings bolder than anything she'd done before. The paintings, relying heavily on red, black, and yellow and short, jabbed lines, seemed to me to express rage, perhaps the artist's response to the terrorists' attacks.

A few days after this, the composer, who had arrived at the colony intending to complete a sonata for string quartet, set the sonata aside and worked instead on a requiem, a musical form he'd never considered writing before.

On the day before I was to leave Hambidge, I wrote the final scene of a novel, a scene in which the characters, having narrowly escaped death, are floating at night on a lake talking to one another, their disembodied voices rising from the darkness. Only on rereading the scene did I realize that my characters were like spirits speaking beyond the barrier separating life and death, and I felt this scene was my response to the events that had accompanied my arrival at the colony.

I have no illusion that the art made at Hambidge in September 2001 will change the world or even make much impact on it. But it is and always has been the nature of art to attempt the impossible. And it has also been the nature of artists to keep trying the impossible. September 11 has not changed this.

SCOTT RUSSELL SANDERS

Sorrow and Solidarity

It will take us all a very long time to absorb the lessons of last week's violence, and to gain some understanding of what it means for our society and ourselves. Anything that I can say or write so soon after the events will inevitably be partial and may be wrongheaded. For what they are worth, here are my early thoughts.

We have a great deal of mourning to do for all those who died or were seriously injured, for their families and friends. For those of us who had never known grievous loss, these events have stripped away our illusion of invulnerability. What follows grief, however, is most likely to be anger, and that seems to me dangerous, for ourselves and for the world.

I think the attack demonstrates the folly as well as the immorality of using violence to impose our will on others, and so I am dismayed to hear so many voices, both inside and outside the government, responding to the atrocity by threatening vengeance, by calling for greater military spending, by promising war. I think the attack demonstrates the folly of building a nuclear missile shield, both because the money for such a technological fantasy will be drained away from humanitarian purposes (at home and abroad), and because there are clearly easier ways to attack a complex technological society than by firing nuclear-tipped missiles. I think the attack illustrates the dangers of gigantism—striving to construct the largest building, corporation, economy, army, or machine—because such gigantism makes a fat target and it also makes our country easy prey to terrorism. I think the attack, and the subsequent run on gasoline, reveals the folly of building an economy so addicted to petroleum that any hint of a disruption in supply throws us into a panic.

Above all, I think the attack demonstrates—if we needed such a demonstration—that United States foreign policy, economic practice, military behavior, and cultural products have inspired passionate hatred in many parts of the world, including within our own borders. I want to understand what I can of that hatred—what caused it, what reasons there may be behind it, and what we might do, as a country and as individuals, to reduce it. This is not a matter of "blaming" America for the attack; nothing whatsoever could justify such mayhem. Rather, I wish to understand what I can of the grievances and suffering that bred the hatred. For I don't accept the view that the people who carried out these monstrous acts were themselves simply monsters—that they were crazy, or brainwashed, or demonic, or evil. I am convinced that if we follow such acts back to their sources, we will find suffering. And only by alleviating suffering can we reduce the likelihood of further violence. The antidote to war is neither missile shields, larger Pentagon budgets, nor bombing raids; the only durable antidote is taking away the causes of war.

I am also troubled by the sometimes reckless search for a culprit, especially by the tendency among some people to demonize whole categories of people—Arabs, Muslims, Afghans, Iraqis, etc. I suspect that precisely this penchant for dividing the world into "Us and Them" helped to inspire the hatred that boiled over in last week's attack. We may get tired of hearing about the necessity for compassion, tolerance, and mutual respect. But we cannot live decently or peacefully in a crowded world without those qualities.

Certain moments in one's life cast their influence forward over all the moments that follow. For all of us, the events of this week will change us forever. How we change will determine whether the terrorists have achieved their goal.

If we become a more fearful, aggressive, and vengeful society, then the terrorists will have won. If we divide among ourselves, judging one another by religion or skin color or accent, then the terrorists will have won. If we respond to this assault on freedom by sweeping aside protection for civil liberties, for other species, and for the soil and water and air; if we respond to violence by becoming more violent, stockpiling weapons, dropping bombs on civilians—then the terrorists will have won.

But if we respond to the terrible events of this week by becoming more loving toward one another and toward innocent people every-where; if we redouble our commitment to the ideals of freedom and equality on which this nation was founded; if we become more compassionate, more aware of the suffering of people in all countries; if we dedicate our own lives to doing useful work and to defending the health of our communities—then the terrorists will have failed.

We cannot bring back those who've died. We cannot wipe away the pain from their families and friends. We cannot undo the monstrous events that have torn the fabric of our society. But we can work to make sure the damage does not creep into our hearts. We can make sure the poison of these cruel acts does not infect our society. We can dedicate ourselves to making peace. And we can only make lasting peace by reducing injustice and misunderstanding and suffering everywhere—beginning in our own households and communities.

During a time of war in Ireland, William Butler Yeats wrote a poem called "The Second Coming," whose opening stanza haunts many of us these days:

Turning and turning in the widening gyre
The falcon cannot hear the falconer;
Things fall apart; the centre cannot hold;
Mere anarchy is loosed upon the world,
The blood-dimmed tide is loosed, and everywhere
The ceremony of innocence is drowned;
The best lack all conviction, while the worst
Are full of passionate intensity.

Truly, "the blood-dimmed tide" was loosed this week, and innocence was drowned. We have seen that the worst of people are "full of passionate intensity," willing to wreak havoc without question or remorse.

Now the rest of us must show that we do not lack conviction. We must show that we possess the courage of our principles. The surest way to defeat terrorism is to dedicate ourselves to the work of healing. The surest way to defeat hatred is to enlarge the sphere of love.

You may be finding it difficult to concentrate on your work in the face of such cruel and shocking events. I certainly do. At the same time, I feel all the more determined to do whatever is in my power to increase understanding and affection. Far from making me despair, these terrible events help clarify for me the only true grounds for hope.

At a dark time in his own life, Robert Frost wrote a poem called "Acquainted With the Night," which opens with these lines:

I have been one acquainted with the night.
I have walked out in rain—and back in rain.
I have outwalked the furthest city light.

I have looked down the saddest city lane.
I have passed by the watchman on his beat
And dropped my eyes, unwilling to explain.

We are all now more deeply acquainted with the night than we were at dawn on September 11. The night is real, it is powerful, it is frightening; but it is not the final truth. Every good impulse in your heart tells you that life is larger than death, that love is stronger than hate. Cling to that knowledge, and carry it with you as medicine for the wounds of this week.

JOANNA SCOTT

Our America

We went early on a bright Sunday: October 28, a day that turned out
to be the first full day scheduled for mourning: a day of silence. We
drove in along I-95 without a map, took a wrong turn, found ourselves heading into Queens. As we crossed the Triboro Bridge Billie
Holiday came on the radio to sing "Autumn in New York." We
remarked upon the coincidence.

The dog woke up as we wove through the streets. She planted her
front paws on the seat beside me, perched there between us as
though she knew what she hoped to see. We crossed into Manhattan
over the Queensboro Bridge and made our way downtown along
Second Avenue. Just past 5th Street my brother slammed on the
brakes. The car behind us squealed. There, my brother said—the
fourth floor window of his old apartment! And there, on the corner,
his favorite diner. Cars honked at us, the dog barked, and we drove
on across Houston, through crowded Chinatown, down Mott Street
lined with toppled boxes of refuse, down toward Fulton, past pairs of
police and roadblocks sealing empty side streets, down toward the
South Street Seaport to the east end of Wall Street.

We parked in front of Pier 11 and walked south. Outside Engine
Company 4, a fireman was loading gear into his car. A memorial had
been set up beside the door—a bookcase filled with Dalmatian beanie
babies, photos of men with arms linked, candles burning in memory, letters written with shaky hands to eight lost firemen: Joseph and
Arthur, Scott L. and Scott K., Eric, Douglas, Thomas, and Richard.

The dog tugged at the leash. We walked on. The breeze carried the
bitter odor of wet sheet-rock. There was too much light for lower

Manhattan, and the streets were too empty. When we reached Battery Park, the bell at the Seton Shrine began to ring—an aching, odd tolling, again, again, too many times, again, again, too early to mark the hour. It was five minutes to nine.

And then the tolling stopped, and the Sunday-morning quiet at Battery Park seemed too quiet, the sky too blue, the motion of a man sweeping the walk mesmerizingly slow. He stopped and asked us where we were going. We told him. He told us we couldn't get nowhere near there cause they was guarding that gold, all that gold, keeping the Mafia away from all that gold. But go ahead, he told us, with obvious contempt. Go on and have a look.

The dog lunged at squirrels as we crossed the park. We made our way along the narrow sidewalk in front of the new Residence skyscraper and the neighborhood of Battery Park. In one of those buildings our mother's gentle friend Ruth has lived for years. Our mother told us that Ruth doesn't like to talk about Sept 11th, but she did say that in the last couple of weeks aid workers have supplied her with a new refrigerator and vacuumed the dust from each and every one of her books.

We walked on. The quiet grew even quieter. A woman wearing a surgical mask crossed the street. Two cyclists propped their bikes against a shed and studied a map. We were surprised there weren't more people here. Yellow ribbons and blockades marked police lines, cordoned off alleys and courtyards. A wrought-iron gate had been knocked askew and bent. A hardhat was nailed to a board below words painted in red: MUST WEAR. The crushed branches of a tree dangled over the street. Broken windows of surrounding buildings had been replaced with plywood. As we walked up West Street we saw the long red arms of the construction cranes and the teetering skeleton wall we'd seen in so many pictures. Water poured in a steady, soundless stream from a firetruck. White steam rose from the pile of broken steel and soot, gray smoke rose from the steam.

There was too much sunlight, and everyone moved too slowly. A small group had gathered near a police officer in front of Gateway Plaza. They spoke in murmurs, their reactions and speculation inaudible. Some were weeping. The officer told us that every time the firemen pulled another beam loose, another fire sprang up. He said this was his first day on the site. He asked me what I was writing in my notebook. I told him. He said, You're looking at buildings that were never designed to come down.

Signs below scaffolds forbade commercial photos. A Red Cross Disaster Relief van rolled along the street. Everything was muffled, restrained, warped. Only our dog seemed to exist in real time. She pulled at the leash, pulled us beyond a barricade into the restricted area. A man wearing a hardhat waved us on. Can we go this way? I asked. He said, Keep going. We kept going, circling an emptiness so vast and senseless it allows no description. We wound our way through the labyrinth of yellow ribbons stamped with caution-caution-caution. We looked for evidence that it all had really happened. We left footprints in the ash.

Back on Broadway and Liberty, where the buildings along the western-most block made a corridor leading directly to the site, a woman who wanted to set up a vending stand was arguing with a policeman. Signs prohibited all photographs and videos. On Wall Street, Sengalese vendors were selling I-Love-NY t-shirts and sweatshirts. A man walking ahead of us lifted his young son onto his shoulders. A security guard shifted restlessly from foot to foot. Scaffolding covered the buildings along the south side of the last block of street. A young woman sat on a grate under a stretch of scaffold, her few belongings spread out around her, her face masked with chalky gray ash.

She wanted to talk. She wanted to tell us that her face was rough. Rough? Rough, yeah, rough, thaz right, and she needed money, but she was plenty warm enough, she said, gesturing to her hot-air grate. She crumpled the money we gave her into a ball and stuffed it in the pocket of her jacket. After that she didn't want to talk anymore. She motioned us to go on, indicating that she had work to do. She lifted up a small pair of sewing shears, reached for a piece of bright-red rayon. As we walked back to the car she continued what she'd already started, skillfully separating the fabric's seam with the point of the shears, undoing it stitch by stitch by stitch.

If this were fiction I would explain how we started to walk away and then turned around just a few steps later to look back. But the woman had disappeared, along with her rags, and the shadows beneath the scaffold were empty.

EDWINA SEAVER

Reconciliation: An Introduction

Invited to introduce this anthology, this in some senses topical anthology (& as such anathema to fiction writers & poets), I've in turn requested, in fact insisted, that my brief remarks be buried within its text.

Does this reveal my desire to level myself with this history, as victims of the terrible day of title were crushed or vaporized, disappeared into its story? And is this anthology's own story a babel of voices, or a new anthem? A bedlam of declaration, of rave & grunt, or Walt Whitman's fervently wished-for *ensemble*? Do we hear America singing? Do we hear America praying? I do not know. We hear America writing.

I once wrote, in a phrase that several reviewers fastened on, that American history "is a timeless, inexorable, trans-spatial, backfolding, lyric progression to the Battle of Little Bighorn." In this gathering, Diane Glancy suggests to us that the World Trade Center towers were for white America what the buffalo were for our first peoples. Several others here locate racism within the abiding matrix of guilt that at this time animates our grief & anger & general befuddlement. It is crucial to notice that this collection appears *in medias res* (where as symbolic construct it hopes always of course to remain) as the digging-out continues, & warplanes strike the oppressive Taliban in Afghanistan, & anthrax & other terrors infiltrate our conventional thought & might. Thus, we credit a certain empathic courage here, for the every instinct of creative writers is toward distance & Wordsworthian emotion recollected in tranquility. Many experience trepidation in speaking now, for Time bleaches words (& skulls) that fail to reach meanings beyond words, & enduring voice comes by way of long-staring, by way of osmotic thought & image over however much time may be necessary. Warrior Custer rushed to his death; in some senses, certainly, his was a suicidal empathy.

September 11, 2001: American Writers Respond can appear now in the way it does because its writers, in general, do not decide what they have to say & then say it, do not orchestrate an outline—even Wendell Berry's paragraphs here are an *in*line, the passionate concentrated in-your-face hammerstrokes of a lifetime's integrated (the poet is one who *integrates*, master Emerson tells us) thinking—but learn what they know & feel by first setting it down & *then* staring with the auditory mind to see if their work continues to give of itself beyond them in their timebound lives, and will. If they have in common nothing else here, their united faith is that human survival itself demands their making the unconscious conscious, as trees do, as they current subsoils into air & light. There must have been, even for George Armstrong at the moment he was shot dead from his horse during such an awesome collision of cultures, such piercing revelation as illuminated all his heavens that dusty whites'— Centennial day.

Only sensing what this gathering could become, the editor wrote his preface. He invoked that now-mythic resident of Walden. By way of karmic resonance, the last contributor here, Paul Zimmer, is also able to begin his own meditation by way of Thoreau. Yes, where are we if not always treading the once-crystalline waters of our central question? But what, asked expatriate Gertrude Stein on her deathbed during a muddier time, *is* the question?

If not *the* question, *one* question is in part answered by the fact here that many writers have answered the editor's call to break the bread of their contexts with us. In so doing, it is as though they recognize that September 11, 2001 was a date that must begin their new attempt, as citizens among us, to be—oh these despised & conflicted words—relevant, understood. Aliki Barnstone tells us that consciousness itself changed for her on that date: "In the past, I was loath to describe the autobiographical sources of my poems because I wanted readers to focus on my poetry as the imaginative transformation of experience, and not as a therapeutic record of my personal life. But after the catastrophe, I think this reserve is a silly theoretical conceit that might even have the dangerous effect of divorcing art from the real and from its power to witness." Make no mistake. Our arts have thrived on remoteness, deflection, over-the-shoulder innuendo, a myriad of aesthetic dispensations, and have (have they?) disdained the masses in need of their sustenance. The editor sensed that creative writing, the life of the imagination itself, was fated to become more & more trivialized by traumatic events in the out-there. This is not a new fear. It is as cyclic as mosquitoes in a region of four seasons. But now these mosquitoes have become killer bees. They have become nuclear warheads kept ready in the bellies of Trident submarines. Yes, to say the least: the enormity of homeland destruction on that ninth-month morning might seem to have banished fiction & poetry to margins beyond heal-all & the monarchs' milkweed. There are various kinds of extraordinarily naked & direct communications here—not all, as are Barnstone's, autobiographical—including many that focus on poetics, the thing in itself, a writer's reason for being itself. And what else is poetry, as the editor of this collection seems to sense—though he himself sometimes for ulterior motives of theme or because of his exhaustion grants dispensations of various kind—what else is poetry but the transmutation, by way of language, of mystical power into rhythmic form?

One of the many riveting durations in this book occurs as the editor prods Steve Kowit, a poet he has apparently never met, to pour his orchestral self into his words. No matter its ostensible subject, Heyen's own poetry has tended toward traditional linear & aural symmetries, as in the acerbic brainbroken 29th section, called "Gifts," of the 1991 Gulf War book Kowit looks forward to seeing:

First day of the fifth week of the war.
"Desert Storm" there, winter storm here.
In Iraq, the removal of bodies & body parts
& fused lumps of unidentifiable remains
from what we call a command bunker
& what they call a civilian bomb shelter

& which was one or the other, or both.
In Brockport, snow outlines pastel ribbons
in my neighbors' trees along our streets
cleared by nightshift plows, & sanded
as we slept. In Baghdad, women in black
search & mourn among the blanketed dead

dragged out of their devastated haven.
Air raid sirens are still keening
while here the snow softens everything

in the fallen world. A White House spokesman
informs us that human life hasn't the "sanctity"
for their president that it does for mine ...

& I don't want to live, sometimes—do you?
The blankets are not khaki, but civilian,
in rich colors & sacred Islamic designs.
All day across this country we'll open
cards & heart-shaped boxes of candy.
Happy Saint Valentine's.

Clothed in balanced stanza & keening rhyme, he asks Kowit, in
whom he senses kindred spirit, for more than what to him, so far, is
just the first draft of what might become a poem, asks for remains-
ribbons-haven-mine-civilian-design-Valentine's, so to speak, for
the sanded & ampersanded inevitabilities so dear to my own heart.
Kowit reconciles, responds not in curses but with a letter sung, or
rather chanted, in flame. We realize here the central editorial candle
faithful between these covers. But not every contribution, in Rainer
Maria Rilke's words, does "break free of its own ideas / like a star."
But most do, & this is not a book to be taken like sleepytime tea, or
aspirins, or cathedrals. In the best work here, there is excruciating
tension as form stands in dread of power—*what the devil*, Emerson
asks, *will he* (power) *do next*?

I have introduced many books. Possibly, one or two contain news
that will remain news over time with successive readings. Even while
extolling them, I harbored inner-complaints about these books. But
let us live with ourselves and listen with our whole being to such
ensemble. That old unfashionable verity, sincerity, is here, text &
subtext throughout. Not one contribution here bases its sought-for
truth, its stays against confusion, on one book only. Not one wishes
to terrorize the others. Every writer here kneels for peace as does the
father-spirit of American poetry at the end of the Civil War. If this
gathering's welcoming poem by W.S. Merwin asks that words somehow, despite every limitation begin to speak, this poem by Whitman,
who called for "nature without check with original energy," might
serve as coda:

Word over all, beautiful as the sky,
Beautiful that war and all its deeds of carnage must in time be
    utterly lost,
That the hands of the sisters Death and Night incessantly softly
    wash again
        and ever again, this soil'd world;
For my enemy is dead, a man divine as myself is dead,
I look where he lies white-faced and still in the coffin—I draw near,
Bend down and touch lightly with my lips the white face in the
    coffin.

DIANE SEUSS

Falling Man

The man falls. I'm told
he jumped; he had no choice,
or two bad choices. Burn
or fall. He chose
falling. His clothes
are the clothes
of a businessman. White
shirt, dark, well-tailored pants.
His tie extends from his throat
and draws a black line
parallel to the horizon. He has
not fallen; he is falling. He
falls. The tail of his shirt
has come untucked. He's pulled it
free, or it's been pulled free
by the wind. He's an elegant
man at the end
of his day. I wouldn't be surprised
to see a briefcase in his hand.
His pants balloon a bit, filled
with wind. His hair is cropped short,
the cut of a professional man. An expensive
cut. I'm told he is falling, but he seems
to be flying. The man flies. He dances in the air.
It's a sophisticated dance. Smooth.
Something out of the '40s, a black
and white film. A man and woman have been dancing,
he's held her in his arms but now he breaks

free. Time for a solo. The bones
of his cheek, his jaw, his chin
are exquisite. I can imagine cupping
that face in my hands. I want
to call after him: Have a good day. Don't work
too hard. I'll see you at dinner. I love you baby boy.
I like to call him that. Baby boy. It works against
who he is. Such a grownup. Competent. A man
who knows how to take care of himself. How
lucky I am to have found him. He is a man
who works and now his work
is falling. He falls well, better than anyone
has fallen before. Such grace.
Such a strong wind in his clothes.
His shirt emits light. His pants foretell
the darkness coming on. His belt
is the circular horizon. The man falls
or he is born. He is entering the world
headfirst. Or he is still, a great stillness,
and it is we who are falling, beautifully falling,
we who will be forever falling.

LAURIE SHECK

Letter

Dear William Heyen,

Michael Atkinson told me about the book you're doing on reactions
to Sept 11th. I look forward to it. Sorry I don't have anything to
contribute. Here, in downtown NYC, things are beginning to feel
more normal, though the wreckage still burns and the smell of it
fills the air on certain days—a smell like burning computers.

I was teaching Emily Dickinson during the weeks after the planes
hit (once the University re-opened that is—it took a number of
days before our part of the city, below 14th street, was no longer
cordoned off from the rest of the city). Those were eerie times—
those days when the streets were closed to traffic, and there was no
mail delivery, and phones weren't working, etc. I guess since
you're doing reactions there's not really a place for Dickinson in
your book—but I can't tell you strongly enough how deeply her
work resonated then for my class and me. Among other things she
is, of course, a poet of how the brain registers shock; of breakage
and slippage in the mind. I have always loved her work, but I find
myself turning to it daily now.

These are strange, disturbing times. A girl my daughter goes to
school with is Muslim and for religious reasons always has her head
covered. But now she's removing her kerchief before leaving school
so as not to be bothered on the street.

"After great pain, a formal feeling comes—," "I felt a Funeral in my Brain," "Pain—has an Element of Blank—" —sustaining words these days.

Looking forward to your book—

All best,
Laurie Sheck

ROSALYNNE CARMINE SMITH

The Poison Birds

A robin whispered in my head
I want you dead I want you dead
Though you're a man or child
I want you dead

A grackle screaked in my head
I want you dead I want you dead
Black white yellow brown or red
I want you dead

A bluebird sliced into my head
I want you dead I want you dead
You're Christian agnostic Buddhist Jew
I want you dead

A hummingbird blurred in my head
Farmer teacher nurse and cop
Mick and kraut and spic and wop
I want you dead

A passenger pigeon extinguished my head
I want you dead I want you dead
Women who show your public face
I need you dead

An eagle taloned in my head
In Texas Maine or Tennessee
L.A. Detroit or bluegrass country
I want you dead

Who taught our birds Osama's song
Towers of fear fall all year long
Feathers of ash could they be wrong
I want you dead I want you dead

ON "THE POISON BIRDS"

Ever since I was a child and from my parents' library read William Blake's *Songs of Innocence and of Experience*, I have had one of the latter lyrics singing in me. Do you remember "A Poison Tree"? It begins, "I was angry with my friend: / I told my wrath, my wrath did end. / I was angry with my foe: / I told it not, my wrath did grow." This wrath becomes a tree which bears an "apple bright." The speaker's foe eats this apple, and dies, and the speaker is glad. But he has himself, it seems, become the poison tree of the title!

Shortly after that insidious orchard of September 11, I read a letter in a local newspaper from someone who said that he'd always been a liberal, who said he knew that the skewed priorities and the injustices of American foreign policy were the root causes of the contempt in which we are held in the Middle East and elsewhere. He said that he, and many of his friends, had worked and lobbied against arrogant and even evil American assumptions and practices. But now, he said, with the September 11 attacks, he understood that the United States was up against an enemy that could not be appeased, would not rest before killing every one of us, no matter our religion, sex, age, ethnic background. You would never be able to dance with this devil of an enemy, he said.

Some days after reading this letter, I woke with stanzas of "The Poison Birds" in my mind, and wrote the whole piece quickly. It seems to me now very sure of itself ... until the last stanza, perhaps, when "song" and "long" called up in my mind—as sounds will—what might be the necessary corrective of the third rhyme. But I'll let you be the judge of that experience.

ELIZABETH SPIRES

The Beautiful Day

We cannot live in Eden anymore.
The wall is broken. The violence done.

We peer beyond the ruin of that day
and see ... what do we see?

No enemy. Just smoke and rubble.
A vacancy terrible to behold.

There is a force, the mauve dragon
of my daughter's nightmares,

that wants to kill, cold as a serpent,
whatever harmless thing comes near.

And time now is of a different order,
        the future nearer, close enough

to touch,
               as a day's never-to-be-forgotten
images repeat on an endless spool:

of those told, *don't look back,*
       who saved themselves by running.

The air behind them
vacant. Full of smoke.
What had been there a moment before. Gone.

*

A month after it happened, my daughter and I
stood in a rose garden a few miles

north of Baltimore. Espaliered pear and apple trees
climbed an old brick wall. It was a beautiful day,

but shadowed and deepened in a way
I could never have imagined before.

The sky was *intensely* blue, just like the day
     it happened.

Roses of every shade and hue
still bloomed, the first frost yet to come.

My daughter, nearly eleven, wished for a garden
like the one we stood in. A rose garden

surrounded by a curving wall.
Maybe someday ... I said.

We stood there, watching weightless white spoors
of milkweed lift in the wind.

Uncountable numbers drifted upward and away,
each shining in the sun.

Like words. But what are words now?

Words are so small. Words have no weight.
And nothing will ever be the same.

        (September/October 2001)

DAVID ST. JOHN

from *The Face*

V.

Black leaves. The notebooks filling with ash. The limbs of the city
Warping toward heaven, the limbs of the angels angling toward the
    earth. Hope
Like the blisters bursting along the soft body of the air, the flakes of
    flint falling
Through laced fingers of flame. Black leaves. *Feuilles de noire ...*
—Where were you, do you remember? (I think the television was
    hanging, still,
In the window of the department store, the silent repetition of lips
    moving
Behind its glass.) The black street filling with black leaves. The
    limbs of the lover
Slowly wrapping the soft body of the other, the char of breath rising
Off the future ... Black sheets sheer as satin, black leaves, black rain
    falling
Along blank window sills. Do you remember? (Now?) Where were
    you? Was I
Beside you beneath the black canopy of limbs? Had you filled your
    notebooks
Yet, or were you dreaming of our bodies falling through black rain,
    like the rain,
Black as the leaves of ash, as the lips moving over the lips of the
    lover, the black
Pages swirling in the ever-swelling book of the dead....

Afterwards, that afternoon and for weeks after, old and young writers all were asking themselves the question asked everywhere in these pages: what now? My young undergraduates as well as my graduate students at USC, my friends and fellow poets, both those who are my contemporaries and those who are my elders, my adult students in the small private workshops I teach—every writer I know was asking him or herself, Where now do I fit, where do I belong, against this horrifying landscape?

*

On the Thursday morning following Tuesday the 11th, a reporter I know from the *Los Angeles Times* calls, a brilliant African-American woman, asking for a quote for an article she's doing—a serious and remarkably brave article on the collapse and misuse of public language by politicians, news reporters, and media personalities of every stripe, in the explosion of hysterical nationalism. A second reporter from the *LA Times* calls, and we talk about the cell phone and air phone calls in those minutes before the planes went down. I tell him how they are, for me, like compressed brilliant elegies in reverse, brief haiku of farewell and departure, *feuilles* of release for those who would now continue, those left behind who would need to go on living. Each of those callers, beyond the moment, understood that the most terrifying of all intimate terrors is, with the death of a loved one, not to know what ("really") happened....

*

The day that both *LA Times* articles appear, a producer for a TV tabloid nightly news journal calls me, asking if I will go on camera the next evening to talk about those cell phone calls. I tell her, I think of myself as a bottom-feeding scum sucker, but even I have certain self-respecting limits.

*

We're all writing letters to the dead.

ABIGAIL STONE

3 War World

Mohammed turns on the radio in his underground cave and leans back against the rock wall. Behind him are the eyes of an antelope in a stone age painting.

"Smoke 'em out and move in any way we can. As for the anthrax, we, uh, I can't say for sure if it's the Al Qaeda network or not. We're treating it as a crime, as an act of ..." Mohammed opens his Afghan-to-English dictionary and looks up the word, "network."

I am sitting on the floor of my living room in a small house in Jerkins, New Hampshire, holding a bottle of Cipro and listening to NPR. "All we DO know is this. He is a rich billionaire's son who has a grudge against the United States, against the entire western world." I am not holding the bottle of Cipro out of fear. I am not a postal worker or a democratic leader of the house. In fact, I don't even HAVE a job. I am holding it because I have a tooth infection.

Mohammed goes out in the early morning after the bombing has stopped briefly. He picks his way through the bombed rubble to where Mahmuud is sitting in his usual spot on the ground, selling grapes. "Got any red grapes this morning?" Mohammed asks in Afghanese.

Mahmuud says no, only white grapes. "The red ones were held up at the Pakistani border," he explains.

"What a night, eh?" Mohammed says.

"You don't know noise until you spend a night in Kabul," Mahmuud responds. He hands Mohammed a cloth bag of grapes and takes the handful of bullets in exchange.

"May God be with you," Mohammed says.

"May God be with you," Mahmuud says back to him.

No one has died yet in Jerkins, New Hampshire, of anthrax I mean. A few men have died in high profile places, like Boca Raton and Washington, but no women yet and no one in Jerkins. I feel safe. But I don't feel great.

Tony Blair rolls over toward his wife. "I did everything I could," he complains. "I went out on the proverbial limb for George. I feel very much as though I've lost face with the entire world over this ... praising him and sending in our British troops, only to be snubbed by his whole administration. I mean, China! Russia! He's dancing around the world going thither-and-yon to every major country except England.... It's not quite cricket, is it?"

Tony's wife sighs. "Your problem is that you care too much, Anthony. It's a war, darling. War can't be chummy, now can it?"

They have sex, but it isn't the same. He would have enjoyed it more if George had been nicer about those ground troops.

The radio station in Jerkins asks us to be on the lookout for any suspicious looking characters. "We have received information that leads us to believe another attack is imminent," Mr. Ashcroft says. It's hard to believe he was the man I wrote to my senator about a few months ago. "Please vote against Ashcroft for attorney general," I wrote, "on account of his suspicious looking past record." Now I listen to his words with increasing alarm. Will the evil-doers leap out at me on the sidewalk and shoot me up with chemical warfare? How does Mr. Ashcroft know they are coming? Who tells him this stuff? How did they know anthrax was going to play a part before it ever surfaced? Am I being anti-American to wonder this?

Mohammed doesn't usually call Osama on his cell phone. These days one can't be too sure. But he wants to know if it's OK to send another smallpox letter to the democratic party. "May I speak to Osama?" he asks when the phone is answered by a female.

"May I ask who is calling?" the female voice requests.

"This is Mohammed the 27th, fifty miles outside of Uzbekistan," Mohammed says. He can hear a shout of anger in the background and then gunfire.

"I told you never to inquire who is calling!" Osama shouts to the woman and then Mohammed is spoken to by the old familiar tyrannical voice, "No interviews."

"It is I, Osama, Mohammed, outside of Uzbekistan, yet within our holy borders."

"Did the grapes get there?" Osama asks, forgoing any hi-how-are-you's.

"They are here. And the grape seller is with them."

"Did you hear my wife? Can you believe it? I almost shot her for that. First they want to discard the burka, then they want to start controlling the VCR and the phone."

"Yes," Mohammed agrees, settling back against the rock wall. "But she DID write that bestseller...."

"Don't talk about that," Osama responds. "Ever since *Dirty War, Dirty Socks* she has forgotten how to be a woman. The cave is a mess, she does nothing but talk on the phone to Terry Gross. Anyway, did you mail the smallpox?"

Audrey Rumsfeldt takes two sleeping pills and starts to cook dinner. Donnie will be home soon and she is making macaroni and cheese. She takes a small vial of anthrax out of the spice cabinet and sprinkles it into the boiling water. The phone rings.

"We're smokin' them outta their caves," President Bush says to a crowd of Republican media. "Make no mistake about that. S M O K E-

I N G. And we're gonna get 'em on the run. But right now I have to go
read a Dick and Jane book to a group of children in an undisclosed
location, so I'm afraid I can't answer but two questions."

"Mr. President? Will you be reading the selection with or without
Sally in it?" a reporter demands.

"Without," the president says, decisively.

"Do you plan on flying to this destination?" another queries.

"Yes, and I encourage all of you to fly," the president says and then he
is whisked off stage, and the paparazzi are left to scribble the answers
in their notebooks before returning to their offices to write up the
briefing.

"I want smallpox, I want diarrhea, I want bladder infections, the
whole shee bang and I want it sent out today, do you understand?"
Osama shouts into the green cell phone. Two wives huddle at his feet
anxiously writing down everything he says.

"I just hope to get this published before the devastating winter
weather hits," the older wife whispers.

"Shut up or I will shoot you!" Osama shouts.

"The tragic events that have led us to consider ground troops are very
apparent," Tony Blair recites. It's all rote now, there is no feeling
in his speeches anymore. His wife stands beside him, looking
concerned and attractive. "We are on the precipice of a new era.
This is not like the old era," Tony says.

My tooth infection has improved. If I had a job, I could probably
go back to work tomorrow; that's how much better it is. I sit in the
living room on the Afghan rug and put the English hot water
bottle on my jaw. It is nippy weather. I am listening to the silence.
I turned off the radio an hour ago. It was just the same old same
old, over and over and over. It didn't make any sense. But that is
because it is not supposed to.

RUTH STONE

Tell Me

"Tell me, Ruth, how is your vision?"
"Lord," I say, "know you not how it is with me?
You who are blind to the sorrows of all things temporal,
You who are not even the wind sliding under the door;
how is it that I hear this echo,
catching even in my blind eye the death throes of a distant star?"
And you say, voiceless as the forests of the mountains
of the Sahara, of the Gobi, of the Kalahari,
"Oom ah, swept away."

The Way of It

I often think of the Kamikaze
in my day dreams, or Shizu
painting the flush of new grass
behind Laguna;
the citron baby hairs
spreading over the yellow gash
of erosion where
the seasonal waters rushed.

I often think of the Luftwaffe
in my sleep,
or the hawks at Laguna,
their shadows crossing the hills
around the reservoir,
while the ground squirrels freeze,
motionless, outside their burrows.

STEVE STREET

Care for the Small Things

A few days after the attack, I began to notice a new attitude in my classes. Even in my composition class—in fact especially among those freshmen, whose attention can be the most difficult to get and keep, pelted as they are by new stimuli in most facets of their lives— I sensed, replacing their common adolescent restlessness and enthusiasm for objections, loopholes, ambiguities or errors in the instructions, a new focus, a new willingness to understand the task that each new day's lesson presents. When classes resumed on September twelfth, I made a few vague remarks intended to settle us after the events that had closed our campus on the eleventh, but I didn't encourage further discussion of the disaster, partly because no brief discussion seemed possible, no easy consensus beyond the immediate sense of shock and horror, and partly because the one thing that seemed clear even in the immediate aftermath is that there will be no lack of talk. On that Wednesday, when the university re-opened, a student stopped by my office to ask whether we would be discussing the attack in the afternoon class she had with me. All her other classes had, she said, and she didn't know how much more she could take. Her chin quivered.

As it happened, in that class we were reading fiction from around the world, and to the extent that literature can foster empathy across cultures, the course has a kind of general and long-range bearing on many of the interlocking causes of the attack as well as on future solutions to the global disparities it indicates, in that same general and long-range way. But I took my cue from my upset student and limited my remarks to just that one. I'd wondered what I could do to alleviate her anxiety and that of others who must have felt similarly.

Should I go easy, lighten up, and give everybody a break during this stressful time, as if admitting how insignificant our lives and activities seemed compared to such enormity close by? Should I drop my teacher role, my professional persona—such as it is, since formality can be anathema in this profession—in favor of an even warmer and more human face?

Better, I decided, just to teach a really good class. Not as a distraction, though even in quieter times addressing the same captive audience three times a week can raise that question—but as an offering of something good, something larger than my students, larger than me, larger than our classroom, maybe larger than the crisis, finally. Offer them a place toward which to direct positive energy. Offer them something capable of sustaining all the attention they can bring to bear on it. Offer them my subject as I know it and love it, in other words, and when I did that I was as invigorated as I believe my students were.

And now, after the initial shock and dismay of those first few days following the attack, when most thought seemed irrelevant, this phenomenon seems to be taking place: instead of the enormity of those events reducing small concerns even further, it seems to be restoring to them a measure of importance. Where does the comma go? What's the effect of the repeated line in this poem? Why does Italo Calvino keep interrupting his own narrator more often at the beginning of this story than at the end? If for no other reason than to avoid more unpleasant situations, to face more unanswerable questions, students not only began answering questions like these, they began raising them. Suddenly it all seems to matter a bit more.

Naturally, students still want to know what will be on the quiz, how many points off for spelling, will they miss anything on Friday, because their ride's leaving before class time, and it's their cousin's wedding, so they've got to be there, and all the other logistical and institutional minutiae can still intervene to make the nature and value of any given subject seem to recede like a footrace to the horizon as a semester goes on. But, for a few weeks already now, that doesn't seem to be happening quite so much.

It'll take our continued conviction, energy, and attention to adjust to the shift in our worldview that occurred when, even far from Ground Zero, what we saw there jarred our sense of what's important. We saw exceptional examples of courage and fortitude as well as the tragedy there. But the long war that's been forecast now will have few more such clearcut front-lines, and we can hope they'll be far between, too. So, between times, most of us will be relegated to positions and duties that will bear an eerie resemblance to the way things have been, though we'll know it's not true. How can we deal with such limbo? How can we live in the interim, between September 11 and...and what?

We can learn from our students, and take care with the small things. We can do them well.

LUCIEN STRYK

Quiet, Please!

Keep still. I'm aching.
Winter's passing flakes
are just too feathery

to cover infamies of this
century. Berries flame
bare twigs, their shadows

bloodying stones and twisted
girders in the wind.
Keep still. Must be reliving

time men inched like rats
from foxholes, aiming shells
from mud. Stared into eyes

that never would stare back.
Keep still. A sharp chill—
last night remembrance

dickered with my ears. The
screaming kettle burned
itself to blazes. Then,

catching bedlam on the morning
news, lost my footing, and
a tray of china shattered

down the stairs. Survival
heaps dead flowers into sleep.
Keep still. I think I'm dreaming.

(10/17/01 London)

Cascades of ivy deepening toward winter bloody the wall outside the
window. How can I write with so much pain dividing nightmare from
reality, as I refeel the anguish of that moment making no sense, as
the world looked on and thousands disappeared within the blinking
of an eye? How can one touch the agony that will forever be their
secret? The philosopher Adorno's assertion that after Auschwitz
there could be no more poetry seems a cop-out. Auschwitz, Pearl
Harbor, September 11, 2001, will be remembered, as were other
tragedies, through a poet's voice. All I can say of "Quiet, Please!" is
so much smaller than a breath, lost in a world that can never be the
same again.

BRIAN SWANN

The Necessary Angel

She stands atop a heap that smokes and shifts.
What looks like rigor is a backward look
as she turns her head. Below her, wings
and little feet, feathers and sharp edges,
mouseparts, cogs and wheels of old machines,
a flower, a hand sans fingers, things sans
everything. Peering past her wing-edge she has
no sense of depth as the deep gray swirls behind
and all around. She has no fingers. Her hands
are stumps. What she'd once grasped now falls away,
lying all around. If she could make a tear her eyes would fill
and not know where she was. She tries to rise
from slag but her feet are no bird's that can grasp
and release, grip and go. They are more a mermaid's,
flowing deeper and blacker into the rock, spreading out like a seam,
holding her precariously in place. Her wings
are stiff. She holds them out like torn parchment
no one can yet read. Beauty burns
and the angel with it in a slow heatless flame.
But she keeps her pose, straining upward. Slowly turning back
to face the wind, she feels in the depths
something moving, struggling upward, making wings.

Brian Swann wrote to the editor: "A few days before I wrote the
poem, I did a painting—& the poem was about the painting: ekphra-
sis. A terrible coincidence that Sept. 11 tapped into my fears, which I
painted before I wrote."

HENRY TAYLOR

Midsummer 2002

The mid-morning sun prepares to play his trumpet,
testing the mouthpiece against his stiffening lip,
shoving and kicking the shadows into the parade
he marches across the lawn below the window
of my study, where I sit gazing
through the glass, carving, in my head,
a fresh point on a goose quill
with a sharp silver penknife.

I would like to be preparing a pen
because today is the President's birthday,
a fact that some might let pass unremarked,
but I want to imagine how it is, there in the Oval Office,
half-listening to the Press Secretary
while somewhere along the plastered wall of memory
he has reassembled the gang of little outlaws
who took turns whacking his bottom eight times
and one to grow on, the day he began
to articulate his firm position
on capital punishment.

                    Now here he is,
President of the United States,
his skin still tingling from the slight abrasions
left behind when his lifelong aversion to excellence
was snatched from him in one unspeakable hour
of human sacrifice and unholy gain.

Since then his sleeplessness has produced
repeating scripts of superhuman strength
and ingenuity, night missions in remote mountains,
in which he infiltrates the armed camp
and carries away, in a special magic container
like an oversized golf bag, the captured
terrorist chieftain, and lugs him back
across mysterious borders into the light
of American justice. He speaks of other things.

The generals do not know about the giant golf bag,
and have not yet remembered whose birthday it is.
They are trying to think of the words in which
to declare what they don't know, and never will.

Everyone has been sagging under the knowledge
that the tapes will not run backwards, never lift
the cloud of dust and glass into the still blue sky,
not shrink the bloom of fire back down to nothing,
nor draw the plane from the vanished tower
like a needle from a mended garment.

Still, there he stands, beginning to hear a little more
of the Press Secretary's brief best wishes for the day,
the Chief of Staff ready to lay out the next few hours.
The weeks, the months, the years. He takes note of them,
ponders how to move on. When you are President,
you might draw strength from what seems to offer it.

KEITH TAYLOR

September 16, 2001

The drive out to the southwestern corner of the county had been spectacular. The sky was a bright, crystalline blue, like it had been all week. We drove out on the back roads, snaking along the gravel lines that often went against the pattern of our usual Midwestern grid. We weren't in a hurry. We just wanted to get to the Nature Conservancy preserve at Sharon Hollow soon enough to take a leisurely hike down to the River Raisin and get back to the car before dark.

By Sunday, five days after the attacks, Christine and Faith and I just wanted to get away from the TV for a while. Like everyone else, we had filled our imaginations with impossible images: airplanes exploding into buildings, fire, ash billowing through streets we knew; and bodies falling. And we wanted to get outside, to identify something—a bird or a wildflower or a tree—that didn't much care about our problems.

There are good, practical reasons to be an environmentalist—economic reasons, public health reasons. But those are not mine. Like many people, I call myself an environmentalist because much of my pleasure and interest center on the natural world—even though I recognize that no one quite knows what that adjective "natural" means. I'm an environmentalist because—in the great Romantic tradition—I go to the natural world for solace. Sometimes I don't know where else I might find it.

But on our walk on Sunday, September 16, 2001, we knew we probably couldn't find it yet. After we parked our car, we followed the path through the oak/hickory woods by the road, through the cleared swath under the pylons and power lines, down into the marsh. Years ago I found a clump of Indian pipes growing here, the simple white stalks and flowers rising out of the leaf mulch, looking ghostly and impossible with their lack of chlorophyll. Down in the marsh from the muddy part of the trail, we had seen, just last spring, an extravagant scarlet tanager screeching from the top of a leafless tree. His red caught the sun and he glowed, the brightest thing in the forest.

On September 16 there were few wild flowers still blooming, some goldenrod and asters, but the bugs were gone. We kept going up, out of the marsh, through the stands of beech and black cherry, down onto the old overgrown farm roads that lead to the banks of the River Raisin. A couple of maple leaves floated lazily down the river, and a blue jay flew over it, calling plaintively.

During the last few weeks some people have said that North Americans have lived for a couple of generations outside of history and that the attacks have brought us back into it in ways that we can no longer avoid. I have always felt, however, that history is immanent, that I live at the vortex of historical forces and events, that they swirl around me constantly, forming and changing everything I am.

Just a couple of hundred yards down river from the spot on the Raisin where my wife and daughter and I watched the maple leaves drift past is an old mill. It is being restored now as the centerpiece of a county park, but it was first built as a small parts plant by Henry Ford. If I remember correctly, six people worked there and made cigarette lighters for the Model T. The lighters were taken over to the gigantic assembly plant on the Rouge River, the assembly plant that changed the way industry worked and that contributed significantly to the conspicuous and occasionally destructive prosperity that helped to elevate us to our status as prime targets. I don't accept for a minute the horrendous suggestion from a couple of fundamentalist preachers or tedious left-wing pundits that these attacks are somehow "our fault." By extension, that would have to put the blame for their own terrible deaths on the people in those planes and buildings, and anyone who can say that seems possessed by a horrifying and twisted morality. On the other hand, our nation's position in the world and the prosperity it so proudly manifests must certainly be part of the reason we find ourselves at the center of the bull's eye.

But that prosperity is not what brought us out to the banks of the River Raisin on September 16. People everywhere sit by rivers to find solace, and they've done it for thousands of years. Among many other examples there is the famous old Psalm of revenge: "By the waters of Babylon, there we sat down and wept, when we remembered Zion."

And even the River Raisin has its hidden memories. A few miles further downstream, close to the mouth of the river and the present day town of Monroe, a great battle was fought along its frozen banks on January 18 and 19, 1813. American troops, mostly Kentucky militia, came north through the snow to try to recapture Detroit from the British. At the first battle on the Raisin, the Americans won, although their losses were heavy, something on the order of 200 dead. The next morning, just before dawn, the British and their Native allies—the Potawatomi, the Miami, and the Wyandot—struck back. The Americans were caught off guard and surrendered. The 700 captives were surrounded by their attackers and massacred. Most of them died.

How many people died along the River Raisin on those two January days? Native American and British dead must have been somewhere around 1000. The stories say that when the snow and the ice melted a few weeks later, the Raisin ran red into Lake Erie. Although a few people in Monroe, Michigan, try to keep the history alive, hardly any of the rest of us who live around here remember those dead.

Yet the river was there on a warm Sunday in early fall, quiet and undisturbed. I felt perhaps a flicker of the solace I wanted. I don't know what Christine and Faith felt, but we all were quiet for a while. Then Faith, not quite 10, started picking up stones and throwing them into the water. I threw a couple myself before we turned and started back to the car.

DOUGLAS UNGER

Terrorism: A Requiem

What comes to mind is a memorial service—a sunny spring day, women and men dressed in white or bright colors. The priest wore a white cassock, a minister a white linen suit, a bearded rabbi covered his head with a white *tallis*. Hundreds gathered in the courtyard of a church—not inside the church but outside, under a beneficent sun. Little girls in stiff white dresses stood in ranks like a first communion choir close to the spiritual leaders and a small podium set up for speakers. The little girls held white flowers—white lilies. Much of this ceremony would be spent listening to them joyously singing.

This was not a funeral. This was a celebration for our dead whose bodies had never been found, even the certainty of whose deaths would never be known. After years of looking for them, interviewing witnesses, searching through archives, hunting down evidence, this is how our Barrio Norte neighborhood near San Miguel church in Buenos Aires finally sent off "the disappeared"—as they were called—victims of state terrorism by the death squads of the military dictatorship that ruled Argentina with such brutality from 1976-1983.

More than ten years later, this memorial service was our coming together for vanished lives, our neighborhood and community honoring of their memories in a ritual acceptance that they were certainly gone. One of my adopted brothers—Álvaro Colombo-Sierra—was listed among "the disappeared." The body of another brother, Alejandro Colombo-Sierra, had been found two years after he vanished, and we had been able to bury him. By my rough calculation, one out of every five of my friends had either been murdered or disappeared during Argentina's "dirty war" of state-sponsored terrorism. In this ceremony in part for Álvaro's memory, and for all the rest of the victims, my family and I hoped for rebirth and renewal, fashioned somehow from absence. We sought a sense of closure, finally to pass through grief toward serenity.

Such serenity didn't last. When the World Trade Center towers collapsed last September 11—like two black dying blooms against the Manhattan skyline—the sudden shock and grief I felt at the loss of so many thousands of lives by terrorism, and more, the sirenlike wailing inside that continues screaming still for such an unsettling of our tranquility—the cross of peace burning again—I was thrown straight back into the years of rage I had suffered at the unresolved murders of my "disappeared" brothers in Argentina; then again at the terrible events of the downing of Pan Am Flight 103, in 1988, by a terrorist bomb, when students I knew and loved, two of them very closely, Christopher Jones and Nicole Boulanger, whose body was never found, went down in flames among the 35 victims on that plane from Syracuse University, where I was teaching. At the time, I was chosen as a designated memorialist for the university, and I've been writing memorials—despite my rage—for the dead from terrorism ever since.

After the World Trade Center and Pentagon attacks in the United States, once again, I found myself in numbed, dumbstruck, grieving circles of families. I think everyone in this nation exchanged squeezes, hugs, hand-holding, tears among neighbors and co-workers, gestures meant to comfort each other in the face of the immense incomprehensible question as to why, why, why.

We were once again afraid. How hard to conceive such a fall of so many lives, so many loved ones, could ever become a pretext for further existence, ever somehow be transformed by our human powers and prayers into an ultimate birth. All this combines now into the same pain. All now—every death by terrorism anywhere—becomes part of the same agonizing spinning of a monstrous cycle of cruelty and violence that threatens to overwhelm the spiritual possibilities of our humanity.

We are now asked as a people—as a nation, yes, but I would hope also as newly conscious citizens of the world—somehow to earn the miracle of putting an end to terrorism. Still, too many of us look to tried and failed responses of the past, and believe that the solution to crime is punishment, the salve to righteous anger is revenge, the further violence of armed reprisals—cruise missiles, air strikes, soldiers, bombs, all-out war—is the only eye-for-an-eye response to terrorism which will ever work. So our society continues to seek answers in the new technologies of war and surveillance, to increasing empowerment of police and intelligence agencies, to ever more restrictive anti-conspiracy, press secrecy, and illicit association laws, all of which further threaten our freedom. This is our response—war and revenge, righteous punishment, threats from world leaders—when surely after this initial "war on terrorism" reaction of rage and reprisal is finished, what we should be tirelessly seeking is some fundamental change for the cause of peace.

Mankind has achieved many transformations of the soul throughout history. Our ancestors practiced ritual human sacrifice, incest was habitual, slavery almost everywhere. These barbaric acts are now universally condemned, not only the result of advances in economies and technology and of increasing political enlightenment among nations, no—but also because we have evolved in our humanity, made huge conceptual leaps in our consciousness as human beings and in the power of our spiritual condition.

Terrorism is a tactic of desperation directed against what is perceived to be an inflexible, powerful authority, without appeal to law or any existing social contract, in the perceived absence of any forum for expressing real grievances with a voice that will be heard. Terrorism is a form of violence of last resort, born of rage and frustration, arising from the conviction that there is no other choice. The current crime and punishment response to fight terrorism can only lead—as it almost always has in modern history—to a further spiraling of violence and more terror, which is precisely the reaction the terrorists themselves wish to achieve. As should be clear to anyone aware of rumblings in the streets through the Muslim world—or to anyone who has studied Bolshevik and Bakunin tactics at the turn of the 20th Century in Russia, or Fidelista actions in Cuba, or the upheaval and murder of the Algerian independence movement in the 1950s—terrorism can also grow into revolution.

The worn-out adage that civilized nations should not negotiate with terrorists is wrong. In the history of terrorist movements, short of revolution or civil war, negotiations have almost always been needed to mark their end. And it is generally the most powerful in these confrontations who must become more self-aware and finally yield and give to the most harmed, even if only symbolically, or achieve political repositioning toward dialogue and compromise. It is in the hands of the powerful to provide opportunities for change, not so much in punishment as with wise and cautious generosity. At the very least, the powerful must learn how to listen.

Could it be true—as poet Rainer Maria Rilke wrote—that by living inside human beings even God learns? This question is frightening, granting as it does so much power to the will of each man and woman—perhaps even the level of will it must have taken to steer a jetliner into a skyscraper and murder thousands of innocent people. But consider in the Judeo-Christian tradition how God may really have learned mercy from Abraham, patience and tolerance from the followers of Moses, forgiveness from the life, death, and resurrection of Christ. So it must be also in those gentler passages of the Holy Koran which teach compassion to enemies hand-in-hand with the rewards of devotion and peace—the cool green gardens of paradise with their flowing waters.

The Dalai Lama of Tibet awakens each morning with a prayer to rid himself of anger and resentment so he can be a more positive influence on the world. Arvil Looking Horse, 19th generation carrier of the Sacred White Buffalo Calf Woman Pipe of the Lakota, a people once murdered and terrorized nearly out of existence, travels all over the globe to wherever there is a crisis—he has even performed pipe ceremonies in Iran and Iraq—praying for healing and peace in his ancient and holy language. What will it take for the enraged and aggrieved of all factions and faiths one day to pass this pipe, or to join together to break bread at the same tables?

Let us gather together dressed in white or bright colors—all peoples of the world—as emblem of our rebirth and renewal, as testimony of our hopes, in memory and honor of our dead, in the knowledge that we are providing their deaths a new and lasting meaning within the significant markers of our civilization. Let us remind ourselves that death is a horizon and a horizon is only a limit to what we can see. Let everyone hear our singing. Let us learn to love ourselves second only to our gentleness. Let us share in the blessing of our gentleness. Let us vow never to stop fighting this prison of terrorism, never, until each woman and man in the world is free, until every man and woman is in the custody of gentleness.

JOHN UPDIKE

[September 13, 2001]

Suddenly summoned to witness something great and horrendous, we keep fighting not to reduce it to our own smallness. From the viewpoint of a tenth-floor apartment in Brooklyn Heights, where I happened to be visiting some kin, the destruction of the World Trade Center twin towers had the false intimacy of television, on a day of perfect reception. A four-year-old girl and her babysitter called from the library and pointed out through the window the smoking top of the north tower, not a mile away. It seemed, at that first glance, more curious than horrendous: smoke speckled with bits of paper curled into the cloudless sky, and strange inky rivulets ran down the giant structure's vertically corrugated surface. The W.T.C. had formed a pale background to our Brooklyn view of lower Manhattan, not beloved, like the stony, spired midtown thirties skyscrapers it had displaced as the city's tallest, but, with its pre-postmodern combination of unignorable immensity and architectural reticence, in some lights beautiful. As we watched the second tower burst into ballooning flame (an intervening building had hidden the approach of the second airplane), there persisted the notion that, as on television, this was not quite real; it could be fixed; the technocracy the towers symbolized would find a way to put out the fire and reverse the damage.

And then, within an hour, as my wife and I watched from the Brooklyn building's roof, the south tower dropped from the screen of our viewing; it fell straight down like an elevator, with a tinkling shiver and a groan of concussion, distinct across the mile of air. We knew we had just witnessed thousands of deaths; we clung to each other as if we ourselves were falling. Amid the glittering impassivity of the many buildings across the East River, an empty spot had appeared, as if by electronic command, beneath the sky that, but for the sulfurous cloud streaming south toward the ocean, was pure blue; rendered uncannily pristine by the absence of jet trails. A swiftly expanding burst of smoke and dust hid the rest of lower Manhattan; we saw the collapse of the second tower only on television, where the footage of hellbent airplanes, exploding jet fuel, and imploding tower was played and replayed, much rehearsed moments from a nightmare ballet.

The nightmare is still on. The bodies are beneath the rubble, the last-minute cell-phone calls—remarkably calm and loving, many of them—are still being reported. The sound of an airplane overhead still bears an unfamiliar menace, the thought of boarding an airplane with our old blasé blitheness keeps receding into the past. Determined men who have transposed their own lives to a martyr's afterlife can still inflict an amount of destruction that defies belief. War is conducted with a fury that requires abstraction—that turns a planeful of peaceful passengers, children included, into a missile the faceless enemy deserves. The other side has the abstractions; we have only the mundane duties of survivors—to pick up the pieces, to bury the dead, to take more precautions, to go on living.

American freedom of motion, one of our prides, has taken a hit. Can we afford the openness that lets future kamikaze pilots, say, enroll in Florida flying schools? A Florida neighbor of one of the suspects remembers him saying he didn't like the United States: "He said it was too lax. He said, 'I can go anywhere I want to, and they can't stop me.'" It is a weird complaint, a begging perhaps to be stopped. Weird, too, the silence of the heavens these days, as flying has ceased across America. But fly again we must; risk is a price of freedom, and walking around Brooklyn Heights that afternoon, as ash drifted in the air and cars were few and open-air lunches continued as usual on Montague Street, renewed the impression that, with all its failings, this is a country worth fighting for. Freedom, reflected in the street's diversity and daily ease, felt palpable. It is mankind's elixir, even if a few turn it to poison.

The next morning, I went back to the open vantage from which we had watched the tower so dreadfully slip from sight. The fresh sun shone on the eastward façades, a few boats tentatively moved in the river, the ruins were still sending out smoke, but New York looked glorious.

ROBERT VAS DIAS

Letter to Michael Heller:Some Thoughts on Intercessions After 11 September

18 Sept. 01

Dear Mike,

The night before the Sunday, 16 September Eucharist at St. James's Church Piccadilly (Church of England/Episcopalian), Maggie and I decided to lead the prayers of Intercession together, alternating the prayers in an antiphonal style. This would have the effect of helping to conserve her energy—the ME, or CFIDS (Chronic Fatigue & Immune Dysfunction Syndrome) she suffers from has been ongoing for almost a year—and also be a joint Anglo-American effort, which we felt would be most appropriate in these circumstances. Incidentally, we have decided to get married early in the new year; more on this next e-mail.

I've never led Intercessions before. In fact, as you know, I'm not a regular churchgoer. I never considered the Church as particularly relevant to me, though I have admired its work and the thought of individual, mostly radical Christians while often deploring those who are unscrupulous bigots and unthinking zealots. The same may be said of the adherents of any faith. I regard a church service, any religious service, as the collective expression of a spiritual need and as a renewal and strengthening of belief. I've always thought that my own spiritual needs haven't been particularly served by such public expressions, and I felt uneasy at mouthing the liturgical elements of a belief I didn't wholeheartedly share.

The characteristic of a church service with which I have been uncomfortable is the sometimes platitudinous formulations that are employed to deal with fear and horror, dismay and grief. It seemed to me that these ritualistic expressions were a pathetically inadequate response to the destructive power of organised and individual examples of human violence.

I cannot get out of my mind how very deliberate the planning and execution of the World Trade Center atrocity was. I read the other day an eyewitness account by a UPI reporter in which he describes the approach of the plane that hit the second tower:

> And then the second plane appeared in the sky, from the direction of the Statue of Liberty. It looked like a commercial airliner, and it sailed in over New York Harbour making a gradual descent towards World Trade Two. For a moment it was pointed directly at me, then about five seconds before impact the pilot made an adjustment and banked about 20 degrees. He was making a correction! To go in at an angle? To make sure he hit the center? I had seen him make the manoeuvre. I had seen him make the perfect correction. I had seen him come in from the only side where he could avoid the black smoke and have a precise target. I had seen him go in at exactly the angle he chose.... He had wanted to die and he had wanted to take thousands with him.... It was that manoeuvre that got to me. That 20-degree bank. He had made certain.

And I was thinking what effect our pitiful words have against the murderously fanatic intent of that crazed will. I thought of the lengthy process of a child's upbringing—the continual reiteration of moral imperatives, warnings, advice, commandments, punishments, as well as advice, praise, reward, love—the protracted process of socialization, education, and training that can lead to such an act of immolation and the sacrifice of thousands to an ideal considered "noble."

But then that is only one kind of idealistic, sacrificial act: "There were firemen going up as we were coming down. They were going up to heaven, effectively" (*Guardian* report, 12 Sept. 2001).

The Intercessions, which, in this Church, are led by lay members, and which occur after the sermon and often refer to points raised in it, range from the general to the particular; that is, from prayers of a universal nature to those pertaining to the members of the church and community: from all peoples, to those named individuals who are sick or suffering or in difficulty. They're simple, direct articulations of matters both of timeless and topical concern. Because the sermon for that day had originally been planned around individuals such as the Venerable Thich Nhat Hahn and Bede Griffiths, who drew spiritual nourishment from more than one faith tradition, and in view of the present atrocity, Maggie and I decided to include prayers drawn from other faiths—Muslim, Jewish, and Buddhist—as part of our Intercessions: "Let us pray that all living beings realize that they are all brothers and sisters and nourished from the same source of life. Let us pray that we ourselves cease to be the cause of suffering to each other." (The Venerable Thich Nhat Hahn) And then, a few moments later: "We pray for all those who have lost family members, friends, and colleagues in New York, Washington, and Pennsylvania, remembering in our prayers especially any who might be with us this morning."

As Maggie and I were praying them, it occurred to me that this litany of prayers and the ritualistic formality of the Intercessions, before a gathering of people who have a certain degree of faith that these things count, seemed useful in some way, even necessary and desirable and should be delivered in the best way I could; not least so I wouldn't disappoint people's expectations; so I wouldn't let Maggie down. I wanted them to "work." Of course a measure of the performer's vanity motivated me, but I must say also that I really felt these things were necessary to say, to feel: this went beyond the actor's ploy that effectively to convey your "lines" you must believe either that they are right, or true, or find an equivalence in which you believe, in order to convey their sprit, to project a sense that they matter and that you're not just repeating them formulaically. I became part of a collective witnessing, as much as though I had an important part to play in a continuing human drama.

How does one oppose evil? I can't answer the question definitively for other people, but if one can help some of them to assent to what one has asked them to consider, or hope for, or work toward, or empathize with, in the belief that it is right to do so and may be of collective value in dealing with tragedy, is this not one effective way of countering despair and anomie?

Don't worry, Mike, I'm not about to be born again. I'm still the sceptic I was but I'm different. Perhaps we all are now.

Yours,
Robert

Song of the Cities

AFTER 9 / 11 / 01

Walt bequeathed himself to the dirt
but small pieces of me are already layered
in dusty London, dead cells have flaked
and danced in the traffic's breeze, and my hair,
snipped in drifts on the hairdresser's floor,
doubtless reposes at this very moment
in a landfill site north of the North Circular Road.

When a boy, blood from my eyebrow poured
down my nose and into the Edgware mud
where I'd slipped as my fingers missed their grip
on a fencepost, and my sweat has rained
onto the pavement as I ran from a loutish gang;
I left a half-pound of flesh, "uniform adipose tissue,
a benign lipoma," ten years ago in a bin
in St. Bartholomew's Hospital from where
it was probably incinerated
and dispersed in the city air we breathe.

My foothold is tenon'd and mortis'd in granite,
and I know what he meant because my invisible
footsteps are impressed forever in New York's
conglomerate and in the tar of its streets
covered and preserved by new tar.
At times late at night returning from some convivial
drinking or even not so convivial drinking,
I have pee'd in the street when caught short
and New York streets were golden with me.

I have helped to wear down the steps to Riverside
Park, thin the already thinning grass of Prospect Park,
I've pruned and cut and planted in the Brooklyn backyard,
the soil has jammed itself under my fingernails and dusted
under my collar. I compose the city where the dust
of thousands is carted off to vast landfills
which shall rise in hills and form the new city.

What is the city but a composition of millions
who have lived and died there. The fallen will be
compacted into the foundations of tall buildings,
and underneath, the subways will thump and vibrate,
a living heart. The city rises in impersonal
commemoration, and we inhabit the idea
resurrected again each time a building falls.

RACHEL VIGIER

Burnt Ground

On this street, a powdery dust
settles on my shoulders
as I think of the moment—just before

when it's still an ordinary morning
on a bright September day
when the skyline

stretches up forever
the glory of space
standing still as workers

milling inside or on the street
each start an ordinary day
in an ordinary way. Now

this is the moment—just after
when I think whose dust is this
blowing across burnt ground?

Suddenly it's important to know names—
the name of the waitress in the donut shop
the name of the clerk in the bookstore
the name of the teller at the bank
the name of the visitor in the elevator
the name of the guard at the door
the name of the janitor on the top floor
the names of all the old men
shuffling backgammon pieces
in the park across the street
the names of all the office workers
jostling in lines by the food carts
even the name of the park and the name
of the statue in the park now covered in ash

MICHAEL WATERS

Fork and Spoon

I live in a cul-de-sac, and during these past two weeks neighbors in the half-dozen houses around mine have planted flags like blooming pyracantha on their front lawns. One neighbor has painted his mailbox red, white, and blue. From my half-acre, such gestures, however well-intentioned, seem as hollow as the rhetoric spouted by President Bush during his television address, the speech that commentators referred to as "rousing." My neighbors, like so many of us, do not have easy access to words in a time of tragedy, to a vocabulary that might allow them to express grief and fear and anger, so in their helplessness to articulate such emotions they rely on symbolic gestures. These days, any empty phrase that smacks of affirmation—"Patriotism is stronger than terrorism"—seems to afford some comfort and suggests, at least, some response. My neighbors' flag-waving means to swell that response.

Other gestures and phrases have come, indirectly so far, from poets. It is striking to note that in the September 24 issue of the *New Yorker*, several correspondents, attempting to come to terms with the destruction, mention or quote Dante and Auden and Larkin. The issue concludes with a poem, translated from the Polish, by Adam Zagajewski, "Try to Praise the Mutilated World," and it is impossible to tell whether the poem was written before or in response to the attacks on the Twin Towers. The September 23 issue of the *New York Times Magazine* includes a poem by David Lehman, "The World Trade Center," written in response to the 1993 bombing, while several writers, including Richard Ford and Robert Stone, quote Auden and Larkin and Yeats.

Why should an Italian poet of the 13th century offer comfort now? Why do dead British and Irish poets have words that seem to speak to this tragedy when so many of our citizens can locate none of their own?

On September 23, the *New York Times* reported that "Poetry suddenly appeared all over: haiku on sidewalks, quatrains on church walls, epics scrawled across sidewalks in chalk," and printed a photograph of one Alexis Ignatovich, 17, scrawling a poem in chalk on a path in Union Square Park. You can make out some of the words: "world will spin ... constant velocity ... we trust that we are safe and sound as long as we keep our eyes open for those little mistakes that we as humans sometime make ... we believe that our lives will be ... prosperous and that tomorrow may bring good fortune for those who wait. Yet little do we know, tomorrow is a mystery and today is a tradgedy [sic]." This adolescent self-expression summoned through poetry seems preferable to the generic gesture of flag-waving. In his unself-consciousness, Ignatovich reminds each of us of the need to confront this tragedy personally—*how will this history lodge itself within me?* We must begin the work of sifting through the debris of image and information, of language heaped before us, to locate our lives in this new estate. Where is F. Scott Fitzgerald's "fresh, green breast of the new world" now? Across which body of water does Gatsby's green light still beckon?

On September 25, the *Baltimore Sun* asked four Maryland poets "to share the verses that have haunted them since Sept. 11, 2001." One poet chose Yeats; two others chose Emily Dickinson's #341: "After great pain, a formal feeling comes—" and, oddly but aptly, May Swenson's "Too Big for Words," dated January 26, 1986, about the Challenger tragedy. One of the four, I chose "Objector" by National Book Award winner William Stafford (1914–1993), who served his country as a conscientious objector in the Civilian Public Service during World War II. This Petrarchan sonnet, both eloquent and modest in its refusal, links us to those "other citizens" who commit themselves to peace through simple and unassuming gestures.

Objector

In line at lunch I cross my fork and spoon
to ward off complicity—the ordered life
our leaders have offered us. Thin as a knife,
our chance to live depends on such a sign

while others talk and the Pentagon from the moon
is bouncing exact commands: "Forget your faith;
be ready for whatever it takes to win: we face
annihilation unless all citizens get in line."

I bow and cross my fork and spoon; somewhere
other citizens more fearfully bow
in a place terrorized by their kind of oppressive state.
Our signs both mean, "You hostages over there
will never be slaughtered by my act." Our vows
cross: never to kill and call it fate.

The gesture evident here remains personal and, unlike flag-waving, calls little attention to itself. One of Whitman's "endless announcements," it counsels communication through, or despite, silence. It assumes *individuals* rather than *nations*. Another poem that came to mind was e.e. cummings' "I sing of Olaf glad and big / whose warmest heart recoiled at war: / a conscientious object-or," which contains Olaf's blunt refusal: "'I will not kiss your f.ing flag.'" One thread of dialogue might begin here.

New York City has witnessed flaming bodies falling from the sky before. Almost one hundred years ago, on March 25, 1911, at the corner of Washington Place and Greene Street in Washington Square, an easy walk from the rubble of the World Trade Center, a fire broke out in the Triangle Shirtwaist Company on the upper floors of the Asch Building. One hundred forty-six people, mostly young immigrant women, died. New Yorkers watched, helpless, as scores of women held hands and leapt from windows to escape the flames.

Here in the new century, the new millennium, while ash still rains upon lower Manhattan—paper ash, human ash—we begin again, as we must, individually, to find ways to reconstitute such debris into words, into language that will bear the burden of becoming the appropriate gesture, the right response, not only to this tragedy, but to future tragedies that await us. In this mutilated world, flag-waving won't help to locate such poetry. The transformation from grief to articulation, from grief to art, might begin when we speak to our neighbors, when we cross our forks and spoons.

September 30, 2001

DAVID WATSON

Poetry, Empire and Catastrophe:
A Letter to American Poets and Artists

When I learned on September 11 that the World Trade Center and the Pentagon had been attacked, I was preparing to teach one of Guillaume Apollinaire's *calligrammes*, or concrete poems, "Little Car," to my high school English class. The poem relates his traveling in France in a motorcar as troops were being mobilized on the eve of the First World War, a war in which he would fight and receive wounds that would later kill him. I was grateful later for the poem's sense of uneasy excitement, of retrospective foreboding and "looming angry giants." Its announcement that "Whole populations were rapidly rushing toward earthshaking encounters," that "The dead were trembling anxiously in their dark dwellings," shimmered uncannily after the September attacks.

As the twentieth century gathered its energies along with great armies about to clash, Apollinaire commented, "We said our farewells to an entire epoch." One inevitably felt the same sensation of disquiet, of nostalgia, and farewell, on September 11. The next morning I wrote in my journal, "We have most certainly entered a new era ... The whole country is reeling...." I too seemed to be saying my farewell to some previous life.

I didn't take Apollinaire to my class that day. I took Wislawa Szymborksa's luminous "The Century's Decline" instead. Her characteristically wise and bittersweet lament describes the mess left toward the end of last century. It "was going to improve on the others," she writes. "It will never prove it now...." War, injustice, and hunger were to have been abolished, of course, but things have not turned out that way:

Anyone who planned to enjoy the world
is now faced
with a hopeless task....

But a focused light can leave background in shadow. And so I worry:
how to mourn and honor people wantonly slaughtered for the political ends of implacable madmen, which poetry can and must do,
without succumbing to an unreflective, ahistorical bathos, a kind of
imperial narcissism? The carnage was horrific, the ruthless single-
mindedness of the suicide bombers disturbing; but I believe the
United States is also administered by madmen, though their madness
is more bureaucratic, impersonal, and superficially rational. In this
war, "civilization" purports to be in conflict with "barbarians." But
this civilization has been, and continues to be, a pretty horrendous
affair. I do not wish to participate in denial and self-delusion.

The day of the attacks, many people gathered around television sets
to watch the news—a media experience that, both in the content of
the images and the experience of watching with a group, offered a
sense of community. This intense focus on the suffering in New
York, simultaneously compassionate and voyeuristic, persuaded
people that they were witnesses, rather than mere spectators, of
someone else's misfortune. The disaster-movie thrill of the
destruction did not nullify the empathy; simply hearing the victims'
individual stories was heart-rending. Nevertheless, I found myself
wondering how Americans might have responded had they been
shown such detailed exposure to the miseries of the people this
country brutalized and killed in Central America over decades, when
they were being told lies about "communist subversion," or, as with
the genocide against the Guatemalan Indians—they were told nothing. Would they have demanded a just peace in Central America, as
many of us were trying to do in the 1980s, or switched the channel?

Thus, paradoxically—since the work of the arts is to gather and thread
the particular to universals—a focus by artists on the particulars of the
September 11 cataclysm risks becoming the iconic estheticization of
American disaster and suffering in a world where the disaster and
suffering of others are not only daily affairs, but in fact, essential
consequences of imperial economic plunder and military domination
from which American elites, and to some lesser degree the majority of
people of the advanced industrial world of the West, benefit. The wide-
spread (and assiduously manipulated) social and historical amnesia
prior to September 11 and afterward should suggest to us that our
claims to innocence, justice, and reason are deeply flawed. I would

hope that September 11 might remind us of the immense, institutionalized global suffering from which we Americans have been largely immune and which it has long been our social and historical responsibility to address and to work to eradicate. But with the subsequent crusade for "infinite justice," and the patriotic frenzy and growing clampdown on liberties that have followed, I am not optimistic.

Life was hardly normal for people around the world before September 11; people have been dying in droves for a long time, some of it even documented fleetingly on television, and it should hardly be controversial (though it seems to be increasingly dangerous) to recall that a very large portion of the dying has been perpetrated by the United States government, either directly or through proxies. During the Vietnam War Martin Luther King, Jr. declared the United States "the greatest purveyor of violence in the world," and that has changed little. U.S. arms industries and markets surpass those of all other countries combined. No other state has its soldiers, ships, and air forces patrolling every continent; no military machine comes even remotely close to having bombed so many countries throughout the century. And is it necessary to list the governments overthrown by the CIA throughout the twentieth century and the human toll that was paid by people from Chile to Indonesia to the Congo to Iran?

One recent vivid example of our relative lack of innocence will suffice to make my point. Since the Persian Gulf War, in which several hundred thousand Iraqi civilians and soldiers were massacred by an army so superior that it suffered only minor, self-inflicted ("friendly-fire") casualties, a war US pilots called "a turkey shoot," a million or more people have died from preventable diseases brought on or aggravated by the hunger, lack of medicine, and clean water imposed by the postwar sanctions against Iraq. Clearly, sanctions are a complicated shadow-theater in which the United States, the Iraqi dictatorship, and the oil sheiks of the Gulf all profit in different ways. This cynicism should come as no surprise; Hussein was a U.S. ally and trading partner even when he was crushing dissent, attacking his neighbors, and gassing his own people in the 1980s. When on the May 12, 1996 broadcast of *60 Minutes* reporter Lesley Stahl asked then-Secretary of State Madeleine Albright if the suffering caused by sanctions, including the death by illness and hunger of about a half a million children, was "worth the price," Albright replied, "I think this is a very hard choice, but the price—we think the price is worth it." Albright's morality of ends and means was identical to that of the September 11 highjackers, except that the number of victims caused by those "sanctions of mass destruction" was vastly greater.

People also die because of business as usual. Worldwide, a billion people are malnourished, a quarter of them children. On September 11, assuming that annual deaths were evenly spread, more than thirty thousand children died of starvation or hunger-related diseases in the so-called developing world. Might Americans learn something from reflecting on the fact that though we are only six percent of the world's population, we consume forty percent of its resources? Might the dizzying economic globalization of everything, and subsequent deleterious effects on the living conditions of the world's poor, have anything to do with wide-spread resentment against the U.S.? Does a U.S. foreign policy that supports and arms Israel in the face of manifest brutality in the occupied territories of Palestine and dozens of ineffectual UN resolutions condemning the occupation, or the fact of the mon-strous sanctions against the people of Iraq, or the fact of US support for corrupt and repressive regimes in the middle east like the Saudi monarchy help in any way to explain why the bin Ladens of the world can recruit young men to kill themselves and us in a jihad? Is there no relationship between the profound injustices this empire has unleashed, or ignored, or to which it has actively contributed, and the nihilism of the enemies that such injustice spawns?

These are massacres no one in this country hovers around televi-sions to observe. People wonder instead why anyone would hate *us*, when, as their president assures them, we are so *good*. But when we consider the immense amount of violence this empire has unleashed on so many countries, one wonders why such violence didn't happen sooner, why Guatemalan Indians or Salvadoran or Vietnamese peasants—all killed in the hundreds of thousands, even in the mil-lions—didn't attempt such acts in revenge for the genocide this country and its clients dealt out to them.

The events of September and afterward are depressing. I am deeply pessimistic, uncertain about where they will lead, other than down-ward. I am unsure about how to live in a time of imperial catastrophe, but I believe that poets and artists, people whose devotion to art should make them loyal not to the cold, cold monster of the state but to life, should be, by avocation and by inclination, anti-imperialist. I don't mean the old Leninist style of anti-imperialism, either; there have been many empires since ancient Mesopotamia, and there can be many styles of resistance. I inherit my anti-imperialism from the ancient Greek philosopher Diogenes, who when told by Alexander the Great, the most powerful man in the known world, that he would grant him any wish, told the emperor to move aside, since he was standing in the way of his light. As poets and artists we have to learn to live and to document the life of the spirit, both from within and against the empire, pushing the emperor out of our way to let the light—and the darkness—in.

Diogenes said: "A man keeps and feeds a lion. The lion owns a man." Every empire comes to this. The same insight is echoed in one of the shrewdest and most prescient literary works of the nineteenth century, Mary Shelley's *Frankenstein*, when Victor Frankenstein's monster, which has escaped the power of the young scientist and has started to run amok, declares to him: "You are my creator, but I am your master." Tragic reversal is faced eventually by every empire, and our looking directly at it will serve us better in the long run than any callous, self-pitying, and disproportionate concentration on American suffering.

In the present circumstances, the wizards at the U.S. Central Intelligence Society (just think of that term!), trying to get their feeble mental grasp on the monsters they themselves played a major role in conjuring in one of their satanic mills—these other murderous madmen who now wreak havoc on the so-called homeland—call this phenomenon "blow-back." This term does recognize the inevitable tragic revenge, the feedback loop of imperial arrogance, with its wanton, hallucinatorily destructive power. This nemesis did what no previous enemy has been able to do—it smashed them in their citadel, the Pentagon, Murder Central, where the genocide against the Vietnamese was organized, where the "turkey shoot" in Iraq was overseen. That is where planners have mapped contingency plans for the invasion of every single country on earth, even so-called friends (as someone notoriously quipped, empires have no friends, only interests), where they plan not only the Third World War but even the Fourth, in which submarines will surface to nuke the ruins of World War Three.

And of course, that is where, at least from the other four sides of their damaged citadel, the most powerful empire in history now carries out the devastation of one of history's saddest, most wretched places, where their exploding cluster bombs scatter thousands more active mines in a country that has been described as the most mined place on earth, where the mere threat of attack sent tens of thousands of people into flight and likely caused countless deaths from hunger and exposure. That is where they scattered packets of mass-manufactured food utterly inadequate in quantity—seven million people are in danger of starvation this winter, and a million are starving now—and completely inappropriate for malnourished people, particularly children. Indeed, they dropped the food over mined areas where one might die chasing the illusive manna from the cruel and capricious gods in the air. Since the United States purposely targeted the civilian infrastructure, particularly the water treatment plants of Iraq (thus unleashing a kind of biological war against the population), and considered the resultant mass death "worth the price," one can only assume that the food drops were done not out of magnanimity but to reassure a domestic public that to its credit, was at least initially queasy about the next wave of victims, despite what opinion polls claimed.

Blowback: I read in the September 24 issue of the *New Yorker* that the FBI director and his staff were meeting when the World Trade Center was hit in New York. According to reporter David Remnick, "The FBI, like many other agencies in Washington, had repeatedly reviewed scenarios of grand-scale attacks involving weapons of mass destruction. But this was not in anyone's plans or imagination." When a plane hit the Pentagon and another was reported high-jacked, destination unknown, an FBI official said, "There was a feeling of helplessness. We were all waiting to see what was going to happen." That's what the rest of us were doing, of course; so much for the "intelligence" of cops. Whatever the immediate outcome of this particular imperial adventure, we should expect more blowback.

This is an example of how domination inevitably turns into impotence. The imperial Death Star can unleash its panoply of megatechnic might, but it cannot stop the gremlins from infecting and undermining the machinery because international industrial-capitalism is too ubiquitous, too porous, too vast to monitor or control.

The highjackers commandeered history with box knives, a bit of technical training (provided by the wondrous free-market to anyone with the money to pay), a few airplane schedules, and the daring of the essentially primitive warrior who fought at Troy. A skyscraper and a jet plane—two quintessential representations of modern mass technology, but also archetypal Trojan Horses to carry the perverse revenge of desperate men—were turned into an enormous fuel-bomb. The burning, collapsed skyscraper itself has now become a technological problem—a smaller, and chemically toxic, disaster, whether they simply leave it where it is or salvage it.

Lower Manhattan is still permeated with some hideous, and undoubtedly toxic, chemical smell. The revenge continues—the revenge of our complex chemical way of life. And yet the crackpot realists of "Homeland Defense" tell us that a vast fabric of complicated, hazardous, industrial interdependency—every nuclear power plant, chemical factory, and other megatechnic-industrial complex—can be protected.

Capitalism moved more populations around than any previous cataclysm in human history, uprooting whole peoples, annihilating others. Now this turmoil and dynamism—what its publicists tell us makes capitalism great—has taken on its own momentum, and the guardians of the temple can only fumble and struggle with the consequences, like Captain Ahab with his ship.

The ship once seemed to encompass the whole of history itself, but now it has begun to shrink dramatically, to look like other empires: brutal, ponderous, brittle, unimaginative, and inevitably impermanent. It will sink, one way or the other, like all imperial civilizations that have come before. No one knows what lies in those depths. That is in fact the definition of catastrophe, both etymologically and in the classic tragedy: a turning downward, the horizon beyond which we cannot see. What is coming, as the official told the reporter, is "not in anyone's plans or imagination." We are all now at least potential collateral damage. That is what changed for Americans, heretofore, largely immune from the ongoing catastrophe, on September 11.

The war in Afghanistan and the wars likely to follow, so representative of the myriad wars that have gone on and on at the end of the last millennium and the beginning of this, all the terrible, wasteful, devastating traumas to human beings, to their cultures and histories, and to the natural world that sustains us, make clear that we are indeed in some new and terrible epoch. In the end, this empire is destined, like the rest, to lie half-buried in the rubble of history like Shelley's Ozymandias in the desert.

What follows, whether it comes to an end in one way, or the other, will depend in some obscure way on all of us, though on no one of us. The American empire cannot and should not survive, but America might. This requires our learning to bear witness to the world's suffering, not only to the suffering of Americans and not only when the television commands us to. It means learning about the causes of such suffering and working to eliminate them—committing ourselves to a vision of peace with justice with the potential to build bridges to those desperate people in the poor shantytowns and slums of the imperial peripheries presently being recruited by the evil enemies of an evil empire. It means continuing to live with ambivalence, with uncertainty, while struggling, paradoxically, with the whole of our being to defend the fragile forces of life.

For poets, it does not mean writing a barren political poetry, though, to his great credit, when Robert Bly was asked long afterward about the dubious quality of some of the antiwar poetry he wrote and published against the war in Vietnam, he replied that he had not written or published enough. And sometimes, if not always, the best poetic strategy is to leave our desks and attend to life. We could start by organizing poetry read-outs and art expositions against the war. At very least, whether at our desks or studios or away from them, we might resist doing anything that legitimates the imperial machine.

Whole populations are again rapidly rushing toward earthshaking encounters, the dead trembling anxiously in their dark dwellings. We are destined to be poets of catastrophe one way or the other. Let us consider not the one way, but the other.

November 2001

DAVID WEISS

The Folded Lie

Who among us didn't feel, on September 11th, stunned, fragile, dwarfed, overshadowed by an eruption of History, which—just like that—made our daily concerns and interests, our pleasures and pains, seem beside the point. Only on occasion have Americans collectively experienced History as a trauma which takes precedence over our individual histories and alters our citizen-identity. At such times, if only for a while, we feel that the world has changed and we with it. Pearl Harbor, The Cuban missile crisis, the assassinations of John F. Kennedy and Martin Luther King, and now The World Trade Center. These events induce a terror and awe made more potent by their communal dimension. They seem to summon up something new and indigestible, a terrible fusion of the real and the symbolic. They engender a strange intimacy. Something has happened to us each and to us all.

Who is to say what it is that's happened? Well, everyone, it seems. Anyone with a microphone in hand, with a byline, with the cameras trained on him. The voices most compelling, though, have been the sight-sickened, the grief-stricken voices, those who called from the planes or the towers to express, near the end, their love. Emptiest have been the voices of politics with their hollow, threadbare public language. Yet we listen, hungering for words that will express something of our common inner life, articulate what we want to understand.

This is often the thing we turn to poetry for. *Poetry Daily*, at poems.com, displayed no poem on September 14th, the day of prayer and remembrance, as though to run a poem would have been inadequate, even disrespectful. This may have been the right thing to do. To highlight a poem oblivious to our new condition—"On my Grandfather's Tractor," for instance—might have seemed egregious, stupid. Nevertheless, it's true that our poetry rarely speaks in a public voice; the private voice is our authentic one, the one we trust. And certainly, because a poem must reach down to a stratum of discovered knowledge, the claims of instant topicality are unfair. A poem is not a speech. Or an address. A poet can only speak for others by speaking for and from him—or herself. "From our quarrels with ourselves we make poetry," wrote Yeats; "from our quarrels with others, we make rhetoric." The president can address the nation, his speech writers hammering out the too familiar words. Far harder for a poet to.

The poem most widely circulated in the aftermath of The World Trade Center and Pentagon attacks seems to have been W. H. Auden's "September 1, 1939," its title the date Germany invaded Poland, an act that commenced the Second World War. But of course it's less the poem's apocalyptic gloom than its setting in New York City that has made the poem feel especially pertinent. It begins "I sit in one of the dives / On Fifty-second Street / Uncertain and afraid / As the clever hopes expire / Of a low dishonest decade"; that first stanza ends, eerily: "The unmentionable odour of death / Offends the September night," an image made literal on 9/11 in a way Auden never imagined.

The poem's current popularity might well be due to this, and to Auden's prophetic attention to New York's tall buildings. His interest resides partly in the fact that radio signals are broadcast from them: "Into this neutral air / Where blind skyscrapers use their full height to proclaim / The strength of Collective Man, / Each language pours its vain / Competitive excuse." Skyscrapers are not for Auden bastions or beacons of freedom. Business is not just another word for liberty. They stand for the monolith, first of fascism and, later in the poem, "Authority." That's why he's in a dive. He's down on the ground, below street level, Antaeus-like.

One of the most striking things in the aftermath of the attack has been the fierce battle for control of its meaning. "Freedom versus fear" as our president miscast it. If in identifying the skyscraper as a sign of the totalitarian, Auden seems, to us, off the mark, the lines, "Each language pours its vain / Competitive excuse," feel particularly germane. Commentators along the political spectrum have remarked on the similarity of Osama bin Laden's rhetoric to the president's: the recourse to language of apocalyptic conflict couched in theologic and biblical terms. Both bin Laden and Bush, each in his own way, are born-agains who speak a mirroring language, so stark and ideological, one is struck by how much of this "war" is a war of words. Words, it should be said, which are aimed not at "the enemy" but their own people.

For Auden, as well, it is a matter of words. "All I have is a voice," he says, "To undo the folded lie." In these lines we hear what we want from poetry. A human voice we trust. It's what we go on. Not "the windiest militant trash / Important Persons shout." But something, rather, down to earth that cuts through "the lie of Authority" as well as "the romantic lie in the brain / Of the sensual man-in-the-street." Whenever Auden wants to say something antidotal, he turns to our origins in childhood and a simple, virtually aphoristic language:

I and the public know
What all schoolchildren learn,
Those to whom evil is done
Do evil in return.

Auden wants to bring us down to size. "Evil" is a simple moral term here, not the Evil figured in Revelations; it means cruel things. Human monstrousness comes out of vulnerable human beginnings. Further on, Auden will say that from our basic wishes bad deeds originate; from our deepest yearnings come a willingness to believe in lies:

For the error bred in the bone
Of each woman and each man
Craves what it cannot have,
Not universal love
But to be loved alone.

And it's childhood, too, that underlies why, even as world-changing events are taking place, "the faces along the bar / cling to their average day": "Lest we should see where we are, / Lost in a haunted wood, / Children afraid of the night / Who have never been happy or good." It's curious how much Auden wants to ground a poem about politics in the pre-political.

What do we want from the voice of public poetry? Hope to be given? Something to celebrate, to affirm? I'm not sure this poem of Auden's, if written today, would be anything but notorious. I don't know who would be satisfied with its isolated speaker, its reduction of large historical forces to small ones, its insistence on the squalling infant audible behind the televised trash talk. In "September 1, 1939," no one comes off well. No one is particularly admirable. There are no heroes.

Or almost none. In the final stanza, there are, however, the Just who "flash out" "ironic points of light." Here is another reason the poem would not be popular now. Auden sides with irony. The poem does end with an affirmation, but the "affirming flame" is the flame not of hope but irony.

Why irony? ("Now with 50% less irony!" reads the sticker on a book in a recent Roz Chast cartoon.) Suddenly, we think so little of it now. As if we are relieved to be able to think and feel with an unchallenged, unequivocal certainty. But the trouble is, as Yeats put it in "The Second Coming," that "the worst are full of passionate intensity." The ironic mind that Auden links to justice is not a cynical one. It's one that looks behind the aroused surface and sees something very different going on. The ironic temper will acknowledge that it is composed "of Eros and of dust" and will call things by their real names, however unflattering, as Auden attempts to do here.

Auden didn't include "September 1, 1939" in his collected poems. He came to dislike the line, "we must love one another or die." "A damned lie!" he called it. But it, too, was written out of a wish, as were the lines that precede it: "There is no such thing as the State/And no one exists alone;/Hunger allows no choice/to the citizen or the police." My guess is that Auden rejected these antitheses, the unironic absolutism of it, its desperate fervor. He even changed the offending line to "we must love one another and die," but in the end, Auden scrapped the entire poem; it was, he wrote, "infected with an incurable dishonesty." I imagine Auden felt the poem too weighed down by the kind of political language he calls up to expose and unmask.

The lines that continue to haunt, however, are these: "All I have is a voice / To undo the folded lie." They are disarmed and undefended. In the paradox of poetry, they come across as strong because of that. By "the folded lie" Auden may have meant the news of the day, what's in the papers. That's what he, that's what we, are up against.

What is this voice, then, that is all we have? It is the one which occupies the subject position, whose words speak not just from that position but for it. For Auden that meant acknowledging we are "lost in a haunted wood, / Children afraid of the night." The Russian poet Marina Tsvetaeva once said that all poets were Jews. By which she meant that poets speak from the hurt, vulnerable, powerless place. Even the voice of public poetry must do that. That voice is tantamount to poetry's Bill of Rights which includes the rights of the dead.

When events of great enormity make poets feel insignificant and wish to toss their poems away, they should remember, however difficult it is, that someone must remain close to the ground, at eye-level, inadequate to the occasion, yet seeking, in words, the means to rise to it.

RICHARD WILBUR

Letter

Cummington, 9 November 2001

Dear Bill,

The only thing I can say right now is this. There is no excuse for the cold inhumanity of 11 September, and there is no excuse for those Americans, whether of the left or of the religious right, who say that we had it coming to us.

Dick

JOHN A. WILLIAMS

September 11, 2001

I saw the second plane.

My wife, Lori, had deserted the radio in the kitchen of our house in Teaneck, New Jersey, having heard something about an explosion in one of the World Trade Center buildings and was now standing before the TV set in the sitting room where I joined her.

The plane circled slowly past the north tower, then, dipping a wing, turned to ram into the south tower three-quarters of the way from its top. The jet disintegrated in a raging bright-orange inferno that billowed out and up against a sun-streaked blue sky, merging with the whirling orange-brown clouds boiling out of the north tower. At that instant I knew I wouldn't be driving Lori into Manhattan for her dental appointment.

On television and radio were a scattering of reports—"breaking news"—most ambiguous, awaiting confirmation or denial. A plane that should not have been was headed to Washington; another plane was maneuvering awkwardly over Pennsylvania. Perhaps it, too, came from Boston—or maybe Newark, according to a couple of reports. Commentators were breaking in on one another on all the channels. Then came the report of a plane crashing into the Pentagon, with heavy loss of life. The aircraft now down in Pennsylvania was confirmed, but there was another said to be headed for the White House in Washington. Was that why the President had been whisked to Louisiana and then to Nebraska before flying to Washington?

And then, about fifty minutes after the first strike, the north and then the south towers of the World Trade Center, without a shudder, collapsed straight down as though sucked into the ground by a thirsty earth.

TV commentators were framing the pictures with talk of terrorism. Speculation continued to run up and down the channels, along with the reports of people jumping out of windows or from the edges of the buildings where they'd found themselves, rather than fry to death in the fuel-drenched flames. I watched knowing I'd snatch my eyes away the moment a really tight shot closed in on people free-falling to their deaths. The sun continued to shine. Terrorism continued to be the topic. Moslem-sounding names continued to be repeated.

We succeeded in reaching family in Washington and friends in Manhattan and then relaxed to the extent we could. Although stunned by the horror, we found it difficult to leave the set.

By the time President Bush reappeared, Osama bin Laden's name especially, the Taliban, and a bit later, his fighting unit, Al Qaeda, were being repeated all over the networks. Mr. Bush looked as uneasy as a lad performing before his elders, some of whom must have also wondered when he was coming out of hiding. Many people interviewed agreed that the suicide bombers' attacks had produced ... war. Bin Laden's name almost became a punctuation mark or a pause for breath, it was mentioned so often. But repetition works. Speak a name often enough and listeners will believe whatever negative association is attached to it.

Two weeks past the disaster and the accumulating evidence reveals that a part of the Third World has very definitely taken on the First. The media bannered the phrase "They *hate* us," frequently and in a variety of slogans. That was the primary response of many Americans, and perhaps that made this holocaust barely tolerable. The number of the dead, missing, and wounded was equal to the decimation of two regiments of troops. That, no doubt, angered more than puzzled us.

Anger is easily aroused; it also gives lift to the ignored, deprived, helpless all over this world of six billion, most of whom are people of color, while the wealthiest and best off are white; ancient prejudices remain strong in this leading democracy. To wit: at the end of September, the *Newark Star Ledger* reported that General Motors paid out $1.25 million to settle a bias suit brought by black employees against it; at about the same time, in Cincinnati where rioting had been heavy during the summer (and not the first summer, either), a white cop was acquitted of killing an unarmed black man; in York, Pennsylvania, the mayor was finally convicted of murdering a black woman over 30 years ago when he was chief of police.

We are an active battlefield. The kamikazes have won very small battles, but will quite probably lose the war, and may only be equal to the "winners" when we have all succumbed to poisoned water, air, and food. Read up on the kamikazes from World War II and you'll see we've been there before. The Japanese said they needed more land in which to expand and we said no, like we owned the universe. So, boom! Pearl Harbor. And later, their pilots, desperate in a losing war, smashed into our battleships and aircraft carriers in what could have been nothing more than a gesture of defiance. Our ultimate revenge was to rain down the world's first atomic death upon the Japanese people, killing 130,000 in Hiroshima on August 6, 1945, and around 75,000 in Nagasaki three days later. The Japanese surrendered that day, August 9. Earlier in the year, in February, we and the British bombed Dresden, killing between 35,000 and ten times that number. No atomic weapons were used against the Germans. I was glad the war was over. I exulted in having survived it as well as the raging racism of the American military.

Nevertheless, these days my soul feels like lead. I don't know how many times those television pictures rerun of their own volition through my memory. Sometimes my eyes grow tears and my soul groans in pain, tells me quite distinctly, *"You know this didn't have to happen! How many next time, stupid?! All you have to be, must be, is fair!"*

But the drum beat continues: *"They (out there) hate us. They're angry that we live so well, are so mightily dominant and have supported Israel for over fifty years. The Moslems, the Arabs, hate us because we're so strong."* In addition, the follow-up has been to paint Islam as an inferior, from the git-go, lousy religion, without *really* comparing it to Christianity, Judaism, Buddhism, Confucianism, Shintoism, or anything else.

What is really going on is the race war—or the next phase of it—that has always been on the horizon of world history, and frequently well beyond it. Russia has gone over to a West that once tended to fear and shun it, for its present well-being. The rest of Europe has always held title to those parts of the globe inhabited by the darker brothers and sisters whom they enslaved and/or colonized with impunity and thus were able to grow rich from their labors and enshrine capitalism. The Europeans, in every way, used every part of the enslaved or colonized persons (and I mean *every* part) to fill their pockets and puff up their psyches. The end of slavery and the later end of colonialism in its most formal sense, left billions of people with nothing but the hope that those who had enslaved them would help them. Forget it. New suit; same funk.

To quote from a reader of the *Weekly Guardian* (Sept. 20–26 2001), "Is it civilized to let four-fifths of the world live in abject poverty while we amass 80% of the world's resources and wealth?"

Our thin attendance at the Durban, South Africa, United Nations Conference Against Racism, Racial Discrimination, Xenophobia and Related Intolerance in August again revealed our reluctance to end racism. The American secretary of state, who was expected to attend, did not, presumably on orders. His president might just as well have spit in his face. Colin Powell's a black man. He should have resigned. The Bush decision not to send him made clear his administration's decision to ignore African Americans' call for an apology on a federal level for slavery and the slave trade, and for reparations. There were few comments about this in the press. Yet reparations have been on the table ever since General William T. Sherman put them there at the tail-end of the Civil War. Other groups have fared somewhat better. The debt to Native Americans has been paid to some very small degree; Japanese Americans were handed $20,000 each for their incarceration during World War II— admittedly pennies, but something, and the U.S. has supported Holocaust claims at home and abroad from their inception. To the descendents of the 40 million enslaved Africans (*Encyclopedia Americana*, 1859) the determination not to recognize the justness of their request for reparations—while everyone else gets at least pittances—hammers home one thing, and that is that racism is not even close to being dead.

On the other side of the globe, while the WTC burned, another familiar incident took place: the Australian government refused to allow 237 Iraqis and 283 Afghans, brownish refugees, to disembark at any port of that country. So they were sent to the bleak Pacific coral island, Naru, instead. The most certain thing about their future is that it will be bleak. Those founding felons never learned to respect the land of the aborigines or blackfellows the British first stole, then later turned over to the convict whites.

The frequent UN requests that well-to-do nations provide asylum for those people (overwhelmingly black and brown) who seek it, have largely gone unheeded. To form a League of Nations or a United Nations and activate hundreds of committees over the years that advise the great powers to do more for the poorer, nonwhite nations—and those powers do little—has brought us to this point where the international situation is so fraught with danger. Confidence in the world body seems at its lowest ebb. The U.S. and Great Britain seem to rule the roost instead. But the Bush adminis-tration, suspect since the questionable 2000 elections, also inspires little assurance in any endeavor it may undertake. I reflect on the present early autumn in New York with its own holocaust, from life to sizzling, crushing, choking, falling, death in seconds. Some survivors were lucky enough to walk away coated in white dust looking like George Segal statues, instead of being gathered up piece-by-piece. The universe has shrunk back to basics, as though contemplating its next Big Bang. It is too late to ask, "Can we talk?" We had damned well better, and not tomorrow, either.

TERRY TEMPEST WILLIAMS

Scattered Potsherds

I.

Seismic activity was reported at Columbia University's Lamont-Doherty Earth Observatory in Palisades, New York, on September 11, 2001. The first pulse registered at 8:46 a.m. Eighteen minutes later, another. Then a third tremor was felt, this one a bit stronger and more sustained. At 9:59 a.m. another, and twenty-nine minutes after that, a final pulse.

John Ambruster, a scientist at the Observatory said, "An earthquake is something that gets out of the Earth and into a building. But this event began with a building and a subsequent effect leaked into the Earth."

II.

We watch the Twin Towers of the World Trade Center struck by our own planes, then collapse under the weight of terror. 110 stories. Thousands of life stories. Gone. Collapsed dreams. Compressed sorrows. Shattered innocence. Blood. They say what they need from us now is blood.

Blood knowledge. What will we come to know that we did not understand before? Who knows how this has entered our bloodstream?

III.

Washington, D.C.: Yellow police tape is wrapped around city blocks like its own terrorist package. I cannot get back to my hotel. For hours, I walk the streets of our nation's capital, alone, never have I felt more alone, far from my home in the redrock desert of Utah. I cannot reach home. All phone lines are jammed.

In my bag, I remember, I have a small piece of sandstone that I brought from home, a talisman from the banks of the Colorado River. I stop in the middle of the sidewalk, find it, and hold it tightly in the palm of my hand like a secret, and then continue walking in the steady stream of people, dazed, distracted, and scared.

Looking into the eyes of individuals on the street as they are fleeing by foot, by car, by any way possible, I see a gaze I have never encountered among my fellow citizens. It isn't fear exactly, closer to disbelief, not yet panic. The only comparable eye-strain I have witnessed before is something akin to a herd of sheep being circled by coyotes in the windy sageflats of Wyoming.

Fighter planes scream overhead, flying low, so low, I can see numbers painted on their bellies. F-16s wheeling right, then left over the Mall, the People's Commons where Martin Luther King, Jr. declared, "I have a dream." Where is our dream? Is this a dream? In this collective nightmare, I keep walking, watching, listening, observing, no place to go, where can I go?

A Palestinian kneels in the middle of the intersection on I Street and Seventeenth, crying, "*I didn't do it, you Americans did it.*" Traffic is halted, creating a barrier. A crowd gathers around him. I feel the stone in my hand. And just where do we go now to believe the myth of our own making, that there are places on this planet immune from suffering?

IV.

It is Saturday morning, September 15, 2001, 4:00 a.m. I call for a cab to take me to the Dulles Airport, where I hope I will finally be able to fly home.

I am standing in front of my hotel. In darkness, a yellow cab arrives. The driver gets out, his head bowed.

"I am from Afghanistan, perhaps you would feel safer in another car."

Our eyes meet. I burst into tears, the tears I have not shed all week. Inside the cab, he tells me his mother has called twice begging him to stay home.

"I cannot stay home, even if I am afraid, I have children to feed."

V.

Home in Utah. The Wasatch Range has never looked more formidable, rising beyond 11,000 feet from the valley floor. The spine of the central Rocky Mountains becomes my own. I check in with my family to see how they are feeling. My niece, Diane, who is eleven, tells me she has been spared.

"How so?" I ask.

"I was at camp in the mountains. I haven't seen what everybody else has seen."

VI.

My husband and I, with a friend, walk down to the river to say prayers. Looking up at the granite peaks, one can almost believe the world has not changed. Perhaps we are looking for guidance, perhaps we have been brought to our knees out of a new vulnerability, desperate to know that there is a world older and wiser that remains unchanged.

I close my eyes. After listening to the voice of rushing water, clear and cold, I open them and rock back on my heels. Instinctively, I pick up a stone. There is blood on the stone. I recoil, immediately placing the stone back in its own bed on the riverbank. There are no other blood-streaked stones around me. This is not what I was looking for, not the answer I was seeking. My mind turns to logic. Fish blood. A cutthroat clasped in the talons of osprey. A fisherman who sliced open the belly of a trout. Surely there is an answer. I did not want this answer.

I leave the river and privately carry the stone in my hand so I will not talk myself out of what I have seen.

VII.

Airstrikes over Afghanistan begin. President George W. Bush has announced he will rid the world of evil. *Osama bin Laden—Osama bin Laden—Osama bin Laden.* His name has become a mantra for all Americans and Muslims alike. We are now learning a new vocabulary: Al Qaeda; Taliban; Quran; Haraket-al Mujahadeen; Mazar-e Sharif; Kandahar; Kabul; Al Jazeera; jihad; hijab; burqa; anthrax; Cipro; bioterrorism.

Meanwhile in a Peruvian newspaper, The Statue of Liberty collapses into the arms of a peasant, a tear streams down her cheek, her torch is pointing downward.

VIII.

A friend, Maya Khosla sends me a poem written by her mother whose husband was the Ambassador to Afghanistan from India during the Russian invasion:

Guns thundering
in the distance
at regular intervals.
Unthinking messengers
of pain and death.
And in sharp contrast,
I absorb
the full bloom of roses
through a darkening dusk
while a single shrike
sits, swaying on a stalk.

—GOURI KHOSLA

IX.

Vernon Masayesva, a Hopi elder, speaks to a community gathering in Boulder, Colorado, on the topic of Indian Sacred Sites. He speaks of loss, how the Hopis sold their water rights under extreme pressure to Peabody Coal in 1966, to fuel rapidly growing cities in the American Southwest, like Phoenix. 3.3 million gallons of water a day is being pumped out of the Hopi Aquifer.

"We've lost over 40 billion gallons of water," he says. "Now we are trying to buy our water back. If we cannot reverse this trend, the aquifer will be dry in another decade, and we as a people will be displaced."

Vernon explains to the audience, largely non-Indians, how it is the belief of the Hopi People that we are now living in the Fourth World and the transition to the Fifth World has already begun.

"It doesn't look good right now," he says. "But that's why we are here to turn the tide, to make things happen. The river is going this direction. We can make it go the other way, each with our own gifts. This is our obligation." He then asks, "Do you want to participate in the shaping of the Fifth World?"

Afterwards, I meet with Vernon and another Hopi named Leonard Selestewa. We continue to share stories, how they had visited the Twin Towers a few weeks before the attacks. "I'm so glad I was able to meet The Twins before they were killed," Leonard says.

Over tea and in time, I share with them my encounter with the river and the blood-streaked stone.

"The Earth showed you the future—" remarks Leonard.

The terror of September 11 returns to my body as every hair on my arms stands on end. The darkness I feel inside is a hollow I cannot find my way through.

Vernon sits still for a long time. "Blood is life—" he says. He pauses. Smiles "This is what I have been taught."

X.

Mayor Giuliani reports that the City of New York will be presenting, to each family of the dead and missing, an urn filled with soil from Ground Zero. Each handful of Earth will be gleaned from members of the Police Department's ceremonial unit, in full dress uniform and white gloves.

"This is now sacred ground," he says.

XI.

What does the Earth feel but cannot say?

XII.

Seismic shift. A shift in consciousness. Is this too much to imagine? Do we have the strength to see this wave of destruction as a wave of renewal?

XIII.

I am home in the desert. There are steep canyons before me carved away by water, by wind. I see an opening in the Earth. I feel an opening in my heart. My hands cradle red dirt and I watch it slip through my fingers creating a small rise on the land. To be present, completely present, in these tender and uncertain days. This is my prayer: to gather together, to speak freely without judgment, to question and be questioned, to love and be loved, to feel the pulse, this seismic pulse—it will guide us beyond fear.

PAUL ZIMMER

The Trains

Henry David Thoreau's tranquility was interrupted daily by the sound of the train passing near Walden, reminding him of things he did not wish to think about. "The whistle of the locomotive penetrates my woods summer and winter, sounding like the scream of a hawk sailing over some farmer's yard." The old clinkers must have been especially invasive, clanging and spouting soot and cinders into the trees and onto the board-and-batten houses near the tracks.

There have been no trains in our valley in southwestern Wisconsin for more than sixty years; the final trip on the 52-mile Kickapoo Valley & Northern branch line tracks from La Farge to Soldiers Grove passed through in 1939. I was five years old and growing up far away in Ohio when the last train ran the bankrupt line. I guess it was a sad occasion and the local band played funeral dirges as the engine paused at each station.

All of the KV & N track was pulled up for scrap metal during World War II, and only a few old stations and traces of the throughway are left. Ben Logan, the novelist who grew up in this area, tells me that on damp days the sound of those old trains winding through the valleys came right up to your ears and made you feel the sadness of the fog. It brought you up from whatever you were doing. Just to imagine that mournful hooting in the woods, makes me understand Thoreau's complaint—but now, strangely, I envy his annoyance. I would give a great deal to be able to grumble about such interruptions. They would provide more frame to the landscape than the remote wisps and distant droning of high-flying jetliners over our ridge.

But I start this piece on September 12, 2001, and today I would give anything to hear the distant drone of the high liners and see their contrails crisscrossing overhead. The skies are empty and we are in national shock, mourning death and devastation as we begin to gain determination. We are at war, and we are told that it is likely to be long and cruel. In a few days or weeks, when we have gathered our wits and resources, we will be mounting our response, sending young men and women off to distant battlefields. Their loved ones will bid them goodbye. It will be the fifth war of my generation's time, and perhaps the worst.

Why do I sit at my writing table at a time like this? Because it is what I know how to do. Perhaps I should admit that I long for another time—sights and sounds I never knew or deserved to know—the steam trains gray and heavy in the rain, or blue and buoyant in the sunlight, the whistle of solemn engines winding through misty woods and fields in the valley below.

My orders in 1955 were to report to the army's base near the atomic test grounds. I was not going to war, but I was headed toward the unknown and particular danger of my era. I had been ordered and prepared to participate with a small group of men as military witnesses to the testing of these ultimate weapons. I did not know what this meant, but I was aware of what the bombs had done to Hiroshima and Nagasaki. The army wanted to test the reactions of soldiers to atomic explosions, and we were to witness detonations at very close range.

What I saw and experienced in Nevada does not matter at this moment. What I want to remember here is what I felt—or what little I felt—as I rode the train west from Ohio. I was twenty years old and this was my first train journey alone. I had taken a few days leave from the army to visit home on my way to Nevada. I said hello and goodbye to my friends. My mother tearfully held me for a long time at our house, but she did not go to the station. My father, who never cried, took me to the train and solemnly shook my hand as I stepped up into the coach. He tried to say something, but the engineer was clearing blast pipes on the big engine, so we smiled and waved at each other through the din. Then he turned and walked away quickly with his head down.

I was a shy, taciturn young person and had learned in basic training to attract as little attention as possible to myself. Frightened and trying to be brave, I was also numb with uncertainty. The trip took several days and I must have changed trains in Salt Lake City, but I remember little of it. We passed through grand vistas, deserts, and mountains I had never experienced, but I recall nothing of this. I nibbled candy bars and ate the sandwiches my mother had packed in a shoebox. Without speaking, I pointed to my selections of soft drinks from the vender's cart. Mostly I kept my head down and talked to no one.

What was I thinking? I cannot recall. I was doing my duty, traveling toward danger, preparing myself to be staunch. I had a book with me, an anthology of great short stories, and I had some vague notion that I wanted to be a writer. This was my first experience of Chekhov, Saki, Huxley, Conrad, Maupassant, Colette, Mann, Turgenev, Salinger, Porter, Hemingway, Faulkner. Frequently I was puzzled by what I read, but when I finished the book, I started it again.

There was a young woman with a baby in the seat across the aisle. The baby was fussy, and she struggled to comfort it. At one point, in frustration, she appealed generally to the passengers, if someone could help her open a can of baby food. She had forgotten a can opener. I carried an army C-ration opener on my key chain. When no one else came forth, I motioned to her that I could give assistance. She smiled with relief and thanked me when I handed the opened can back to her. She told me that her husband was also in the army; she wanted to have a friendly chat, but I did not know how to respond. I blushed and put my nose back into my book of stories. I must have opened half a dozen cans for her during the trip, working the sharp little blade around their rims, then handing them back without a word.

When I made my way to the restroom at the end of the car, I kept my eyes straight ahead and looked at no one. How can I explain my extreme reticence? I was so lonely and unpracticed, so far from home. I did not know how to speak, nor did I have anything to say. Occasionally I gazed out the window, but mostly I read.

I remember pondering Joseph Conrad's story, "Youth," the old man's narrative of his perilous experience as a young seaman on a storm-wracked, burning coal liner. I wondered what he meant when he said toward the end: "I remember my youth and the feeling that will never come back any more—the feeling that I could last forever, outlast the sea, the earth, and all men; the deceitful feeling that lures us on to joys, to perils, to love, to vain effort—to death."

I think about myself as that disoriented young man on the train, as I think of the young people who are loading their gear, saying good-byes, and heading toward the highly ambiguous future with so little knowledge of the past. I think of what they must do in the days and months ahead, their silence and strength, their fear and determination. I stand in a meadow and look up, wishing for vapor trails in the crisp, autumn sky. I listen longingly for the clatter of old trains in the valley below.

NOTES ON CONTRIBUTORS

TAMMAM ADI, from childhood, has loved God and languages. When the Syrian government invited the young man to spy on minorities, he fled to the West. Only in America, he has said, was he free to understand and live out his faith. Now he is an interfaith activist and the director of the Islamic Cultural Center of Eugene, Oregon. He is also the inventor of a cross-lingual search engine. Of his American-born wife, Patricia, he says, "I taught her about Islam and she taught me how to be free.

AI is the author of several books of poetry including *Cruelty* (1973), *Killing Floor* (1979), *Sin* (1986), *Fate* (1991), and *Greed* (1993). *Vice: New and Selected Poems* won the 1999 National Book Award (Norton). Among other prizes, she has won Guggenheim and Radcliffe Fellowships. She is a professor at Oklahoma State University. A new book, *Dread*, is forthcoming, also from Norton.

JOHN ALLMAN is a poet and fiction writer who has recently retired from college teaching. He received the Helen Bullis Prize from Poetry Northwest, and NEA fellowships in 1984 and 1990. His latest books are *Descending Fire & Other Stories* (New Directions, 1994) and *Inhabited World: New & Selected Poems* (Wallace Stevens Society Press, 1995). He is currently working on a collection of poems on the *film noir* period and another on the South Carolina low country.

MELISSA ALTENDERFER grew up in Sarasota, Florida, and graduated with a degree in English Writing from Loyola University in New Orleans. She has worked as a college instructor, lingerie saleswoman, SAT prep teacher, mailing list broker, communications manager for a biotech company, cookware retailer, and book store manager. She lives in Pittsburgh, where she is the Public Reading Series Coordinator for the International Poetry Forum.

ANTLER, from Milwaukee, called by Gary Snyder "one of the half-dozen or so truly committed wilderness poets in American letters," is author of *Selected Poems* (Soft Skull Press, 2000), *Ever-Expanding Wilderness* and *Deathrattles vs. Comecries*. Winner of a Pushcart Prize, the Witter Bynner Prize, and the Walt Whitman Award, his work also appears in many anthologies including *Wild Song: Poems from Wilderness*, *Reclaiming the Heartland: Lesbian & Gay Voices from the Midwest*, and *American Poets Say Goodbye to the 20th Century*.

PHILIP APPLEMAN, an Air Force veteran of World War II and a former Merchant Marine seaman, is Distinguished Professor Emeritus, Indiana University. He has published seven volumes of poetry, including *New and Selected Poems, 1956–1996* (Univ. Arkansas Press, 1996); three novels, including *Apes and Angels*; and several nonfiction books, including the Norton Critical Editions of *Darwin* and Malthus' *Essay on Population*.

MICHAEL ATKINSON's first book of poems, *One Hundred Children Waiting for a Train* (WordWorks), won the 2002 Washington Prize. His poetry has appeared in *The Best American Poetry 1993*, and in many periodicals including *Crazyhorse*, *New Letters*, *Michigan Quarterly Review*, and *The Threepenny Review*. He teaches at Long Island University/C.W. Post, and works as a film critic for *The Village Voice*.

DAVID BAKER is the author of eight books, most recently a volume of criticism, *Heresy and the Ideal: On Contemporary Poetry*, and the collections of poetry *Truth About Small Towns* and *Changeable Thunder* (Univ. Arkansas Press, 2000, 1998, 2001). Among his honors are fellowships and awards from the John Simon Guggenheim Memorial Foundation, the NEA, and the Poetry Society of America. He teaches at Denison University and in the MFA program for writers at Warren Wilson College, and is Poetry Editor of *The Kenyon Review*.

ALIKI BARNSTONE edited *Voices of Light: Spiritual and Visionary Poems by Women Around the World from Ancient Sumeria to Now* (Shambhala 2000). Her two most recent books of poems are *Madly in Love* (Carnegie Mellon, 2001) and *Wild With It* (Sheep Meadow, 2001). She is a Professor of English at the University of Nevada, Las Vegas.

WILLIS BARNSTONE's recent and forthcoming books are *The Secret Reader: 501 Sonnets* (Univ. Press of New England, 1996), *New & Selected Poems, 1948–1998* (Sheep Meadow, 1999), *The New Covenant: The Four Gospels & Apocalypse* (Penguin Putnam, 2002), *The Gnostic Bible* (Shambhala, 2002), and *Life Watch: A Circle of 61 Nights* (BOA, 2003). His poems continue to appear widely in periodicals.

WENDELL BERRY has lived on and worked a Kentucky farm for more than three decades. "Such history as my family has," he writes, "is the history of its life here. All that any of us may know of ourselves is to be known in relation to this place." He is the author of more than thirty books of poetry, fiction, and essays, including *Recollected Essays 1965–1980* (North Point Press, 1981), *Collected Poems 1957–1982* (North Point Press, 1985), and *The Selected Poems of Wendell Berry* (Counterpoint, 1998). Recent prizes include the T.S. Eliot Award, the John Hay Award, the Lyndhurst Prize, and the Aiken-Taylor Award for Poetry from *The Sewanee Review*.

PATRICK BIZZARO is the author of eight books and chapbooks of poetry, most recently *Fear of the Coming Drought* (Mount Olive College Press, 2001). He has won the Madeline Sadin Award from *New York Quarterly* and the *Four Quarters* Poetry Prize. His criticism includes *Dream Garden: The Poetic Vision of Fred Chappell* (Louisiana State Univ. Press, 1997). His pedagogical work includes *Responding to Student Poems: Applications of Critical Theory* (NCTE, 1993). He is currently Director of University Writing Programs and teaches writing and literature at East Carolina University.

KAREN BLOMAIN's books of poetry include *Borrowed Light* and *Normal Ave.* (Nightshade Press, 1992, 1998). She edited *Coalseam: Poems from the Anthracite Region* (Univ. of Scranton Press, 1995). *A Trick of Light* (Toby Press, 2001), her first novel, is in development for a CBS movie. She has conducted writing workshops in France, Austria, Russia, and across the U.S. She teaches in the Professional Writing Program at Kutztown University of Pennsylvania.

BRUCE BOND is Professor of English at the University of North Texas where he is Poetry Editor for *American Literary Review*. His most recent collections of poetry include *The Throats of Narcissus* (Univ. Arkansas Press, 2001) and *Radiography*, which received the Natalie Ornish Award (BOA, 1997). He has received fellowships from the National Endowment for the Arts, the Texas Commission on the Arts, and other organizations.

EMILY BORENSTEIN lives in Middletown, NY, with her husband, Morris. She has published three poetry chapbooks—the latest being *From a Collector's Garden* (Timberline Press, 2001)—and two full-length collections, *Cancer Queen* (Barlenmir House, 1979) and *Night of the Broken Glass* (Timberline Press, 1981). Her poetry has also appeared in several anthologies. She is a psychotherapist and counselor.

JONAH BORNSTEIN moved with his wife and two sons to Ashland, Oregon, from NYC in 1989. In 1995 he co-founded, and currently directs, the annual Ashland Writers Conference. He has published a chapbook, *We Are Built of Light*, and is co-author with three other poets of *A Path Through Stone*. His poems have appeared widely in periodicals, and he received the inaugural Southern Oregon Poetry Prize for Service to the Community. He works as an editor and teaches private poetry workshops.

DANIEL BOURNE is the author of a collection of poems, *The Household Gods* (Cleveland State Univ. Press, 1995), and a collection of translations of the Polish political poet Tomasz Jastrun, *On the Crossroads of Asia and Europe* (Salmon Run Press, 1999). The recipient of a Fulbright to Poland in 1985–1987 to translate younger Polish poets, he currently teaches at the College of Wooster in Ohio and edits the literary journal *Artful Dodge*.

PHILIP BRADY is the author of two books of poems, most recently, *Weal*, the 1999 winner of the Snyder Prize from Ashland Poetry Press. He has received fellowships in Ohio, New York, California, Ireland, Scotland, Spain, and the Czech Republic. He has taught at the University of Lubumbashi in the Congo and University College Cork, Ireland. Currently he teaches at Youngstown State University, where he directs the Poetry Center.

DAVID BUDBILL is the author of, among other books, *Why I Came to Judevine* (White Pine Press, 1987), *Judevine: The Complete Poems* (Chelsea Green, 1991), and *Moment to Moment* (Copper Canyon Press, 1999). He has published widely in periodicals. He lives in Wolcott, Vermont.

FRED CHAPPELL is the author of some twenty-five books of poetry, fiction, and criticism including, recently, the novel *Farewell, I'm Bound to Leave You* (Picador USA) and *Spring Garden: New and Selected Poems* (Louisiana State Univ. Press). His writing has received many prizes, including the Bollingen Prize in Poetry (shared with John Ashbery), the Ingersoll Foundation's T.S. Eliot Award, the Aiken/Taylor Award from the University of the South, and the Award in Literature from the National Institute of Arts and Letters. He Teaches at the University of North Carolina in Greensboro.

KELLY CHERRY's most recent collection of poems is *Rising Venus* (Louisiana State Univ. Press, 2002). Her most recent book of fiction, *The Society of Friends: Stories*, received the *Dictionary of Literary Biography Yearbook* Award for a Distinguished Volume of Short Stories. She is Eudora Welty Professor Emerita of English and Evjue-Bascom Professor Emerita in the Humanities at the University of Wisconsin-Madison and recently served as Eminent Scholar at the University of Alabama in Huntsville.

VINCE CLEMENTE, a SUNY English Professor Emeritus, is a poet-biographer whose books include *John Ciardi: Measure of the Man* (Univ. Arkansas Press, 1986), and the poetry volumes *Snow Owl Above Stony Brook Harbor*, *Songs from Puccini*, and *A Place for Lost Children*, among others. He is founding editor of *Long Pond Review*, *West Hills Review*, and *John Hall Wheelock Review*. His work has also appeared widely in newspapers, literary periodicals, and anthologies.

LUCILLE CLIFTON, whose *Blessing the Boats* (BOA, 2000) received the National Book Award for Poetry, serves as Distinguished Professor of Humanities at St. Mary's College of Maryland. Other of her books include *The Book of Light* (Copper Canyon, 1994), and *Quilting* and *The Terrrible Stories* (BOA, 1991, 1996). Ms. Clifton serves on the board of Chancellors of the Academy of American Poets and is a Fellow of the American Academy of Arts and Sciences.

CHRISTOPHER CONLON is the author of *Saying Secrets: American Stories* (Writers Club Press, 2000). His work has appeared in *America Magazine*, *The Washington Post*, *Tennessee Williams Annual Review*, and *The Long Story*, among other newspapers and magazines. His latest publication is a chapbook, *What There Is: Poems* (Argonne House Press, 2001). He lives in Maryland. His web site can be accessed at www.christopherconlon.com.

LUCILLE LANG DAY is the author of four poetry collections: *Infinities* (Cedar Hill Publications, 2002), *Wild One* (Scarlet Tanager Books, 2000), *Fire in the Garden* (Mother's Hen, 1997), and *Self-Portrait with Hand Microscope* (Berkeley Poets' Workshop and Press, 1982), which received the Joseph Henry Jackson Award in Literature. She also has a poetry chapbook in the "Greatest Hits" series from Pudding House Publications, and her work has appeared widely in magazines and anthologies. She is the founder and director of Scarlet Tanager Books, and the director of the Hall of Health, a museum in Berkeley.

ALISON HAWTHORNE DEMING is the author of *The Monarchs: A Poem Sequence*, and *Science and Other Poems* (Louisiana State Univ. Press, 1997, 1994) which was selected by Gerald Stern to receive the 1993 Walt Whitman Award. She edited *Poetry of the American West: A Columbia Anthology* (1996), and has published three books of prose: *Writing the Sacred into the Real* (Milkweed Editions, 2000), *The Edges of the Civilized World: A Journey in Nature and Culture*, and *Temporary Homelands* (Picador, 1998, 1994). She teaches literature and creative writing at the University of Arizona.

RICHARD DEMING, an editor/publisher at Phylum Press, is currently a doctoral candidate in American literature and poetics at SUNY Buffalo. His poems and reviews have appeared in such journals as *A.Bacus*, *American Studies International*, *Field*, *The Journal*, *Quarter After Eight*, and *Sulfur*.

ROSEMARIE DiMATTEO is an alumna of SUNY Brockport, and has taught at Illinois State Univesity where she is pursuing her English Studies doctorate. She lives in Hilton, New York, with her family. She has published poetry and criticism in several newspapers and journals.

ELIZABETH DODD's books include *Archetypal Light* (Univ. Nevada Press, 1991) and *Like Memory, Caverns* (NYU Press, 1992). She has published widely in periodicals. She grew up in Southeastern Ohio and lives in Eastern Kansas where she is Professor of English at Kansas State University.

WAYNE DODD's new book of poems, entitled *Is*, will be published by BOA Editions in early 2003. Among his recent books are *The Blue Salvages*, *Toward the End of the Century*, and *Of Desire & Disorder*. For many years, he was editor of *The Ohio Review* at Ohio University. In 2001 he received the Ohio Governor's Award for the Arts.

SHARON DOUBIAGO has published two volumes of stories—*The Book of Seeing with One's Own Eyes* (1988) and *El Niño* (1989)—and several collections of poetry including *Hard Country* (1982), *Psyche Drives the Coast: Poems 1975–1987* (1990), which won the Hazel Hall Oregon Book Award for Poetry, and the book-length *South America* Mi Hija (1992). She has traveled very widely, and has served as writer and artist-in-residence at numerous schools and colleges. She considers the West Coast of the United States her home

BART EDELMAN is a professor of English at Glendale College in California, where he edits *Eclipse*, a literary journal. His poetry has appeared widely in newspapers, journals, anthologies, and textbooks. Collections of his work include *Crossing the Hackensack* (Prometheus Press, 1993), *Under Damaris' Dress* (Lightning Press, 1996), *The Alphabet of Love* and *The Gentle Man* (Red Hen Press, 1999, 2001).

KARL ELDER is a Pushcart Prize recipient and has been included in The Best American Poetry series. He is the author of *Phobophobia* and *A Man in Pieces*. His recently completed sequence, *The Geocryptogrammatist's Pocket*

Compendium of the United States, has been published by Robert Schuricht Endowment Editions. He is the editor of the literary journal *Seems*, and is a professor of English at Lakeland College in Wisconsin.

Marcia Falk is the author of two books of poems and several volumes of poetry translations from Hebrew and from Yiddish. Among her books are *The Song of Songs: A New Translation and Interpretation* (Harper, 1990) and *The Book of Blessings* (Harper, 1996; pb Beacon, 1999). The latter is a re-creation of Jewish prayer as contemporary poetry in English and Hebrew. She has taught Creative Writing and Hebrew and English literature at SUNY Binghamton, the Claremont Colleges, Hebrew Union College, and Stanford.

Richard Foerster, who lives in York Beach, Maine, was the Amy Lowell Poetry Travelling Scholar for 2000/2001. For over twenty years, he edited the literary journal *Chelsea*. He is the author of four collections of poetry including, most recently, *Trillium* and *Double Going* (BOA, 1999, 2002).

Nora Gallagher is the author of the memoir *Things Seen and Unseen: A Year Lived in Faith*, and is presently under contract with Knopf for a second memoir, *A Book of Hours*. Her essays, book reviews and journalism have appeared in the *New York Times Magazine*, the *Los Angeles Times Magazine*, *Utne Reader*, the *Village Voice*, *Mother Jones*, and elsewhere. She lives in San Francisco.

Tess Gallagher is the author of the poetry collections *Portable Kisses, Instructions to the Double, Moon Crossing Bridge*, and *Willingly*. She has published two short-story collections, *The Lover of Horses* and *At the Owl Woman Saloon*, and a collection of essays, *A Concert of Tenses: Essays on Poetry*. *Soul Barnacles: Ten More Years with Ray* (Univ. Michigan Press, 2000) gathers diary entries, memoirs, letters and poetry celebrating her marriage and literary partnership with the late Raymond Carver. She lives in Port Townsend, Washington.

Brendan Galvin is the author of twelve collections of poetry. His most recent are *The Strength of a Named Thing* and *Sky and Island Light* (Louisiana State Univ. Press, 1999, 1997), and the narrative poem *Hotel Malabar*, winner of the 1997 Iowa Poetry Prize (Univ. Iowa Press, 1998). His translation of Sophocles' *Women of Trachis* appeared in the Penn Greek Drama Series in 1998. His awards include NEA and Guggenheim fellowships, the Sotheby Prize of the Arvon Foundation (England), and the Charity Randall Citation from the International Poetry Foundation. He has taught at many universities, and regularly reads and gives poetry workshops around the United States. He lives in Truro, Massachusetts.

Dan Giancola is the author of two books of poetry, *Powder* and *Echo* (Canio's Editions, 1991) and *Songs From the Army of the Working Stiffs* (Karma Dog, 1998). His poems appear widely in periodicals. He teaches at Suffolk County Community College on Long Island and is also the proprietor of A Cool of Books.

Daniela Gioseffi is the author of eleven books of poetry and prose. She won The American Book Award 1990 for *WOMEN ON WAR: International Voices for the Nuclear Age*, recently reissued by The Feminist Press; a World Peace

Award from The Ploughshares Fund for *On Prejudice: A Global Perspective* (Anchor/Doubleday, 1993); two awards in poetry from The New York State Council for the Arts; and a Pen Syndicated Fiction Award, 1990. Her latest book of poetry is *Symbiosis* (Rattapallax Press, 2001).

DIANE GLANCY is Professor of English at Macalester College in Minnesota where she teaches Native American literature and creative writing. She is the author of several volumes of poetry. Her latest novel is *The Man Who Heard the Land* (Minnesota Historical Society Press, 2001). Forthcoming novels are *The Mask Maker* (Univ. of Oklahoma Press, 2002) and *Designs of the Night Sky* (Univ. Nebraska Press, 2002). A collection of plays, *American Gypsy*, will be published by the Univ. of Oklahoma Press in 2002.

PATRICIA GOEDICKE is the author of, among other books, *Paul Bunyan's Bearskin*, *Invisible Horses* (Milkweed, 1992, 1996), and *As Earth Begins to End* (Copper Canyon, 2000). Her work has appeared widely in periodicals such as *Kenyon Review*, *Hudson Review*, and *Gettysburg Review*. She is a professor at the University of Montana in Missoula.

LAURENCE GOLDSTEIN is the author of three books of poetry, most recently *Cold Reading* (Copper Beech Press, 1995), three books of literary criticism, and seven edited or coedited volumes including *The Faber Book of Movie Verse* (1994). He is Professor of English at the University of Michigan where, since 1977, he has been Editor of *Michigan Quarterly Review*.

RAY GONZALEZ teaches in the MFA Creative Writing Program at The University of Minnesota in Minneapolis. He is the author of *Memory Fever*, a memoir about growing up in the Southwest, and of *The Underground Heart: Essays from Hidden Landscapes* (Univ. Arizona Press, 1999, 2002). His many volumes of poetry include *Turtle Pictures*, also from Arizona (2000), and *The Heat of Arrivals*, *Cabato Sentora*, and *The Hawk Temple at Tierra Grande* (BOA, 1997, 2000, 2002). He has also written two collections of short stories, *The Ghost of John Wayne* (Univ. Arizona Press, 2001) and *Circling the Tortilla Dragon* (Creative Arts, 2002). Editor of twelve anthologies, he has won many awards including a 1998 Colorado Governor's Award for Excellence in the Arts, a 1993 Before Columbus Foundation American Book Award for Excellence in Editing, and a 1998 Illinois Arts Council Fellowship in Poetry.

GAIL GRIFFIN teaches literature and writing at Kalamazoo College. She is the author of two volumes of nonfiction: *Calling: Essays on Teaching in the Mother Tongue* and *Season of the Witch: Border Lines, Marginal Notes*. She has also published essays and poetry and is at work on a volume of brief creative nonfiction called *Heart Rendering*.

KIMIKO HAHN is the author of *Air Pocket* (1989), *Earshot*, which won an Association of Asian American Studies Literature Award (1992), *The Unbearable Heart*, which won an American Book Award (1995), *Volatile* (1999), and *Mosquito and Ant* (1999). She has received a Lila Wallace-Readers Digest Writers Award, and fellowships from the New York Foundation for the Arts and the National Endowment for the Arts. She wrote ten portraits of women for an HBO production, *"Ain't Nuthin' but a She Thing."* She currently teaches at Queens College/CUNY.

Joy Harjo (Muscogee/Tallahassee Wakokaye Grounds) is a poet, musician, writer, and performer. *How We Become Human: New and Selected Poems* appeared from Norton in 2002. Harjo also performs nationally and internationally, solo, and with her band Joy Harjo and Poetic Justice (now called Joy Harjo and Her Real Revolution Band) for which she plays saxophone. Her first CD, *Letter From the End of the Twentieth Century* was released by Silverwave Records in 1997. In 1998 the CD was honored by the First Americans in the Arts with the award for Outstanding Musical Achievement. A second CD, *Crossing the Border*, appeared in 2002.

Samuel Hazo is Director of the International Poetry Forum in Pittsburgh where he is also McAnulty Distinguished Professor of English Emeritus at Duquesne University. His latest books are *The Holy Surprise of Right Now* and *As They Sail* (poetry), *The Rest Is Prose* and *Spying for God* (essays), *Stills* (fiction), and *Feather* (play). Translations include Denis de Rougemont's *The Growl of Deeper Waters*, Nadia Tueni's *Lebanon: Twenty Poems for One Love*, and Adonis' *The Pages of Day and Night*. *The Autobiographers of Everybody* appeared from the International Poetry Forum in 2000. He has been a National Book Award finalist and was chosen the first State Poet of the Commonwealth of Pennsylvania in 1993, a position he still holds.

Michael Heller is the author of six volumes of poetry, including *In the Builded Place* (Coffee House Press, 1989) and *Wordflow: New and Selected Poems* (Talisman, 1997). His memoir, *Living Root*, was published in 2000 by State Univ. Press of New York and re-issued in paperback in 2001. His libretto for the opera *Benjamin*, based on the life of Walter Benjamin, was set to music by Ellen Fishman Johnson and performed at the 2000 Philadelphia Fringe Festival.

Al Hellus is a poet and arts activist living in Saginaw, Michigan. His poetry chapbooks include *A Vision of Corrected History with Breakfast* (Mayapple Press, 1995), and *Alternative Baseball & Other Poems* and The *Legend of the Turnips* (Ridgeway Press 1997,1999) He collaborates with six local musicians who constitute the Plastic Haiku Band. They have produced, to date, one CD, *Raw Haiku*, and their second, *5/7/5* is in the works. He was indeed born on a September 11.

Geof Hewitt was born in New Jersey. He moved to Vermont in 1970, where he has worked ever since as a writer in the schools, and, for a real living, as an arts and education administrator. In addition, he currently teaches as an adjunct at the University of Vermont and at Vermont College. He has published two books for teachers, *A Portfolio Primer* and *Today You Are My Favorite Poet* (both from Heinemann Publishers in Portsmouth, NH), and three books of poems—*Stone Soup, Just Worlds* (both from Ithaca House), and, most recently, *Only What's Imagined* (The Kumquat Press).

William Heyen is Professor of English/Poet in Residence Emeritus at SUNY Brockport. A former Fulbright Lecturer in American Literature in Germany, he has won NEA, Guggenheim, American Academy & Institute of Arts & Letters, & other fellowships and prizes. He edited *American Poets in 1976* (Bobbs-Merrill, 1976) and *The Generation of 2000: Contemporary American Poets* (Ontario Review Press, 1984). Books of poetry include *Long*

Island Light (Vanguard, 1979); *Erika: Poems of the Holocaust* (1991), *Ribbons: The Gulf War* (1991), and *The Host: Selected Poems 1965–1990* (1994) (Time Being Books); and *Crazy Horse in Stillness*, winner of 1997's Small Press Book Award (BOA, 1996). BOA also published his *Pig Notes & Dumb Music: Prose on Poetry* (1998).

JOANNA HIGGINS was born in Alpena, Michigan, studied at Aquinas College, The University of Michigan, and later at Binghamton University, graduating with a Ph.D. in literature. Her fiction and essays have appeared in various journals and anthologies. In 1998 The Permanent Press brought out her first novel, *A Soldier's Book*. Earlier, Milkweed editions published a collection of her short fiction, *The Importance of High Places: Stories and a Novella*. She lives in Vestal, New York, with her husband and child, and is now at work on another novel.

LAURA HINTON is the author of *The Perverse Gaze of Sympathy: Sadomasochistic Sentiments from* Clarissa *to* Rescue 911 (SUNY Press 1999), and co-editor (w. Cynthia Hogue) of *We Who Love to Be Astonished: Experimental Women's Writing and Performance Poetics* (Univ. Alabama Press 2001). She has published essays in literary and film studies, on topics including Hitchcock's *Vertigo* and feminism, Henry James and sadomasochism, and women's postmodern novels. She is a professor of contemporary literature and women's studies at CCNY. She lives in Manhattan and Woodstock, New York, and is currently working on a book about fetishism in women's experimental fiction and is writing fiction herself.

H. EDGAR HIX is a poet who has kept his day job, letting writing be just for the joy of it. He loves the winter snows in Minnesota but misses the thunderstorms in his home, Oklahoma. He has been a warehouseman, a lay minister, and a missionary. He finished his first freshman composition course in 1972 and his second in 2001. After six colleges and universities, he has recently graduated with an A.A.S. He looks so much like Santa Claus that children stop him to ask him if he is. He always says yes.

H. L. HIX's most recent poetry books are *Rational Numbers* and *Surely As Birds Fly*. His essay collection *As Easy As Lying* is forthcoming from Etruscan Press. He is Director of the School of Liberal Arts at the Kansas City Art Institute.

CYNTHIA HOGUE has published two collections of poetry, most recently *The Never Wife* (MAMMOTH Books, 1999). Her new collection is *Flux* (New Issues Press 2002). She is the editor of a critical book on American women's poetry entitled *Scheming Women: Poetry, Privilege, and the Politics of Subjectivity*. She lives in Pennsylvania, where she directs the Stadler Center for Poetry and teaches English at Bucknell University.

TOM HOLMES received his MA in English from SUNY Brockport in 1995. Since then, he has evolved from a coffee slinger to a professional editor, writer, and grant writer. He has also had his poems published in a handful of magazines and journals. Recently, he and his fiancé, Michelle, moved from Brockport, New York to Spokane, Washington, where he currently washes dishes.

John Hoppenthaler's poetry appears in such journals as *Ploughshares*, *The Southern Review*, *New Letters*, *Connecticut Review*, *The Bloomsbury Review*, *Chelsea*, *Poet Lore*, and *Tar River Poetry*. His essays, interviews, and reviews also appear widely. He is the poetry editor of *Kestrel*. He has most recently edited a collection of essays and interviews on the poetry of Jean Valentine (Wesleyan Univ. Press, 2002).

Mark Irwin is the author of *The Halo of Desire*; *Against the Meanwhile*; *Quick, Now Always*; and most recently, *White City* (BOA, 2000), which was nominated for the National Book Critics Circle Award and won a Colorado Book Award. He has taught at many universities and colleges in the U.S., and he spends a part of each year on a wilderness ranch in southern Colorado.

Mark Jarman's latest collection of poetry is *Unholy Sonnets* (Story Line, 2000). His previous collection, *Questions for Ecclesiastes*, won the Lenore Marshall Poetry Prize for 1998. A collection of his essays and reviews, *The Secret of Poetry*, was published by Story Line Press in 2001. Another collection, *Body and Soul*, will be published by the Univ. of Michigan Press in its Poets on Poetry series in 2002. He teaches at Vanderbilt University.

Denis Johnson is the author of *The Name of the World*, *Already Dead*, *Jesus' Son*, *Resuscitation of a Hanged Man*, *Fiskadoro*, *The Stars at Noon*, and *Angels*. *The Throne of the Third Heaven of the Nations Millennium General Assembly: Poems Collected and New* appeared from HarperCollins in 1995. Among many other awards, he has received a Lannan Fellowship and a Whiting Writer's Award. He lives in northern Idaho.

Erica Jong is the author of several best-selling novels including *Fear of Flying* and *Any Woman's Blues*; seven books of poetry including *Ordinary Miracles* and *Becoming Light*; a children's book, *Fanny: Being the True History of the Adventures of Fanny Hackabout-Jones*; and memoirs including *The Devil at Large: Erica Jong on Henry Miller* and *Fear of Fifty: A Midlife Memoir*. She lives in New York City and in Weston, Connecticut.

X. J. Kennedy is a free-lance writer who lives in Lexington, Mass. He is co-author (with Dana Gioia) of *An Introduction to Poetry* (8th Edition, Longman, 2002). His verse, which includes *Dark Horses: New Poems* (Johns Hopkins Univ. Press, 1992) has received several recognitions, most recently the Aiken-Taylor Award of the University of the South and *The Sewanee Review*, and the Award for Excellence in Children's Poetry of the National Council of Teachers of English.

Maxine Hong Kingston won the National Book Critics Circle Award for her first book, *The Woman Warrior: Memoirs of a Girlhood Among Ghosts* (Knopf, 1976). *China Men*, a sequel (which also received this award) was published four years later. She has taught at several schools and universities, including Mid-Pacific Institute and the University of California at Berkeley. *Tripmaster Monkey: His Fake Book*, her first novel, appeared from Knopf in 1989.

Steve Kowit lives and teaches in San Diego. He is the author of, among other books, *Confessions* (Carpenter Press, 1983) and *Pranks* (Bloody Twin Press, 1990). His latest collection of poetry is *The Dumbbell Nebula*. He is also the author of a teaching manual, *In the Palm of Your Hand: The Poet's Portable Workshop*. A former animal rights organizer, he has been working for several years on a study of mass persuasion, self-deception, and social terror.

NORBERT KRAPF a native of southern Indiana, directs the C.W. Post Poetry Center of Long Island University, where he has taught English since 1970. A former senior Fulbright lecturer, he won the Lucille Medwick Memorial Award from the Poetry Society of America. He is the author, editor, or translator of eighteen books, including the poetry collections *Somewhere in Southern Indiana, Bittersweet Along the Expressway, The Country I Come From*, and *Blue-Eyed Grass*, which concludes with a cycle about World War II and the Holocaust.

NANCY KUHL is the author of *In the Arbor*, a collection of poems published by Kent State University Press. Her work has appeared in *Verse, The Cream City Review, Poetry Northwest, Quarter After Eight, Alaska Quarterly Review, Puerto del Sol*, and other magazines. She is the Assistant Curator of the American Literature Collection at Yale University's Beinecke Rare Book and Manuscript Library.

KELLY LEVAN studied at SUNY Brockport, then earned a B.A. in English from Western New Mexico University, and is currently working toward her M.F.A. in Creative Writing at Emerson College in Boston. She works as a webmaster for a local Massachusetts paper, tutors writing at Emerson, and edits a webzine for experimental writing and artwork, *Noochbomb*.

CLAUDE LIMAN was born in Mt. Kisco, New York, and attended Deerfield Academy, Dartmouth, New York University and the University of Colorado. He has taught American literature and creative writing in Canada since 1973. He is a professor at Lakehead University in Thunder Bay, Ontario. His books are *Landing* (1976), *Becoming My Father* (1988), and the forthcoming *Home-Made Hill*.

ANN LoLORDO who attended the Writing Seminars program at Johns Hopkins, is currently a features editor at the *Baltimore Sun* where she previously served as the newspaper's Middle East correspondent. Her poems have appeared in *The Greensboro Review, Puerto Del Sol, Southern Poetry Review*, and other journals. She lives in Crownsville, Maryland.

JAMES LONGENBACH is the author of, among other studies, *Stone Cottage: Pound, Yeats & Modernism* and *Wallace Stevens: The Plain Sense of Things* (Oxford Univ. Press, 1988, 1991). His most recent books are *Modern Poetry After Modernism: Essays on Contemporary American Poetry* (Oxford Univ. Press, 1997) and *Threshold*, A Collection of Poems (Univ. of Chicago Press, 1999). He has published widely in periodicals. He is Joseph H. Gilmore Professor of English at the University of Rochester.

ADRIAN C. LOUIS was born and raised in Nevada and is a member of the Lovelock Paiute Tribe. He is the author of several books of poetry including *Blood Thirsty Savages* (1994), *Vortex of Indian Fevers* (1995), *Ceremonies of the Damned* (1997), and *Bone & Juice* (2001). His *Fire Water World* won the 1989 Poetry Center Book Award from San Francisco State University. His novel

Skins (1995) will soon be a motion picture. He has won NEA, Lila Wallace-Reader's Digest Fund, and other awards. He currently resides in Minnesota and teaches at Southwest State University.

DAVID ZANE MAIROWITZ is the author of *BAMN, The Radical Soap Opera* (1974), *In the Slipstream: Short Stories* (1977), *Wilhelm Reich for Beginners* (1986), *Introducing Kafka*—with Robert Crumb (1993), and *Introducing Camus* (1998). His plays for the theatre have been produced widely. He is the author of numerous radio dramas and documentaries, produced in 20 European countries. His 3-part radio dramatization of *Moby Dick* was broadcast on the BBC in 2000, and has been published as an audio cassette as part of the BBC Radio Collection.

PAUL MARIANI is a poet, biographer (of William Carlos Williams, John Berryman, Robert Lowell, Hart Crane), and critic. His most recent books are *Thirty Days: On Retreat with the Exercises of St. Ignatius* (Viking, 2002) and *God and the Imagination: On Poets, Poetry, and the Ineffable* (Univ. of Georgia Press, 2002). For over thirty years he taught at the University of Massachusetts/Amherst, and currently holds a Chair in English at Boston College.

DAVID MASON's books of poems include *The Country I Remember* and *The Buried Houses* (Story Line Press, 1996, 1991). He is also the author of a collection of essays, *The Poetry of Life and the Life of Poetry*. He has published widely in journals such as *Georgia Review, New Criterion, Harvard Review*, and *American Scholar*. He teaches at The Colorado College.

DAN MASTERSON is the author of several volumes of poetry including *World Without End* and *All Things, Seen and Unseen: New and Selected Poems* (Univ. of Arkansas Press, 1991, 1997). He has won many awards, and was elected to PEN in 1986. His website, Poetry Master, http://www.poetrymaster.com is a valuable resource for advanced poets interested in revision and publication. The site is connected with Manhattanville College's graduate writing program. He is the recipient of two Pushcart Prizes, and his work has appeared widely in periodicals.

JACK MATTHEWS has published 22 books of essays, poetry, drama and fiction. Among his novels are the well-known *Hanger Stout, Awake!*, *The Charisma Campaigns*, and *Pictures of the Journey Back*. His most recent is *Schopenhauer's Will*, which he refers to as "a rather eccentric production," but one scheduled to appear soon in a Czech translation, even though it still awaits publication in English. He has also published several volumes on the collecting of rare books. Matthews is Distinguished Professor of English at Ohio University, in Athens, where he lives with his wife, Barbara.

JEROME MAZZARO recently relocated to New York City, having retired from the University at Buffalo in 1996. His books include three volumes of poetry, including *Rubbings* (Quiet Hills Press, 1985), as well as several books of criticism. He was the recipient of a Guggenheim Fellowship in poetry, and edited *Modern Poetry Studies* (1970–1978). His most recent books are *Mind Plays: Essays on Luigi Pirandello's Theater, Robert Lowell and Ovid*, and *War Games* (Xlibris, 2000, 2001, 2001).

JAY MEEK has published seven books of poetry and fiction with Carnegie-Mellon Univ. Press, including *Windows, Headlands*, and, most recently, *The Memphis Letters* (2002). A member of the writing faculty at the University of North Dakota, he is co-editor with F.D. Reeve of *After the Storm: Poems on the Persian Gulf War* (1992).

W. S. MERWIN's most recent books of poetry are *The Vixen* (1996), *Flower & Hand* (1997), *The Folding Cliffs: A Narrative* (1998), *The River Sound* (1999), and *The Pupil* (2001). His volumes of prose include *Unframed Originals* (1982) and *The Lost Upland* (1992). His most recent of some twenty volumes of translation is *Dante's Purgatorio* (2000). One of America's most distinguished men or letters, he has won the Pulitzer Prize, the Bollingen Prize, and the Tanning Prize for mastery in the art of poetry, among others. For many years, he has made his home on Maui, Hawaii, where he raises rare palm trees. "To the Words" was the first poem he wrote after September 11, 2001.

BRUCE MILLS teaches American literature at Kalamazoo College in Michigan. He has published a monograph on nineteenth-century reformer Lydia Maria Child and an edition of her essays on New York (*Cultural Reformations: Lydia Maria Child and the Literature of Reform* and *Letters from New-York*). He is currently working on a collection of essays exploring how his autistic son's vision of the world has altered his own way of knowing.

JUDITH MINTY is the author of eight books of poetry, most recently *Walking with the Bear: Selected and New Poems* (Michigan State Univ. Press, 2000). Her first book was recipient of the United States Award of the International Poetry Forum. She reads her poetry and directs workshops widely. She has taught at universities across the country. She lives with her husband and yellow dog named River in Michigan.

ROBERT MOONEY's short fiction has appeared in numerous literary magazines and his novel *Father of the Man* will be published by Pantheon Books in September 2002. He is director of the creative writing program and a member of the English faculty at Washington College in Chestertown, Maryland. For four years he edited the journal *New Myths/MSS*, and served as senior editor at New Myths Press. He and his wife Maureen and two children divide their time between the Eastern Shore of Maryland and their native upstate New York.

FRED MORAMARCO edits *Poetry International* at San Diego State University where he teaches literature and creative writing. He is co-author of *Modern American Poetry* (Univ. of Massachusetts Press) and *Containing Multitudes: Poetry in the United States Since 1950* (Twayne). With Al Zolynas he co-edited *Men of Our Time: Male Poetry in Contemporary America* (University of Georgia Press), and is currently at work on a sequel, *A Man's World: An International Anthology of Male Poetry*.

ANDY MOZINA has published short fiction in *Alaska Quarterly Review, Fence, Mississippi Review, The Massachusetts Review* and elsewhere. He teaches literature and creative writing at Kalamazoo College in Michigan.

HOWARD NELSON is a teacher at Cayuga Community College in Auburn, New York. He is the author of several collections of poetry, his most recent being *Bone Music* (Nightshade Press). His critical essays appear in *The Hollins Critic*, and he recently edited *Earth, My Likeness: Nature Poems of Walt Whitman* (Woodthrush Books).

NAOMI SHIHAB NYE has for many years worked as a writer-in-the schools across the United States, and has also been a visiting writer at many universities, including Berkeley and Hawaii. She is much-traveled in the Middle East and Asia. She published a volume of essays, *Never in a Hurry* (1996), and is the author of many volumes of poetry, including *Different Ways to Pray* (1980), *Hugging the Jukebox* (1982), *The Yellow Glove* (1986), *Red Suitcase* (1994), *Words Under the Words: Selected Poems* (1995), and *Fuel* (1998). Among her many awards are the I. B. Lavin Award from the Academy of American Poets and a Guggenheim Fellowship.

HUGH OGDEN has published several books, including *Two Roads & This Spring* (1993), *Windfalls* (1996), *Gift* (1998), and *Natural Things* (1998). He teaches full time at Trinity College in Connecticut, and also teaches a course at a magnet high school, the Hartford Academy of the Arts.

ALICIA OSTRIKER's *The Imaginary Lover* (Univ. of Pittsburgh Press) won the 1986 William Carlos Williams Prize from the Poetry Society of America. As critic, she is the author of *Vision and Verse in William Blake* and editor of the Penguin edition of *Blake's Complete Poems*. Her writing on women poets includes the essays published in *Writing Like a Woman* and *Stealing the Language: The Emergence of Women's Poetry in America*. She has received grants from the NEA, the Rockefeller Foundation, and the Guggenheim Foundation. Her most recent volumes of poems, *The Crack in Everything* and *The Little Space: Poems Selected and New* (Univ. of Pittsburgh Press, 1996,1998) were both National Book Award finalists. She is Professor of English at Rutgers University.

ERIC PANKEY is Professor of English at George Mason University in Virginia. His first book of poems, *For the New Year*, winner of the Academy of American Poets' Walt Whitman Award, appeared from Atheneum in 1984, which published his second book, *Heartwood*, four years later; *Apocrypha* (1991), *The Late Romances* (1997), and *Cenotaph* (1999)—as a whole, a triptych—have followed from Knopf. He has won fellowships from the NEA and the Ingram-Merrill Foundation.

BETTE PESETSKY is the author of two short story collections, *Stories Up to a Point* and *Confessions of a Bad Girl*, and of several novels including *Author from a Savage People, Digs, Midnight Sweets, The Late Night Muse*, and, most recently, *Cast a Spell*. Her books have consistently been listed by the *New York Times* as Notable Books of their years. She has taught at the Iowa Writers Workshop, University of California, Wichita University, St. Lawrence University, and elsewhere. She is currently at work on a novel about Leon Trotsky.

ROBERT PINSKY former Poet Laureate of the United States and creator of the Favorite Poem Project, teaches in the graduate writing program at Boston University. Poems from four previous books were brought together for his

The Figured Wheel: New & Collected Poems 1966–1996 (Farrar, Straus & Giroux, 1996). His books of essays include *The Situation of Poetry* (1977) and *Poetry and the World* (1988). His translation of *The Inferno of Dante* (FS & G, 1994) received the *Los Angeles Times* Book Prize and the Harold Morton Landon Translation Prize of the Academy of American Poets, which also awarded him the Lenore Marshall Poetry Prize in 1998. He collected *The Handbook of Heartbreak: 101 Poems of Lost Love and Sorrow* (William Morrow, 1998). His *The Sounds of Poetry: A Brief Guide* appeared from FS & G the same year.

STANLEY PLUMLY is a Distinguished University Professor at the University of Maryland. His most recent collection of poems is *Now That My Father Lies Down Beside Me: New & Selected Poems, 1970–2000* (Ecco/HarperCollins, 2000). His work has been honored with the Delmore Schwartz Memorial Award, nominations for the National Book Critics Circle Award, the William Carlos Williams Award, and the Academy of American Poets' Lenore Marshall Poetry Prize.

JEFF PONIEWAZ (pronounced Poe-nYEAH-vAHsh, Polish for "because") is the PEN Discovery Award-winning author of *Dolphin Leaping in the Milky Way*. He teaches "Literature of Ecological Vision" at University of Wisconsin-Milwaukee. His poems have appeared in many periodicals, and in anthologies including *Earth Prayers* and *Prayers for a Thousand Years*. He's currently trying to get a major orchestra to perform the *"Song of the Rainforest"* concert he brainstormed.

MAJ RAGAIN was born in 1940 in Olney, southeastern Illinois, and now lives in Kent, Ohio, along the Cuyahoga river. He has published several collections of poetry, the most recent being *Twist the Axe: A Horseplayer's Story* (Bottom Dog Press, 2002). In the summer of 2001, he was resident poet at the Fine Arts Work Center in Provincetown.

DAVID RAY is the author of many books of poetry, including, most recently, *Wool Highways* (Helicon Nine Editions, 1993), *Kangaroo Paws* (Thomas Jefferson Univ. Press, 1995), *Demons in the Diner* (Ashland Poetry Press, 1999), and a Holocaust collection, *One Thousand Years* (Holy Cow! Press, 2002). He received the Nuclear Age Peace Foundation 2001 Poetry Award.

ISHMAEL REED is the author of nine novels, including *The Last Days of Louisiana Red* (1974) and *Flight to Canada* (1976); four books of poetry including *New and Collected Poetry* (1988); five plays, and four books of essays including *God Made Alaska for the Indians: Selected Essays* (1982) and *Writing is Fighting: Thirty-Seven Years of Boxing on Paper* (1988). His latest book is *The Reed Reader*. His latest awards are The Chancellor's Award for Community Service and The Integrity Award from The Oakland Women's Chamber of Commerce. He lives in Berkeley, California.

F. D. REEVE was a New York City longshoreman before he became a poet, novelist, critic, translator, and teacher. His most recent books of poetry include *The Moon and Other Failures* (which includes the secular oratorio "Alcyone") and *The Urban Stampede and Other Poems* (Michigan State Univ. Press, 1999, 2002)—the latter includes his latest long poem for music. The e-book *A World You Haven't Seen* (Ratapallax, 2001) is a book of selected poems. He is co-editor, with Jay Meek, of *After the Storm: Poems on the Persian Gulf War* (Maisonneuve Press, 1992). He lives in Wilmington, Vermont.

HELEN MORRISSEY RIZZUTO is the author of two collections of poetry, *Evening Sky on a Japanese Screen* and *A Bird in Flight*. Her work has appeared widely in literary journals. She was a resident fiction writer and poet for New York State Council on the Arts' Poets-In-Public-Service, and has taught writing at University College, Hofstra University for twenty years. She teaches English at Townsend Harris High School in the NYC School System and is an adjunct professor at Queens College.

MARY ELSIE ROBERTSON is the author of a children's book, a collection of short fiction, and of several novels including *Family Life* (Atheneum, 1987) and *What I Have to Tell You* (Doubleday 1989). Her novel-in-progress is entitled *Wire Walking*. She has taught creative writing workshops across the country. She lives in upstate New York.

SCOTT RUSSELL SANDERS is the author of *Secrets of the Universe, Staying Put, Writing from the Center*, and, most recently, *Hunting for Hope, The Country of Language*, and *The Force of Spirit*. His work has been selected for *Best American Essays*. He has won the John Burroughs Award for best essay in natural history, and the Lannan Literary Award. He is Distinguished Professor of English at Indiana University, in the White River Valley.

JOANNA SCOTT is the author of several novels, including *The Manikin* (1996) and *Make Believe* (2000), and of a collection of short fiction, *Various Antidotes* (1994). Her honors include the Lannan Literary Award, the Aga Kahn Award, the Rosenthal Award from the Academy and Institute of Arts and Letters, and a MacArthur Fellowship. She is Roswell Smith Burrows Professor of English at the University of Rochester.

EDWINA SEAVER is Amerigo Vespucci Professor of Religious Studies and Comparative Literature at City University of New York. Of books published under her own name, she is best known for her volume of collected poems, *Liberty's Helmet* (Ellis Island, 1985), which won several awards in America and England's prestigious Brittinghill Prize, and for her monumental study *1876 & All That*, first published by Univ. Press of the Southwest in 1976 and reissued as a 25th anniversary edition in 2001 by Harcourt-Collins.

DIANE SEUSS is the author of *It Blows You Hollow* (New Issues Press, 1998). Her work has appeared widely in such magazines as *Poetry Northwest, Alaska Review, The Georgia Review*, and *Indiana Review*. She teaches in the creative writing program at Kalamazoo College in Michigan.

LAURIE SHECK's volumes of poetry include *Amaranth* (Univ. Georgia Press, 1981), *Io at Night* (Knopf, 1990), and, most recently, *Black Series* (Knopf, 2001). Her work has appeared widely in such periodicals as *New Yorker, Poetry*, and *Iowa Review*. She lives and teaches in New York City.

ROSALYNNE CARMINE SMITH is the pseudonym of a much-published novelist, short story writer, playwright, essayist, and poet who prefers on this occasion to remain anonymous.

ELIZABETH SPIRES is the author of four books for children, including, most recently, *The Mouse of Amherst*, a *Publishers Weekly* Best Book of 1999, and *I Am Arachne: Fifteen Greek and Roman Myths* (Farrar, Straus & Giroux, 1999, 2001). Her books of poetry include *Globe, Swan's Island, Annonciade* (which received the Sara Teasdale Poetry Award from Wellesley College), and *Worldling* (Norton, 1995). A professor at Goucher College, she has received many other honors, including a Guggenheim Fellowship and a Whiting Writers' Award.

DAVID ST. JOHN's *Study for the World's Body: New and Selected Poems* (HarperCollins, 1994) includes poetry from four previous books. His most recent collections are *The Red Leaves of Night* (HarperCollins, 1999) and *In the Pines: Lost Poems, 1972–1997* (White Pine Press, 1999). White Pine Press also published his *Where the Angels Come Toward Us: Selected Essays, Reviews and Interviews* (1995). He has won Prix de Rome, NEA, Guggenheim and other fellowships. He lives in Venice, California.

ABIGAIL STONE is the author of the novels *Recipes from the Dump* (Norton/Avon paperback) and *Maybe It's My Heart* (Lincoln Springs Press). She also writes short stories and songs. She lives in Middlebury, Vermont.

RUTH STONE has been a Fellow of the Radcliffe Institute, a Pulitzer nominee, won the Shelley Award from the Poetry Society of America, and was twice a Guggenheim Fellow. She is the author of many collections of poetry from *In an Iridescent Time* (1951), *Topography and Other Poems* (1970), and *Cheap* (1972), to *Who Is the Widow's Muse* (1991), *Second-Hand Coat:Poems New and Selected* (1991), and *Ordinary Words*. She has taught at Wellesley, Brandeis, the University of Wisconsin, the University of California at Irvine, Indiana University, and SUNY Binghamton.

STEVE STREET, the son of teachers and the brother of a teacher, teaches writing and literature at SUNY Brockport. He's lived in four other states, in France, and in Egypt. His short fiction has appeared in *The Quarterly, Exquisite Corpse, Another Chicago Magazine*, and elsewhere. His collection *Compass: Stories About East and West, Up and Down, Toward and Apart* focuses on Americans in contemporary Egypt, and he's working on a novel, *The Murther of Blick Mancoosh*.

LUCIEN STRYK lives in Lake Bluff, Illinois. His distinguished translations and editions include *Zen: Poems, Prayers, Sermons, Anecdotes, Interviews* (with Takashi Ikemoto); *World of the Buddha: A Reader—from the Three Baskets to Modern Zen; Afterimages: Zen Poems of Shinkichi Takahashi; The Awakened Self: Encounters with Zen; The Dumpling Field: Haiku of Issa*; and *Where We Are: Selected Poems and Zen Translations*. His most recent books are *And Still Birds Sing: New and Collected Poems* and *Zen Poetry: Let the Spring Breeze Enter*.

BRIAN SWANN is Professor of English at the Cooper Union for the Advancement of Science and Art, and poetry editor of *OnEarth*. He recently edited *Poetry Comes Up Where It Can*, an anthology of poems from that journal, and *Coming to Light: Contemporary Translations of the Native Literatures of North America*. He is the author of *Wearing the Morning Star: Versions of Native*

American Song-Poems, and of many volumes of his own poetry and prose. He lives in New York City and in Delaware County, New York.

HENRY TAYLOR won the Pulitzer Prize in 1986 for his third collection of poetry, *The Flying Change*. His first two collections, *The Horse Show at Midnight* and *An Afternoon of Pocket Billiards*, are available in one volume from LSU Press, which published his *Compulsory Figures: Essays on Recent American Poets* (1992), and also his *Understanding Fiction: Poems 1986–1996* and *Brief Candles: 101 Clerihews* (1996, 2000). He is professor of literature at the American University in Washington, D.C.

KEITH TAYLOR's most recent book is the co-edited collection *What These Ithakas Mean: Readings in Cavafy* (Athens, Greece: E.L.I.A., 2002). He was also co-editor of the anthology *The Huron River: Voices from the Watershed* (Univ. Michigan Press, 2000). He has published five chapbooks of poetry and one collection of very short stories. He works part-time as the co-ordinator of the undergraduate program in Creative Writing at the University of Michigan.

DOUGLAS UNGER is the author of the novels *Leaving the Land* (Harper & Row, 1984/Bison Books, 1995), *El Yanqui* (Harper & Row 1986/Ballantine 1988), *The Turkey War* (Harper & Row 1988/ Ballantine, 1991), and *Voices from Silence: A Novel of Repression and Terror in Argentina* (Wyatt/St. Martin's, 1995). His stories have appeared widely. Since the attack in 1988, he has served as memorialist and spokesperson for Syracuse University and the victims of Pan Am Flight 103 and is currently at work on *The Lockerbie Trial: Terrorism and Its Shadows*, awaiting the outcome of the final appeals process of the Scottish Court in the Netherlands sometime in 2002.

JOHN UPDIKE since 1958, has published more than fifty volumes of fiction, poetry, and essays. Twice a winner of the Pulitzer Prize—for *Rabbit Is Rich* (1981) and *Rabbit at Rest* (1990)—he has also won the American Book Award and the National Book Critics Circle Award, among others. He was presented with the National Medal of the Arts in 1989. Volumes of non-fiction include *Assorted Prose* (1965), *Picked-Up Pieces* (1975), *Hugging the Shore* (1983), *Just Looking: Essays on Art* (1989), *More Matter* (1999), and the memoir *Self-Consciousness* (1989). His *Collected Poems 1953–1992* appeared in 1993. Well-known novels include *The Couples* (1968), *The Witches of Eastwick* (1984), *Brazil* (1994), *In the Beauty of the Lilies* (1996), and *Gertrude and Claudius* (2000). He lives with his wife in Beverly Farms, Massachusetts.

ROBERT VAS DIAS, an Anglo-American poet currently living in London, has published five collections in the US and UK since his first major book of poetry, *Speech Acts & Happenings* (Bobbs-Merrill, 1972); his anthology *Inside Outer Space* appeared in 1970 from Doubleday Anchor Books. He was founding director of the Aspen Writers' Workshop in Colorado, Poet-in-Residence at Michigan's Thomas Jefferson College, where he also directed the National Poetry Festival, and taught at Long Island Univesity, New York University, and in the UK in the Writing Program of Antioch University and in the European Division of the University of Maryland. He recently co-organized two conferences for Gresham College in London, "Sensing the Poem" (1999) and "Verbal inter Visual" (2001).

RACHEL VIGIER is the author of a collection of poems, *On Every Stone* (Pedlar Press, 2002). Her *Gestures of Genius: Women, Dance and the Body* (The Mercury Press, 1994), is an examination of voice inside women's bodies, muscle, flesh, movement. She was raised on a farm in Manitoba, Canada and now lives and works in New York City where she was injured during the September 11 attack on the World Trade Center.

MICHAEL WATERS is Professor of English at Salisbury University in Maryland. Recent books include *Parthenopi: New & Selected Poems* (BOA, 2001) and (with the late A. Poulin, Jr.) *Contemporary American Poetry: Seventh Edition* (Houghton Mifflin, 2001). His six previous books of poetry include *Green Ash, Red Maple, Black Gum* (BOA, 1997), *Bountiful* (1992), *The Burden Lifters* (1989), *Anniversary of the Air* (1985)—these three titles from Carnegie Mellon Univ. Press—and *Not Just Any Death* (BOA, 1979). He has received a Fellowship in Creative Writing from the NEA, several Individual Artist Awards from the Maryland State Arts Council, and two Pushcart Prizes.

DAVID WATSON has been a key contributor to the radical journal *Fifth Estate* since the mid–1970s. He has published poems, essays, and translations in various other journals and magazines as well. His third book, *Against the Megamachine: Essays on Empire & Its Enemies* (Autonomedia, 1998), is a collection of some of his major essays on politics, ecology, and culture. *Pandemonium: Reflections on the Kosova War and the New World Disorder* (Black & Red), is due out in the spring of 2002.

DAVID WEISS has published two books of poetry, *The Fourth Part of the World*, winner of the George Ellison Prize, and *A Pail of Steam*. His novel, *The Mensch*, appeared in 1998. His work has appeared widely in periodicals. With Deborah Tall, he is co-editor of *The Poet's Notebook*. He teaches at Hobart and William Smith Colleges.

RICHARD WILBUR, a veteran of World War II, is the author of many volumes of poetry, translation, and criticism. From *The Beautiful Changes and Other Poems* (1947), *Ceremony and Other Poems* (1950) and *Things of This World* (1956) to *New and Collected Poems* (1988) and *Mayflies:New Poems and Translations* (2000), his work has been awarded two Pulitzer Prizes, the National Book Award, and Guggenheim and Prix de Rome fellowships. He is a former Poet Laureate of the United States. An expanded edition of his *Responses: Prose Pieces 1953–1976* was published in 2000.

JOHN A. WILLIAMS, a Navy veteran of WWII, is the prolific author of dozens of novels, plays, and collections of non-fiction. A few of his better-known books are the novels *The Man Who Cried I Am* (1967), *!Click Song* (1982), and *Jacob's Ladder* (1987), his collections of essays *Flashbacks* (1973) and *Minorities in the City* (1975), and his study of Martin Luther King, Jr., *The King God Didn't Save* (1970), lauded as a "courageous honoring of truth." In 1982 he was honored with the Lindback Award for Distinguished Teaching at the Newark College of Arts and Science where he was a Professor of English. He was inducted into the New Jersey Literary Hall of Fame in 1987.

TERRY TEMPEST WILLIAMS is the author of *Pieces of White Shell: A Journey to Navajoland* (1984), *Coyote's Journey* (1989), *Refuge: An Unnatural History of Family and Place* (1991), *An Unspoken Hunger: Stories from the Field* (1994), *Desert Quartet: An Exotic Landscape* (1995), *Leap* (2000), and most recently, *Red: Passion and Patience in the Desert* (2001). She was inducted into the Rachel Carson Institute's Honor Roll. The recipient of a Lannan Literary Fellowship, a Guggenheim Fellowship, and a Conservation Award for Special Achievement from the National Wildlife Federation, she lives with her husband in Grand County, Utah.

PAUL ZIMMER has published a dozen books of poems, including *Family Reunion: Selected and New Poems* (Univ. of Pittsburgh Press, 1983), *The Great Bird of Love* (Univ. of Illinois Press, 1989), and *Big Blue Train* (Univ. of ArkansasPress, 1993). His most recent book is a volume of collected essays, *After the Fire: A Writer Finds His Place* (Univ. of Minnesota Press, 2002). He lives with his wife, Suzanne, on a farm near Soldiers Grove, Wisconsin and often serves as a visiting writer at universities.

GRATEFUL ACKNOWLEDGMENT IS MADE TO THE AUTHORS AND/OR PREVIOUS PUBLISHERS AND/OR AGENTS FOR PERMISSION TO REPRINT CERTAIN CONTRIBUTIONS HERE:

WENDELL BERRY's "Thoughts in the Presence of Fear," Alison Hawthorne Deming's "Waking to the World's Pain," and Scott Russell Sanders' "Sorrow and Solidarity" first appeared in *Orion Online*. For more information on Orion, see also the Terry Tempest Williams entry below.

DAVID BUDBILL's poem "What Issa Heard" first appeared in his *Moment to Moment: Poems of a Mountain Recluse* (Copper Canyon Press, 1997).

ELIZABTETH DODD's poem "Zero" first appeared in *OnEarth* (Winter 2002).

MARCIA FALK's "After Astounding Evil, The Promise of More to Come" first appeared in *The Forward*.

RICHARD FOERSTER's poem "Resolve" first appeared in *The York Independent* (Maine).

An early draft of DIANE GLANCY's "Lamentations" appeared in a booklet— *Beyond Words, September 11, 2001, Minnesota Writers Respond*—published by The Loft in Minneapolis and handed out on September 22, 2001.

Two of KIMIKO HAHN's poems, "Her Very Eyes" and "After Forty-eight Hours," first appeared in *The Clarion: Newspaper of the Professional Staff Congress/CUNY*.

SAMUEL HAZO's poem "September 11, 2001" first appeared in Pittsburgh's *Post-Gazette*.

WILLIAM HEYEN's "Elegy" first appeared in *OnEarth* (Winter 2002).

DENIS JOHNSON's observations are reprinted by permission; © 2000 Conde Nast Publications, Inc. Originally published in the *New Yorker*. All rights reserved.

W. S. MERWIN's "To the Words" first appeared in the *New Yorker* (Oct. 8, 2001).

FRED MORAMARCO's "Messages from the Sky: September 11, 2001" first appeared in *San Diego Reader*.

ROBERT PINSKY's "Enormity and the Human Voice" first appeared in *Boston Magazine*.

STEVE STREET's "Care for the Small Things" first appeared in *The State University Journal*.

JOHN UPDIKE's observations are reprinted by permission; © 2000 John Updike. Originally published in *The New Yorker*. All rights reserved.

DAVID WEISS's "The Folded Lie" first appeared in *The Bookpress*.

TERRY TEMPEST WILLIAMS's "Scattered Potsherds" is copyright © 2001 by Terry Tempest Williams. Originally published in OrionOnline.org, the website of Orion and Orion Afield magazines, under the feature headline "Thoughts on America." The list of contributing writers continues to grow. Reprinted by permission of Brandt & Hochman Literary Agents, Inc. All rights reserved.

COVER ART: *Entry Gate Creek (1999)*. Raku-fired earthenware. By Wayne Higby (b. 1943).

About this work, the artist writes: "I consider these tile-sculptures to be a distillation of the concepts, materials, and processes that I have been pursuing for the past thirty years."

Higby's work as artist, teacher, and leader in the field of ceramics establishes him as one of America's premier ceramists. His work is an expression of his intense interest in the external world and the merging of manmade forms with transcendent concepts.

"Today," he says, "I am thinking more about architecture, but essentially I am concerned with landscape imagery as a focal point of meditation. Space, both real and implied, is of utmost importance. I strive to establish a zone of quiet coherence—a place full of silent, empty space where finite and infinite, intimate and immense intersect...."

The cover image is used with the permission of the artist and of Memorial Art Gallery (Rochester, New York), Grant Holcomb, Director.

Founded in 2001 with a generous grant from Stephen M. and Jeryl Oristaglio, Etruscan Press is a non-profit cooperative of poets and writers working to produce and promote books that nurture the dialogue among genres, that achieve a distinctive voice, and that aim to reshape the literary and cultural histories of which we are a part. *September 11, 2001: American Writers Respond* is the first book published by Etruscan Press.

www.etruscanpress.org